Growing Up Postmodern

Culture and Politics Series
General Editor: Henry A. Giroux, Pennsylvania State University

Postmodernity's Histories: The Past as Legacy and Project (2000)
Arif Dirlik

Collateral Damage: Corporatizing Public Schools—A Threat to Democracy (2000)
Kenneth J. Saltman

Public Spaces, Private Lives: Beyond the Culture of Cynicism (2001)
Henry A. Giroux

Beyond the Corporate University (2001)
Henry A. Giroux and Kostas Myrsiades, editors

From Art to Politics: Octavio Paz and the Pursuit of Freedom (2001)
Yvon Grenier

Antifeminism and Family Terrorism: A Critical Feminist Perspective (2001)
Rhonda Hammer

Welcome to Cyberschool: Education at the Crossroads in the Information Age (2001)
David Trend

Surpassing the Spectacle: Global Transformations and the Changing Politics of Art (2002)
Carol Becker

Ethics, Institutions, and the Right to Philosophy (2002)
Jacques Derrida, translated, edited, and with commentary by Peter Pericles Trifonas

Forthcoming

Dangerous Memories: Educational Leadership at a Crossroads
Barry Kanpol

Growing Up Postmodern

Neoliberalism and the War on the Young

EDITED BY RONALD STRICKLAND

ROWMAN & LITTLEFIELD PUBLISHERS, INC.
Lanham • Boulder • New York • Oxford

ROWMAN & LITTLEFIELD PUBLISHERS, INC.

Published in the United States of America
by Rowman & Littlefield Publishers, Inc.
An Imprint of the Rowman & Littlefield Publishing Group
4720 Boston Way, Lanham, Maryland 20706
www.rowmanlittlefield.com

12 Hid's Copse Road, Cumnor Hill, Oxford OX2 9JJ, England

British Library Cataloguing in Publication Information Available

Library of Congress Cataloging-in-Publication Data

Growing up postmodern : neoliberalism and the war on the young / edited by
Ronald Strickland.
p. cm.
Includes bibliographical references and index.
ISBN 0-7425-1650-4 (alk. paper)—ISBN 0-7425-1651-2 (pbk. : alk. paper)
1. Youth—United States. 2. Youth—Government policy—United States. 3. Young consumers—United States. 4. Consumption (Economics)—Social aspects—United States. 5. Postmodernism—Social aspects—United States. I. Strickland, Ronald.

HQ796 .G75 2002
305.235'0973—dc21

2002069688

Printed in the United States of America

™ The paper used in this publication meets the minimum requirements of American National Standard for Information Sciences—Permanence of Paper for Printed Library Materials, ANSI/NISO Z39.48-1992.

For Ian, Robert, and Stephanie

Contents

Acknowledgments

Some of the essays included in this collection were first delivered as papers at Border Subjects IV: Growing Up Postmodern, a conference held at Illinois State University in October 1999. I would like to express my gratitude to the Provost's Office, the College of Fine Arts, the University Galleries, Global Review, the Minority Professional Opportunities Program, and the departments of English, Foreign Languages, Philosophy, and Curriculum and Instruction for their financial and institutional support, and to my colleagues Sophia McClennen and Victoria Harris for their help in organizing the conference.

1
Introduction: What's Left of Modernity?

Ronald Strickland

Growing Up Postmodern takes its inspiration from Paul Goodman's *Growing Up Absurd*, an indictment of postwar American society's failure to provide the necessary conditions for boys to grow up into an emotionally healthy and dignified adulthood. Writing at the end of the 1950s, hard upon the emergence of both the "youth culture" and the socioeconomic and cultural conditions that we now identify as postmodernity, Goodman saw modern American society as suffering from a long list of compromised revolutions. In *Growing Up Absurd* he called for a revival of progressive efforts in areas such as urban planning, social welfare, workplace democracy, freedom of speech, racial harmony, sexual freedom, popular culture, and public education to produce a society that could inspire young people, an adult society worth joining.

In many ways the problems Goodman identifies are still with us today. He describes a postwar American society that was unwilling to fund adequate public education, and unable to provide meaningful and dignified employment for most of its citizens. At the turn of the century, despite the pro-education rhetoric of recent political campaigns, public education is still suffering after more than two decades of systemic underfunding from the 1970s into the 1990s. And during the high employment boom years of the 1990s the largest growth was in low-paying, dead-end service-sector jobs. Goodman describes a postwar society that was alarmed by youth violence and responded with increasingly punitive treatment of young offenders while the root causes of youth disaffection and hopelessness were ignored. In the last two decades, even as public education funding has stagnated, budgets for new prison construction are exploding and children barely in their teens are being held responsible as adults for criminal behavior. Goodman describes a postwar society in which young people have "a little extra spending money," so they "get around more and are exposed to the expensive glamour, but this is precisely not attainable by them unless they take short cuts."[1] At the end of the twentieth century the youth marketing industry that Goodman observed in its infancy has long since come of age. Contemporary youth are prematurely affluent—they have money for consumer electronics, fashion apparel, movies, and music cd's, but they linger in dependence upon their parents' assistance for basic living expenses, educational costs, etc. According to economic forecasts, many of them will not attain the level of economic security achieved by their parents.

These chronic problems of modernity have become the accepted status quo of postmodernity; to many people they now appear no longer as problems but as the natural and unchangeable order of things. Indeed, for some contemporary cultural critics postmodernity is a revolutionary new social order in which the political projects and goals of the enlightenment—democratic political empowerment, progressive social policy, high-quality public education, etc.—have been rendered obsolete. In the consumerist theory of Jean Baudrillard, for example, the freedom to consume has replaced political freedom. In postmodern society, according to Baudrillard, subjectivity is formed and expressed through consumption. Postmodern consumption exceeds the fulfillment of need, expressing the subject's desire at the level of the "political economy of the sign," which is taken to supercede the society's economic relations of production.[2] A broad (if tacit) coalition of mainstream political leaders from the center-right to the center-left has come together under the banner of "neoliberalism," the hegemonic ideology of postmodern consumerism. Neoliberalism revives Adam Smith's "invisible hand of the market," seeking, as Rosemary Hennessy has observed, "to free up the operation of the capitalist market from public (state) controls and regulations," and at the same time "to extend the rationality of the market—its schemes of analysis and decision-making criteria—to areas of social life that have not been primarily economic."[3] The corporate-political strategies of neoliberalism have been gaining prominence since the economic downturn of the early 1970s. Under expanded free-trade agreements industrial production has been displaced from "rust belt" U.S. cities to the "maquiladora" region of northern Mexico and other "underdeveloped" locations where cheap labor, weak or nonexistent environmental protection regulations and undemocratic governments enable greater corporate profits and leverage for corporations to squeeze further concessions from U.S. workers.

One of many harmful effects of neoliberal social and economic policy in the U.S. has been the corporate-sector demand for a curriculum of narrowly defined skills training in public schools and universities, undermining public education's role as a democratic social institution. Neoliberal attempts to limit state and federal funding for education and to divert tax revenues to private schools have also taken a toll. Schools in poor rural areas and inner-city neighborhoods are scandalously underfunded in comparison with affluent suburban schools. Meanwhile, right-wing politicians call for "school choice" voucher schemes that would make tax dollars available to subsidize families who send their children to parochial schools. "School choice" advocates employ the neoliberal rhetoric of marketization, arguing that forcing the public schools to compete in a "free market" would improve the quality of public schools, and arguing that all students should have the right to choose the school that best suits their needs. But the proposed voucher funds are never sufficient to pay the full cost of private schooling. Therefore, the inevitable result would be subsidies for middle-class families who can afford private schooling while poorer children are left in even more seriously underfunded public schools.

SUBVERSIVE CONSUMPTION AND HYPERCONFORMITY

Beyond the effects of social disinvestment on public education, both consumerism and neoliberalism shape the lived experiences of young people and the subjectivities available to them in postmodern society. As Bill Osgerby details in his chapter in this volume, consumerism developed in conjunction with the emergence of a new social agent—the "teenager." In the era of industrial capitalism social subjectivity was predicated upon the adult male worker's productive capacity; the subjectivities of women and children were constituted in relation to that of the adult male worker. According to the conventional logic of modernity, teenagers were not productive workers, hence they were not social agents. But they did become agents-as-consumers after World War II. The teenager is, in fact, the ideal subject of an economic order in which consumer demand for services and nondurable goods seemingly generates profits out of thin air. Teenagers are primarily consumers rather than producers, and most of their income is "disposable" income that can be spent on leisure-oriented consumer goods rather than basic necessities.

In addition to its emphasis on consumer demand—or "desire"—neoliberalism is marked by a tendency to obscure the relations of production of contemporary capitalism. Following Daniel Bell's highly influential *The Coming of Post-Industrial Society* (1973), neoliberalism argues that we have entered a new phase of capitalism in which information processing is more important than material production.[4] In the new information-driven economy, it is asserted, technological breakthroughs (primarily the development of virtually instantaneous global communications) have enabled the compression of time and space such that a surplus of material wealth is produced, making basic "needs" increasingly irrelevant for more and more people, and elevating "desire" as the principal concern of the postmodern subject. In the books of conservative futurists like Bell these conditions are taken as almost a fait accompli. But they tend to assume that industrial production has disappeared, when actually it has simply been restructured and relocated.

In his early writings Baudrillard argues that the distinction between use value and exchange value is no longer tenable in late capitalism, thus rejecting Marx's critique of "commodity fetishism" and the concept of alienation. Both the concepts of use value (expressing human needs) and exchange value (expressing human desires) are "*an organized extension of productive forces*" (Baudrillard, 46) and, as such, both express the "puritan" disciplinary ethos of capitalism. In the contemporary "information society" Baudrillard asserts, this disciplinary ethos leaves very little room for political agency. Confronted with a glut of information, the masses are entangled in a network of media discourses, completely "informed" by the media, which is the same thing as being "formless" (218). The individual is in a "double bind," which, he argues, is exactly like the situation faced by young people in the transition to adulthood:

> They are at the same time told to constitute themselves as autonomous subjects, responsible, free, and conscious, and to constitute themselves as submissive objects, inert, obedient, and conformist. The child resists on all levels, and to these contradictory demands he or she replies by a double strategy. When we ask the child to be object, he or she opposes all the acts of disobedience, of revolt, of emancipation; in short, the strategy of a subject. When we ask the child to be subject, he or she opposes just as obstinately and successfully a resistance as object; that is to say, exactly the opposite: infantilism, hyperconformity, total dependence, passivity, idiocy. (218)

Autonomous "subject resistance" is generally considered positive "in the same way as in the political sphere only the practices of liberation, of emancipation, of expression, of self-constitution as a political subject are considered worthwhile and subversive." But the "strategic resistance" of refusal of meaning and of speech, "of the hyperconformist simulation of the very mechanisms of the system," is, Baudrillard concludes, the "winning" strategy of postmodernity, "because it is the most adapted to the present phase of the system" (218-19).

This "silent" resistance, Baudrillard emphasizes, is not at all "passive" (215). But many cultural critics remain unconvinced. Following the lead of Michel de Certeau, cultural studies scholars have examined the neoliberal marketization of everyday life, searching for instances of symbolic resistance and "subversive consumption" in discursive practices such as youth fashion and popular music.[5] In *Postmodernism and Popular Culture*, for example, Angela McRobbie analyzes "the role of the rag market" and the ongoing popularity of "retro" fashion as an implicit critique of consumerism and the social inequities of late capitalism. In *Black Noise* Tricia Rose describes how rap music's production concepts evolved significantly in the context of the mid-1970s bankruptcy crisis in New York. Faced with the widespread retrenchment of music programs in the public schools, young people created a new hybrid musical form through "sampling" of existing records and the use of playback and production technologies (such as the turntable and the soundboard) as instruments in themselves. In Rose's discussion of hip-hop culture there is an emphasis on the overtly pedagogical and polemical force of the discourse that distinguishes her analysis from other critics who treat the random nonconformism of youth subcultural styles as self-evidently subversive.

Absent this self-consciously polemical and pedagogical dimension, however, subversive consumption has obvious limitations as a resistance strategy. In the words of Dick Hebdige, youth subcultural styles are "meaningful mutations," capable of embodying a symbolic refusal of the social consensus on which western democracies depend, but in the end, "no amount of subcultural incantation can alter the oppressive mode in which the commodities used in subculture have been produced."[6] The problems with the "freedom to consume" argument are fairly evident. The power to consume is distributed very unevenly, notwithstanding the claims of the dominant ideology. Even for the affluent the power to consume never meets the desire produced by the advertising industry. By definition the consumer gratification dulls the critical edge, leaving us stalled in the effort to produce a better world, unaware that conditions could be different.

NEOLIBERALISM AND LABOR

A somewhat different argument for the revolutionary implications of postmodernity is found in Antonio Negri and Michael Hardt's recent book, *Empire*.[7] Like both conservative futurists and left-liberal cultural studies scholars, Negri and Hardt argue that capitalism has entered a new stage—or "new times" in the phrase popularized by the British journal *Marxism Today*. But they emphasize the importance of understanding late modernity as "crisis" and they focus on labor rather than leisure as the driving force of subject-formation in postmodernity. In their view, the synthesis of Taylorism, Fordism, and Keynesianism that coalesced under Roosevelt's New Deal produced a "factory society"—"the highest form of *disciplinary* government"—in which "the entire society, with all its productive and reproductive articulations, is subsumed under the command of capital." In the disciplinary society of late modernity, "productive subjectivities are forged as one-dimensional functions of economic development," but during the 1960s "the expansion of welfare and the universalization of discipline in both the dominant and subordinate countries created a new margin of freedom for the laboring multitude," accompanied by key moments of dissent and political destabilization such as the Civil Rights and decolonization struggles, the Vietnam War, and the feminist and gay rights movements (243). In the dominant capitalist countries, they argue, the social struggles of the 1960s raised the costs of labor to the point at which it eventually forced a change in the "quality and nature" of labor itself:

> The disciplinary regime clearly no longer succeeded in containing the needs and desires of young people. The prospect of getting a job that guarantees regular and stable work for eight hours a day, fifty weeks a year, for an entire working life, the prospect of entering the normalizing regime of the social factory, which had been a dream for many of their parents, now appeared as a kind of death. The mass

> refusal of the disciplinary regime, which took a variety of forms was not only a negative expression but also a moment of creation, what Nietzsche calls a transvaluation of values. (273-74)

In order for this revolution to be achieved Negri and Hardt identify three positive demands implicit in this "mass refusal": the right to global citizenship, the right to a social wage and a guaranteed income, and the right to reappropriation of the means of production (400-407). These are modernist, enlightenment-inspired goals of the sort that Paul Goodman could subscribe to, but, in Negri and Hardt's analysis, postmodernity presents the conditions for the achievement of these goals. They see the demand for global citizenship, for example, as the inevitable result of a labor regime in which corporations seek to exploit the labor of "under-developed" regions. Inadvertently, or perhaps the better term is "collaterally," these ventures sometimes result in campaigns for unionization, skills training that translates to (post)industrial jobs abroad, and higher standards of living that enable workers in the dispersed industries to contest oppressive local regimes and to emigrate to metropolitan regions. Of course, both the industrialized countries and the "developing" countries attempt to control these steps toward global citizenship through immigration quotas and the creation of "international industrial zones" aimed at discouraging unionization. Nonetheless, the counterresponses themselves indicate that the trend toward the "globalization" of labor threatens to undermine the use of national sovereignty as a means of controlling the freedom of workers.

The "new proletariat" of postmodernity is "not a new industrial class." The industrial working class of modernity, Negri and Hardt argue, represented only a temporary stage in the history of the proletariat, a stage at which "capital was able to reduce value to measure." Production under the conditions of contemporary global capitalism, by contrast, is more elusive; they call it "biopolitical." In postmodernity "the production of capital converges ever more with the production and reproduction of social life itself; it thus becomes ever more difficult to maintain divisions among productive, reproductive, and unproductive labor." In calling for a "social wage" and a guaranteed annual income for all, Negri and Hardt are opposing in particular the modernist concept of a "family wage," the "fundamental weapon of the sexual division of labor by which the wage paid for the productive laborer is conceived also to pay for the unwaged reproductive labor of the worker's wife and dependents at home" (402). Since, in post-Fordist flexible production, labor has become increasingly collective and social, conditions are favorable for "the demand that all activity necessary for the production of capital be recognized with an equal compensation such that a social wage is really a guaranteed income, or, effectively, a 'citizenship income'." This biopolitical regime of production also gives a distinctive emphasis to the fundamental Marxist demand for the worker's right to control the means of production. In the context of the "informatization of production" in postmodernity, all global citizens must also have "free access to and control over knowledge, information, communication, and affects" (407).

Attributing the current developments in global capitalism at least partly to the pressure of proletarian resistance rather than simply to capital's escalating need for expanded profits, Negri and Hardt shift the discussion of "desire" from the terrain of consumption to that of production. This move points toward a more focused, active potential for a postmodern revolutionary struggle, one in which the resources and opportunities made available for young people are crucially at stake, and one in which young people might conceivably be mobilized to play a more active role than sullen rejection or subversive consumption. But the "new proletariat" Negri and Hardt describe still leaves out huge sectors of the global population. There is an immediate and urgent need to resist further privatization of resources and other kinds of social disinvestment. And, in their neglect of "desire as consumption" they leave aside the question of how to resist the ideological power of consumerism as well as the question of how to marshall the oppositional force—however limited—of "subversive consumption." These issues are related to the adverse conditions of postmodernity and neoliberalism that make it difficult for young people to take control of their own lives—the relentless pressure to consume, the social disinvestment in education, the harsh responses to youth crime, and the continuing climate of intolerance for cultural diversity that falls heavily on the young. The following chapters seek to intervene against these conditions and to continue the struggle for a better future.

CONSUMERS AND CRIMINALS

First, Bill Osgerby shows how post-1950s American advertisers successfully used images of "youth as fun" as a metaphor for a new consumer value system promoting commodity consumption and immediate gratification to the middle class as a whole. These transformations in marketing practices were essential features of a new middle-class faction characterized by its pursuit of "liberated" lifestyles that laid emphasis on the achievement of self-expression and individuality through the consumption of "distinctive" products. From the beginning of the "teenager" phenomenon critics have recognized that the commercial interests ostensibly serving the teenage market were in fact "creating" the market and even the social concept of the "teenager" through their market research methods and media strategies. Osgerby traces the historical development of this criticism from the pessimistic "mass culture" studies of the 1960s and 1970s through the "subversive consumption" arguments of the 1980s and 1990s. Throughout this period he finds an ongoing ambivalence toward youth in the larger society: "almost simultaneously youth is *both* vilified as the most deplorable evidence of cultural bankruptcy *and* celebrated as the exciting precursor to a prosperous future" (Osgerby, 23). This dualistic attitude is borne out in the ways neoliberal policies of social disinvestment depend upon the construction of teenagers as a "market." Public education, and especially extracurricular programs such as music and art education, and services such as health care, recreation, and rehabilitation programs for juvenile offenders and other troubled youth are seen as programs and services that a consumer might choose or not choose (assuming ability to pay, of course), rather than as generally beneficial programs and service to which every citizen should have access.

Following Osgerby, Henry Giroux describes the effects of the corporatization of public education on high school students. Ironically, as Giroux points out in his chapter included here, "the corporate model of educational reform wraps itself in the democratic principles of freedom, individualism, and consumer rights," but "it fails to provide the broader historical, social, and political contexts necessary to render such principles meaningful and applicable" (Giroux, 39). Faced with ongoing budget difficulties, many school administrators have opened up their captive student markets to fast-food, soft-drink, and athletic-wear companies in order to secure program funds that should have been provided by tax revenues. Zero tolerance policies have streamlined the process for expelling kids from school while laws have been passed in all fifty states allowing juveniles to be tried as adults in the criminal justice system. Meanwhile, in the popular media, young people—especially the poor and young people of color—are demonized as violent and marked as disposable. Some of the examples of this media hysteria are truly sobering; Giroux cites a spate of recent anti-youth films like *187*, a *Death Wish*-inspired revenge fantasy in which Samuel L. Jackson plays a beleaguered teacher who systematically murders his problem students. In response to the "war on the young" waged by the corporate culture of neoliberalism, Giroux calls for an educational policy that protects students from coercive consumer appeals and the abandonment of public support for education.

The effects of neoliberal ideology upon inner-city youth are considered in Jerry Phillips's reading of Richard Price's *Clockers*, a 1992 novel which was later made into a film by Spike Lee. Phillips criticizes postmodern social theory's conception of the inner city as an "urban jungle," existing outside of history and economic relations. Modernist writers like Marx and Goodman considered youth alienation in historical and social contexts, but contemporary postmodern writers often invite us to think of inner-city youth in biological determinist and social Darwinist terms—as a "breed" of "dangerous animal beings devoid of human conscience" (Phillips, 48). By contrast, Price's novel relentlessly insists upon the fundamental humanity of young people struggling on the margins of the postindustrial city. The sad revelation of the novel is that while we may have passed beyond modernism in the form of liberal statism or Fordist industrial production, we still remain trapped within the horizon of social possibilities as determined by capitalist political economy.

As Giroux's list of violent anti-youth films demonstrates, one of the most prevalent media images circulating in public discourse during the last decade has been that of the teenager as sociopath. These media images reflect a tendency to replace rehabilitative correctional programs with merely punitive criminal justice for teenage offenders. In "Remorseless Young Predators" Gary Smith discusses this critical erosion of the juvenile justice system in the United States. At the end of the nineteenth century social reformers in Chicago established an alternative court structure that would become a national model for the rehabilitative treatment of juvenile offenders, but at the end of the twentieth century more and more teenagers are tried in adult courts with mandatory sentence laws that prevent judges from considering their youth or circumstances. At the same time, the economic impact of youth incarceration is significant. The construction of new prisons means jobs and prosperity for economically depressed rural communities. Inside the prisons, inmates produce products and services for token wages. This neoliberal regime of social disinvestment and "market solutions" to social problems helps keep taxes low and labor costs down, while the social costs of writing off so many young people as unredeemable criminals goes uncalculated.

In "Growing Up Incarcerated" Elizabeth Kleinfeld offers a loosely ethnographic discussion of the literacy struggles of typical prisoners. Kleinfeld shows how juvenile correctional facilities and prisons limit prisoners' literacy by systematically regulating prisoners' reading and writing. Seventy percent of prisoners in this country are illiterate, and research shows that when correctional facilities do provide educational opportunities for prisoners, recidivism rates decrease. Nonetheless, correctional institutions are reducing, not increasing, their educational programs. There is no coherent literacy program or other educational programming in our prisons, resulting in haphazard approaches and conflicting philosophies from state to state and prison to prison. In addition, none of the existing educational programs are designed specifically for prisoners. Mass literacy is a distinctly modernist phenomenon that, by all accounts, is declining in the visually oriented culture of postmodernity. Yet, the prisoners interviewed by Kleinfeld see their literacy struggles as vitally important. For these prisoners who confront an oppressive social and institutional order without the mediating release of consumerist escapism, literacy means power against the system.

INTERPELLATION AND SUBJECTIVITY

Andrew Kurtz's and Tim Scheie's chapters explore different modes of interpellation in the gray area between modernist and postmodernist subjectivity. In the complex mix of ideological and interpellative effects of "first-person shooter" video games Kurtz sees a replication of the "manichean ideologies in which the only 'other' in the game is an enemy to be destroyed" that permeate most media and political discourses in the United States. In the public sphere these reductive oppositions and the simplistic responses they evoke are able to become hegemonic and yet also are held in check because they are "filtered through larger discursive structures such as humanism, democracy, and globalism" (Kurtz, 107). But these modernist values are absent from the violent video games. These games give the player a false sense of being in control of his environment through the deployment of a prosthetic device (the joystick) that is very much like the experience of carrying a firearm. For the overwhelming majority of players, the video game experience functions symbolically to resolve contradictions symptomatic of the perceived breakdown of white male hegemony in the contemporary information-based economy. Of course, this symbolic resolution is not always sufficient; Kurtz notes the references to the video game *Doom* made in a video left behind by the Columbine High School killers. Other observers have made this connection, but Kurtz's interest is in explaining the relationship between symbolic and real violence in the context of the inability of late capitalism to deliver on its promise of personal freedom and happiness through consumerism.

In the following chapter Tim Scheie analyzes *Roland Barthes by Roland Barthes*, a book of childhood photos with commentary by Barthes. By inviting the reader to approach the childhood photographs as texts of pleasure, Scheie argues, Barthes has engaged in a provocatively "queering" gesture: he invites and even coerces the reader to consider a child who is not the guarantor of a future in the form of biological progeny (this, Scheie argues, is a key function of children in the family photo albums of the modern era). Scheie concludes with a speculative discussion of how Barthes's elegant but rather passive theorizing stands as a sort of "cautionary shadow" to the more aggressive "in-your-face" attitude of contemporary queer activism. While noting that Barthes's rethinking of youth outside the bounds of the regime of reproduction was a fundamental gesture, Scheie doesn't see Barthes as a sort of "proto-queer" thinker. Barthes lacked the implicit optimism that underlies more recent invocations of queerness.

CONSUMERISM, FEMINISM, HYPERMASCULINITY

In "The Big Business of Surfing's Oceanic Feeling" Margaret Henderson analyzes the evolution of the Australian surfing magazine, *Tracks*, from its beginnings as a vanguard text of the counterculture to its current incarnation as a "glossy, commercialized, rebelliously adolescent and hypermasculine" organ of postmodern consumerism. In Henderson's reading, the thirty-year history of Australian surfing subculture is interpreted through mapping the conjunctions of several discourses where the relationship between modernity and postmodernity is textualized—the 1960s counterculture, the professionalization of leisure as sport, second- and third-wave feminisms and the attendant backlashes, and the consumerist hypermasculinity of corporate-sponsored youth "anarchy" all packaged especially for young male readers and surfers. These conjunctions can be read in *Tracks*, Henderson argues, because throughout its history the magazine has, however ambivalently, attempted to reconcile the growing contradictions between surfing as a countercultural lifestyle and surfing as a highly commodified professional sport. Over the decades, *Tracks* has steadily undermined the oppositional political force of the surfing counterculture by hardening its patriarchal ideology and masculine symbolic identities against the increasing demands by women for a place in the sport. Australian surfing is a textbook-worthy example of the containment of an oppositional discourse through a consumerist invocation of patriarchal ideology.

In the following chapter, Angela Hubler discusses shortcomings in the representation of the "crisis" of female adolescence in writings by both academic and popular writers. Some contemporary observers locate the source of these problems, as Paul Goodman would, in the "sick culture" that teaches girls that their value lies only in their appearance and sexuality. Nonetheless, they respond to the problems in narrowly psychological terms, offering therapeutic remedies that place the responsibility for the problems on the victims themselves and fail to develop a transformative critique of the social system. Mary Pipher's best-selling trade book, *Reviving Ophelia*, is a characteristic example. Pipher understands the self-mutilation, eating disorders, depression, multiple unplanned pregnancies, and suicide attempts of the girls she sees as socially induced problems. She provides suggestions for helping girls to develop the self-esteem to survive in a patriarchal society, and she calls for cultural changes such as better sexual harrassment policies and a redefinition of manhood to counter the traditional association of masculinity and violence. But her individualist orientation precludes a discussion of the collective social efforts necessary to change the society that she describes as sick. The problem with analyses like Pipher's, Hubler argues, is also the secret to their success—they simplify, psychologize, and individualize the effects of capitalist patriarchy on adolescent girls, and thereby present a palatable if not very useful version of the crisis of female adolescence for readers.

Concluding this cluster of essays, Jennifer Drake explores the contradictory forces of "third-wave," "capitalist," or "power" feminism. Though it is strongly influenced by the anti-feminist backlash against the feminist movement of the 1960s and 1970s, third-wave feminism also represents a progressive feminist response to the backlash, drawing on critiques of mainstream academic feminism from working class women and women of color. Power feminism attracts many young people across lines of race and class at least partly because it offers success stories rather than victim stories. But the transformative potential of this hopeful, capitalist version of third wave feminism is easily subsumed under the logic of acquisitive individualism. "Within the dominant culture," Drake observes, "'power feminism' has been privileged as the new feminism because it shores up competive individualism, meritocracy, consumerism, and catfighting, its motto being 'work, buy, and/or claw your way to the top'" (Drake, 184). Drake sees more promise in the "Girl Culture" movement, an aggressively sexy feminist music and 'zine culture that has emerged in the 1990s. Though it began as a grass-roots movement, Girl Culture was almost immediately colonized by the mass consumer products industry. Some observers, Drake points out, see benefits behind this curse—Girl Culture circulates more widely and becomes a more popular discourse through the capitalist marketing apparatus. Drake is skeptical about this, but she explores two examples of third wave feminist polemic and what might be called a revolutionary public pedagogy in the music of Lauryn Hill and Ani DiFranco. In the work of Hill and DiFranco, she demonstrates, Girl Culture intersects with history-saturated oppositional discourses—hip-hop culture for Hill and the folk and punk countercultures for DiFranco—to produce spaces where community and collective action can be imagined and made.

COUNTERCULTURE AND 1968

In "Post-'68: Theory Is in the Streets" Astra Taylor reacts to the recent wave of anti-global capitalism protests from the perspective of the post-1968 student generation. Her generation, she observes, has come of age in a period during which the forms and goals of civil disobedience that had been so successful in the 1960s had to be reevaluated. Taylor interprets the institutionalization of academic postmodern theory and technological developments such as the Internet as conditions that have suddenly made possible a new kind of student resistance movement based on situated action, nonhierarchical associations, and contingent tactics. The protests are decentralized. In place of what would have been the "protest headquarters" in years past one now finds a "convergence center" in Seattle. Environmentalists and Teamsters march side by side. Compulsory unity has been abandoned in favor of a more fluid form of coalition building based on "affinity groups" and depending on the Internet for communication. The Websites published by the activists provide news and updates, but they also serve as forums for discussion of the movement as it progresses. These developments have captured the imaginations of contemporary students who have grown up in the era of postmodernity and enabled new tactics appropriate to their specific historical moment. Whether the protests of 2000-2001 will inaugurate a new revolutionary era of civil disobedience and progress remains to be seen.

In "To Be Young, Countercultural, and Black," David Jones notes that the term "countercultural" has sometimes been associated with hedonism and lack of ambition—characteristics with which black people have been denigrated historically. Partly for this reason, most African American political and cultural activists have not claimed the term "countercultural." But Jones points to a historical tradition of innovative counterculture including predominantly black and integrated movements from the ragtime era through the Harlem Renaissance, jazz, rock and roll, and into the hip-hop era. And, he argues, while the term "counterculture" has too often been associated with an urge toward individual self-expression and self-gratification it should also be recognized as encompassing an urge toward collectivism and community. Jones offers this broader definition of "countercultural" as a way beyond the racial essentialism of much African American political and cultural activism. Noting that the most widely circulated images of black culture continue to privilege urban, usually coastal settings, hip-hop music, and a small number of national figures as representatives and spokespersons for black cultural generally, Jones urges a more pluralistic African American cultural activism that would be

WHAT'S LEFT OF MODERNITY?

As the essays collected here will demonstrate, this question is urgent in several senses. Despite the claims of neoliberalism and consumerism, postmodernity is not inherently to the "left" of modernity—postmodernity, in political and economic terms, is no more revolutionary than it is reactionary. The social transformations of postmodernity represent global capitalism's attempt to maintain a regime of profit against the challenge of a new proletariat produced by modernist social institutions. The modernist ideal of a good society, with universal access to education and other social services, is an important, even necessary, stage in the progress toward replacing a realm of necessity with a realm of freedom for all humans. Postmodernity has not achieved those goals, nor rendered them obsolete. In this context it is important to take stock of what remains of modernity—what remains of enlightenment values and institutions—that can be preserved and adapted to help young people to resist the new forms of exploitation and social disinvestment characteristic of neoliberalism. Postmodern theories of resistance, generally framed in the context of semiotic and consumerist theories of subjectivity, fall short in neglecting to consider the social relations of production, the true source of profit in capitalism. The argument that surplus wealth can be generated without labor always depends upon the concealment of labor through geographical displacement or the redefinition of congealed labor such as private property or information as existing outside the relations of production. Analyses of practices such as subversive consumption can be helpful insofar as they identify sites of potential resistance to oppression. But subversive consumption must be a part of a larger organized resistance in order for it to avoid being easily co-opted by corporate marketing strategies. Finally, the fact that subversive consumption is widely seen as the only viable mode of resistance to global capitalism is in itself alarming; the discourses of youth culture are already so thoroughly saturated with the ideology of consumerism that it is increasingly difficult to imagine alternatives. This book is conceived as a critical and polemical response to this assault upon the public imagination. Reclaiming the right for young people to grow up in a safe, supportive, and tolerant social environment is an important step to resist the subsumption of an ever-increasing proportion of social consciousness under the logic of neoliberalism.

NOTES

1. Paul Goodman, *Growing Up Absurd: Problems of Youth in the Organized System*. New York: Random House, 1960, 57.

2. For a representation of Baudrillard's thought over the past thirty years see Jean Baudrillard, *Selected Writings* (trans. Mark Poster). Stanford: Stanford University Press, 1988. For a detailed critique of Baudrillard's semiotic displacement of "production" see Mas'ud Zavarzadeh, "Post-ality: The Dis-simulations of Cyber-capitalism," in Mas'ud

Zavarzadeh, Teresa Ebert, and Donald Morton, eds., *Post-ality: Marxism and Postmodernism*. Washington, D.C.: Maissonneuve Press, 1995.

3. Rosemary Hennessy, *Profit and Pleasure: Sexual Identities in Late Capitalism*. London: Routledge, 2000, 75.

4. Daniel Bell, *The Coming of a Post-Industrial Society: A Venture in Social Forecasting*. New York: Basic Books, 1973, 212.

5. Michel de Certeau, *The Practice of Everyday Life*. Berkeley: University of California Press, 1984.

6. Dick Hebdige, *Subculture: The Meaning of Style*. London: Methuen, 1979, 130.

7. Antonio Negri and Michael Hardt, *Empire*. Cambridge, Mass.: Harvard University Press, 2000.

BIBLIOGRAPHY

Barthes, Roland. *Roland Barthes*. Trans. Richard Howard. New York: Hill and Wang, 1977.

Baudrillard, Jean. *Selected Writings*. Stanford, Calif.: Stanford University Press, 1988.

Bell, Daniel. *The Coming of a Post-Industrial Society: A Venture in Social Forecasting*. New York: Basic Books, 1973.

de Certeau, Michel. *The Practice of Everyday Life*. Berkeley: University of California Press, 1984.

Goodman, Paul. *Growing Up Absurd: Problems of Youth in the Organized System*. New York: Random House, 1960.

Hebdige, Dick. *Subculture: The Meaning of Style*. London: Methuen, 1979.

Hennessy, Rosemary. *Profit and Pleasure: Sexual Identities in Late Capitalism*. London: Routledge, 2000.

McRobbie, Angela. *Postmodernism and Popular Culture*. London: Routledge, 1994.

Negri, Antonio, and Michael Hardt. *Empire*. Cambridge, Mass.: Harvard University Press, 2000.

Pipher, Mary. *Reviving Ophelia*. New York: Ballantine, 1994.

Rose, Tricia. *Black Noise: Rap Music and Black Culture in Contemporary America*. Hanover, N.H.: Wesleyan University Press/University Press of New England, 1994.

Zavarzadeh, Mas'ud, Teresa Ebert, and Donald Morton, eds. *Post-ality: Marxism and Postmodernism*. Washington, D.C.: Maissonneuve Press, 1995.

2
"A Caste, a Culture, a Market": Youth, Marketing, and Lifestyle in Postwar America

Bill Osgerby

> The high school set makes its own decisions about what to buy and where to buy it, often dragging their parents along in their wake. Thus teen-age boys have created the vogue for button-down collars, Bermuda shorts, cashmere sweaters, sport shirts, "Ivy League" jackets and loafers. And the junior miss . . . leads the way in endorsing "separates," "man-tailored" shirts, ballet slippers, and skintight "stem" skirts or ballooning layers of petticoats.
>
> Eugene Gilbert, in *Harper's Magazine*, November 1959

Writing in *New Yorker* in November 1958 cultural critic Dwight Macdonald drew readers' attention to what he depicted as a startlingly new social phenomenon—the American teenager. "Teenagers," the author affirmed, were now "not just children growing into adults but a sharply differentiated part of the population."[1] As a generational cohort of unprecedented numbers, with unique levels of disposable income and an apparent thirst for the exciting opportunities opened up by postwar affluence, it did not seem unreasonable for Macdonald to conclude that young people represented an exceptional social formation. Proclaiming the advent of a "teenage revolution," he argued that American youth had "a style of life that was fast becoming *sui generis*."[2] In these terms the 1950s had seen youth emerge as both a potent economic force and a compelling cultural influence, Macdonald opining that the American teenager had now taken discrete and distinctive shape as "a caste, a culture, a market."

For Macdonald it was their unparalleled spending power that, above all else, marked out 1950s teenagers as "a new American caste." "Economically," Macdonald advised his readers, teenagers constituted "the latest—perhaps the last—merchandising frontier." Before 1958 was out, Macdonald estimated, America's seventeen million teenagers would have spent at least nine-and-a-half billion dollars, an annual spending that was set to rise by a further five billion dollars by 1965.[3] And this financial power seemed all the more impressive for the way it was unencumbered by domestic responsibilities or restraints—teenage consumption being concentrated in the realms of leisure, style, and hedonistic pleasure. As Macdonald put it, the distinctive feature of the teenage market was that it was "free money":

> Free from all claims except the possessor's whim. . . . Some teenagers actually have more free money to spend than their parents, who must meet all kinds of fixed obligations, among them the support (and the allowances) of the teenagers in question.[4]

Nor was Macdonald a voice in the wilderness. Throughout the late 1950s and early 1960s the scale and character of youth consumption was a regular topic for awestruck media comment. In 1959, for example, a breathless edition of *Life* announced "A New $10-Billion Power: The US Teenage Consumer"—the magazine recounting how American youth had "emerged as a big-time consumer in the US economy. . . . Counting only what is spent to satisfy their special teenage demands, the youngsters and their parents will shell out about $10 billion this year, a billion more than the total sales of GM [General Motors]."[5] In 1964, meanwhile, *Newsweek* averred that "the country's 28 million youngsters between the ages of 13 and 22 control a collective purchasing power that has long since ceased to be child's play, with US youngsters expected to spend more than $24.5 billion in 1964."[6] And two years later the teenage market was still a hot topic—*Newsweek* devoting a special edition to a survey of the young generation's tastes and lifestyles, the magazine concluding that "the high school set has graduated from the ice-cream, soda-fountain and bicycle circuit into the big leagues of US consumption."[7]

During the late 1950s and early 1960s commercial interests scrambled to cash in on the gold mine represented by young people's spending. The range of products geared to the young was literally boundless, consumer industries interacting with and reinforcing one another in their efforts to woo the youth market. Rather than neutrally "reflecting" consumer demand, however, manufacturers and marketeers played an active role in shaping and disseminating the tastes, styles, and attitudes of "teenage" America. Moreover, the process of interpellating youth as a discrete consumer group was integral to the transformation of the American marketing industry. In recognizing "teenagers" as a distinct market segment, with specific tastes and interests, the strategies of youth marketing developed by postwar advertising gurus pioneered the concepts of "consumer lifestyle" and "niche marketing" that became central to the regeneration and revitalization of Madison Avenue.

The manner in which consumer industries represented and responded to the youth market during this period was also fundamental to broader patterns of cultural change. Mobilized as a signifier for dynamic modernity and stylish individualism, the iconography of "youth as fun" was central to a new consumer value system that prioritized commodity consumption and immediate gratification. This cultural infatuation with "youthful hip" was especially pronounced within an emergent faction of the American middle class—a group that sought to distinguish itself as a distinct class formation through the pursuit of expressive, "liberated" lifestyles that laid emphasis on the achievement of self-expression and individuality via the consumption of distinctive cultural goods and signifiers.

YOUTH IN THE JAZZ AGE

The existence of a commercially based youth culture was not a feature unique to America during in the 1950s. An embryonic youth market was already discernable in the universe of commercial entertainment that took shape in the burgeoning cities of the late nineteenth century. And during the consumer boom of the 1920s a more fully formed, youth-oriented leisure culture became recognizable—a phenomenon heavily indebted to the concomitant expansion of higher education. Once the preserve of a relatively small elite, colleges and universities saw a threefold increase in enrollments between 1900 and 1930, nearly 20 percent of the college-age population attending some kind of educational institution by the end of the 1920s. In her meticulous survey of this growing student body, Paula Fass shows how "the first modern American youth culture" coalesced during the Jazz Age amid the budding network of student fraternities and a world of proliferating dance halls, cinemas, cafeterias, and other campus hangouts.[8]

The student culture chronicled by Fass weathered the lean years of the 1930s, but overall American youth was hard hit by the Depression. Young people represented 27.5 percent of those unemployed in 1930, and by 1937, 16 percent of the total youth population was still out of work. Even those from relatively well-to-do backgrounds were hard hit—this reflected in the 10 percent decline that took place in college enrollments between 1932 and 1934.[9] During the 1940s, however, youth culture was reenergized by the labor demands of the wartime economy. The economic pressures of the war drew increasing numbers of young people into the workforce, partially reversing trends towards extended schooling and dependency on parents. In 1944, Census Bureau statistics showed that over two in five young men aged between sixteen and seventeen were gainfully employed—35 percent of these having left school altogether to enter full-time work.[10] As a consequence, greater disposable income was delivered into young hands. By 1944 American youth was believed to account for a spending power of around $750 million, much of it discretionary.[11] This economic muscle not only helped crystallize notions of young people as possessing unprecedented cultural autonomy, but also provided the basis for a significant expansion of the commercial youth market—and thereby laid the foundation for the rise of the "teenager" as a cultural phenomenon.

THE TEENAGE MARKET

Clearly, a distinct youth culture associated with particular tastes and patterns of consumption existed before the Second World War. But the specific concept of the "teenager" only began to coalesce during the 1940s. Since the 1600s it had been common to refer to an adolescent as being someone in their "teens," yet it was only in 1941 that an article in *Popular Science* magazine featured the first published use of the word "teenager."[12] During the 1940s the term was increasingly utilized in the world of advertising and marketing, steadily leaking into popular discourse where it was used to denote a new breed of affluent, young consumers who prioritized fun, leisure, and the fulfillment of personal desires.

The runaway success of *Seventeen* magazine was one of the first pointers to the rise of distinctly "teenage" consumption. Helen Valentine, *Seventeen*'s first editor, had originally developed the idea of a publication geared to college girls while working as promotions editor of *Mademoiselle* magazine. In 1944 she perfected the concept with the launch of *Seventeen*—its premier edition of 400,000 copies selling out within two days and its circulation topping the million mark within sixteen months. Keen to maximize her venture's commercial potential, Valentine hired a professional research team—Benson and Benson from Princeton—to survey her readership's buying habits.[13] With this information at their disposal, *Seventeen*'s editorial team could tempt merchandisers with valuable information on the tastes and desires of a demographic market that was shaping up as one of the most lucrative in modern America.

By the 1950s the developing scope and scale of the youth market seemed spectacular. The growth was partly indebted to demographic trends, wartime increases in the birthrate, and a postwar "baby boom" ensuring that the teen population spiraled from 10 to 15 million during the 1950s, eventually hitting a peak of 20 million by 1970. The postwar expansion of education, meanwhile, further accentuated the profile of young people as a distinct social group. During the 1950s the high school system was expanded considerably, but it was in colleges and universities that the most dramatic growth took place. In 1950 about 41 percent of high school graduates went on to college, but by 1960 this had risen to 53 percent, the trend giving a new lease of life to the campus culture that had first surfaced between the wars.[14] The vital stimulus behind the growth of the commercial youth market, however, was economic. Wartime increases in young people's spending power were sustained throughout the fifties. Though peacetime saw a decline in full-time youth employment, young people's consumption was sustained by a combination of parental allowances and part-time work. Hyperbole undoubtedly crept into some of the more extreme claims made for the magnitude of youth's spending, but the general trend was undoubtedly upwards—some estimates suggesting that young people's average weekly income had risen from just over two dollars in 1944 to around ten dollars by 1958.[15]

Commerce quickly grasped the potential of this market. Following in the footsteps of Helen Valentine and *Seventeen* magazine, a legion of marketeers developed strategies to zero in on the wallets of young consumers. A young entrepreneur from Chicago led the field. An enterprising nineteen year old in 1945, Eugene Gilbert was working as a shoe store clerk when he noticed that few youngsters shopped in the store, even though it was stocking the latest styles. After persuading the owner to advertise more directly to young buyers, Gilbert was struck by the sudden rise in sales and began to consider market research among his peers as a viable business proposition. By 1947 his research organization, Youth Marketing Co., was prospering. With plush offices in New York, the company employed a battalion of market researchers and boasted accounts with such prestigious clients as Quaker Oats, Maybelline, Studebaker, and United Airlines. Gilbert himself became a figure of some celebrity. Profiled by national magazines like *Newsweek* and *Harper's*, he was hailed as a leading spokesman for, and interpreter of, modern youth culture. Pronouncements in his syndicated newspaper column—"What Young People Think"—charted the whims and caprices of the young, while his book *Advertising and Marketing to Young People* (1957) became a manual for those hoping to court adolescent spending. With missionary zeal Gilbert evangelized youth as a commercial market of unprecedented importance. As he explained to *Advertising Age* in a 1951 interview:

> Our salient discovery is that within the past decade teenagers have become a separate and distinct group within our society, enjoying a degree of autonomy and independence unmatched by previous generations.[16]

Not everyone, however, shared the young adman's enthusiasm. In its 1957 special issue on youth, for example, *Cosmopolitan* magazine rhetorically asked "Are Teenagers Taking Over?"—the inside copy only half jokingly conjuring with images of "a vast, determined band of blue-jeaned storm troopers forcing us to do exactly as they dictate."[17] These anxieties were constituent in a broader climate of uncertainty. Although postwar economic growth had brought prosperity for many, the 1950s saw a wide body of academic and popular opinion revile what was regarded as the malignant cultural fallout of the consumer boom. Across the political spectrum authors decried the rise of a debased "mass culture" they perceived as the corollary of modern consumerism—processes of cynical marketing and mass consumption delivering a cultural life bereft of meaning and individuality. For the mandarins of mass culture theory the flourishing youth market offered the starkest evidence of the consumer society's blanket of oppressive uniformity. For example, in 1950 (the same year that he lamented the "other-directed" conformism of *The Lonely Crowd*) David Reisman condemned a pop music industry that had the power "to mold popular taste and to eliminate free choice by consumers."[18] Dwight Macdonald, too, saw the young generation as falling easy prey to the wiles of commerce. "These days," he dolefully explained in his commentary for *New Yorker*, "merchants eye teenagers the way stockmen eye cattle."[19] And, even though fascinated awe was the underlying tone of *Esquire*'s 1965 special edition on "The Affluent Teen" ("In the time it takes you to read these lines the American Teen-Ager will have spent $2,378.22"), a distinct sense of unease also crept in.[20] Profiling the new wave of youth marketeers, *Esquire* was ambivalent. The magazine was spellbound by their business acumen but, gathered together in a group portrait, the high priests of the youth market seemed to be presented in a more ominous light. Shot against a shadowy background, Helen Valentine, Eugene Gilbert, and their confederates cast a sombre gaze at the camera—configured, perhaps, as the manipulative Pied Pipers of teenage consumption.

The mass society pessimism of figures such as Reisman and Macdonald starkly contrasts to the more positive accounts of commodity consumption offered by many cultural theorists thirty years later. During the 1980s a number of authors sought to emphasize dimensions of agency (even transgression) in the domain of consumer practice. Here, social actors were interpreted as activating their own values and meanings through their patterns of consumption, creatively using the market machine to engineer their own cultural space and identities.[21] Elements of this approach were especially evident in analyses of youth culture, with theorists such as Paul Willis seeing young people as actively generating their own cultures and forms of self-representation by "creatively selecting and appropriating the raw texts and artefacts made available by the commercial market."[22] For critics such as Jim McGuigan,[23] however, this approach drifted dangerously close to a celebration of the unqualified pleasures of consumer sovereignty in the marketplace and subsequently other theorists have called for renewed attention to the political economy of the culture industries and to the "interplay between the symbolic and the economic."[24]

This, however, does not entail sliding back into notions of marketing Svengalis leading passive and undiscriminating consumers by the nose. In the analysis of youth culture, for example, it is important to retain recognition of young people's capacity as active agents in the authorship of their culture. At the same time, this is a process underpinned by an engagement with the machinery of the commercial market—youth culture being formed through an intersection with the media, commercial entrepreneurs, and market institutions. As Steven Miles argues, therefore, while a reciprocal and "mutually exploitative" relationship exists between youth and the commercial market, the boundaries of this relationship are largely set by commercial interests. As Miles elaborates:

> The proposition that young people actively engage with the mass media and to a degree forge it in their own image is a sound one, but is only ever partially realized. Ultimately, the parameters within which young people are able to do so, are set down for them by a mass media that is inevitably constructed first and foremost on the need to sell magazines, programmes and what is essentially a consumerist way of life. Young people are therefore liberated and constrained by the mass media at one and the same time—it provides them with the canvass, but the only oils they can use to paint that canvass are consumerist ones.[25]

In these terms, then, there was at least a grain of truth to Dwight Macdonald's 1958 contention that "the teenage market—and, in fact, the very notion of the teenager—has been created by the businessmen who exploit it."[26] Indeed, the 1950s saw American industry devote increasingly assiduous attention to this process of creation. In 1956, for example, the *Wall Street Journal* reported that Hires Root Beer was using part of its 3 million dollar promotions budget to pay popular high school girls to ask for Hires soft drinks on their dates. The tobacco firm R.J. Reynolds, meanwhile, were ensuring that their brand of Camel cigarettes were heavily promoted on Alan Freed's CBS radio show, "The (Camel) Rock 'n' Roll Dance Party."[27]

This was a field in which Eugene Gilbert developed particular expertise. Drawing on Elihu Katz and Paul Lazarsfeld's influential study of "opinion leaders,"[28] Gilbert argued that the surest way of finding a market among teenagers was "to sell a product to the leaders in school; what they approve of counts far more than what Mom and Dad approve at home."[29] Rather than simply manipulating the market, however, strategies of investigation and research were also central to Gilbert's approach. Early in his career Gilbert recognized that young people themselves were best placed to gauge the tastes and interests of the teenage market and, in a pioneering move, he recruited an army of students to canvass the opinions and consumer preferences of their peers.[30] As such, Gilbert's techniques of marketing and promotion can be seen as anticipating later trends towards qualitative consumer research and "post-Fordist" niche-marketing. Gilbert's attention to the attitudes and feelings of young consumers was a foretaste of moves away from "number-crunching" empiricism towards the kind of attitudinal and motivational research that would become widespread in American marketing during the 1960s.[31] Moreover, in developing the model of a specifically "teenage" market, Gilbert's work can be seen as part of a broader structural shift taking place within American marketing. By the late 1950s notions of monolithic and homogenous "mass" consumption were increasingly abandoned as advertisers began coining the term "lifestyle" to denote the distinctive consumption practices of a spectrum of nuanced consumer groupings.[32] In these terms the rise of "teenage" marketing was one (very visible and influential) aspect of a wider move by American business to address an increasingly diverse range of "lifestyle" markets.

Surveying structural changes in western economies since the 1970s, many commentators have identified the emergence of a new, "post-Fordist" era.[33] Here, the systems of mass production, standardized products, uniform markets, and concentrations of capital typical of the modern, Fordist economy are seen as giving way to a new, consumption-oriented era of flexible production processes and fragmented markets. In this narrative of economic change, consumption occupies a pivotal role—authors such as Frank Mort arguing that manufacturers, marketeers, and retailers have resorted to "[g]reater market segmentation [which] demands different methods of communication. . . [with an] upbeat stress on design and visual awareness."[34] The rise of the teenage market in postwar America, however, suggests that such developments did not suddenly materialize during the 1980s and 1990s, but were already pronounced traits of the consumer economy that emerged in the United States after the Second World War.

The rise of "teenage" consumption also impacted upon Madison Avenue's creative practice. During the late 1950s American advertising had been beset by a sense of malaise, the industry perceiving itself as woefully lacking in innovative flair. The early 1960s, however, saw a "creative revolution" in advertising strategy as a new generation of admen began to identify with the contemporary youth scene. Their aim was partly to appeal to the growing youth market but, as Thomas Frank cogently argues, the "creative revolution" was also distinguished by the way it traded on youth as an icon of rebellious autonomy.[35] In employing the concept of "youthfulness" as a shorthand signifier for self-fulfillment and "hip" nonconformity, advertisers appealed to new consumer value systems that aspired to break away from stodgy conformity and explore new horizons of individuality and excitement—an ethos of hedonism and personal gratification that was especially significant within ascendant factions of the American middle class.

THE ETHIC OF FUN

For much of the 1950s notions of "youth" were surrounded by largely negative social meanings and connotations. Wartime perceptions of a frightening rise in levels of juvenile crime continued apace and prompted, in 1953, the launch of a Senate Subcommittee to Investigate Juvenile Delinquency. The Subcommittee hearings continued until the end of the decade, its concerns mirrored by a plethora of exposés in magazines, newspapers, and newsreels—all purporting to show a new form of delinquency that was chilling in its extent and severity.

Yet, as James Gilbert demonstrates, rather than being rooted in a genuine explosion of adolescent vice, the 1950s alarm around juvenile delinquency (or the "J.D." phenomenon, as it was dubbed) was a product of broader anxieties about the nature of social and cultural change. According to Gilbert, the J.D. "moral panic" of the 1950s had a powerful "metaphorical" dimension, serving as a symbolic focus to "a vaguely formulated but gnawing sense of social disintegration," fears of juvenile depravity serving as a vehicle for wider concerns in the face of rapid and disorienting change.[36] Developments in the world of youth seemed to exemplify those forces deemed most threatening to social stability. Perceptions of a more permissive sexual code among young people stoked fears of moral disarray, while the expansion of a commercially based and peer-oriented youth culture challenged dominant ideologies of family-centered "togetherness." Young people's affluence and the growth of a commercial youth market were perceived as weakening the family's cohesive power—adolescent taste seeming to be increasingly independent of parental influence. Moreover, the popularity of cultural forms such as rock 'n' roll prompted particular fear as white, middle-class youngsters appeared to fall under the spell of lower-class and black cultural values.

Nevertheless, rather than being entirely negative, social and political responses to youth are characterized by a recurring duality. Almost simultaneously youth is *both* vilified as the most deplorable evidence of cultural bankruptcy *and* celebrated as the exciting precursor to a prosperous future—contrasting images that Dick Hebdige terms "youth-as-trouble" and "youth-as-fun."[37] Both are distorted and exaggerated stereotypes with tenuous relation to social reality. But, since the 1940s, they have wielded tremendous connotative power, serving as key motifs around which dominant interpretations of social change have been constructed. Amid the "J.D. panic" of the 1950s it was notions of "youth-as-trouble" that tended to hold sway, but by the end of the decade anxieties were dissipating and a more positive set of youth stereotypes came to the fore. By the beginning of the 1960s young people were portrayed, celebrated even, as an excitingly new and uplifting social force. This was an iconography powerfully marshaled by John F. Kennedy in both his public persona and political rhetoric, where the rising generation was deployed as an avatar of progress in a new era of bold confidence.[38] At the same time commercial interests also helped foster an upbeat iconography of youth—James Gilbert arguing that the rise of more positive social responses to young people during the late 1950s and early 1960s was to a large part "derived from a further extension of the market economy in American cultural life."[39] Central to this process was the galloping success of commercial leisure industries specifically geared to young consumers, together with the efforts of the new army of advertisers and marketeers who worked both to gauge and to exploit the desires of this "teenage" market.

The early hyphenation of the word "teen-ager" is suggestive of its initial novelty, but by the late 1950s the "teenager" had become a familiar archetype as advertisers and social scientists (along with an avalanche of books and magazine and news features) revealed to the American public what appeared to be a new generational strata with its own language, culture, and values. The concept of the "teenager," however, amounted to more than simply a descriptive term for a generational group. Written into notions of "teenage" tastes and lifestyles was a specific ideological construction of social change. Configured as the embodiment of modern prosperity, the teenager became symbolic of wider shifts in American life. While some commentators, as we have seen, derided "teenage" culture as the worst example of commercial massification, more widely the late 1950s and early 1960s saw the teenager cast in radiant terms. "Come Alive! You're in the Pepsi Generation" entreated a Pepsi ad campaign in 1963, advertisers and manufacturers habitually identifying their products with the vitality and independence of youth. Here, young people were taken as the epitome of an America in which the sheer pace of economic growth seemed set to engender a newly prosperous age of fun, freedom, and social harmony. In these terms "teenagers" were presented as being at the sharp end of the new consumer culture, distinguished not simply by their youth but by a particular style of conspicuous, leisure-oriented consumption.

And it was among the American middle class that this upbeat "re-branding" of youth registered greatest impact. In the rhetoric of marketeers and social scientists alike, the "teenager" was presented as essentially classless—an image redolent of the wider Cold War mythologies of universal abundance. In reality, however, the modes of consumption that defined the "teenage" lifestyle were relatively specific to the white middle class. As sociologist Jessie Bernard observed in his 1961 survey of the American youth scene, "teen-age culture" was "essentially the culture of a leisure class":

> Youngsters of lower socioeconomic classes are in the teen-age culture only in their early teens. They are more likely than children of higher socioeconomic class to enter the labor force or the armed forces or to get married soon after high school and, thus, to disappear into the adult world. This exit from the teen-age world by youngsters of lower class background means that those who remain are disproportionately from the higher socioeconomic class background.[40]

The burgeoning commercial youth market of the late 1950s and early 1960s, therefore, was largely a middle-class province. The array of "teen-" products and advertisements geared to Eugene Gilbert's "teenage consumer" were pitched to a relatively well-heeled and respectable market of middle-class, white youngsters. But perhaps even more significant was the way in which the ethos of hedonism and hectic consumerism central to the "teenage" experience also set the pace for the new values and lifestyles evident among an ascending section of the American middle class.

The "traditional" middle class world that had originally emerged during the eighteenth and nineteenth centuries—with its emphasis on family life, the work ethic, moderation, and probity—had been a powerful force, but by the 1920s was already losing some of its authority as American capitalism steadily prioritized consumption, leisure, and immediate gratification.[41] In the period after the Second World War these changes intensified, middle-class culture becoming more thoroughly permeated by a leisure-oriented consumer ethos. These shifts were especially pronounced within an emergent middle-class faction. The American economy's growing dependence on the servicing of consumer demand brought with it a major expansion in the number of salaried managerial and technical workers and "culture producers" of all kinds—administrators, academics, journalists, advertisers (Eugene Gilbert, for example), and other professions whose economic role centered on the production and dissemination of symbolic goods and services. Despite its occupational diversity, Barbara and John Ehrenreich argue that this professional-managerial group was bound together by common experiences, interests, and worldview, coming to represent a distinct and recognizable middle-class formation that constituted roughly 20 percent of the American population.[42] Moreover, in contrast to the reserve and diligent work ethic of the traditional middle class, this ascendant faction was distinguished by its embrace of the pleasures of commodity consumption and its hunger for "youthful" fun.

In making sense of these transformations the insights of French cultural theorist Pierre Bourdieu are illuminating. In *Distinction*, his analysis of changes in the fabric of French bourgeois culture, Bourdieu argues that postwar France saw the rise of a new form of capitalist economy in which power and profits were increasingly dependent not simply on the production of goods, but also on the continual regeneration of consumer desires.[43] To sustain its survival, therefore, this new economic order demanded the emergence of a new sociocultural formation which championed the cause of commodity consumption and judged people "by their capacity for consumption, their 'standard of living' [and] their life-style, as much as by their capacity for production."[44] Lacking the economic, cultural, or social capital that distinguished the traditional petite bourgeoisie, this new class faction established its own distinctive status by colonizing new occupations based on the production and dissemination of symbolic goods and services—Bourdieu coining the term "cultural intermediaries" to denote the new petite bourgeois cohort that rose to dominate fields such as the media, advertising, journalism, fashion, and so on. Moreover, in its quest to secure its class position and status, the new petite bourgeoisie broke away from the puritanical and production-oriented "morality of duty" associated with the traditional middle class. In its place was elaborated an "ethic of fun"—a new "morality of pleasure as a duty," in which it became "a failure, a threat to self-esteem, not to 'have fun'."[45]

Bourdieu's original study was focused exclusively on developments within the French social structure during the late 1960s, but since the 1980s a growing body of authors have drawn on his work to analyze a broad range of contemporary cultural formations. For example, Paul Bagguley and his associates, Mike Featherstone, Scott Lash, and John Urry, have all deployed Bourdieu's terms of analysis in their accounts of "postmodern" cultures in the late twentieth century.[46] However, while these authors have focused their attentions on cultural shifts in contemporary Europe, it is also possible to see middle-class culture in America during the 1950s and 1960s as evidencing many of the qualities characteristic of Bourdieu's new petite bourgeoisie.[47]

Like Bourdieu's "cultural intermediaries" of 1960s France, the ascending middle class of 1950s America established their status as a social formation through their skills in "the art of living." They defined their social status and sense of cultural identity through distinctive, consumption-driven lifestyles—their values and codes of behavior laying an accent on stylistic self-expression, self-conscious display, and (to use Bourdieu's terminology) an "ethic of fun." Indeed, the emergence of "lifestyle" as a marketing concept was largely predicated upon the developing consumer tastes of this new middle class. As Joseph Bensman and Arthur Vidich later explained, by the 1960s marketeers and advertisers were most often using the notion of "lifestyle" to denote the mores of "a new middle class of college-bred administrators, professionals and managers" who were oriented to a culture of "play, fun and excitement" and who took "endless delight in pursuing a light-hearted existence of interpersonal repartee and pleasure based on a moral code that bore no relationship to babbitry and its protestant morality."[48]

In pursuing its "ethic of fun," the new middle class took many of its cultural cues from the developing world of youth consumption. As Eugene Gilbert recognized in 1957, teenagers' tastes not only influenced their parents' household spending but were a source from which

> almost all mass buying trends originate. The mass adult market may not feel all the trends in this storm center, but most of those that reach the adult market have their beginnings here.[49]

This was particularly true of the cultural forms and texts associated with the new middle class. In the case of advertising, for example, Thomas Frank shows how the "creative revolution" of the 1960s was underpinned by an attempt to mobilize "youth" as a signifier of hip individualism and hedonistic fulfillment that could appeal to newly affluent and upwardly mobile consumers.[50] Frank demonstrates that the trend registered across a wide range of products and advertising campaigns, but it was probably best encapsulated by the success of the Ford Mustang. The sporty Mustang first rolled off assembly lines in April 1964 and was an instant sensation. Ford's first-year sales estimate of 100,000 units was surpassed in just four months, with some 22,000 orders taken on the first day of availability and more than 417,000 Mustangs sold in twelve months—then a record for first-year car sales. The Mustang phenomenon was indebted to Ford's deft marketing. The Mustang was designed to be a "youth" car—a product that could exploit the increasingly profitable youth market, but which could also appeal to consumers who sought to identify with "youthful" themes of adventure and fun. Both strategies were a big success. As expected, the Mustang sold enormously well to the young, with more than half of the car's first-year buyers aged under thirty-four. But the car was also a hit with older age groups, 16 percent of sales going to men in the forty-five to fifty-five age group—the "young at heart" clambering aboard the bandwagon of "youthful" and exciting consumerism. The success of the Mustang, then, is testimony to the way in which "youth" had become a motif for the dreams, desires, and ideals of the hedonistic, middle-class consumer.

Frank is correct to argue that the marketing move towards "this more hip style" was fully established by 1965.[51] But it was amid the countercultural ferment of the late 1960s that the "hip" consumer really came into his own. While the most politically conscious elements of the counterculture undoubtedly presented a challenge to the dominant order, the libertarian 1960s ethos of "doing your own thing" offered a code of optimism, excitement, and stylishness that was commensurate with the lifestyle sensibilities of the new middle class. Indeed, rather than representing the antithesis of the consumer society, the counterculture can itself be seen as a developmental phase in the evolution of the new, consumption-oriented petite bourgeoisie. As Frank observes, rather than representing the nemesis of advanced capitalism, "the counterculture may be more accurately understood as a stage in the development of the values of the American middle class, a colorful instalment in the twentieth century drama of consumer subjectivity."[52] Pointing the way to a more liberal set of social, sexual, and cultural mores, the counterculture helped give free rein to the new middle class as they strived for "hip" individuality and sensuous indulgence through hedonistic and "youthful" patterns of consumption. It was, for example, this "ethic of [youthful] fun" that particularly caught *Newsweek*'s eye when the magazine surveyed the male fashion scene in 1968:

> Seldom has male fashion switched, twitched and disported itself with the urgency of today. Money and leisure are part of the reason; the suburban man wants—and can afford—bright togs to fit his weekend fun. A more energetic and pervasive influence is youth. Hipped on color and cacophony, whether it's psychedelic art or discothèques, young people dress to fit their milieu—and their elders are picking up the beat. "It used to be that the son sneaked in to borrow his father's tie," says James K. Wilson Jr., president of Hart Schaffer and Marx Clothes. "Now the father is sneaking in to borrow his son's turtleneck."[53]

THE LAST MERCHANDISING FRONTIER

At the end of the 1990s a group of young entrepreneurs announced an innovative marketing breakthrough. Under the moniker "Sputnik" they presented themselves as the thrusting Young Turks of American market research. Drawing on their "network of young correspondents across the country," Sputnik claimed they were uniquely placed to "get to the streets, the neighborhoods, the clubs, the basements and the playgrounds, and talk to the street cultures." By mining its rich seam of qualitative research data, Sputnik argued, it could get "inside the minds and souls of this largest growing consumer group,"[54] offering business an unparalleled opportunity "to turn to the progressive trendsetters, to get close, to understand what they are doing culturally and socially by tracking the shifts, where they are going or what they will be doing next."[55]

With a client base that included high-profile clients such as Reebok, Pepsi, and Levi Strauss, there was no doubting Sputnik's credentials as an influential player in the field of youth marketing. But in many ways their approach was not especially groundbreaking. For all their brash sales talk, Sputnik were really just the latest installment in the saga of American business's attempts to understand, tap into, and draw influence from the youth market. The drive towards qualitative research focused on the tastes, attitudes, and lifestyles of young people had been initiated by American marketeers over forty years earlier, while the 1950s had seen Eugene Gilbert make his name from "getting close" to the young consumer, deciphering the styles and preferences that were laying the seeds for the Next Big Thing.

In 1958 Dwight Macdonald had speculated that the growth of teenage spending might mark "the last merchandising frontier." In many ways, however, the rise of the teenage market represented a prologue rather than a finale to the development of modern consumerism. With its emphasis on "hip" nonconformity and unabashed pleasure seeking, the "teenage" phenomenon of the late 1950s and early 1960s initiated and experimented with new cultural forms and lifestyles that laid the basis for a rising middle-class habitus—a way of life oriented around personal consumption, stylish display, and a hedonistic "ethic of fun."

NOTES

1. Dwight Macdonald, "A Caste, a Culture, a Market I," *New Yorker*, 22 Nov. 1958, 57. This was the first instalment of a two-part feature. The second instalment followed in the 29 November edition of the magazine.

2. "A Caste, a Culture, a Market I," 57.

3. "A Caste, a Culture, a Market I," 73.

4. "A Caste, a Culture, a Market I," 74.

5. "A New $10-Billion Power: The US Teenage Consumer," *Life*, 31 Aug. 1959, 77.

6. "The $25 Billion-a-Year Accent on Youth," *Newsweek*, 30 Nov. 1964, 66.

7. Richard Thomas, "Pleasures of Possession," *Newsweek*, 21 March 1966, 45.

8. Paula Fass, *The Damned and the Beautiful: American Youth in the 1920s* (Oxford: Oxford University Press), 1978, 122.

9. Richard Reiman, *The New Deal and American Youth: Ideas and Ideals in a Depression Decade* (Athens: University of Georgia Press), 1992, 59.

10. John Modell, *Into One's Own: From Youth to Adulthood in the United States, 1920-1975* (Berkeley: University of California Press), 1989, 165-66.

11. Michael Adams, *The Best War Ever: America and World War II* (Baltimore, Md.: Johns Hopkins University Press, 1994), 127.

12. Thomas Hine, *The Rise and Fall of the American Teenager* (New York: Avon), 1999, 8-9.

13. Grace Palladino, *Teenagers: An American History* (New York: Basic Books, 1996),

103-4.

14. Modell, *Into One's Own*, 266.

15. Macdonald, "A Caste, a Culture, a Market I," 60. See also Eugene Gilbert, *Advertising and Marketing to Young People* (New York: Printer's Ink, 1957), 21, tables 1-6.

16. "Everybody Talks about Youth Advertising. . . ," *Advertising Age*, 26 Feb. 1951, 1.

17. Richard Geham, "That Nine Billion Dollars in Hot Little Hands," *Cosmopolitan*, Nov. 1957, 72.

18. David Reisman, "Listening to Popular Music," *American Quarterly*, Vol. 2, Winter 1950: 361.

19. Macdonald, "A Caste, a Culture, a Market I," 70.

20. "In the Time It Takes You to Read These Lines the American Teen-Ager Will Have Spent $2,378.22," *Esquire*, July 1965, 65.

21. This approach was exemplified in the work of John Fiske. See his *Understanding the Popular* (Boston: Unwin Hyman, 1989) and *Reading the Popular* (Boston: Unwin Hyman, 1989).

22. Paul Willis, *Common Culture* (Milton Keynes: Open University Press, 1990), 157.

23. Jim McGuigan, *Cultural Populism* (London: Routledge, 1992).

24. Graham Murdock, "Cultural Studies at the Crossroads," in Angela McRobbie (ed.), *Back to Reality? Social Experience and Cultural Studies* (Manchester: Manchester University Press, 1997), 68.

25. Steven Miles, *Youth Lifestyles in a Changing World* (Buckingham: Open University Press), 2000, 85.

26. Dwight Macdonald, "A Caste, a Culture, a Market II," *New Yorker*, 29 Nov. 1958, 58.

27. "Teenage Consumers," *Wall Street Journal*, 6 Dec. 1956.

28. Elihu Katz and Paul Lazarsfeld, *Personal Influence: The Part Played by People in the Flow of Mass Communications* (Glencoe: Free Press), 1955.

29. "Catching the Consumers at a Critical Age," *Business Week*, 26 Oct. 1957.

30. See "Teen-Age Tasters," *Newsweek*, 3 Dec. 1951.

31. See Sean Brierly, *The Advertising Handbook* (London: Routledge, 1995), 36-39; and Stephen Fox, *The Mirror Makers: A History of American Advertising and Its Creators* (New York: Vintage, 1985), 183-87.

32. By 1963 market segmentation and concepts of lifestyle were leading topics on the agenda of the Winter Conference of the American Marketing Association. See William Lazer, "Life Style Concepts and Marketing," and Eugene Kelly, "Commentary on Life Style," both in Eugene Kelly and William Lazer (eds.), *Managerial Marketing: Perspectives and Viewpoints* (Homeward, Ill.: Irwin, 1967).

33. Michel Aglietta was among the first theorists to suggest that the structures of Fordism typified by the American economy were facing crisis. From the late 1960s, Aglietta argued, declines in productivity and demand had prompted moves into more flexible forms of production and business organization. See Michel Aglietta, *A Theory of Capitalist Regulation: The US Experience* (London: Verso, 1979). Subsequently, many other authors have used the term "post-Fordism" to denote what they see as a new economic order based around flexible production and market segmentation. See, for example, Robin Murray, "Fordism and Post-Fordism," in Stuart Hall and Martin Jacques (eds.), *New Times: The Changing Face of Politics in the 1990s* (London: Lawrence and Wishart), 1990.

34. Frank Mort, "The Politics of Consumption," in Hall and Jacques (eds.), *New Times*,

167-68.

35. Thomas Frank, *The Conquest of Cool: Business Culture,Counterculture, and the Rise of Hip Consumerism* (Chicago: University of Chicago Press, 1977).

36. James Gilbert, *A Cycle of Outrage: America's Reaction to the Juvenile Delinquent in the 1950s* (Oxford: Oxford University Press, 1986), 77. More generally, Joe Austin and Michael Nevin Willard have also highlighted the symbolic or "metaphorical" dimensions to public debate about "youth," such discourse representing "important forums where new understandings about the past, present, and future of public life are encoded, articulated, and contested." In these terms, "youth" is mobilized as "a metaphor for perceived social change and its projected consequences, and as such it is an enduring locus for displaced social anxieties." See Joe Austin and Michael Nevin Willard, "Introduction," *Generations of Youth: Youth Cultures and History in Twentieth-Century America* (New York: New York University Press, 1988), 1.

37. Dick Hebdige, "Hiding in the Light: Youth Surveillance and Display," in Dick Hebdige, *Hiding in the Light: On Images and Things* (London: Routledge, 1988), 19.

38. For a discussion of the aura of "youthful" idealism and energy that surrounded the Kennedy presidency, see John Hellmann, *The Kennedy Obsession: The American Myth of JFK* (New York: Columbia University Press, 1997), 105.

39. James Gilbert, *Cycle of Outrage*, 214.

40. Jessie Bernard, "Teen-Age Culture: An Overview," *The Annals of the American Academy of Political and Social Science*, Vol. 338, Nov. 1961: 2.

41. Discussion of the history and character of the American middle class prior to the impact of 1950s consumer affluence can be found in Burton Bledstein and Robert Johnston (eds.), *The Middling Sorts: Explorations in the History of the American Middle Class* (London: Routledge, 2001).

42. From a neo-Marxist perspective the Ehrenreichs define the professional-managerial class as "salaried mental workers who do not own the means of production and whose major function in the social division of labor may be described broadly as the reproduction of capitalist culture and capitalist class relations." See Barbara Ehrenreich and John Ehrenreich, "The Professional-Managerial Class," in Pat Walker (ed.), *Between Capital and Labor* (Boston: South End Press, 1979), 12. Conservative commentators have also identified an emergent social formation of middle-class professionals. For example, B. Bruce-Briggs provides comprehensive occupational and educational data to illustrate the ascendancy of the professional-managerial group during the 1960s. See B. Bruce-Briggs, *The New Class?* (New Brunswick, N.J.: Transaction, 1979), 217-25.

43. Pierre Bourdieu, *Distinction: A Social Critique of the Judgement of Taste*, trans. R. Nice (London: Routledge, 1984), 310.

44. Bourdieu, *Distinctions*, 310.

45. Bourdieu, *Distinctions*, 367.

46. See Paul Bagguley et al., *Restructuring: Place, Class, and Gender* (London: Sage, 1990); Mike Featherstone, *Consumer Culture and Postmodernism* (London: Sage, 1991); and Scott Lash and John Urry, *The End of Organized Capitalism* (Cambridge: Polity, 1987).

47. Admittedly, there are problems with transposing Bourdieu's account of the transformation of the French bourgeoisie during the late 1960s onto a postwar history of the American middle class. Michèle Lamont, for example, notes important differences between the contemporary French and American upper-middle classes in terms of their use of distinctive tastes as a mark of social distinction. For Lamont, cultural perimeters are more

strongly demarcated in France than in America, where the presence of powerful ideologies of egalitarianism has meant that such boundaries are weaker and more loosely defined. See Michèle Lamont, *Money, Morals, and Manners: The Culture of the French and American Upper-Middle Class* (Chicago: University of Chicago Press, 1992), 4-5. Nevertheless, though differences obviously exist between the national cultures of France and America, Bourdieu's account of a shift from a "morality of duty" to an "ethic of fun" remains broadly useful as a framework for understanding the postwar transformation of American middle-class life during the 1950s and 1960s.

48. Joseph Bensman and Arthur Vidich, "Changes in the Life-Styles of American Classes," in Arthur Vidich (ed.), *The New Middle Classes: Life-Styles, Status Claims, and Political Orientations* (London: Macmillan, 1995), 249-52 (originally published 1971).

49. Gilbert, *Advertising and Marketing*, 28.

50. Frank, *Conquest of Cool,* 1997.

51. Frank, *Conquest of Cool,* 133.

52. Frank, *Conquest of Cool,* 120.

53. Pat Smith, "Male Plumage '68," *Newsweek*, 25 Nov. 1968, 70.

54. Janine Lopiano-Misdom and Joanne de Luca, *Street Trends: How Today's Alternative Youth Cultures Are Creating Tomorrow's Mainstream Markets* (New York: Harper Collins, 1998), 10.

55. Lopiano-Misdom and de Luca, *Street Trends*, xv; 8.

BIBLIOGRAPHY

Adams, Michael. *The Best War Ever: America and World War II*, Baltimore, Md.: Johns Hopkins University Press, 1994.

Advertising Age. "Everybody Talks about Youth Advertising ...," 26 Feb. 1951, 18.

Aglietta, Michel. *A Theory of Capitalist Regulation: The US Experience*, London: Verso, 1979.

Austin, Joe, and Michael Nevin Willard. *Generations of Youth: Youth Cultures and History in Twentieth-Century America*, New York: New York University Press, 1998.

Bagguley, Paul et al. *Restructuring: Place, Class, and Gender*, London: Sage,1990.

Bensman, Joseph, and Arthur Vidich. "Changes in the Life-Styles of American Classes," in Arthur Vidich (ed.), *The New Middle Classes: Life-Styles, Status Claims, and Political Orientations*, London: Macmillan, 1995 (1971), 238-60.

Bernard, Jessie, "Teen-Age Culture: An Overview," *The Annals of the American Academy of Political and Social Science*, Vol. 338 (Nov. 1961): 1-12.

Bledstein, Burton, and Robert Johnston (eds). *The Middling Sorts: Explorations in the History of the American Middle Class*, London: Routledge, 2001.

Bourdieu, Pierre. *Distinction: A Social Critique of the Judgment of Taste*, trans. R. Nice, London: Routledge, 1984.

Brierly, Sean. *The Advertising Handbook*, London: Routledge, 1995.

Bruce-Briggs, B. *The New Class?* New Brunswick, N.J.: Transaction, 1979.

Business Week. "Catching the Consumers at a Critical Age," 26 Oct. 1957, 88.

Ehrenreich, Barbara, and John Ehrenreich. "The Professional-Managerial Class," in Pat Walker (ed.), *Between Capital and Labor*, Boston: South End Press, 1970, 5-45.

Esquire. "In the Time It Takes You to Read These Lines the American Teen-Ager Will Have Spent $2,378.22," July 1965, 65-68.

Fass, Paula. *The Damned and the Beautiful: American Youth in the 1920s*, Oxford: Oxford University Press, 1978.

Featherstone, Mike. *Consumer Culture and Postmodernism*, London: Sage, 1991.

Fiske, John. *Understanding the Popular*, Boston: Unwin Hyman, 1989.

———. *Reading the Popular*, Boston: Unwin Hyman, 1989.

Fox, Stephen. *The Mirror Makers: A History of American Advertising and Its Creators*, New York: Vintage, 1985.

Frank, Thomas. *The Conquest of Cool: Business Culture, Counterculture, and the Rise of Hip Consumerism*, Chicago: University of Chicago Press, 1997.

Geham, Richard. "That Nine Billion Dollars in Hot Little Hands," *Cosmopolitan,* Nov. 1957, 72-73.

Gilbert, Eugene. *Advertising and Marketing to Young People*, New York: Printer's Ink, 1957.

———. "Why Today's Teen-Agers Seem So Different," *Harper's Magazine*, Nov. 1959, 76-79.

Gilbert, James. *A Cycle of Outrage: America's Reaction to the Juvenile Delinquent in the 1950s*, Oxford: Oxford University Press, 1986.

Hebdige, Dick. "Hiding in the Light: Youth Surveillance and Display," in Dick Hebdige, *Hiding in the Light: On Images and Things*, London: Routledge, 1988, 17-36.

Hellmann, John. *The Kennedy Obsession: The American Myth of JFK*, New York: Columbia University Press, 1997.

Hine, Thomas. *The Rise and Fall of the American Teenager*, New York: Avon, 1999.

Katz, Elihu, and Paul Lazarsfeld. *Personal Influence: The Part Played by People in the Flow of Mass Communications*, Glencoe: Free Press, 1955.

Kelly, Eugene. "Commentary on Life Style," in Eugene Kelly and William Lazer (eds.), *Managerial Marketing: Perspectives and Viewpoints*, Homeward, Ill.: Irwin, 1967 (1963), 42-45.

Lamont, Michèle. *Money, Morals, and Manners: The Culture of the French and American Upper-Middle Class*, Chicago: University of Chicago Press, 1992.

Lash, Scott, and Urry, John. *The End of Organized Capitalism*, Cambridge: Polity, 1987.

Lazer, William. "Life Style Concepts and Marketing," in Eugene Kelly and William Lazer (eds.), *Managerial Marketing: Perspectives and Viewpoints*, Homeward, Ill.: Irwin, 1967 (1963), 33-41.

Life, "A New $10-Billion Power: The US Teenage Consumer," 31 August 1959, 78-80.

Lopiano-Misdom, Janine, and Joanne de Luca. *Street Trends: How Today's Alternative Youth Cultures Are Creating Tomorrow's Mainstream Markets*, New York: HarperCollins, 1998.

Macdonald, Dwight. "A Caste, a Culture, a Market I," *New Yorker*, 22 Nov. 1958, 57-94.

———. "A Caste, a Culture, a Market II," *New Yorker*, 29 Nov. 1958, 57-107.

McGuigan, Jim. *Cultural Populism*, London: Routledge, 1992.

Miles, Steven. *Youth Lifestyles in a Changing World*, Buckingham: Open University Press, 2000.

Modell, John. *Into One's Own: From Youth to Adulthood in the United States, 1920-1975*, Berkeley: University of California Press, 1989.

Mort, Frank. "The Politics of Consumption," in Stuart Hall and Martin Jacques (eds.), *New Times: The Changing Face of Politics in the 1990s*, London: Lawrence and Wishart,

1990, 160-72.
Murdock, Graham. "Cultural Studies at the Crossroads," in Angela McRobbie (ed.), *Back to Reality? Social Experience and Cultural Studies*, Manchester: Manchester University Press, 1997, 58-73.
Murray, Robin. "Fordism and Post-Fordism," in Stuart Hall and Martin Jacques (eds.), *New Times: The Changing Face of Politics in the 1990s*, London: Lawrence and Wishart, 1990, 38-53.
Newsweek. "The $25 Billion-a-Year Accent on Youth," 21 March 1964, 66-68.
———. "Teen-Age Tasters," 3 December 1951, 77-79.
Palladino, Grace. *Teenagers: An American History*, New York: Basic Books, 1996.
Reiman, Richard. *The New Deal and American Youth: Ideas and Ideals in a Depression Decade*, Athens: University of Georgia Press, 1992.
Reisman, David. *The Lonely Crowd: A Study of the Changing American Character*, New Haven, Conn.: Yale University Press, 1950.
———. "Listening to Popular Music," *American Quarterly*, Vol. 2 (Winter 1950), 359-71.
Smith, Pat. "Male Plumage '68," *Newsweek*, 25 Nov. 1968, 70-73.
Thomas, Richard. "Pleasures of Possession," *Newsweek*, 21 March 1966, 45-46.
Wall Street Journal. "Teenage Consumers," 6 December 1956, 11.
Willis, Paul. *Common Culture*, Milton Keynes: Open University Press, 1990.

3
The War on the Young: Corporate Culture, Schooling, and the Politics of "Zero Tolerance"

Henry A. Giroux

> It's almost ten years after the wilding in Central Park, and what people had stigmatized as a black criminal mentality they now have to look at in Colorado and Arkansas. When white youths display the rage of what they'd panned off as black pathology, they now have to look at it as an American pathology—as a country diseased at its core when children step out to kill. They're literally using their lives as revenge against the culture. And I don't think that we can ignore that and keep saying it's an individual pathology or it's because of the family. The country creates the family. People, for the most part, don't create their own values; the culture gives values–that's the purpose of culture.
>
> Sapphire[1]

Within the last decade, youth have become public enemy number one—blamed for nearly all of our major social ills extending from violence and drug use to the breakdown of family values. On the cultural front, the media constantly depicts youth, especially youth of color, as more troubling than troubled. Hollywood films such as *The Substitute*, *Dangerous Minds*, *187*, *Belly,* and *Black and White* are premised on the assumption that brown, black, and poor kids are not only outside of the purview of respect and decency, but also pose a threat to society because they embody rampant criminality, sexual degeneracy, and excessive drug abuse. In these films, youth are both demonized and marked as disposable, literally murdered as part of a "cleaning up" operation to make the public schools and urban streets safe for a largely white, middle-class adult population whose well-being and security are allegedly under siege. Rather than being *at risk* in a society marked by deep economic and social inequalities, youth have become *the risk.* Such representations signal a growing shift in the public's perception of young people.

No longer simply a symptom of systemic economic, social, and political inequalities, youth have become a social menace—a root cause of all that is wrong with American society. This perception of youth as ultraviolent, predatory, and morally depraved serves largely to eradicate any notion of adult responsibility for youth, offering few possibilities for analyzing how teens view themselves and their own sense of agency, experience their relations with others within diverse social spheres, and mediate power relations with adults. As corporate culture gains ascendency in all facets of American life, such representations of youth become more credible and less problematic as the rhetoric of cynicism, disdain, and containment are divorced from broader considerations of social responsibility.

Compassion for troubled youth has given way to "zero tolerance" policies that often translate into an easy excuse to punish kids rather than attempt to work with them and make an investment in their psychological, economic, and social well-being.[2] A growing number of cities are passing sweep laws—curfews and bans against loitering and cruising. Such laws are not only designed to keep youth off the streets, but to make it easier to criminalize their behavior as part of a broader effort to shift responsibility to the police and the courts for dealing with youth. Curfew arrests nationwide doubled between 1988 and 1997, and the brunt of such policies have fallen on youth of color. For instance, "according to the Center on Juvenile and Criminal Justice, Ventura County, California, arrests Latino and black youths at over seven times the rate of whites. In New Orleans, blacks are arrested at 19 times the rate of whites."[3] In spite of the fact that national homicide rates have dropped over 40 percent in the last seven years, youth of color are being incarcerated at record levels as indicated by the fact that while "whites make up 68 percent of all juveniles, 63 percent of youths in custody facilities are of color. In California, 86 percent of wards in the California Youth Authority are of color."[4] All fifty states have passed laws that allow juveniles—in some cases as young as eleven—to be tried as adults, and forty-three states have laws on the books making it easier to transfer children charged with crimes to adult courts. One recent study, the "Color of Justice," confirms that such laws are not only Draconian, but that such get-tough policies disproportionately punish disenfranchised minority youth.[5] The statistics are disturbing: "Minority youths are more than twice as likely as their white counter-parts to be transferred out of California's juvenile justice system and tried as adults. . . . [Moreover], once transferred to the adult system, young African-American offenders were 18.4 times more likely to be jailed than were young white offenders."[6] Dan Macallair, the coauthor of the study, claims that "California has a double standard: throw kids of color behind bars, but rehabilitate white kids who commit comparable crimes."[7] It gets worse. Cities such as Los Angeles are developing data bases to identify young "suspects" before they commit an actual crime. Ryan Pintado-Vitner and Jeff Chang are right in arguing that "youth of color have been turned into a generation of suspects."[8] All of this echoes a recent report by the Public Agenda policy group which found that "58 percent of those surveyed think children and teens will make the world a worse place or no different when they grow up."[9] More than three-quarters of the adults who responded to this survey used derogatory labels and negative terms in referring to teens as "rude," "irresponsible," or "wild."[10] There is a tragic and cruel irony in the fact that in many states kids need their parents' permission to get a tattoo, buy cigarettes, or get their ears pierced, while the same states see no contradiction in trying them as adults. It must seem strange to young people to live in a society that prevents them from getting their ears pierced without adult permission but has no qualms about placing them in jails with adults, subjecting them to rape, assault, and a range of other dehumanizing indignities.

Zero tolerance as both an ideology of disdain and a policy of containment increasingly reaches across a variety of public spheres that bear down on teens, extending from the criminal justice system to the public schools. Questions of school safety now become more important than issues of academic quality, even though by all accounts the public schools are just about the safest places available for children. Unfortunately, any sense of perspective appears to be lost, as school systems across the country clamor for metal detectors, armed guards, see-through knapsacks, and in some cases armed teachers. As *Boston Globe* columnist Ellen Goodman points out, zero tolerance has become a code word for a "quick and dirty way of kicking kids out" of school.[11] As compassion and understanding give way to rigidity and intolerance, more and more kids are being either suspended or expelled from the public schools. And the racial consequences of such policies are glaring. For example, in a recent study of twelve large public school districts, black youth were "suspended or expelled at a higher rate than their white peers."[12] But zero tolerance policies do more than turn schools into an adjunct of the criminal justice system; they also further rationalize misplaced legislative priorities that have a profound social cost. For instance, many states now spend "more on prison than on university construction. Operating prisons in the year 2000 will cost about $40 billion."[13] Young people are quickly realizing that schools have more in common with boot camps and prisons than they do with other institutions in American society. The hidden curriculum here is that learning is about conformity and adaptation, and that resistance means punishment and containment.

Demonized by the media, turned into a generation of suspects by the criminal justice system, and warehoused in economically depressed and overcrowded public schools, young people often find themselves inhabiting a social landscape in which public space is replaced by commodified spaces. As social space disappears and the welfare state is dismantled, teens find themselves without the benefit of youth programs, recreational facilities, health care, and basic support services. As the state is hollowed out and public services are dismantled, non-commodified spheres are replaced by privatized play areas, militarized urban spaces, a proliferation of malls and fast food restaurants, and an economic landscape offering low-skill, low-wage jobs. The adult world provides few markers for negotiating this terrain. Unfortunately, educators have ever-shrinking access to public forums to address the ongoing attacks on youth. In part, this is because the dominant discourses of neoliberalism and evangelical conservatism privilege the market-driven language of entrepreneurship and a ruthless bootstrap morality over the language of social responsibility, equity, justice, and democracy.

THE CRISIS OF AMERICAN SCHOOLING

The attack on the rights of children is nowhere more evident than in the increasingly powerful attempts to decimate the public school system as part of a broader assault on the welfare state and the democratic foundations of political, social, and cultural life. American youth and public schooling have not fared well in the political culture of the 1980s and 1990s. By calling into question the relationship between schooling and equity, many politicians and academics have redefined the role of education in terms that accentuate the language of privatization and standardization. Removed from the skills and knowledge of public service, many educational spokespersons have attempted to redefine the public school as an adjunct of the corporation, offering its services to the highest corporate bidder. In stark contrast to established educational philosophies ranging from John Dewey to W. E. B. Du Bois to Paulo Freire, schooling has become a private enterprise rather than a public good, a new market for investment opportunities that benefits the individual consumer rather than all members of society.

Growing up corporate has become a way of life for American youth. As commercial culture replaces public culture, the language of the market increasingly becomes a substitute for the language of democracy. The cost of this shift is high and can be seen in the power of an ever-expanding commercial culture to undermine the democratic foundation of civil society, particularly as the function of schooling shifts from being seen as a universal right to a privatized interest in which training increasingly replaces any vestige of critical education. Consumerism now appears to be the only kind of citizenship being offered to children and adults. Within this discourse, schooling offers no language for educating young people to defend vital public institutions, define citizenship as a social rather than privatized affair, and link learning to democratic social change.

Strapped for money, many public schools have had to lease out space in their hallways, buses, restrooms, and school cafeterias, transforming such spaces into glittering billboards for a variety of business interests. Invaded by candy manufacturers, breakfast cereal makers, sneaker companies, and fast food chains, schools increasingly offer the not-so-subtle message to students that everything is for sale—including student identities, desires, and values. Seduced by the lure of free equipment and money, schools all too readily make the transition from allowing advertising to providing commercial merchandise in the form of curricular materials designed to build brand loyalty among members of the captive public school audience. In this context, administrators and classroom teachers experience the humiliations of restructuring and the loss of autonomy as their roles shift from the demands of enlightened leadership to the pragmatics of the sales pitch, from the challenge of critical teaching to the spectacle of aping the hard sell.

While the corporate model of educational reform wraps itself in the democratic principles of freedom, individualism, and consumer rights, it fails to provide the broader historical, social, and political contexts necessary to render such principles meaningful and applicable, particularly with respect to the problems facing public schools. For instance, advocates of privatization and choice have little to say about the relationship between choice and the systemic relations of economic inequality; nor do they provide any context to explain public school failure in recent decades—ignoring factors such as joblessness, poverty, racism, crumbling school structures, and unequal school funding. Largely indifferent to the financial inequities that haunt public schools, the ideas and images that permeate this corporate model of schooling reek with the rhetoric of insincerity and the ruthless politics of social indifference.[14]

TOWARD A RADICAL EDUCATIONAL PRACTICE

In opposition to the corporatizing of public schools, progressive educators need to define public and higher education as a resource vital to the democratic and civic life of the nation. At the heart of such a task is the need for academics, cultural workers, and labor organizers to join together and oppose the transformation of the public schools and higher education into commercial spheres, to resist what Bill Readings has called a consumer-oriented corporation more concerned about accounting than accountability.[15] Schools need to provide students with possibilities for linking knowledge, social responsibility, and collective agency.

In addition to redefining the purpose and meaning of schooling as part of a broader attempt to struggle for a radical democratic social order, progressive educators need to reassess what it means to define the conditions under which they work in ways that provide them with a sense of dignity and power. Defending public and higher education as a vital sphere is necessary to develop and nourish the proper balance between democratic public spheres and commercial power, between identities founded on democratic principles and identities steeped in forms of competitive, self-interested individualism that celebrate selfishness, profit making, and greed. Progressives also need to reconsider the critical role educators might take up within public and higher education. This suggests that progressive educators strongly oppose those approaches to forms of schooling that corporatize and bureaucratize the teaching process, processes that deskill as they disempower. A radical pedagogy should, in part, be premised on the assumption that educators vigorously resist any attempt on the part of liberals and conservatives to reduce them to either the role of technicians or multinational operatives. Instead, progressive educators need to define their roles as engaged public intellectuals capable of teaching students the language of critique and possibility as a precondition for discovering their ability to become social agents. Such a redefinition of purpose, meaning, and politics suggests that educators critically interrogate the fundamental link between knowledge and power, pedagogical practices and social consequences, and authority and civic responsibility.

The question of what educators teach is inseparable from what it means to invest in public life and to locate oneself in a public discourse. Implicit in this argument is the assumption that the responsibility of educators cannot be separated from the consequences of the knowledge they produce, the social relations they legitimate, and the ideologies they disseminate to students. Educational work at its best represents a response to questions and issues posed by the tensions and contradictions of public life; it attempts to understand and intervene in specific problems that emanate from the material contexts of everyday existence. Teaching in this sense becomes performative and highlights considerations of power, politics, and ethics fundamental to any form of teacher-student interaction.

A radical pedagogy points to the connections between conception and practice, and it honors students' experiences by connecting learning to their everyday lives. Within such an approach, theoretical rigor is connected to social relevance, knowledge is subjected to critical scrutiny and engagement, and pedagogy is seen as crucial to the production both of individual and social agency. Struggles over pedagogy must also be seen as part of a broader struggle over institutional and material relations of power, and it is only by linking the institutional conditions for the organization of schooling to the production of critical pedagogical practices that teaching and leaning can take place as a concrete affirmation of dignity, meaning, and empowerment. This suggests that struggles over pedagogy must be accompanied by sustained attempts on the part of progressive educators collectively to organize and oppose current efforts to disempower teachers through the proliferation of standardized testing schemes, management by objectives designs, and bureaucratic forms of accountability. This requires that radical educators and other progressives organize against the corporate takeover of schools, fight to protect the power of unions, expand the rights and benefits of staff personal, and put more power into the hands of faculty and students. Accordingly, progressive educators and social activists should reject forms of schooling that marginalize students who are poor, black, and least advantaged. This suggests developing school practices that recognize how issues related to gender, class, race, and sexual orientation can be used as a resource for learning rather than being contained in schools through a systemic pattern of exclusion, punishment, and failure. Similarly, if curricular justice suggests that school knowledge be organized around the needs of the least advantaged, then school and classroom authority should rest in the hands of teachers and communities and not be under the control of "experts," imported from the business community or the world of for-profit schools. In addition, assessments in schools should draw upon multiple sources, be attentive to the cultural resources of the communities in which students live their daily lives, ai that any viable approach to assessment is as much about the discourse o and fair distribution of resources as it is about issues of testing and accou In this perspective, the conditions for teaching and learning cannot be se ated from the how and what students learn. Public schools don't need standardized curricula and testing. On the contrary, they need curricular justice—forms of teaching that are inclusive, caring, respectful, economically equitable, and whose aim, in part, is to undermine those repressive modes of education that produce social hierarchies and legitimate inequality while simultaneously providing them with the knowledge and skills needed to become well-rounded critical actors and social agents.

At the level of higher education, it is crucial for progressive educators not only to wage battles over access for poor and minority students, but to shift power away from bureaucracies to faculty, and also address the exploitative conditions under which many graduate students work—often constituting a de facto army of service workers who are underpaid, overworked, and shorn of any real power or benefits.[16] Simply put, the what, how, and why of teaching cannot be separated from the basic conditions under which educators and students labor. This means rethinking how teaching functions as a form of academic labor within iniquitous relations of power and how schooling can be addressed as a crucial site of struggle.[17] As long as teachers and students increasingly bear the burden of overcrowded classes, limited resources, and hostile legislators, progressive educators and students need to join with labor organizations, community people, and others in forming social movements that resist the corporatizing of schools, the rollback in basic services, and the exploitation of teachers and students.

At the very least, radical pedagogical work proposes that education is a form of political intervention in the world and is capable of creating the possibilities for social transformation.[18] Rather than viewing teaching as technical practice, radical pedagogy in the broadest terms is a moral and political act premised on the assumption that learning is not about processing received knowledge but actually transforming it as part of a more expansive struggle for individual rights and social justice. This implies that any viable notion of pedagogy should illustrate how knowledge, values, desire, and social relations are always implicated in relations of power, and how such an understanding can be used pedagogically and politically by students to expand further and deepen the imperatives of economic and political democracy. The fundamental challenge facing progressive educators within the current age of neoliberalism is to provide the conditions for students to address how knowledge is related to the power of both self-definition and social agency. Central to such a challenge is providing students with the skills, knowledge, and authority they need to inquire and act upon what it means to live in a radical multicultural democracy, to recognize antidemocratic forms of power, and to fight deeply rooted injustices in a society and world founded on systemic economic, racial, and gendered inequalities.

Addressing the problems youth currently face suggests that rigorous educational work needs to respond to the dilemmas of the outside world by focusing on how young people make sense of their experiences and possibilities for decision making within the structures of everyday life. The motivation for scholarly work cannot be narrowly academic; such work must connect with "real life social and political issues in the wider society."[19] This requires, in part, that progressive educators address the practical consequences of their work in the broader society while simultaneously making connections to those too-often-ignored institutional forms, social practices, and cultural spheres that position and influence young people. Moreover, it is crucial for critical educators to recognize that the forms of domination that bear down on young people are both institutional and cultural, and that one cannot be separated from the other. Within this approach to cultural politics, the effects of domination cannot be removed from those wider pedagogical conditions and popular spheres in which such behavior is learned, appropriated, or challenged.

As committed educators, progressives need to respect the lives of children by asking important questions such as what schools and other public spheres should accomplish in a democracy and why they fail, and how such a failure can be understood within a broader set of political, economic, spiritual, and cultural relations. We should remind ourselves in this time of rapacious capitalist mergers and downsizing that market-driven knowledge should not be the only discourse that schools offer to young people, that citizenship is not an entirely privatized affair, and that capitalism and democracy are not the same thing. Against dominant corporate ideology and relations of power, progressives must enter a wider public conversation around school policy and begin to argue forcefully in multiple cultural spheres that schools should function to serve the public good and not be seen merely as a source of private advantage removed from the dynamics of power and equity. At the same time, such arguments need to take place as part of a reconstituted defense of the welfare state and radical democracy. Progressive educators need to reappropriate the belief that academic work matters in its relationship to wider public practices and policies. In part, this suggests they address the crisis of vision and power that currently characterizes all levels of schooling and culture in the United States. The crisis of vision registers the political, social, and cultural demise of democratic relations and values in American institutions and culture while the crisis of power points to the necessity for educators and others to link educational work, both within and outside of schools, to "what it means to expand the scope of democracy and democratic institutions, [and to] address [how] the very conditions of democracy are being undermined."[20] Such work holds the promise for understanding not just how power operates in particular contexts, but also how the knowledge and skills produced and learned within diverse locations "will better enable people to change the contexts and hence the relations of power"[21] that inform the inequalities that undermine any viable notion of democratic participation in a wide variety of cultural spheres, including public and higher education.

Learning takes place in a variety of public spheres outside of the schools, and while we need to defend public and higher education against the ravaging influence of corporate culture, which means defending it as a public asset rather than as a private investment, we must also connect what is taught in the larger culture to the problems of youth and the challenges of radical democracy in a newly constituted global public. Progressive education in an age of rampant neoliberalism requires an expanded notion of the public, pedagogy, solidarity, and democratic struggle. Crucial here is a conception of the political that is open yet committed, respects specificity and difference without erasing global considerations, and provides new spaces for collaborative work engaged in productive social change. The time has come for progressive educators to develop a more systemic political project in which power, history, and social movements can play an active role in constructing the multiple and shifting political relations and cultural practices necessary for connecting the construction of diverse political constituencies to the revitalization of democratic public life.

At the beginning of the new millennium, educators, parents, and others should reevaluate what it means for children to grow up in a world that has been radically altered by a hyper-capitalism that monopolizes the educational force of culture as it ruthlessly eliminates those public spheres not governed by the logic of the market. Such a task demands new theoretical and political tools for addressing how pedagogy, knowledge, and power can be analyzed within and across a variety of cultural spheres, including but not limited to the schools, especially as such spheres frame the intersection of language and bodies as they become "part of the process of forming and disrupting power relations."[22] At the same time, progressive educators should work with parents, community organizers, labor organizations, and other groups to better understand how public discourses about youth have become synonymous with the language of control, surveillance, and demonization. Interrogating how power works through such discourses and social relations, particularly as they affect youth who are marginalized economically, racially, and politically, provides opportunities for progressives to challenge dominant ideologies and regressive social policies that undermine the possibilities for connecting the crisis of youth and the struggles over education to the broader crisis of radical democracy and social and economic justice. For many youth, the future appears to be a repeat of the present, a period not unlike what Gil Scott-Herron once called "winter in America." The time for radical change has never been so urgent since the fate of an entire generation of young people is at stake.

NOTES

1. Fran Gordon, "Breaking Karma: A Conversation with Sapphire," *Poets and Writers,* Jan.-Feb. 2000, 26-27. See my commentary on the culture of cynicism in Henry A. Giroux, *Public Spaces/Private Lives: Beyond the Culture of Cynicism* (Lanham, Md.: Rowman and Littlefield, 2001).

2. For a perceptive analysis of the recent attacks on youth within the media and other spheres see Carol Tell, "Generation What?" *Educational Leadership* 57, no. 4 (Dec. 1999/ Jan. 2000): 8-13.

3. Tell, "Generation What?" 13.

4. Tell, "Generation What?" 11.

5. As I write this essay, California has put into law Proposition 21, which shifts power away from judges to prosecutors in deciding whether juveniles fourteen years or older should be charged as adults. The law also calls for expanding penalties for youths fourteen and over who are convicted of felonies. Such youths would automatically be put in adult prison and be given lengthy mandated sentences. The law would largely eliminate intervention programs, increase the number of youth in prisons, especially minority youth, and keep them there for longer periods of time. The law is at odds with a number of studies that indicate that putting youth in jail with adults both increases recidivism and poses a grave danger to young offenders who, as a recent Columbia University study suggested, are "five times as likely to be raped, twice as likely to be beaten, and eight times as likely to commit suicide than adults in the adult prison system." Cited in Evelyn Nieves, "California Proposal Toughens Penalties for Young Criminals," *New York Times,* 6 March 2000, A1, A15.

6. Tamar Lewin, "Racial Discrepency Found in the Trying of Youths," *New York Times,* 3 Feb. 2000, A14.

7. Lewin, "Racial Discrepency . . . ," A14.

8. Ryan Pintado-Vertner and Jeff Chang, "The War on Youth," *Colorlines* (Winter 1999-2000), 12.

9. Public Agenda, *Kids These Days 1999: What Americans Really Think about the Next Generation* (New York: Public Agenda, 1999), 3.

10. Public Agenda, *Kids These Days,* 11.

11. Ellen Goodman, "'Zero Tolerance' Means Zero Chance for Troubled Kids," *Centre Daily Times* (Tuesday, Jan. 4, 2000): 8.

12. Tamar Lewin, "Study Finds Racial Bias in Public Schools," *New York Times,* 11 March 2000, A14.

13. Cited in Anthony Lewis, "Punishing the Country," *New York Times,* 21 Dec. 1999, A31.

14. A classic example of such mean-spirited indifference can be found in James Traub, "What No School Can Do," *New York Times Magazine,* 16 Jan. 2000, 52-57, 68, 81, 90-91.

15. Bill Readings, *The University in Ruins* (Cambridge, Mass.: Harvard University Press, 1996).

16. See Cary Nelson, ed., *Will Teach for Food: Academic Labor in Crisis* (Minneapolis: University of Minnesota Press, 1997).

17. I have taken this up in Henry A. Giroux, *Impure Acts: The Practical Politics of Cultural Studies* (New York: Routledge, 2000). See also, Stanley Aronowitz, *The Knowledge Factory* (Boston: Beacon Press, 2000).

18. I discuss this in great detail in Henry A. Giroux, *Pedagogy and the Politics of Hope: Theory, Culture, and Schooling* (Boulder, Colo.: Westview Press, 1997).

19. Tony Bennett, "Cultural Studies: A Reluctant Discipline," *Cultural Studies* 12, no. 4 (1998): 538.

20. Cornel West, "America's Three-fold Crisis," *Tikkun* 9, no. 2 (1994): 41-42.

21. Lawrence Grossberg, "Cultural Studies: What's in a Name?" in *Bringing It All Back Home: Essays in Cultural Studies* (Durham, N.C.: Duke University Press, 1997), 252-53.

22. Cindy Patton, "Performativity and Spatial Distinction," in Eve Kosofsky Sedgwick and Andrew Parker, eds., *Performativity and Performance* (New York: Routledge, 1993), 183.

BIBLIOGRAPHY

Aronowitz, Stanley. *The Knowledge Factory.* Boston: Beacon Press, 2000.

Bennett, Tony. "Cultural Studies: A Reluctant Discipline," *Cultural Studies* 12, no. 4 (1998): 528-46.

Giroux, Henry A. *Pedagogy and the Politics of Hope: Theory, Culture and Schooling.* Boulder, Colo.: Westview Press, 1997.

———. *Impure Acts: The Practical Politics of Cultural Studies.* New York: Routledge, 2000.

———. *Public Spaces/Private Lives: Beyond the Culture of Cynicism.* Lanham: Rowman and Littlefield, 2001.

Goodman, Ellen. "'Zero Tolerance' Means Zero Chance for Troubled Kids," *Centre Daily Times,* 4 Jan. 2000, 8.

Gordon, Fran. "Breaking Karma: A Conversation with Sapphire," *Poets and Writers* (Jan.-Feb. 2000): 24-27.

Grossberg, Lawrence. *Bringing It All Back Home: Essays in Cultural Studies.* Durham, N.C.: Duke University Press, 1997.

Lewin, Tamar. "Racial Discrepency Found in the Trying of Youths," *New York Times,* 3 Feb. 2000, A14.

———. "Study Finds Racial Bias in Public Schools," *New York Times,* 11 March 2000, A14.

Lewis, Anthony. "Punishing the Country," *New York Times,* 21 Dec. 1999, A31.

Nelson, Cary, ed. *Will Teach for Food: Academic Labor in Crisis.* Minneapolis: University of Minnesota Press, 1997.

Nieves, Evelyn. "California Proposal Toughens Penalties for Young Criminals," *New York Times,* 6 March 2000, A1, A15.

Patton, Cindy. "Performativity and Spatial Distinction," in Eve Kosofsky Sedgwick and Andrew Parker, eds., *Performativity and Performance.* New York: Routledge, 1993, 173-96.

Pintado-Vertner, Ryan, and Jeff Chang. "The War on Youth," *Colorlines* (Winter 1999-2000).

Public Agenda. *Kids These Days 1999: What Americans Really Think about the Next Generation.* New York: Public Agenda, 1999.

Readings, Bill. *The University in Ruins.* Cambridge, Mass.: Harvard University Press, 1996.

Tell, Carol. "Generation What?" *Educational Leadership* 57, no. 4 (Dec. 1999-Jan. 2000): 8-13.

Traub, James. "What No School Can Do," *New York Times Magazine,* 16 Jan. 2000, 52-57, 68, 81, 90-91.

West, Cornel. "America's Three-fold Crisis," *Tikkun* 9, no. 2 (1994): 41-42.

4
Richard Price and the Ordeal of the Postmodern City

Jerry Phillips

> Armed and dangerous, prowling the concrete jungle in search of ourselves, we were children who had grown up too quickly in a city that cared too little about its young.[1]

> Teenagers are the normal children of today's adults. They act in much the same way as the adults who raised them, and for much the same reasons. . . . In light of the rapidly deteriorating social conditions to which modern youth are subjected, most adolescents act better than we have a right to expect. If adults don't like the way teenagers act, the solution is not to turn a generation over to the professional treaters and imprisoners who have markedly worsened matters over the last decade, but to change our behaviors and the conditions in which youth are raised.[2]

> I always felt a mixture of pity and envy for kids. Childhood was hell, but I swear I'd give anything to start all over again.[3]

In a 1992 *Time* magazine article, Kevin Fedarko pondered the grim social conditions of the postindustrial city. Fedarko's prose aims at a sort of ethnographic impressionism, but his tone of voice evokes distilled melodrama rather than disinterested social science. Consider, for example, his lurid portrait of Camden, New Jersey: "Night puts a dark mask on this city's abandoned row houses, gutted factories and boarded shops. . . . Camden is a city of children. . . boys who blind stray dogs after school. . . whores who get pregnant at 14 only to bury their infants."[4] One could analyze this passage to show the conventional rhetorical moves of urban ethnography. Note, for instance, that the passage evokes a timeless urban scene in which there are no concrete individuals, only stereotypes, namely, teenage mothers and predatory schoolboys. However, what concerns me for the purposes of this essay is Fedarko's contention that "Camden is a city of children." What is meant by this phrase? How does the reduction of the urban scene to a cruel adolescent society throw light upon the postindustrial city, and the pains of growing up post-modern?

Fedarko's portrait of Camden draws from a storehouse of mythic images of the city: Sodom, Babylon, Necropolis, the modern wasteland, and the atavistic urban "jungle." These archetypical images preclude other ways of viewing the post-industrial urban milieu. Camilo Jose Vergara reminds us that Camden is "the poorest city in New Jersey," and that its resident population consists of people, not predatory animals.[5] The myth of the urban jungle blinds us to the human face of the post-industrial city. How, then, does the image of the ghetto teenager, as one who is cruel and amoral, blind us to the human faces of our children?

I propose to get at this question by analyzing Richard Price's *Clockers* (1992), a novel which compellingly explores the relationship between youth and post-industrial urbanism.[6] Set in the fictional New Jersey city of Dempsy, a decaying industrial "wasteland" of "three hundred thousand mostly angry blue-collar and welfare families" (31), *Clockers* tells the story of Strike, a young African American drug dealer who is "torn between visions of paradise and survival" (65) in his commitment to the illegal cocaine trade of the streets. Where Fedarko invites us to consider inner-city youth as dangerous animal beings devoid of human conscience, Price labors mightily to capture the irredeemably human aspect of the black ghetto, the dreams of its residents, their hopes and fears, and their struggles with "the giants of drugs, alcoholism and poverty" (473). Before embarking on my analysis of the novel, with a view to contextualizing the issues that the novel addresses, I want to consider the significance of the phrase "Camden is a city of children."

YOUTH AND THE CITY: MIRRORS OF ALIENATION

> Adolescence is a time of turbulence marked by rapid physical, sexual, social and emotional development. It is a time of confusion and rebellion.[7]

> The contacts of the city may indeed be face to face, but they are nevertheless impersonal, superficial, transitory, and segmented. The reserve, the indifference, and the *blasé* outlook which urbanites manifest in their relationships may thus be regarded as devices for immunizing themselves against the personal claims and expectations of others.[8]

If traditional culture yielded a fairly coherent model of historical process (the present finding itself in the past with the future in mind), then the characteristic note of modernity is discontinuity, the increasing separation of present practice from past. As David Harvey puts it, modernity "not only entails a ruthless break with any or all preceding historical conditions, but is characterized by a never-ending process of internal ruptures and fragmentations within itself."[9] In the attempt to theorize the discontinuous logic of modernity, social commentators have often viewed the capitalist metropole as a central modernizing force.

For example, Friedrich Engels noted that the great towns of nineteenth-century English capitalism, even as they concentrated individuals in vast numbers, dissolved human community into tens of thousands of "monads," each with a "separate purpose" and each brutally indifferent to the welfare of others. One can only wonder, mused Engels, "how the whole crazy fabric still holds together."[10] Writing a half-century after Engels, Georg Simmel contended that "the inner meaning of specifically modern life" can be gleaned from the symbolic terrain of "metropolitan phenomena."[11] Like Engels, Simmel viewed the modern metropolis as the appropriate social form for a "money economy" that threatens to obliterate authentic personhood. In short, for both theorists, the city becomes the objective correlative for the condition of alienation under capitalism.

To the extent that the city, in the words of Murray Bookchin, "reflects and even exaggerates the social irrationalities of our time,"[12] it has a symbolic logic that parallels the concept of "youth" as employed by writers, social scientists, pedagogues, and the like. For where childhood is typically associated with innocence, adolescence is often equated with alienation. Thus, Paul Goodman's *Growing Up Absurd* (1960) evokes the category of "youth" (which for Goodman means troubled young men) in such a way as to offer a sharp critique of modern society for being "deficient in many of the most elementary objective opportunities and worthwhile goals that could make growing up possible."[13] For Goodman, the "organized system" of commerce, industrialism, state bureaucracy, and mass culture has brought on a crisis of human purpose, "of how to be useful and make something of oneself" (*Growing Up*, 18), and nowhere is this crisis better revealed than in the travails of youth. In fine, like the urban scene of social theory, Goodman's delinquent youngster, the youth who belongs nowhere, who confronts absurdity in all directions, does nothing so much as symbolize the wayward, alienating culture of capitalist modernity.[14]

Youth and the city are mirrors of alienation to the degree that modern writers interpret human development in terms of an adequate human environment that is historically formed. In *Capital* Karl Marx drew attention to "the vile housing conditions" which the urban working class was subjected to in nineteenth-century England.[15] Marx's critique of the unheavenly city was part of his general denunciation of what he called "the anthropology of the capitalists [which held that] the age of childhood ended at 10, or at the outside 11" (*Capital*, 392), so that a little adult of twelve might be expected to labor long hours! The industrial city prepared its working class inhabitants for factory work and for little else. Said city was particularly ill suited for the training up of children—its barbaric qualities ensured that many children would grow up alienated and abused. Now when Kevin Fedarko writes of postindustrial Camden as a hellish "city of children" it isn't entirely clear whether the children are the cause or the effect of moral disintegration. This ambiguity speaks volumes about mainstream theories of human development in the era of late monopoly capital.

For where modernists like Marx and Goodman were wont to place the condition of youth alienation in a historical and social setting, many contemporary writers resort to biological or genetic models of the human character. The focus on naturalistic causes rather than sociohistorical processes tends to normalize the status quo with all its manifold social problems; and, more insidiously, it transforms the condition of youth into a dysfunctional or pathological state. Robert Hill and Dennis Fortenberry suggest that "The creation of adolescence as an age-based pathological condition" contributes to "the masking of factors" that are the sources of youth alienation and juvenile delinquency: "racism, the juvenilization of poverty, underemployment, inadequate education, and declining per-capita resources for dependent children and youth."[16] Consider, for example, Barbara Kantrowitz's comment in an article on juvenile delinquincy: "Some social scientists argue that teenage aggression is natural. . . . But other researchers who have studied today's violent teens say they are a new and more dangerous breed."[17] The lazy terminology employed here (with its implication that teenagers are a sort of "breed" apart) recalls G. Stanley Hall's developmental model of "the adolescent races" whose perverse behavior originates in the forces Sturm und Drang (storm and stress). Hall's adolescent was a kind of natural savage who has to be socialized ("civilized") into responsible adult identity. Mike Males points out that Hall's theory of adolescent behavior necessarily implies a disciplinary adult subject, for "if adolescence is defined as a disease state, it must be cured" (*Scapegoat Generation*, 219).

G. Stanley Hall was a social Darwinist, and if any one premise defined social Darwinism it was the ideological notion that competitive liberal capitalism approximated the natural order of species life.[18] A sociobiological outlook was therefore indispensable to social scientific researches. In our postmodern times, where the rule of Capital approaches absolutism (and thus a "natural" status), biological arguments for social inequality and the like have once again taken root, and nowhere more so than in discussions of race, poverty, crime, and inner-city youth. In *The War against Children of Color*, Peter Breggin and Ginger Breggin contend that the Federal Violence Initiative, housed at the National Institute of Mental Health, epitomizes the return of biological models of social problems and social control: "Perpetrators of violence in the inner-city are seen [by researchers] as biochemically and genetically defective, and plans are developed for identifying supposedly violence-prone children before they grow into dangerous youth and adults."[19] The orientation of the Federal Violence Initiative reinforces the journalistic stereotype of the natural-born teen criminal, the superpredator of the streets who stands today as the extreme version of alienated youth. This is the stereotype that Fedarko panders to when he describes Camden as a city of cruel children.

In *Clockers* Richard Price disavows the stereotype of the natural-born black criminal. If mainstream social science and journalism all too often place adolescents at a moral distance by confining them in a spurious category of "nature" (such as race), then a work like *Clockers* draws us nearer to our children by showing that they are what we have made them, and that we do them great evil when we oblige them to grow up in social environments that frustrate and deform their human potential. I now turn to the novel to explore this thesis in more detail.

STRIKE: POSTMODERN RAGGED DICK

> In the street life of the metropolis a boy needs to be on the alert, and have all his wits about him, or he will find himself wholly distanced by his more enterprising competitors for popular favor. To succeed in his profession, humble as it is, a boot-black must depend upon the same qualities which gain success in higher walks of life.[20]

Clockers captures the ordeal of postmodern urbanism in its treatment of Strike's subjective life-world, his coming to terms with the objective conditions of his existence. The lack of genuine human purpose in the black ghetto is registered in Strike's habitual feelings of unfocused rage: "Sometimes he found it impossible to keep straight what exactly it was that was pissing him off from day to day, hour to hour" (76). Strike's rage lacks focus because his plight is owing to a complex of social factors rather than a single cause. Which is to say, it is the condition of being *poor and black and young in a dying city* that leaves him prey to feelings of absurdity. Dempsy is the only world Strike has known, and yet he is plagued by the idea of a paradisial life, where "palm trees and ocean" replace "empty lots and broken buildings" (161) as the landscape for self-realization.

Like all human beings, Strike desires autonomy, the freedom to become on his own terms. However, Price shows us that freedom is not simply a matter of individual will but is very much a social question bound up with objective necessity. We are told that Strike "never considered himself a criminal: clocking [i.e., drug dealing] was just what he did, what he considered his best shot at having a life, like going into the army or working for UPS" (69). Strike considers drug dealing a pathway to autonomy; he associates low-paid work and military service with unfreedom. *Clockers* asks us to ponder the question of how it is that criminality or heteronomy are the only life choices on offer for inner-city youth. In order to answer this question we have to consider objective necessity in the light of the social totality, which is to say, we have to attend to the economic system that confronts the individual as he comes of age.

The fundamental objective fact that looms over working class youth as they enter the adult world is that the distribution of property and wealth under capitalism (which decrees that the necessities of life can only be purchased at the marketplace) obliges the worker to sell his or her labor power for another's benefit.[21] However, what if the labor power of the worker cannot be profitably used by the owning class? The worker remains bereft of the necessities of life and has no means by which to purchase them. Working class resistance over the ages has forced capitalists to concede some protection to workers from the worst failures of the market, in the form of social welfare programs or "safety nets." However, in the last few decades Capital has launched a relentless counteroffensive, severely curtailing the power of the State to intervene in the "natural" workings of the market, especially as it affects the value of labor power.[22] Nowhere has this counteroffensive been felt with greater pain and urgency than in the black ghettos of urban America. Here, then, is the context for *Clockers*' treatment of objective necessity, more specifically, the form it assumes in the illicit cocaine trade, which has transformed the streets of Dempsy into the various territories of drug crews and gangs.

Deborah Prothrow-Stith rightly points out that "the drug problem that is decimating our inner-city neighborhoods is much more than a drug problem. It is also a job problem. A housing problem. . . . A problem of hope and hopelessness."[23] The cocaine trade employs so many black youngsters because, starved of investment, the ghetto offers few, if any, legitimate opportunities for the sale of one's labor power. Within the ghetto, pauperism swells and an informal economy of crime, barter, and the like grows in due time. Thus, Strike might be viewed as a typical or representative character as described by Terry Eagleton: "a protagonist who incarnates historical forces without thereby ceasing to be richly individualized."[24] The absurd paradox which dogs Strike is that far from making him autonomous, his drug dealing only confirms his heteronomous state. Strike recognizes that he lacks the ruthlessness to succeed on his own in the drug trade, and because of this he will always be someone else's lackey. As symbolized by his stomach ulcer, Strike's despair eats away at him. The frenzied promise that he makes to himself that "If I don't step up, I'm stepping out. I can't take it no more" (14), gives us insight into pain that is unmistakably human.

The novel shows that while Strike finds it impossible to remain within the cocaine trade, he does not know how to extricate himself. He dreams of rising out of the informal economy of crime into social reputability. However, because he wants to avoid the attention of the police, Strike "was afraid to do anything with [his] money, didn't want to flaunt it or acquire anything that could be taken from him, so all he had to show for his hard work was cash, more cash than he could count" (20). Paul Goodman notes that meaningful growth from adolescence to maturity requires "adequate objects in the environment" (*Growing Up*, 12). With this standard in mind, one immediately sees the absurdity of Strike's predicament: money is the only object of his criminal activities because money under capitalism is the key to personal autonomy; however, Strike cannot use his money to attain a legitimate social status; all he can do is accumulate it ad infinitum. In *Clockers*, money symbolizes the existential divide between subject and object that is at the heart of alienation.

In one respect, Strike is a postmodern Ragged Dick. In Horatio Alger's *Ragged Dick* (1867), the central character is an impoverished orphan who had "earned his own living ever since he was seven years old" (*Ragged*, 88) as a bootblack on the streets of New York. Ragged Dick makes his way through a largely heartless world by sheer force of moral character. He refuses the temptations of crime and embraces the discipline of self-culture. He is finally rewarded with wealth and social reputability. Alger portrays Dick as a type of the entrepreneur in order to convey the message that an individual's fate, under capitalism, is solely of his or her own making. "Poverty," says Dick's sponsor, "is no bar to a man's advancement" (*Ragged*, 108).

Of course, Alger's novel is a puerile fantasy of the assimilation of the so-called dangerous classes to the bourgeois social order. In Alger's world vision the individual, of whatever class background, is superior to the objective social relations that he finds himself in. Herein lies the appeal of Alger's novel as modernist myth.[25] In sharp contrast, *Clockers* dramatizes a world into which the individual is simply thrown (as the phenomenologists say) without any transcendent meaning. In *Clockers*, the lowly individual might bring his character to bear on his situation (like Ragged Dick), but there is no necessary connection between virtue and social mobility. The novel makes this abundantly clear in its treatment of two characters: Victor Durham, Strike's elder brother, and Rodney Little, the druglord to whom Strike owes allegiance.

Like Strike, Victor dreams of escape from the public housing projects that form Dempsy's black ghetto. "Victor never did anything but work his whole life, never even hung out on the street" (247). He holds two jobs, and works from daybreak to nightfall. And yet Strike makes more money in one month selling drugs than Victor makes in two years of legitimate employment. The absurdity of capitalism as a system of human value starkly reveals itself: the low-paid worker forever has a foot in the "swamp of pauperism" (*Capital*, 796), so he ends up living to work rather than working to live. From a rational choice perspective, Strike's decision to sell illegal narcotics makes sense because the sole point of economic activity in the capitalist marketplace is to maximize the monetary value of one's labor. However, as we have seen, Strike is unable to translate his economic capital into social capital. Little wonder, then, that Strike finds it hard "to draw a picture of himself that could be entitled 'Making It.' He couldn't imagine what he would be doing in that picture, what he would be holding, wearing, even what the expression on his face would be" (205). Both Strike and Victor possess many of the virtues of Horatio Alger's Ragged Dick; they are resourceful, temperate, and hard working. But where Dick was able to walk into the future of his dreams, neither of the Durham brothers is truly able to imagine a hopeful future. Theirs is a world of limits rather than possibilities.[26]

Ragged Dick reaps the advantages of "self-denial and judicious economy" (*Ragged*, 193), but he is helped on his way by a bevy of benevolent, respectable adults who recognize true virtue when they see it. This sentimental formula of the virtuous, ambitious youth and his worthy patron (so beloved by Victorian writers) appears in *Clockers* in a grotesquely modified form: the relationship between Strike and Rodney, the young drug dealer and his captain. Price portrays Rodney as a sort of diabolic tempter, who forces Strike to recognize himself as one capable of crime. Significantly, the narrator calls Rodney a "ghetto capitalist," for Rodney conceives of himself as a "businessman" in the self-made tradition of Benjamin Franklin. Rodney's paternalistic advice to his teenage drug crew calls to mind the practical wisdom of Franklin's famous treatise, *The Way to Wealth*: "a dime's a dime"; "that's the most important thing a man owns, his word"; "a man who can't do nothing for himself, shit, he can't do nothing for anybody"; and "you gotta start respecting yourself." Rodney's aphorisms take the metaphysic of possessive individualism (which holds that the individual is "essentially the proprietor of his own person or capacities, owing nothing to society for them"[27]) to its solipsistic extreme. Rodney survives the brutalities of the cocaine trade because "he understood that there were no real lives out here on the streets, no real lives other than his own, and that what really mattered was coming first in all things, in all ways and at all costs" (340). Through the character of Rodney, Price shows the human toll exacted when social values collapse leaving only a hyper-capitalist ethos of individualism in their wake.

This is the tragedy of the drug trade in the postindustrial milieu: the drug trade takes hold because capitalism has failed the inner city, and yet the effect of the drug trade is not necessarily to call into question the "natural" workings of the market (and thus generate interest in an alternative social arrangement), but rather it works to shore up competitive capitalist values.[28] We learn that "A lot of young boys around the projects liked to tear and fold paper until they had a stack of blank pretend money, and could play dope dealer, whipping out their roll, hiking one foot up on a bench and counting out loud like it was a good night. Strike thought such behavior . . . in young kids was just sadder than shit" (195). The drug trade has created the spectacle of "fifteen year old kids driving new cars, wearing gold" (528). Such youths are drawn to the drug trade by the canon of conspicuous consumption that makes itself felt at all levels of capitalist society.[29] "The idea of all these things to be had" (18); the "concept of possession" that leaves the individual "crazed with wanting" (19)—these are the social values that underlie the willingness to commit crime.

When the journalist Alex Kotlowitz proposed writing a book about children growing up in inner-city Chicago, he was told by an adult resident that "there are no children here. They've seen too much to be children."[30] Price hints at the disappearance of childhood innocence in the contemporary urban world in his depiction of the children playing dope dealer. That the social environment of the postindustrial city robs children of their childhood only confirms Neil Postman's thesis that "the dividing line between childhood and adulthood is rapidly eroding."[31] The child of our postmodern times is always already a youth or little adult who knows too much, has seen too much, and is capable of all good and evil.

THE NEW AMERICAN GHETTO AND THE OBSOLESCENCE OF THE BLACK POOR

> Within ghetto walls a new generation is growing along with new activities, ideologies, institutions and drugs. Crack sells briskly across the streets from drug treatment centers, and children walk past homeless shelters. . . . Houses, turned into fortresses, stand alone, enclosed by fences. Dozens of cities are falling into ruin, and along their streets billboards plead for people to stop killing one another.
>
> (*New American*, 22)

> Strike hated posters. If you were poor, posters followed you everywhere—health clinics, probation offices, housing offices, day care centers, welfare offices—and they were always away at you with warnings to do this, don't do that. (407)

> [The] symbol of the megalopolis is rapidly becoming the police badge superimposed by a gun.
>
> (*Limits*, 139)

The emphasis on semiology in postmodern urban theory encourages blindness to the fundamental reality of the urban scene: that before a city is a "text," a drama of eloquent signs, it is a set of social and spatial relations established by politico-economic factors (chief of which is capital accumulation).[32] Postmodern urbanists are wont to make the Central Business District and the entertainment avenues, with their skyscrapers, shops, billboards, museums, theaters, and hotels, the foci of their analysis of the city as text.[33] However, the postmodern city looks very different in theoretical terms if one begins one's analysis in the residential areas of the urban working class. From this angle, the city as a set of social relations framed by Capital cannot be gainsaid.

Dempsy's landscape of "gas stations and highways and housing projects" (204) is precisely the urban world that is missing from celebrations of the postindustrial city as postmodern text. Indeed, *Clockers* obliges us to compare and contrast the city of finance, information, and consumerism with its counterpart of indigence, racial segregation, and ruins, the one a primary circuit of investment capital, the other an economic desert. What Vergara calls "the cityscape of poverty" (*New American*, xv) forms the background to the action of the novel.

Strike's drug territory takes in Roosevelt Homes, a public housing project made up of "thirteen high rises, twelve hundred families over two square blocks" (4-5). That the projects are named for President Franklin D. Roosevelt is not coincidental. In the folklore of modern capitalism, FDR is associated with the round of welfare state policies termed the New Deal, which, as Sidney Lens remarks, "turned America from *laissez faire* to controlled capitalism."[34] Whether or not the New Deal was an economic success is debatable, but on the ideological front it represented the partial victory of social values over market values. Which is to say, the indigent were viewed in New Deal social policy as having a legitimate claim on the wider community when the market failed them. However, as noted above, welfare statism has been ruthlessly discarded by the ruling class, and laissez-faire capitalism is once again the reigning orthodoxy.

Modernist urban policy and welfare statism went hand in hand as regards the construction of public housing projects like the Roosevelt Homes. But with the decline of the latter, the former's influence has waned, so that mass-produced public housing is now fairly a thing of the past. In its depiction of Roosevelt Homes, *Clockers* makes one cognizant of the fact that those housing projects which remain are no longer (if they ever were) monuments of an ideal "city of tomorrow."[35] Rather, in their increasing decrepitude, the projects herald "the coming of the post-urban era" (*New American*, 205), wherein the liberal model of inclusive social pluralism is unlikely to survive. Consider this description of JFK Boulevard, Dempsy's main street: "two miles of funk: storefront churches, deserted lots, hair salons and private day-care centers. Most of the store signs were hand drawn . . . cameras on every telephone pole to monitor drug transactions" (118-19). The reference to surveillance cameras alludes to what Camilo Jose Vergara has termed "the New American Ghetto"—a repressive politics of space in which fortification, panopticism, and paramilitarized policing play determinate roles in confining the racially oppressed to de facto "reservations of the destitute."[36]

In his study of American apartheid, Douglass Massey points out that "racial segregation concentrates deprivation in black neighborhoods by restricting the poverty created in economic downturns to a small number of minority neighborhoods."[37] Black youth like Strike feel imprisoned by their neighborhoods, and with good reason, for there are active social forces at work to separate the ghetto from the rest of the city. The chief agency in this regard is the police. Under the aegis of the War Against Drugs, the police perform the necessary work of social control of the ghetto. As pauperism within the ghetto increases, the police become more actively involved in all aspects of ghetto life. Price captures something of this social logic in casting a police officer as one of his central characters. The novel gives us the drug war as experienced by both the young ghetto resident and the white police officer who comes from without. From countless newspaper articles and prime-time crime reports, this pairing of social types is now so familiar that one can almost describe it as the essential mythic encounter in the postindustrial city, wherein the black youth symbolizes lawlessness, degeneracy, and savagery, while the police officer stands for law and order and civility.[38] To be sure, much of the moral beauty of *Clockers* as a work of art resides in the fact that although it uses the broad lineaments of this mythic narrative, it rejects the racist ideology that gives the myth its potency. Price portrays his youthful black characters as complexly human in all aspects of their lives.

At one point in the novel, Rocco Klein, the detective paired with Strike as a paradigmatic urban figure, watches some junkies scavenge on a garbage dump "like insects programmed for a life task and knowing nothing else" (215). Klein reflects, "It's like fucking Bhopal [the scene of a major industrial disaster]." Most of the junkies suffer from AIDS. Klein entertains a "half-serious theory of the Virus as a weapon against crime" (219). Klein's apocalyptic vision of the ghetto as populated by "bloody burning children and walking dead parents" (256) brings into focus the sociobiological attitude toward the urban milieu, which works to normalize the catastrophic results of social inequality. If AIDS can be viewed as nature's revenge on people "at the bottom of the junkie chain" (215), then the social Darwinist vision of life as perpetual struggle, wherein the weakest go to the wall (a vision that has long attended laissez-faire capitalism), comes into its own. In short, the AIDS epidemic in the inner city becomes part of a deliberate Malthusian final solution to the problem of an obsolete surplus populace.[39]

Sidney Wilhelm observes that automation of the labor process in heavy industries has consigned large numbers of working class African Americans to economic obsolescence. Which is to say, a significant stratum of the black labor force has been rendered into a permanent surplus population. "Stripped of his economic usefulness," Wilhelm argues, "the negro becomes a nonentity whose body must be 'taken care of'—ignored within the ghetto reservation, or, in the event of physical resistance, exterminated."[40] Marx noted that "a surplus population is a necessity of modern industry" (*Capital*, 787): what he called "the reserve industrial army" is one of the great weapons that capitalists have at their disposal in their efforts to regulate the value of labor power and its effects on the rate of profit. However, the black surplus populace is in some ways unique. For not only are blacks economically worthless in accordance with the "logic of surplus," they are also a racially despised people. The combination of economic worthlessness and social inferiority makes the genocidal option towards blacks increasingly attractive.

You will say that I exaggerate, but consider the telling observation made by Richard Rubenstein about genocide in the modern era: "The history of the twentieth century has taught us that people who are rendered permanently superfluous are eventually condemned to segregated precincts of the living dead or are exterminated outright."[41] The awful condition of many inner-city neghborhoods and the remarkable rate of black imprisonment are strong evidence that Rubenstein's first option of intense segregation has already been adopted in the social treatment of superfluous blacks. That we cannot dismiss the second option of extermination is made plain by the strong return of scientific racism, which makes of blacks creatures of nature who can hardly be civilized.[42] In *The War against Children of Color*, Peter Breggin and Ginger Breggin cite the words of Dr. Frederick Goodwin, a top official at the National Institute of Mental Health. According to Goodwin, black youth in the cities exhibit behaviors that are comparable to "male monkeys, especially in the wild. . . . Maybe it just isn't careless use when people call certain areas of certain cities jungles . . . we may have gone back to what might be more natural without all the social controls . . . [of] civilization" (*War*, 8). It need harldy be pointed out, with the example of the Nazi doctors firmly planted in our minds, that what the Breggins call "biomedical social control" of black youth could well be the prelude to something far more sinister. Certainly, many African Americans consider themselves under threat of extermination. "Everywhere we have gone," write the Breggins, "from Harlem to Watts and from Washington, D.C. to Fort Lauderdale, . . . African Americans tell us that white America is increasingly genocidal toward them" (*War*, 163). And Camilo Jose Vergara notes that "A national mood of desperation and resentment, expressed by words like 'genocide,' 'concentration camps,' and 'apartheid,' has developed [in the inner cities] to account for the condition of our ghettos" (*New American*, 22).

"A NEW LIFE"

At the close of *Clockers*, Detective Rocco Klein decides to give Strike a chance at "a new life" by encouraging him to leave Dempsy. Strike doesn't know whether to head for the South or the West, but he feels that his future has at last become meaningful. He sees possibilities where formerly he had seen only limits. The ending of the novel can be criticized on the grounds that the narrative fails to follow through on the social vision it has entertained, a vision of inner-city youth trapped in an absurd world, and instead offers the familiar American myth, as in *Huckleberry Finn*, of individual escape. The plight of children and youth today hardly permits the consolation of myth. "Our time," notes George Lipsitz, "is a time of crisis for youth, a time of unprecedented damage and danger to young people."[43] The great virtue of *Clockers* is that it makes us *feel* the crisis as only a novel can. However, Price offers few, if any, solutions to the problems he has so powerfully diagnosed.

In contemporary Brazil, indigent and orphaned children are cleansed from the streets as so much social waste by fascistic death squads, many of whose members are police officers.[44] The United States has yet to arrive at this juncture, but the possibility of such an arrival, at some date in the future, cannot be ruled out. To summarize the message that has been the burden of this essay, I can do no better than close with the warning words of Peter and Ginger Breggin:

> If white America cannot find the heart to empathize with the plight of its black children, and if the black community cannot find some hope for surviving and ultimately thriving in America, our society as we know it cannot be maintained. . . . America will either fall apart or become a genocidal police state, or both, if it does not deal equitably with its Americans.
>
> The fate of the black child may turn out to be the single most important indicator of the future of America—a future that is inseparable from that of the black child.
>
> How goes the black child? So goes America. [45]

NOTES

1. Sanyika Shakur, *Monster: The Autobiography of an L.A. Gang Member* (New York: Penguin, 1993), 111. Hereafter cited as *Monster*.

2. Mike A. Males, *Scapegoat Generation: America's War on Adolescents* (Monroe, ME: Common Courage, 1996), 275. Hereafter cited as *Scapegoat Generation*.

3. Richard Price, *Ladies' Man* (Boston: Houghton Mifflin, 1978), 9.

4. Cited in Males, *Scapegoat Generation*, 77.

5. Camilo Jose Vergara, *The New American Ghetto* (New Brunswick, NJ: Rutgers University Press, 1995), 14. Hereafter cited as *New American*.

6. Richard Price, *Clockers* (Boston: Houghton Miflin 1992). Subsequent references to this text are in parentheses.

7. Flint E. Scheingold, "Teen Suicide," *The New Physician* (March 1987), 35. Cited in Males, *Scapegoat Generation*, 77.

8. Louis Wirth, "Urbanism as a Way of Life," in Paul K. Hatt and Albert J. Reiss, eds. *Reader in Urban Sociology* (Glencoe, IL: Free Press 1951), 40.

9. David Harvey, *The Condition of Postmodernity: An Enquiry into the Origins of Cultural Change* (Cambridge, MA: Blackwell, 1990), 12.

10. Friedrich Engels, *The Condition of the Working Class in England* (Harmondsworth: Penguin, 1987 [1845]), 69.

11. Georg Simmel, "The Metropolis and Mental Life," in Kurt H. Wolff, ed., *The Sociology of Georg Simmel* (New York: Free Press, 1950), 409-24.

12. Murray Bookchin, *The Limits of the City* (New York: Harper & Row 1974), viii. Hereafter cited as *Limits*.

13. Paul Goodman, *Growing Up Absurd: Problems of Youth in the Organized Society* (New York: Vintage, 1960), 12. Hereafter cited as *Growing Up*.

14. For a study which links youth alienation to suburbia, the dominant model of settlement in the contemporary United States, see Donna Gaines, *Teenage Wasteland: Suburbia's Dead-End Kids* (New York: Harper, 1990).

15. Karl Marx, *Capital, Vol. I: A Critique of Political Economy,* trans. Ben Fowkes (New York: Vintage, 1977 [1867]), 813. Hereafter cited as *Capital*.

16. Cited in Males, *Scapegoat Generation,* 219.

17. Barbara Kantrowitz, "Wild in the Streets," *Newsweek,* 2 August 1983, 45.

18. Herbert Spencer makes the classic argument for this theory. See his "The Proper Sphere of Government" in *Spencer: Political Writings* (Cambridge: Cambridge University Press, 1994), 1-59. On the ideological aspect of social Darwinism see Richard Hofstadter, *Social Darwinism in American Thought* (Boston: Beacon Press, 1955 [1944]); R. Jackson Wilson, *Darwinism and the American Intellectual: An Anthology* (Chicago: Dorsey Press, 1989); and Robert C. Bannister, *Social Darwinism: Science and Myth in Anglo-American Social Thought* (Philadelphia: Temple University Press, 1979).

19. Peter Breggin and Ginger Breggin, *The War against Children of Color: Psychiatry Targets Inner-city Youth* (Monroe, ME: Common Courage 1998), xv. Hereafter cited as *War*.

20. Horatio Alger, "Ragged Dick," in *Ragged Dick and Mark, the Match Boy* (London: Collier McMillan, 1962), 205. Hereafter cited as *Ragged*.

21. For an insightful treatment of the subjective and objective dimensions of growing up

working class, see Paul E. Willis's classic *Learning to Labor: How Working Class Kids Get Working Class Jobs* (London: Gower, 1977).

22. See Edward S. Herman, *Triumph of the Market: Essays on Economics, Politics, and the Media* (Boston: South End Press, 1995).

23. Deborah Prothrow-Stith, *Deadly Consequences* (New York: Harper, 1991), 113.

24. Terry Eagleton, *Marxism and Literary Criticism* (London: Methuen, 1976), 29.

25. See John G. Cawelti, *Apostles of the Self-Made Man: Changing Concepts of Success in America* (Chicago: University of Chicago Press, 1965), 101-23.

26. Compare Goodman: "The delinquent fatalism is the feeling of no chance in the past, no prospect for the future, no recourse in the present; whence the drive to disaster" (*Growing Up*, 211).

27. C. B. Macpherson, *The Political Theory of Possessive Individualism: Hobbes to Locke* (Oxford: Oxford University Press, 1962), 3.

28. Thus Sanyika Shakur says of his career on the streets as an "original gangster": "I had as much ambition, vitality, and ruthlessness to succeed as any corporate executive planning a hostile takeover" (*Monster*, 15). For an informative (though uneven) ethnography which illuminates the everyday economics of the drug trade, see Terry Williams, *The Cocaine Kids: The Inside Story of a Teenage Drug Ring* (Reading, MA: Addison Wesley, 1989).

29. I draw here from Thorstein Veblen, *The Theory of the Leisure Class: An Economic Study of Institutions* (New York: New American Library, 1953 [1899]), 60-80.

30. Alex Kotlowitz, *There Are No Children Here* (New York: Doubleday, 1991), x.

31. Neil Postman, *The Disappearance of Childhood* (New York: Vintage, 1992 [1984]), xii.

32. I am following the lead of David Harvey, *The Urban Experience* (Baltimore, MD: Johns Hopkins University Press, 1989), 256-78.

33. See, for example, Jean Baudrillard, *America,* trans. Chris Turner (London: Verso, 1988), 13-24.

34. Sidney Lens, *Poverty: America's Enduring Paradox* (New York: Thomas Y. Crowell Co., 1971), 257.

35. For the classic statement of modernist ideals in urban planning, see Le Corbusier, *The City of Tomorrow and Its Planning* trans. Frederick Etchells (New York: Dover, 1987 [1927]).

36. Camilo Jose Vergara, "A Guide to the Ghettos," *The Nation* (13 March 1993): 339.

37. Douglas S. Massey, "American Apartheid: Segregation and the Making of the Underclass," *American Journal of Sociology* 96, no. 2 (Sept. 1990): 356.

38. For a work which conveys the police officer's view of the (mythic) urban scene, see Mark Baker, *Cops: Their Lives in Their Own Words* (New York: Simon and Schuster, 1985).

39. In the second edition of *On Population* (1803), Thomas Malthus proposed an overtly genocidal policy for reducing the numbers of the poor: "[Far from] recommending cleanliness to the poor, we should encourage contrary habits. In our towns we should make the streets narrower, crowd more people into the houses and court the return of the plague." Cited in Murray Bookchin, *Re-Enchanting Humanity: A Defense of the Human Spirit against Anti-Humanism, Misanthropy, Mysticism, and Primitivism* (London: Cassell, 1995), 70. For an outstanding study of the dismal effects of Malthusianism throughout the modern era, see Allan Chase, *The Legacy of Malthus: The Social Costs of the New Scientific Racism* (Urbana: University of Illinois Press, 1980).

40. Sidney Wilhelm, *Who Needs the Negro?* (Hampton, VA: UB and US Communications

Systems, 1993 [1970]), 224. Another work which advances the thesis that African Americans are in danger of being exterminated is Samuel Yette's *The Choice: The Issue of Black Survival in America* (New York: Berkeley Medallion Books, 1971). Note that even a political liberal like William Julius Wilson is forced to acknowledge the economic obsolescence of the black poor. The major difference between Wilhelm and Wilson is that the former sees the present moment as the inevitable result of the history of black dehumanization, whereas the latter rejects what he derisively calls "the easy explanation of racism." Wilson's argument is surely too economistic, paying insufficient attention to the ideological and cultural functions of racist discourse and practice. See William Julius Wilson, *The Truly Disadvantaged: The Inner-city, The Underclass, and Public Policy* (Chicago: University of Chicago Press, 1987). For a powerful refutation of Wilson's argument that race is declining in its social significance, see Joe R. Feagin and Melvin P. Sikes, *Living with Racism: The Black Middle Class Experience* (Boston: Beacon, 1994).

41. Richard L. Rubenstein, *The Cunning of History: The Holocaust and the American Future* (New York: Harper, 1975), 96.

42. Graphs, charts, and pseudo-scientific jargon cannot disguise the fact that this is the essential message of Charles Murray's and Richard Hernstein's *The Bell Curve: Intelligence and Class Structure in American Life* (New York: Free Press, 1994). That this ponderous and pretentious book was taken seriously in some quarters is an ominous sign of the growing respectability of scientific racism.

43. Cited in Henry A. Giroux, *Fugitive Cultures: Race, Violence, and Youth* (New York: Routledge, 1996), 10.

44. See Nancy Scheper-Hughes and Daniel Hoffman, "Kids Out of Place," *NACLA: Report on the Americas* 27, no. 6 (May-June 1994): 16-23.

45. Breggin and Breggin, *War against Children*, 161.

BIBLIOGRAPHY

Alger, Horatio. *Ragged Dick and Mark, the Match Boy.* London: Collier McMillan, 1962.

Baker, Mark. *Cops: Their Lives in Their Own Words.* New York: Simon & Schuster, 1985.

Bannister, Robert C. *Social Darwinism: Science and Myth in Anglo-American Social Thought.* Philadelphia: Temple University Press, 1979.

Baudrillard, Jean. *America* trans. Chris Turner. London: Verso, 1988.

Bookchin, Murray. *The Limits of the City.* New York: Harper and Row, 1974.

———. *Re-Enchanting Humanity: A Defense of the Human Spirit against Anti-Humanism, Misanthropy, Mysticism, and Primitivism.* London: Cassell, 1995.

Breggin, Peter, and Ginger Breggin. *The War against Children of Color: Psychiatry Targets Inner-city Youth.* Monroe, ME: Common Courage, 1998.

Cawelti, John G. *Apostles of the Self-Made Man: Changing Concepts of Success in America.* Chicago: University of Chicago Press, 1965.

Chase, Allan. *The Legacy of Malthus: The Social Costs of the New Scientific Racism.* Urbana: University of Illinois Press, 1980.

Corbusier, Le. *The City of Tomorrow and Its Planning,* trans. Frederick Etchells. New York: Dover, 1987 (1927).

Eagleton, Terry. *Marxism and Literary Criticism.* London: Methuen, 1976.

Engels, Friedrich. *The Condition of the Working Class in England.* Harmondsworth: Penguin,

1987 (1845).
Feagin, Joe R., and Melvin P. Sikes. *Living with Racism: The Black Middle Class Experience.* Boston: Beacon, 1994.
Gaines, Donna. *Teenage Wasteland: Suburbia's Dead-End Kids.* New York: Harper, 1990.
Giroux, Henry A. *Fugitive Cultures: Race, Violence, and Youth.* New York: Routledge, 1996.
Goodman, Paul. *Growing Up Absurd: Problems of Youth in the Organized Society.* New York: Vintage, 1960.
Harvey, David. *The Urban Experience.* Baltimore, MD: Johns Hopkins University Press, 1989.
——.*The Condition of Postmodernity: An Enquiry into the Origins of Cultural Change.* Cambridge, Massachusetts: Blackwell, 1990.
Herman, Edward S. *Triumph of the Market: Essays on Economics, Politics, and the Media.* Boston: South End Press, 1995.
Hofstadter, Richard. *Social Darwinism in American Thought.* Boston: Beacon Press, 1955 (1944).
Kantrowitz, Barbara. "Wild in the Streets," *Newsweek,* 2 August 1983, 45.
Kotlowitz, Alex. *There Are No Children Here.* New York: Doubleday, 1991.
Lens, Sidney. *Poverty: America's Enduring Paradox.* New York: Thomas Y. Crowell Co., 1971.
Macpherson, C. B. *The Political Theory of Possessive Individualism: Hobbes to Locke.* Oxford: Oxford University Press, 1962.
Males, Mike A. *Scapegoat Generation: America's War on Adolescents.* Monroe, ME: Common Courage, 1996.
Marx, Karl. *Capital, Vol. I: A Critique of Political Economy,* trans. Ben Fowkes (New York: Vintage, 1977 (1867).
Massey, Douglas S. "American Apartheid: Segregation and the Making of the Underclass," *American Journal of Sociology* 96, no. 2 (Sept, 1990).
Murray, Charles, and Richard Hernstein. *The Bell Curve: Intelligence and Class Structure in American Life.* New York: Free Press, 1994.
Postman, Neil. *The Disappearance of Childhood.* New York: Vintage, 1992 (1984).
Price, Richard. *Clockers.* Boston: Houghton Mifflin, 1992.
Prothrow-Stith, Deborah. *Deadly Consequences.* New York: Harper, 1991.
Rubenstein, Richard L. *The Cunning of History: The Holocaust and the American Future.* New York: Harper, 1975.
Scheper-Hughes, Nancy, and Daniel Hoffman. "Kids Out of Place," *NACLA: Report on the Americas* 27, no. 6 (May/June 1994): 16-23.
Shakur, Sanyika. *Monster: The Autobiography of an L.A. Gang Member.* New York: Penguin, 1993.
Simmel, Georg. "The Metropolis and Mental Life," in Kurt H. Wolff, ed. *The Sociology of Georg Simmel.* New York: Free Press, 1950.
Spencer, Herbert. "The Proper Sphere of Government," in *Spencer: Political Writings.* Cambridge: Cambridge University Press, 1994, 1-59.
Veblen,Thorstein. *The Theory of the Leisure Class: An Economic Study of Institutions.* (New York: New American Library, 1953 (1899).
Vergara, Camilo Jose. "A Guide to the Ghettos." *The Nation* (March 13, 1993): 339.
——. *The New American Ghetto.* New Brunswick, NJ: Rutgers University Press, 1995.
Wilhelm, Sidney. *Who Needs the Negro?* Hampton, VA: UB and US Communications

Systems, 1993 (1970).

Williams, Terry. *The Cocaine Kids: The Inside Story of a Teenage Drug Ring.* Reading, MA: Addison Wesley, 1989.

Willis, Paul E. *Learning to Labor: How Working Class Kids Get Working Class Jobs.* London: Gower, 1977.

Wilson, R. Jackson. *Darwinism and the American Intellectual: An Anthology.* Chicago: Dorsey Press, 1989.

Wilson, William Julius. *The Truly Disadvantaged: The Inner-city, the Underclass, and Public Policy.* Chicago: University of Chicago Press 1987.

Wirth, Louis. "Urbanism as a Way of Life," in Paul K. Hatt and Albert J. Reiss, eds. *Reader in Urban Sociology.* Glencoe, IL: Free Press, 1951.

Yette, Samuel. *The Choice: The Issue of Black Survival in America.* New York: Berkeley Medallion Books, 1971.

5
"Remorseless Young Predators": The Bottom Line of "Caging Children"

Gary L. Smith

In June 2000, a Chicago teenager was sentenced to 50 years in prison for his role in a crime that occurred when he was 15. Leon Miller, who was 17 when sentenced, had served as a lookout in a gang fight in which two young men were shot and killed by someone else in a housing project in 1997. Even his trial judge later remarked on his "minimal involvement" in the killings. But at 15, Miller had been the age at which Illinois law required that his case be transferred automatically to adult criminal court, rather than being handled in a juvenile proceeding. He was charged with two counts of first-degree murder and found guilty under an accountability theory holding an accomplice equally responsible as the person who pulled the trigger.

But when Miller's case made Chicago headlines and caused one more minor stir in this country's continuing, contentious debate over juvenile crime, it was by no means because of the severity of his sentence. It was, in effect, the *leniency.* Under Illinois law, a person in Miller's position faced a mandatory life prison term without possibility of parole. For convictions of more than one murder, among some other offenses, the state's General Assembly had determined that the trial judge should have no discretion in determining a sentence—just as the judge had none in the transfer of the case to adult court or the charges lodged there. The teen was hit by "a triple whammy," in the words of a University of Chicago law professor who argued that a mandatory life sentence for a juvenile accomplice would violate U.S. constitutional protections against disproportionate punishment and international law standards prohibiting life sentences for offenders under 18. The Cook County judge who presided over the case agreed. Granted no sentencing leeway by the law, he declared it unconstitutional.[1]

That decision was immediately appealed, of course, and this in a jurisdiction where the state's highest court had previously upheld mandatory life terms for juvenile murderers. So it is quite possible that Miller's reprieve to a half-century term will be short-lived. But whatever the ultimate outcome of that case, it was just one extreme example of the extreme lengths to which legislators had been going for some time to ensure increasingly punitive treatment, and specifically more and longer incarceration, for kids who break the law. Other examples abounded nationwide, even as the Miller case was going on. In Florida, for example, a 13-year-old boy accused of killing a teacher was being prosecuted under a statute calling for a mandatory life term. In Michigan, an 11-year-old boy was exposed to that sentence after being convicted of murder, though a judge used that state's judicial discretionary power to impose a lesser penalty. And in California, a 16-year-old boy had just become the first juvenile charged with murder under a recently approved law requiring that he be prosecuted in criminal court and face a life sentence.

Yet there was a particularly dark irony in the fact that the Miller case called attention to Illinois for having such penalties as mandatory life terms for teenagers. For this was the state that had first forged formal principles of crafting judicial outcomes to fit the specific circumstances of youthful offenders. It was in Chicago, in 1899, that the efforts of social reformers had led to the creation of the world's first juvenile court. It was a creation dedicated to the proposition that children and adults are not equal, and that both justice and sound social policy demand that they almost always be treated differently in courts of law. That basic precept had become the foundation for a nationwide juvenile court structure that generally emphasized an ideal of rehabilitation over punishment, and specifically sought to look closely at the often difficult life circumstances of offenders as well as the characteristics of the offense in determining case dispositions. To what extent the juvenile court's actual operation has measured up to such standards has been a matter of debate for a long time. But it is a system that has been replicated in many other countries and spawned many personal success stories by offering "second chances," the phrase used in the title of a book published in 1999 to commemorate the court's centennial.[2] Among the figures represented are Olympic and professional athletes, authors, a big city prosecutor, a judge, a college administrator, and a former U.S. senator, who have credited the juvenile court with helping them turn their lives around at a critical point.

It was telling, however, that the book's publication was often heralded in commentaries attacking a juvenile crime bill then before Congress. That bill, which included such measures as making 13 year olds subject to adult prosecution and making federal block grants subject to similar action at the state level, did not immediately pass, but it was symptomatic of the process in which the procedures and protections afforded by the juvenile court system had been attacked and repudiated during the past several years. Just between 1992 and 1997, for instance, 44 states and the District of Columbia made it easier for minors to be prosecuted as adults. Penalties were increased, and long-standing policies of confidentiality were eroded or eliminated. Even the minimum age for execution was lowered in some jurisdictions, and the United States was already the only death penalty nation that had refused to sign an agreement prohibiting execution of offenders under the age of 18. As the centennial approached, accordingly, a leading legal scholar and juvenile court defender was moved to wonder "whether there will be a birthday cake and a celebration or a funeral pyre."[3]

Meanwhile, somewhat lost in the shuffle while legislators have been "trying to out-tough each other on juvenile justice reform,"[4] in the words of an attorney for the Citizens' Committee for Children of New York, is the fact that their actions have had little or no rationale. Although more juveniles than ever before were being arrested and charged as the century neared an end, the rate of serious violent crime by youthful offenders was actually less than twenty years earlier, according to the federal government's Office of Juvenile Justice and Delinquency Prevention. Furthermore, studies in Florida, New Jersey, New York, and Pennsylvania suggest that such "get tough" measures as prosecuting juveniles as adults have actually increased recidivism rates among youthful offenders. "At the turn of the century the Juvenile Court . . . in Chicago was developed in large part because of the horrible experiences children were being subjected to in adult jails," observed Steven Drizin of Northwestern University's Center on Children and Family Justice, "and as we approach another turn of the century we are moving in the direction of placing more and more children—and younger children—in adult prisons."[5]

An understanding of the management of youthful offenders at this turn of the century cannot be achieved without attention to the historical modulations of the juvenile court system. The first part of this essay, accordingly, is devoted to highlighting some of the key points in the evolution of that institution and some of the meanings that have been attached to them. The second part provides an overview of policy and practice alterations that have been instituted over roughly the last two decades as children have been increasingly shunted into the adult criminal court system or exposed to more severe penalties in juvenile proceedings, often under rationale of reforming or repudiating juvenile court principles. Outlined in that part are some of the economic and human costs of those changing practices. In the third and final section, the treatment of juveniles is situated within the larger context of the criminal justice system and its important role in advanced capitalism. In that context, "caging children"[6] can be seen to serve powerful ideological and economic interests.

WHO IS SAVED?

As legal scholar Barry Feld has observed, there is no such thing as a single or univocal history of the juvenile court, for accounts of its origins range widely from a "progressive-liberal" position to a "critical-revisionist" stance that began to take shape shortly after a 1967 U.S. Supreme Court ruling involving the court's procedures. "The former view juvenile courts as benevolent humanitarian efforts to save children from social disorder and to protect them from their own flawed development and the criminal justice system," Feld notes, while revisionists characterize those courts as "expansive agencies of social control that used their discretionary powers primarily to impose sanctions on poor and immigrant children."[7] Because much debate about youth crime has been organized partly around perceived failures of the juvenile court, it is important to distinguish between these two readings of the tribunal's history.

In the progressive-reform version, social reformers in late nineteenth-century Chicago were appalled that criminal courts had jurisdiction over children as young as ten, yet had no specialized procedures for dealing with them or institutions for confining them. As a result, children were sent to the city jail for offenses ranging from burglary to playing ball in the street.[8] Seeing children alongside adults in such circumstances both horrified and invigorated reformers like Jane Addams, Lucy Flower, and Judy Lathrop. To these reformers, the last thing a civilized society should do to its children was to process and punish them like adults in the criminal justice system. They believed that the State had a moral responsibility to act as "kind and just parents" to each of its children. In the context of a court system, this meant that children should receive individualized attention, under the watchful eyes of trained and sensitive judges and probation officers, in a system premised on rehabilitation rather than on the crippling punishments of the adult system.[9]

In fact, alternatives to adult jail confinement had long existed in the form of the reformatories and industrial schools established in the mid-nineteenth century. But what was unique about the Illinois Juvenile Court Act of 1899, soon to be duplicated in some form by most other states, was the institutional enactment of a separate forum with a set of principles and procedures intended to serve the best interest of the child. Installed in the court was the judicial philosophy of *parens patriae*, in which the court is configured as a surrogate parent for the wayward child. As one early juvenile court judge in Chicago described the court's goals in a *Harvard Law Review* article, "The child who must be brought into court should, of course, be made to know that he is face to face with the power of the state, but he should at the same time, and more emphatically, be made to feel that he is the object of its care and solicitude."[10]

That the child "should be made to feel" goes to the core of the critical-revisionist attitude toward the origins of the juvenile court. The subtle coercion embedded in that clause is seen as revealing a social-control agenda on the part of its founders and defenders. One of the first and most articulate statements of this view was set out in 1969 by sociologist Anthony M. Platt in *The Child Savers*: *The Invention of Delinquency.* Using the term "child savers" to refer to a group of reformers who "regarded their cause as a matter of conscience and morality, serving no particular class or political interests," Platt argued that they were actually trying to do for the justice system "what industrialists and corporate leaders were trying to do for the economy—that is, achieve order, stability, and control, while preserving the existing class system and distribution of wealth." This book destroys the myth that the child-saving movement was successful in humanizing the criminal justice system, rescuing children from jails and prisons, and developing dignified judicial and penal institutions for juveniles. It argues that, if anything, the child savers helped to create a system that would subject more and more juveniles to arbitrary and degrading punishments.[11]

Although the founders of the juvenile court came largely from the middle and upper class, the revisionist critique of the court does not rest on an attribution of conscious motives or deliberate efforts at exploitation. The reformers saw the tribunal as an instrument that could transform society by transforming some of its members. Child saving was "part of a larger social movement which went beyond mere instrumental reforms and set as its goal the revitalization and salvation of society."[12] The argument, rather, is that this transformation was imagined largely in terms of inculcating lower-class children, particularly those of immigrants who arrived in U.S. cities in large numbers in the late nineteenth century, with middle-class values compatible with industrial capitalism, and that measures removing children from jurisdiction of the criminal court system actually led to a considerable increase in state control of youths, particularly poor and minority youths.

This came about through the *parens patriae* principle of judicial determination of the best interests of the child. Along those lines, the court developed a rehabilitative ideal based on a "medical" model construing wrongdoing as correctable, given the proper diagnosis and methods of treatment. And from the beginning, it sought to bring together a wide range of multidisciplinary and multiagency collaboration in an effort to change juvenile behavior. The central concern of the child savers was not "the austerity of the criminal law and criminal institutions," Platt argues, but "the normative behavior of youth—their recreation, leisure, education, outlook on life, attitudes to authority, family relationships, and personal morality."[13] The finding of "delinquency" then is seen as a move that justifies judicial intervention and control extending into areas far beyond the specific acts bringing juveniles before the court—and all in *their* best interest. "The juvenile court functioned as a coercive treatment agency," writes Feld:

> Because juvenile courts could not rely solely on juveniles' voluntary compliance with their treatment program, they required the power to impose restraints. And youths' criminal violations provided the most common basis for the courts' coercive intervention. . . . This unresolvable tension between coercion and treatment represented one of the fundamental criminological fault lines underlying the court.[14]

A significant tremor occurred on that fault line in 1967, when the U.S. Supreme Court reviewed a case in which a 15-year-old boy had been sentenced to an industrial school for allegedly making a lewd telephone call to a neighbor. The key issues in the case of *In re Gault* revolved around the fact that he had been ruled delinquent on the basis of statements he made at an informal hearing at which he was not advised of any right to remain silent or to be represented by counsel. In a review of the history of juvenile proceedings, the Warren Court found that rehabilitative rhetoric had often been translated into punitive realities to such an extent that the juvenile court could not claim to be noncriminal or nonadversarial. In that context, the stance of acting in the minor's best interest could not justify denial of rights of due process. In a decision that effectively recognized juveniles as "persons" under the 14th Amendment, the court held that accused delinquents must be accorded such procedural rights as formal notice of charges, assistance of counsel, the chance to confront witnesses, and to avoid self-incrimination.[15]

The Gault case is often perceived as a leading example of the Warren Court's view that expanding the range of constitutional rights and requiring adversarial procedures could help restrict the coercive powers of the state. But that has not been the result in the juvenile court, according to some critics, who argue that the court's continuing power of intervention under its *parens patriae* role leaves juveniles with watered-down versions of procedural rights. In most states, for instance, juveniles are not entitled to jury trials but are tried in closed, informal bench trials. Juvenile courts, Feld argues, "provide youths with fewer and less effective safeguards than those afforded adult criminal defendants in order to maximize the courts' social control."[16] Arguing that the goals of social welfare and criminal social control are fundamentally inconsistent, Feld goes so far as to advocate abolishing the juvenile court and handling all cases in criminal proceedings, while giving a "youth discount" in sentencing to minors found guilty. "A sentencing policy that recognizes youthfulness as a mitigating factor and provides a youth discount fosters greater honesty about the role of the justice system and greater realism about young people's developmental capacity and criminal responsibility."[17]

One of the more curious things about Feld's proposal is an assumption that seems to underlie it. Whereas he faults the juvenile court's informal procedures and individualized sentencing practices for often contributing to racial and class differentiations in outcomes, he seems to suppose that judges applying a "youth discount" as a mitigating factor would somehow guarantee more consistency. This does not seem self-evident.

But this is not the place to analyze that proposal in detail. What is important to point out is that the juvenile court Feld criticizes is not the same juvenile court that has been under attack by proponents of "get tough" approaches to youth crime. Within that rhetorical sphere the problems are "leniency" and "coddling," not the protection of procedural rights, and the solution is to hand down sentences that are inflated, not discounted. So contemporary defenses of the juvenile court need to be seen in that context. Even if its control of a youth's life has considerable breadth, in terms of covering more than individual acts of wrongdoing, it also has less depth, or length, in that the control typically ends at age 21. In that respect, the juvenile court serves as a sort of fire wall, a last line of defense against prison terms that some would like to see extend through most or all of a young person's life.

HUGGING THE JUVENILE "TERRORIST"

The title of this essay comes from comments made about a federal juvenile crime bill proposed in the U.S. House of Represenatives in 1997. The measure had initially been introduced the year before by Bill McCollum, then a Florida representative (he gave up his seat to run for the U.S. Senate in 2000 but lost that race), as the Violent Youth Predator Act, and was then brought back as the more nuanced Juvenile Crime Control Act. It proposed not only treating some 13-year-old federal offenders as adults—a measure that would have little practical impact—but also denying federal funds to states that do not do the same, and also abolishing the federal agency responsible for trying to prevent juvenile crime. When Democrats on the House Judiciary Committee tried to modify the bill, then-Princeton University political scientist John DiIulio objected that "head-in-the-sand word games won't obviate the fact that this nation is threatened by large numbers of remorseless young predators."[18]

This is the same John DiIulio who was appointed by U.S. President George W. Bush in early 2001 to head a new federal office established to promote the further integration of religious organizations into federally funded social services. That appointment followed his conversion to the view that churches hold the key to saving inner-city youths from drugs and crime, because "attachment to religious institutions" helps them do so. "We think the spiritual dimension here is real and important," he said in a published interview. "The at-risk kids, like all kids, need adults in their lives who are there because they see in the child not just another statistic or body but a spiritual being who needs to be saved, saved from the horrors of the streets and saved spiritually."[19]

This is the same John DiIulio who had warned a few years earlier of "a rising wave of superpredators" among youth, and had posed in a leather jacket in front of a graffiti-covered wall to help illustrate a *Time* cover story on "A Teenage Time Bomb." That was during the heyday of the young predator predictions in the mid-1990s, and articles from the period show how media coverage helped etch those speculations into fact in the consciousness of the public. In one of the other leading examples of the genre, *U.S. News & World Report* weighed in with a story titled "Crime Time Bomb," and subheaded, "Rising juvenile crime and predictions that it is going to get worse." The article mentioned public officials "responding to the grim statistics and depressing stories," and said "victims of underage felons are demanding changes in the juvenile justice system." Not that there appeared to be much hope, to judge from the conclusion: "The tragic fact is that it may take an even greater blood bath to force effective crime solutions to the top of the nation's agendas."[20]

When the superpredator bloodbath did not really materialize, DiIulio and some other prophets seemed to distance themselves from the predictions and calls for increased imprisonment. "Most kids who get into serious trouble need adult guidance. And they won't find suitable role models in prison," DiIulio wrote in one op-ed piece.[21]

But finding "suitable role models" did not exactly seem the primary goal of legislation and rhetoric calling for more and longer prison sentences for younger children. They "are not children anymore. They're the most violent criminals on the face of the earth," McCollum said in defense of his bill. And interestingly, much the same tone was taken by another man who would later become part of the Bush administration. That was John Ashcroft, the religious and political conservative who survived token opposition to become U.S. Attorney General under Bush. As a U.S. Senator from Missouri in 1997, Ashcroft denounced the juvenile justice system and demonized its clients while endorsing the Violent and Repeat Offender Act:

> We are living with a juvenile system that reprimands the crime victim for being at the wrong place at the wrong time, and then turns around and hugs the juvenile terrorist, whispering ever so softly into his ear, "Don't worry, the state will cure you."[22]

Beyond this sort of rhetoric, there have been significant changes in laws, policies, and judicial practices as youthful offenders have been increasingly shunted into adult criminal court or exposed to more severe penalties through juvenile proceedings. Government, university, think tank, and advocacy organization reports reveal the statistical skeleton of the phenomenon. In 1998, for instance, Amnesty International concluded that about 200,000 minors (under 18) were being prosecuted as adults every year. Although many states set a minimum age for adult criminal prosecution, most ranging from 14 to 16, at least 22 states had no minimum at all. Conventional wisdom casts this as a response to teen violence. But a University of Maryland study found that slightly over half of all such cases involved drugs or other nonviolent offenses. Minors in juvenile custody numbered 163,200 by 1997, an increase of 56 percent over a decade. And more than 17,000 juveniles were in adult prisons by 1998, with 3,500 of them in general populations with adult offenders, according to Steven Drizin, supervising attorney for Northwestern University's Children and Family Law Center. "We should be ashamed of these statistics and should not continue to disgrace ourselves by adding to them," Drizin writes.[23]

The treatment of youthful offenders, in both juvenile and adult court, also replicates racial disparities that are well documented in the prosecution and incarceration of all Americans. To rehearse a few of the latter figures, African American men in the United States are imprisoned at a rate nearly six times higher than white men. They make up about 6 percent of the country's population, but nearly half the male prison population. Bureau of Justice statistics suggest that nearly 3 of every 10 black men face the prospect of being sent to prison during their lifetime. And though raw numbers are smaller, proportions are similar for women. Whereas 20 white women out of every 100,000 are in prison, the rate for black women is 143 of every 100,000—more than seven times as high.[24]

Likewise, minorities also are overrepresented at every stage in the juvenile justice process, according to a report by the federal government's Office of Juvenile Justice and Delinquency Prevention. Although minorities constituted only a third of juvenile population in 1997, for instance, they represented *two-thirds* of the residents of secure juvenile custody. Of juveniles prosecuted as adults, 67 percent are black, and 77 percent of those sent to prison are minorities, according to a Bureau of Justice report. Although statistics show a slightly higher rate of drug use among white teenagers than minorities, 75 percent of the juveniles prosecuted on drug charges are black, and a staggering 95 percent of those sent to prison are minorities.[25] Such patterns seem likely to "continue the trend of African American male incarceration well in to the 21st century," as the journal *African American Male Research* stated in another context.[26] Indeed, if the present rate of growth of imprisonment continues along with these racial proportions, Vivien Stern observes in a recent study of prison systems worldwide, "4.5 million black men will be in prison in the U.S. by the year 2020."[27]

Getting tough on teen crime does not come cheap, in economic, social, or human terms. Some of the numbers are staggeringly large. For instance, between 1993 and 1998, a period when juvenile crime dropped about a third, annual state spending on juvenile justice increased 65 percent to a total of $4.2 billion, according to a study by the National Association of State Budget Officers. Some numbers, however, are very small. Only 8.4 percent of that total was spent on prevention, and only 3.6 percent on follow-up supervision of teens newly released from lockups. Two-thirds of it went for secure custody. That $4.2 billion was slightly more than total government expenditures on child care that year. In the spring of 2000, when Florida legislators were debating a bill requiring offenders as young as 16 to serve a minimum 10-year prison term for certain offenses, a state corrections official pointed out that "it's cheaper to put a person in state prison than in a juvenile facility."[28]

And what do those dollars sometimes buy? A 1999 report by Human Rights Watch (HRW) found some Maryland jails holding children in abusive condition, including poorly lit, cockroach-infested cells; not enough food; and inadequate medical and mental health care and educational services. Nearly half of all incarcerated juveniles need mental health treatment, a separate study has found.[29] But in Maryland, HRW found, there were no specific services for juveniles, and those placed in mental health units were "likely to be stripped of their clothing and given only a paper blanket to cover themselves."[30] In early 2000, a federal judge suspended the operating contract of a private prison firm, Wackenhut Corrections Corporation, at a Louisiana juvenile facility on the basis of a Department of Justice investigation. The probe found inmates often had to fight over basic necessities like food, shoes, and clothing, and were subjected to chemical controls and gas grenades as well as excessive force; one 17-year-old boy had been so severely beaten by staff that some of his intestines had tumbled into his colostomy bag.[31] Juveniles in adult prisons, meanwhile, were twice as likely to be beaten by staff, five times more likely to be sexually assaulted, and 7.7 times more likely to attempt suicide, according to a 1999 report by the Sentencing Project. "Few adult correctional agencies provide special programming for this age group and most states do not provide special training on handling juvenile offenders," the report pointed out.[32]

Because the assault on youth has continued and even been ratcheted up in the face of a declining crime rate, it's necessary to look elsewhere for explanations for the perception that violent crime demands even more severe responses. One, obviously, can be found in media coverage that sensationalizes outbursts of violence. Another is the tendency of public figures to demonize youthful offenders, like DiIulio's "remorseless young predators" and Ashcroft's "juvenile terrorist," as a rhetorical strategy to simplify complex issues. Sometimes this is done in more subtle ways, as it was by their boss, President George W. Bush, early in his administration. When he put forward a public education program, he included proposals for school safety, such as providing federal money for enforcing tough discipline and for character education. The accompanying rhetoric went, "We must face up to the plague of school violence, with an average of three million crimes committed against students and teachers inside public schools every year." Obviously the president was appealing to a public rightly horrified by recent highly publicized school shootings, such as in Colorado and Arkansas. But as a *New York Times* analysis showed, this notion of a plague "is more myth than reality."[33]

That number of three million, the *Times* pointed out, was derived by a rounding upwards of figures in a Census Bureau survey in which teenagers said they were victims of 2.7 million "crimes." But the teens were urged to identify events as crimes even if they didn't know whether they fit that category, and even then fewer than 10 percent of the incidents were described by the survey as "serious," much less violent. For all of the attention given to a few terrible events, the paper observed, out of some 2,000 killings of children each year, only about 10 typically occur in or near schools. That is the basis on which youths are characterized by the president as perpetrators of a "plague" of violence.

As the *Times* also noted, one of the major factors in real teen violence, when it does occur, is the access to guns. Unfortunately, such straightforward evidence is often overlooked or omitted from high-pitched rhetoric about plagues and predators. Even during periods when most juvenile crime rates stayed flat or decreased, for instance, one category that increased sharply was handgun killings, as when "youth homicide rates surged in the mid-1980s as a result of the growth of the crack cocaine drug industry and the diffusion of handguns among urban youths. . . . Young people committed more than three-quarters of their homicides with firearms, handguns accounted for 80 percent of all gun homicides, and gun deaths accounted for nearly the entire increase in youth homicides."[34]

But Massachusetts, a state with strict handgun controls, has had a low rate of violent juvenile crime. Juvenile homicides in Washington, D.C., dropped by almost two-thirds after neighboring Virginia and Maryland put new restrictions on gun sales. "Academics and politicians should have the guts to admit responsibility for being wrong," argue Vincent Schiraldi and Mark Kappelhoff. "They need to go to the president, the congress, the media, and say, 'It's the guns, stupid.'"[35]

Also largely overlooked are alternatives to state incarceration for serious offenders. Variations on "youth courts" and "teen courts" have multiplied rapidly during the 1990s and have earned regard for their results with nonviolent, first-time offenders. No one has proposed institutionalized peer pressure as an adequate response to every crime juveniles might commit. Yet agencies philosophically committed to rescuing the more serious offenders often find themselves with less and less public support for their efforts, pointing to opportunities lost, abandoned, or never seized. A small but conspicuous case in point involves a facility called Salem Children's Home, a century-old children's service agency in rural Illinois. Like many similar institutions, Salem was founded as an orphanage by a church denomination, but has become a private nonprofit organization providing a wide range of residential and community-based services to youths of all ages. Seeing a desperate need to provide high-risk juveniles intensive short-term treatment in a secure setting yet separate from a youth prison, Salem had secured initial commitment for utilization contracts from the Illinois Department of Corrections and other agencies for a forty-bed diagnostic and stabilization unit. After the foundation had been completed, however, the state department's position gradually changed from "significant encouragement" to "noncommittal to our project altogether," Salem president Stephen Yahnig reported in a 1999 newsletter. Though he went on to analyze various political variables that might have influenced the change, he still found some reasons "murky," since "everyone seems to agree that the Salem Stabilization Unit is needed." So Salem would proceed with trying to raise more funds through donations.[36]

Yet even as Salem was pressing ahead to raise private funds to carry out its essentially public purpose, the governor of Illinois, George Ryan, was announcing plans to construct a new $34 million, 288-bed juvenile prison in a small town in western Illinois. This was barely a trickle in the stream of prisons going up across the country, and would scarcely dent even the 50 percent overcrowding in that state's existing juvenile facilities, which had doubled in population since 1980. But it was a big event in the little town of Rushville, population about 3,200, and Ryan revealed why as he announced the site selection. "This new state of the art juvenile center will not only help the state solve overcrowding problems within our correctional system, but it will provide a badly-needed economic boost for the citizens of Western Illinois."[37]

"NOWHERE ELSE IN THE WORLD"

That George Ryan's announcement was quite literally greeted by cheers and applause in Rushville was one sign of how successfully the contemporary prison system has been integrated into society's social and economic value systems. Twenty-seven Illinois communities, most in relatively poor rural areas, had vied vigorously in the state's periodic "prison sweepstakes" for either the youth prison or an 1,800-bed, $80-million women's prison to be built at the same time. (The women's facility happened to wind up in the governor's home county, Kankakee, south of Chicago.) In Rushville, seat of a county with the highest unemployment rate in western Illinois, the prison project would mean 250 construction jobs, then some 300 permanent positions at a facility with an $11 million budget. A project that once might have elicited cries of "Not In My Back Yard" was met by invitations and inducements declaring "*Please* In My Back Yard."

As Christian Parenti has pointed out in his important book, *Lockdown America: Police and Prisons in the Age of Crisis*, this joining of "little town and big prison . . . is a marriage that has been replicated scores of times in recent years." His observations are worth quoting at length:

> From Bowling Green, Missouri, to rural Florida, economically battered towns are rolling over for new prisons. Nationally, the tab for building penitentiaries has averaged about $7 billion annually over the last decade; in 1996 alone contractors broke ground on twenty-six federal and ninety-six state prisons. Estimates for the yearly expenses of incarceration run between $20 and $35 billion annually, and one report has more than 523,000 full-time employees working in American corrections—more than in any *Fortune* 500 company except General Motors. In the American countryside punishment is such a big industry that, according to the National Criminal Justice Commission, 5 percent of the growth in rural population between 1980 and 1990 was accounted for by prisoners, captured in cities and exiled to the carceral arcadia.[38]

To understand the economic importance of the prison industry, it is necessary to get a perspective on its scale. In February 2000, the U.S. prison population passed the two million mark. "We have less than five percent of the world's population but 25 percent of the world's prisoners."[39] A staggering and unprecedented number of 532,448 Americans were newly incarcerated just during the 1990s. Of that total, more than 60 percent, or more than 1.2 million, have been sentenced for nonviolent offenses, often involving drugs. In 1999, the costs of keeping those people in prison was slightly over $39 billion.[40] "Nowhere else in the world is there a comparable situation," writes Vivien Stern in a study of prison systems worldwide.

> Never discussed is the fact that most people convicted of a criminal offense in most Western countries do not go to prison. A dramatic exception is the U.S., where 70 percent of all offenders convicted of a felony in state courts . . . are sentenced to incarceration.[41]

What are the future implications of those present facts and figures? Bernardine Dohrn, the 1960s radical activist who now advocates for children as director of the Children and Family Justice Center at the Northwestern University School of Law, expresses it this way: "I'm really afraid that we are building ourselves into something that we're not going to be able to unbuild."[42]

Beyond a facility's direct impact at the local level in places like Rushville, and the political advantage that politicians like Ryan gain from that, two other components of the contemporary prison system show the clear, strong, and far-reaching economic interests of both government and private corporations in maintaining and increasing imprisonment. One is the burgeoning business of prison industry in which a panoply of products are made by inmates typically working for token wages at best. Some of these operations are joint ventures enabled by the Federal Prison Industries Enhancement (PIE) Act of 1979, which made it possible for private companies to operate for-profit businesses within, and under contract to, correctional institutions. Although the companies must pay prisoners the "prevailing" (usually minimum) wage, inmates typically receive much less, because a large part of their "pay" is set aside for room and board for their cells, as well as for restitution, fines, and court costs incurred in the criminal proceedings that led to their imprisonment.[43]

A separate and larger subsector of prison industry consists of the remarkably diverse enterprises owned and operated by the correction arms of state and federal government. Illinois Correctional Industries alone, for instance, offers a literal catalog of products and services, ranging from clothing, food, furniture, eyeglasses, building maintenance supplies, and playground materials, to telemarketing and data entry services. These state-owned entities generally can only sell to other government agencies, but some operate within a captive economy in which other public institutions are required to purchase prison-produced goods and services, whenever available, rather than buying in the outside market. The largest of these is Federal Prison Industries, which operates under the business name of Unicor, and employs some 18,000 inmates in turning out about 150 products. In 1998, Unicor produced $502 million worth of goods and services.[44]

Besides the impact on local and regional economies and the growth in prison industry, a third economic factor in imprisonment is the rapidly accelerating privatization of prisons, which entails facilities being run by for-profit companies. To be sure, the basic idea of prison-for-profit is nothing new in the United States, as inmates are known to have been leased out to private companies at least as early as the 1840s. But the contemporary version that has taken shape in the late twentieth century grew out of both the practical need to squeeze a rapidly growing supply of inmates into cell space and the general fascination with "privatizing" as a better or more efficient way to handle government functions. The phenomenon began with private firms operating detention centers for illegal immigrants but gradually spread to other types of incarceration. Within fifteen years, corporations were operating more than a hundred lockups with over 100,000 prisoners nationwide.[45]

Vivien Stern reports on a conference held for investment managers in Dallas in 1996 on the profit opportunities waiting in the prison industry. People were invited with a brochure promising "profits from crime":

> Dear Executive,
> Can you afford to bypass a tremendous opportunity to invest in stocks showing great performance and high returns? Privatization of correctional facilities is the newest trend in the area of privatizing previously government-run programs that can offer such optimal rewards. . . .
> While arrests and convictions are steadily on the rise, profits are to be made—profits from crime. Get in on the ground floor of this booming industry now![46]

The invitation might read like pure satire to some readers, but there is nothing facetious about the statement. In one index of the industry's success, Wackenhut, the second-largest for-profit prison firm and the company involved in the Louisiana juvenile facility investigation in 2000, reported early that year that its 1999 revenues were $438 million, up from $312.8 million the year before, and that net profits had quadrupled from $5.3 million to $21.9 million.[47] Industry leader Corrections Corporation of America, with 52 percent of the market, was regarded a "secure" investment with strong growth even after private prison scandals in 1996. "To maintain market dominance CCA does things the old fashioned way: giving generously to politicians and buttering up the press," Parenti remarks, and adds that the major for-profit firms are "led by people—powerfully connected men—with sophisticated political agendas and who are positioning for long-term growth and political influence."[48]

Because some of the information from the past few paragraphs is drawn from Parenti's book, it should be noted that he downplays the importance of these economic factors in prison growth even as he calls attention to them. He emphasizes, for instance, that the for-profit sector is still a very small presence in U.S. incarceration overall; that a relatively small portion of all inmates are involved in prison industries, and that those operations often tend to be inefficient in spite of their low labor costs; and that the new prisons being sited in depressed rural areas bring only a limited form of economic revival. Prison growth is best explained not in terms of "*direct involvement of specific economic interests*" (emphasis original) but as a social control mechanism for managing "surplus populations" that cannot be profitably integrated into capitalism. "At the heart of the matter," he writes, lies an important contradiction in a class society:

> [C]apitalism needs the poor and creates poverty, intentionally through policy and organically through crisis. Yet capitalism is also directly and indirectly threatened by the poor. Capitalism always creates surplus populations, yet faces the threat of political, aesthetic, or cultural disruption from those populations. Prison and criminal justice are about managing those irreconcilable contradictions.[49]

But it is important to notice that "specific economic interests" in the prison industry extend far beyond for-profit management firms or in-house prison businesses. Stern surveys the organ of the American Correctional Association, *Corrections Today*, and notes the vigorous promotion of the huge list of products that a growing roster of companies make for use in the administration of contemporary prisons: electric locks and electronic monitoring systems; X-ray body search machines; restraint devices ranging from leather and nylon straps to "violent prisoner chairs"; tear gas dispensers and grenades, projectiles, and impact cartridges; protective helmets for staff; razor wire and electrified fences; bulletproof inmate security transportation vehicles; even "modular detention facilities [which] can give you a prison up and running in 120 days." As Stern observes, "A whole sector of U.S. industry is now devoted to the war against U.S. citizens."[50]

Further evidence that more than social control is involved lies in a significant trend that emerged in imprisonment in the 1990s. Historically, prison populations have fluctuated with social and economic conditions. In the past decade that trend changed, and it began to increase steadily. It rose "in good times and bad times, independent of whether the crime rate rose or fell," as the Justice Policy Institute reports. "As doors to new cells opened, the number of prisoner and jail inmates soared."[51]

And there is reason to believe it will keep soaring. With prisons embraced for the profit potential they offer to business and the economic benefits they bring to some areas, it has long since become impossible to perpetuate the myth that they are ultimately trying to put themselves out of business by rehabilitating wrongdoers. They are in the business of perpetuating and reproducing themselves. Such sentencing practices as mandatory life terms for youthful offenders, or for adults with "three strikes," are boons to that business. And as those are relatively recent innovations, there is no reason to doubt that even more punitive strategies could be implemented. As Stern says:

> The question has to be asked: why should there be any limit? These processes need never stop. More and more people can go to prison. The logic of three strikes and you're out could equally apply to two strikes and you're out. What is the argument then against one strike and you're out? The logic that follows from this

> is that if you come from a one-strike-and-you're-out family, you are likely to follow in your father's footsteps, so let us take you out now, before the first crime is committed.[52]

Calling attention to such points is by no means to minimize the importance of social control in explaining growth in the incarceration industry, but is rather to expand and amplify it. When prisoners create profit potential for a growing number of corporations; when they generate political capital for politicians by bringing steady jobs and economic growth to depressed areas; and when they demonstrate to law-abiding citizens that prisons are not just confining people but are putting them to work in useful industries, then those prisoners are no longer truly a surplus population. They are *assets*, like raw materials or the means of production, and they are being put to increasingly better advantage and more profitable use.

The existence of such high stakes for the growing number of powerful public and private entities clearly suggests a further explanation, then, for the increasing incarceration of children and other components of the "get tough" approach to juvenile crime. Prison industries, whether publicly or privately owned, need a literally captive labor supply, and private prison companies need "correctional centers" to manage. Because the prison industry, like any in a capitalist economy, is driven by a logic in which success requires steady expansion, the supply of those commodities will have to increase as the industry grows. Teenagers sentenced to life in prison, or very long terms, fulfill a dual purpose. They become part of the labor and commodity supply, and they also ideologically reinforce the social logic in which further prison expansion is necessary. As for youthful offenders not immediately subjected to long-term incarceration, the relatively high rates of recidivism among those exposed to adult jurisdiction indicates that many will eventually become part of the adult prison population. Thus, getting tough on kids could help ensure that prison growth will continue along the path that has made the United States "the great incarcerator." That is a potential that has not been overlooked by the private sector, as glaringly highlighted in the investment brochure cited earlier:

> The brochure had a heading, "Understand why the private prison industry is one of the fastest growing markets today." The answer was clear. "Just consider the current inmate populations in adult facilities combined with population growth at juvenile detention centers." Young criminals would become older criminals. The future was bright.[53]

SOME QUESTIONS

Serious questions remain on issues that figure to be influential factors in juvenile justice for the foreseeable future. First, a concrete and very foreboding one: Who will represent the interests of current and coming generations of marginalized children whose life circumstances make it likely that they will be exposed to harsher and harsher treatment at younger and younger ages? The juvenile court system—whether characterized as a magnanimously sweeping protective cloak or a subtle social control mechanism—has increasingly come to entail "representation" in a fairly narrow legal sense: the appointment of a public defender to stand up and speak during court appearances and to negotiate outcomes as favorable as possible. And ironically, even that important step of trying to protect the procedural rights of baffled kids also has the effect of increasing the workload of a tribunal already being widely criticized for being ineffectual even as its resources are siphoned away.

"When juvenile courts are given adequate resources, they can be effective in curtailing juvenile crime," maintains J. Dean Lewis, a Virginia judge who is past president of the National Council of Juvenile and Family Court Judges.[54] But even the most ardent advocates of the traditional juvenile court cannot overpower state legislatures that strip their budgets or take more and more matters out of their hands through such mechanisms as automatic transfer to adult criminal court or mandatory life terms. "Historically and currently, public officials deny juvenile courts adequate resources because of pervasive public antipathy to their clients, those who are poor, disadvantaged, and minority offenders."[55]

Secondly, how, if at all, will the widespread perception of juvenile offenders as a profoundly ominous and evil scourge, which threatens order and safety in American society, be adjusted in the future? Long-since discredited predictions of an emerging generation of teenage "superpredators" have continued to hold sway over the popular and political imagination. One poll by *American Demographics* found that 74 percent of respondents considered teen violence a major problem in society, and 53 percent saw it as a big problem in schools. But only 30 percent saw it as a problem in their local schools, and only 18 percent in their own neighborhoods.[56] "The public believes crime is rampant, except in their own neighborhoods and communities, because the media interpret the world outside to them," observes University of Richmond law professor Robert E. Shepherd Jr.[57] The publication of *Second Chances,* the book about "success stories" stemming from juvenile court intervention, was a calculated effort to change such perceptions. Will it or other strategies be effective?

A final and fundamental question really involves the framework in which the other two are posed. Namely, to what extent is it possible to reform an exploitative incarceration system that is a symptomatic component of an exploitative economic system? This is not an original question, obviously, and it is not intended to deny or minimize the profound impact that reform measures can have on people's lives. Countless demonstrations of that impact emerge from stories of the juvenile court, itself a reform institution. But it does suggest the difficulties in defining and achieving reform goals within an incarceration system that is becoming ever more pervasive, interconnected, and truly systemic, particularly as prisons are welcomed as good neighbors throughout middle America even as their residents are hated and feared. Even as law professor Feld winds up his energetic defense of shifting all youthful offenders into criminal court as a way of better protecting them, he also calls attention to things that could not be accomplished by that or any other reform of the judicial system:

> An affluent society that values its own future assures all young people of access to quality education, health care, adequate nutrition, and affordable housing without insisting on either parental failure or youthful criminality as prerequisites of assistance. A society that seeks racial harmony and social justice must address the structural inequality, concentrated poverty, racial segregation, and cultural isolation that excludes many members of minority communities and maintain "two societies, one black, one white, separate and unequal."[58]

How can those conditions best be addressed? Such questions are not merely academic. The answers could determine whether future "success stories" come down to celebrating sentences of *only* 50 years.

NOTES

1. "Mandatory Life Term for Teen Rejected," *Chicago Tribune*, 22 June 2000.

2. *Second Chances, 100 Years of the Children's Court: Giving Kids a Chance to Make a Better Choice,* a joint project of the Justice Policy Institute, Washington, D.C., and the Children and Family Justice Center at Northwestern University School of Law, Chicago, Ill.

3. Robert E. Shepherd Jr., "The Juvenile Court at 100: Birthday Cake or Funeral Pyre?" *Juvenile and Family Court Journal* 50, no. 4 (1999): 10.

4. Gabrielle Kreisler, "A Mostly Sensible Approach to Juvenile Crimes and Punishment," *Criminal Justice,* http://www.abanet.org/crimjust (8 May 2001).

5. Steven Drizin, quoted in *The Advocate* 21, no.3 (May 1999), http://dpa.state.ky.us/library/advocate/may99/juv100.html (8 May 2001)

6.Bernardine Dohrn, in a lecture titled "Think Globally, Act Locally" and delivered Oct. 19, 2000, at Illinois State University, cited the explosion of punishment and incarceration as one of the five main challenges to democracy today. Referring to the increasing criminalization of youths, she said, "We must stop caging children."

7. Barry Feld, *Bad Kids: Race and the Transformation of the Juvenile Court* (Oxford: Oxford University Press, 1999), 56.

8. Feld, p. 62; also, see Anthony M. Platt, *The Child Savers: The Invention of Delinquency*, second edition (Chicago: University of Chicago Press, 1977), 127.

9. *Second Chances,* 2.

10. Julian Mack, from "The Juvenile Court," quoted in Shepherd, "The Juvenile Court at 100," 109.

11. Anthony M. Platt, *The Child Savers: The Invention of Delinquency*, second edition (Chicago: University of Chicago Press, 1977), xvii, xxii, 3.

12. Platt, 55.

13. Platt, 99

14. Feld, 69.

15. *In re Gault*, 387 U.S. 1 (1967).

16. Feld, 163.

17. Feld, 303.

18. Quoted in Vincent Schiraldi and Mark Kappelhoff, "As Crime Drops, Experts Backpedal—Where Have the 'Superpredators' Gone?" *Jinn Magazine* (2 May 1997) http://www.pacificnews.org/jinn (8 May 2001).

19. Quoted in Michael Cromartie, "Kids Who Kill: A Conversation with John DiIulio," *Books & Culture* (January/February 1997), 10.

20. Ted Gast with Victoria Pope, "Crime Time Bomb," *U.S. News & World Report* (25 March 1996).

21. Quoted in Schiraldi and Kappelhoff.

22. Quoted in Vivien Stern, *A Sin against the Future: Imprisonment in the World* (Boston: Northeastern University Press, 1998), 168. The statement previously appeared in *Criminal Justice Newsletter* 28.3 (February 1997), 2.

23. Steven A. Drizin and Vincent Schiraldi, "Crime, Punishment, and Children: Give Kids a Chance at Redemption," *Chicago Tribune* (12 August 1999).

24. Stern, 50-51.

25. "Juvenile Felony Defendants in Criminal Courts," *Bureau of Justice Statistics*, September 1998, http://www.ojp.usdoj.gov/bjs/ (12 May 2001).

26. Christopher Booker, "New Juvenile Justice Bill Promises Further Increase in African American Male Incarceration," *African American Male Research* 1.3 (6 May 1997), http://www.pressroom.com/~afrimale/juvjustc.htm (12 May 2001).

27. Stern, 304.

28. National Association of State Budget Officers, *State Juvenile Justice Expenditures and Innovations,* http://www.nasbo.org (12 May 2001).

29. "State Watch," American Bar Association, http://abanet.org/juvejust/state.htm (12 May 2001).

30. Human Rights Watch, http://www.hrw.org/reports/1999/maryland (12 May 2001).

31. *Prison Privatization Report* 34 (March/April 2000).

32. J. Fagan, M. Frost, and T. S. Vivona, "Youth in Prisons and Training Schools: Perceptions and Consequences of the Treatment-Custody Dichotomy," *Juvenile and Family Court,* no. 2 (1989): 1-13, cited by the Sentencing Project.

33. Richard Rothstein, "Of Schools and Crimes, and Gross Exaggeration," *New York Times,* 7 February 2001.

34. Feld, 339.

35. Schiraldi and Kappelhoff, "As Crime Drops."

36. *Cadence*, a Newsletter of Salem Children's Home, no. 8 (August 1999).

37. Quoted in "Ryan Sites New Juvenile Correctional Center in Schuyler County," a News Release from the State of Illinois Department of Corrections (9 December 1999).

38. Christian Parenti, *Lockdown America: Police and Prisons in the Age of Crisis* (London: Verso, 1999), 213.

39. Dohrn, "Think Globally."

40. Justice Policy Institute, *America's Prison Population,* http://www.cjcj.org/jpi (12 May 2001).

41. Stern, 278, 319.
42. Dohrn, "Think Globally."
43. Parenti, 230-31.
44. Parenti, 231.
45. Stern, 292-93; Parenti, 218.
46. Stern, 290.
47. *Prison Privatization Report.*
48. Parenti, 219-20.
49. Parenti, 238-39.
50. Stern, 303.
51. Justice Policy Institute.
52. Stern, 303.
53. "The Great Incarcerator" is the title of Stern's chapter on U.S. imprisonment, pp. 36-63.
54. "An Evolving Juvenile Court: On the Front Lines with Judge J. Dean Lewis," *Juvenile Justice* (December 1999).
55. Feld, 291.
56. Ira Apfel, "Crime—Teen Violence: Real or Imagined," *American Demographics* (June 1995), 22.
57. Robert Shepherd Jr., "False Images? The News Media and Juvenile Crime," *Annual Report of the Coalition for Juvenile Justice* (1997).
58. Feld, 341-42.

BIBLIOGRAPHY

American Bar Association. "State Watch," http://abanet.org/juvejust/state.htm (12 May 2001).

Anon. *Prison Privatization Report* 34 (March/April 2000), http://www.stateaction.org/issues/privateprisons/index.cfm (12 May 2001).

———. "An Evolving Juvenile Court: On the Front Lines with Judge J. Dean Lewis," *Juvenile Justice* (December 1999), 3-12.

———. "Juvenile Felony Defendants in Criminal Courts," *Bureau of Justice Statistics*, September 1998. http://www.ojp.usdoj.gov/bjs/ (12 May 2001).

Apfel, Ira. "Crime—Teen Violence: Real or Imagined," *American Demographics* (June 1995), 22-23.

Booker, Christopher. "New Juvenile Justice Bill Promises Further Increase in African American Male Incarceration," *African American Male Research* 1.3 (6 May 1997), http://www.pressroom.com/~afrimale/juvjustc.htm (12 May 2001).

Cadence, a Newsletter of Salem Children's Home, no. 8 (August 1999).

Cromartie, Michael. "Kids Who Kill: A Conversation with John DiIulio," *Books & Culture* (January/February 1997), 10.

Drizin, Steven A., quoted in *The Advocate* 21, no.3 (May 1999), http://dpa.state.ky.us/library/advocate/may99/juv100.html (8 May 2001).

Drizin, Steven A., and Vincent Schiraldi. "Crime, Punishment, and Children: Give Kids a Chance at Redemption," *Chicago Tribune* (12 August 1999), 25.

Fagan, J., M. Frost, and T. S. Vivona. "Youth in Prisons and Training Schools: Perceptions and Consequences of the Treatment-Custody Dichotomy," *Juvenile and Family Court*, no. 2 (1989): 1-13.

Feld, Barry. *Bad Kids: Race and the Transformation of the Juvenile Court* (Oxford: Oxford University Press, 1999).

Gast, Ted, with Victoria Pope. "Crime Time Bomb," *U.S. News & World Report* (25 March 1996), 28-36.

Human Rights Watch. http://www.hrw.org/reports/1999/maryland (12 May 2001).

Justice Policy Institute. *America's Prison Population,* http://www.cjcj.org/jpi (12 May 2001).

———, and the Children and Family Justice Center at Northwestern University School of Law. *Second Chances, 100 Years of the Children's Court: Giving Kids a Chance to Make a Better Choice,* Chicago, Ill.: Justice Policy Institute, 1999.

Kreisler, Gabrielle. "A Mostly Sensible Approach to Juvenile Crimes and Punishment," *Criminal Justice,* http://www.abanet.org/crimjust (8 May 2001).

"Mandatory Life Term for Teen Rejected," *Chicago Tribune*, 22 June 2000.

National Association of State Budget Officers. *State Juvenile Justice Expenditures and Innovations,* http://www.nasbo.org (12 May 2001).

Parenti, Christian. *Lockdown America: Police and Prisons in the Age of Crisis* (London: Verso, 1999).

Platt, Anthony M. *The Child Savers: The Invention of Delinquency*, second edition (Chicago: University of Chicago Press, 1977).

Rothstein, Richard. "Of Schools and Crimes, and Gross Exaggeration," *New York Times,* 7 March 2000, B9.

Shepherd, Robert, Jr. "False Images? The News Media and Juvenile Crime," *Annual Report of the Coalition for Juvenile Justice* (1997), http://www.juvjustice.org/publications/1997ar.html (8 May 2000).

———. "The Juvenile Court at 100: Birthday Cake or Funeral Pyre?" *Juvenile and Family Court Journal* 50, no. 4 (1999): 9-19.

Stern, Vivien. *A Sin against the Future: Imprisonment in the World* (Boston: Northeastern University Press, 1998).

6
Growing Up Incarcerated: The Prison-Industrial Complex and Literacy as Resistance

Elizabeth Kleinfeld

Nearly two million Americans are currently in prison or jail. The Bureau of Justice Statistics reported that in 1999, 3.1 percent of all adult U.S. residents were on probation, in jail, or in prison.[1] The prevailing notion is that this fact is responsible for another fact: violent crime is down across the country. In some major metropolitan areas, major crime is down to the levels of the 1970s. Not surprisingly, politicians of both major political parties are claiming the low crime rates prove that the war on crime is being won by their party.[2] Both parties advocate imprisoning more people and for longer periods of time to continue this downward trend, although as Michael Tonry, professor of law and public policy at the University of Minnesota, points out, "You could choose another two million Americans at random and lock them up, and that would reduce the number of crimes, too."[3] Eric Schlosser, writing for the *Atlantic Monthly*, notes that Canada's violent crime rate has gone down as well, "while their incarceration rate has risen only slightly."[4] The dip in the crime rate is most likely linked to the drop since 1980 in the number of males aged 15-24; historically, when this population rises, so do crime rates.

Whether or not incarceration reduces crime, it serves an important function in a capitalist system. Imprisonment can be seen as a ruling class social control formation, a construction of the ruling class to control the other classes.[5] One way this works is through the disenfranchisement of convicts. Because minorities and the poor are disproportionately imprisoned, they are also disproportionately stripped of their right to vote through the disenfranchisement that often accompanies imprisonment. In some states, people convicted of felonies lose their right to vote *forever*, even after their sentence has been served. Thirteen percent of adult African Americans cannot vote because of felony convictions.[6] Minorities receive longer sentences for similar crimes than whites do, and low-income defendants receive prison sentences twice as often as high-income defendants do for similar crimes.[7] The National Council on Crime and Delinquency's report, *And Justice for Some,* shows that minority youths are significantly more likely than white youths to be arrested, jailed, brought to trial, and convicted.[8] According to the report, a black juvenile with no criminal record is 48 times more likely to be imprisoned for a drug offense than a white juvenile with no record. The *Nation*'s David Cole found that "from 1986 to 1991, for example, the number of white drug offenders in state prisons increased by 110 percent, but the number of imprisoned black drug offenders increased by 465 percent."[9] The people who suffer the most in the current system are denied their right to vote; in other words, they are made impotent to change the system.[10] Youths who are incarcerated now may never be able to vote, an especially chilling idea considering how crucial just a few votes in Florida turned out to be in the 2000 presidential election.

Who benefits from the imprisonment of large segments of the population? The prison-industrial complex. In his insightful article, "The Prison Industrial Complex," Schlosser gives an accurate and detailed definition of the prison-industrial complex:

> a set of bureaucratic, political, and economic interests that encourage increased spending on imprisonment, regardless of the actual need . . . it is a confluence of special interests that has given prison construction in the United States a seemingly unstoppable momentum. It is composed of politicians, both liberal and conservative, who have used the fear of crime to gain votes; impoverished rural areas where prisons have become a cornerstone of economic development; private companies that regard the roughly $35 billion spent each year on corrections not as a burden on American taxpayers but as a lucrative market; and government officials whose fiefdoms have expanded along with the inmate population.[11]

He goes on to describe those enmeshed in the prison-industrial complex: everyone from architects who design prison compounds to companies that manufacture security cameras. Another important component is private prisons.[12]

The prison-industrial complex depends on a steady supply of prisoners. In this essay, I will discuss some ways in which the prison-industrial complex ensures this steady supply, focusing on the systematic production and maintenance of prisoner illiteracy. I will also show how some of the current trends in the juvenile justice system—including a growing emphasis on punishment and the lowering of the age at which juveniles can be prosecuted in the adult justice system—fulfill the prison-industrial complex's ideology, functioning to keep prisons full and prisoners illiterate. The prison-industrial complex intentionally keeps prisoners, beginning with juveniles, illiterate to further its economic and social control agendas. Two of the ways the prison-industrial complex accomplishes this are the systematic regulation and censorship of reading and writing materials and opportunities in prisons and the incoherency of educational programming in prisons. Illiteracy serves to produce a permanent prisoner class, solidifying and stabilizing the power and control of the prison-industrial complex.

Schlosser estimates 70 percent of prisoners to be illiterate in terms of reading and writing ability. A plethora of research reveals that when prisons provide educational opportunities for prisoners, recidivism rates decrease.[13] In spite of this, Citizens United to Rehabilitate Errants reports that "more than half of all state prison systems have reduced educational and vocational training since 1989. . . . Post secondary programs which have generated incentives and have a demonstrated track record in substantially reducing recidivism have been eliminated in virtually all state and federal prisons."[14] There is no coherent literacy program or other educational programming in this country's prisons, resulting in haphazard approaches, redundancy in programming that does exist, and conflicting philosophies from state to state and prison to prison. In addition, none of the existing programs or materials used in those programs were designed specifically for prisoners.[15] No coherency means reduced effectiveness and maintenance of illiteracy. Depriving prisoners of education keeps them both textually and culturally illiterate. Illiteracy helps to produce a permanent prisoner class, solidifying and stabilizing the power and control of the prison-industrial complex.

MY STUDY

Interested in how prisoners can and do resist these institutional efforts to keep them illiterate, I interviewed twelve male prison inmates about the history and development of their literacy in the prison system. I located most through ads placed by them on the Internet for pen pals. Two of them entered juvenile facilities at the age of 14, two at the age of 15, and one each at the ages of 16 and 17. Three men entered correctional facilities at 18, and three were over 18 when they entered. All of the men are in their 20s or 30s now, currently serving time in adult correctional facilities. Nine are serving sentences for violent crimes, and all are serving their sentences in medium or high security facilities. I gathered the data in written form from all prisoners; in addition, I conducted two brief telephone interviews. The demographics of my sample are quite limited:[16] I spoke with four Hispanic men, four white men, two African Americans, and two Native Americans.

My study was somewhat hindered by the fact that I had to correspond with these men instead of conducting face-to-face interviews; whenever I needed a response clarified, I had to write a letter and then wait up to a month for a response. Another problem that came up is that during the time of our correspondence, six men were transferred from one prison to another, resulting in misrouted prisoner mail, long delays in prisoners' receipt of mail, and bounced mail. Only one man had requested the transfer. And finally, my study is clearly limited by the small number of prisoners surveyed. My sample may not be representative of the prison population in its demographics or literacy, but these men illustrate several key concepts of my argument. First, they show why the prison-industrial complex is so intent on keeping prisoners illiterate. Second, they illustrate why the systemic oppression of the prisoner class through illiteracy is doomed to fail. And finally, they illustrate some concrete ways in which this oppression breeds resistance.

CENSORSHIP AND LITERACY

Most prisons curtail prisoners' access to literacy. Not only is literacy education limited; prisons regulate and limit the number of books in a prisoner's cell at one time and censor incoming and outgoing mail and publications. The ACLU recently filed a suit against Colorado's prison system for banning *Westword*, a general interest weekly publication that routinely covers prison issues; *Rolling Stone* (the magazine allegedly contains gang related symbols); guides to sign language (gang members use sign language to communicate with each other); and the novel *Like Water for Chocolate* (the book allegedly contains recipes for explosives).[17] In addition to regulating and limiting access, the prison environment discourages reading and writing, with constant interruptions and noise and lack of good lighting.

Almost all the prisoners I interviewed cited institutional censorship and other limitations on reading material. One prisoner, Jerry,[18] says his facility does not allow *The Source*, a rap magazine, because the staff alleges that the magazine contains gang propaganda. Prisoners are not allowed to receive any books on topics deemed "revolutionary" by the administration, including some books on legal matters, and prisoners may not have more than ten books at a time in their cells, which makes legal research and independent study difficult. Another prisoner, Pete, reports that while obscene materials are not censored in his prison, most legal materials are limited. He says most of the law books have been removed from the law library. Red Bear, another prisoner, reports that his prison no longer even has a law library. He has trouble receiving materials in the mail pertaining to his Native American heritage, especially items about Native American religious practices. Last year, he sent out letters to thirty organizations asking for information on Native American religious festivals, and did not receive a single response. He suspects that either the prison staff read his outgoing letters and did not allow them to be mailed, or that the staff confiscated the requested information when it arrived. He says, "To adequately express myself in writing is impossible here. All outgoing mail is read," which makes him hesitant to express himself fully even in personal letters to family.

All twelve cited limitations imposed by their imprisonment on their writing. Several correspondents specifically mentioned keeping a journal as something they would like to do and would find beneficial for personal reflection and growth, but they have many concerns about the consequences of such personal writing. Manuel worries that a journal would be read by a guard. He is considered an active gang member, although he has not been involved in any gang activities in at least eight years, and he is concerned that something he might write in a journal would be misinterpreted as proof of gang activity. Jerry's cell is searched regularly and so he is careful to not write anything that could be construed as revolutionary or gang related. He has also had cellmates read his personal papers. Angel just began keeping a journal a few months ago, but has recently become concerned that prison authorities may read it. He is hesitant to give it up because he feels so much more in touch with his thoughts and feelings now but the prospect of having the journal read by a staff member is disturbing, and he finds himself writing in his journal less and less. Red Bear reports, "I can't keep a journal because staff will find it in a shake down, take it, read it, copy it, and [put it in my file to use against me first chance they get]." Red Bear feels that prison authorities do everything to take away the prisoner's voice.

In recent years, many prisoners have turned to prisoner pen pal services, which print advertisements from prisoners looking for pen pals. Many of these services now post prisoner advertisements on the Internet, and although most prisoners do not have Internet access, they can mail advertisements to Web-based pen pal services who will post their ads. Charles Sparks, director of an Internet-based prisoner pen pal service, says that the states of New York and Arizona have prohibited prisoners from receiving any information in the mail about pen pal services.[19] New York is considering prohibiting prisoners from receiving any mail from people not on a preapproved list, which would make correspondence with pen pals found through a service like Sparks's difficult. Many states do not allow prisoners to receive printouts of Internet sites in the mail. Some prisons, such as Virginia's Keen Mountain Facility, do not allow inmates to receive any photocopied materials.[20] California's Corcoran State Prison does not allow inmates to receive newspaper clippings or photocopies of newspaper clippings.[21] These prisons claim that allowing photocopied materials or newspaper clippings would somehow jeopardize the prisoners' safety. The *New York Times*'s Dirk Johnson reports that New York and Arizona have made it illegal for prisoners to post pen pal ads on the Internet. Johnson speculates that one reason authorities may be trying to limit these services is that they often serve to publicize cases like Mumia Abu-Jamal's.[22] Perhaps officials fear the sense of empowerment prisoners can find in correspondence.

CONSEQUENCES OF LITERACY

Study after study reveals education to be rehabilitative for prisoners. In the late nineteenth century, the National Prison Association advocated education for prisoners because of its ability to enhance self-respect and make prisoners better citizens.[23] Literacy is also recognized as a deterrent to recidivism. The California Youth Authority's Mitchell Jancic found that prisoners who completed GED requirements while incarcerated had lower recidivism rates than those that did not. He reports that the State of New York Department of Correctional Services studied 4,226 prisoners released in 1986 and 1987 and found that those with GEDs recidivated at a rate 5 percent lower than the general prison population.[24] Dennis J. Stevens, Professor and Director of Criminal Justice at Mount Olive College, and Charles S. Ward, Education Program Director of Eastern Correctional Institution in North Carolina, found that inmates who were able to earn college degrees had a significantly lower recidivism rate than other prisoners.[25] In a study of inmates in North Carolina, they found the recidivism rate among the general prison population to be 40 percent; however, among inmates with at least an associates degree, the rate was only 5 percent.[26] They found similar statistics when they reviewed research done in Alabama, Maryland, New York, and Texas. Stevens and Ward surveyed studies on the relationship between education and recidivism between 1969 and 1993 and found that 85 percent of the studies reported that education reduces recidivism.[27] Red Bear contends that "the prisons in Arizona do not want the inmates to be smarter than the staff who work at the prisons. When the ADOC realized inmates going to school and reading educational books were becoming smarter than their staff, they stopped all schooling."

Researchers Ross and Fabiano found that effective programs do exist, and that successful education programs in corrections facilities encourage critical thinking.[28] Anabel P. Newman, Warren Lewis, and Caroline Beverstock found that successful literacy programs "educate broadly, [are] governed for the sake of the learners, make prison life more livable . . . improve the quality of life, provide a new reader's library." Newman also found that successful programs encourage prisoners to develop several types of literacy, "[including] social literacies: cultural literacy . . . gender literacies, civil literacy, [and] consumer literacy."[29] Newman found that prisoners who were encouraged to become literate were better adjusted in prison, reporting that "the ability to relax and enjoy a good book reduces the stress level, increases tolerance for over-crowded conditions, causes the inmates to require less supervision."[30] These prisoners are also less likely to recidivate.

Literacy can have a dramatic effect on a prisoner. Writing of his first experience with imprisonment, which also became his first experience with literacy, poet Jimmy Santiago Baca remembers,

> With shocking speed I found myself handcuffed to a chain gang of inmates and bused to a holding facility to await trial. There I met men, prisoners, who read aloud to each other the works of Neruda, Paz, Sabines, Nemerov, and Hemingway. Never had I felt such freedom as in that dormitory. Listening to the works of these writers, I felt that invisible threat from without lessen—my sense of teetering on

> a rotting plank over swamp water where famished alligators clapped their horny snouts for my blood. While I listened to the works of the poets, the alligators slumbered powerless in their lairs. Their language was the magic that could liberate me from myself, transform me into another person, transport me to other places far away.[31]

Baca found that literacy made prison life more tolerable. Literacy became one of the tools Baca would use to rehabilitate himself and prevent himself from returning to prison, which is consistent with the findings of Jancic, Stevens, and Ward. Newman emphasizes, "the case is clear for the relationship between illiteracy and criminality in adult inmates, but it is even clearer in juveniles."[32] But the prison-industrial complex cannot profit without full prisons.

In a survey of research on the role of literacy instruction in preventing juvenile crime, Newman found that "the 'right kind' of literacy instruction, especially where the parents become supportive, is the knock-out punch against juvenile crime"[33] and goes on to describe "the right kind" of instruction:

> The right kind of instruction, as revealed in these studies, can be summarized as early-intervention, individualized, small-class, closely monitored, culturally responsive, success-oriented, highly motivating, self-esteem-building instruction that is delivered by caring and competent, well-trained and dedicated, street-wise and savvy teachers and counselors.[34]

These same characteristics should, as much as possible, be present in programs in juvenile facilities. (It is outside the scope of this essay to discuss the role of the prison-industrial complex in defunding and in other ways hindering literacy instruction in urban areas.)

Although there is much compelling evidence that educating prisoners reduces crime and the need for prisons, education in the prison system in general is in a woeful state. Newman laments, "Despite a near-universal awareness of education's high potential for habilitative success among juvenile offenders, in very many situations—especially local jails—the laws mandating educative remediation are being ignored."[35] For example, in Maryland, Newman found that many of the county jails did not offer any education opportunities to juveniles, and in several of the jails that did provide classes, juveniles in administrative segregation were not permitted to attend classes. Newman also found that some local jails had no books in their libraries except Bibles.[36] Adding to the problem is the fact that laws governing education in correctional facilities differ in all fifty states.

Often when educational programming is available to juvenile offenders and prison inmates, it is inappropriate for them. Thom L. Felton conducted a study to determine the preferred learning methods for prisoners. He found that more than 50 percent preferred a hands-on method.[37] Newman's findings are similar:

> Assessments of offenders have pointed to a high incidence of learning difficulties. Offenders also seem to differ markedly from non-offending populations in preferred learning styles; they favor an intense, hands on approach rather than the more passive, visual methods practiced in our schools.[38]

Many prisons, however, citing security concerns, will not allow an instructor to conduct small group work with students, have students complete collaborative assignments, or use kinesthetic methods. When asked about the education available to him in a juvenile facility, Antonio says all he remembers is having to sit still for long periods of time and being reprimanded for fidgeting. Many of my correspondents shared similar memories of the classrooms in the juvenile facilities they were in.

Jerry's story vividly shows how the incoherency in educational programming hurts prisoners. Jerry dropped out of school when he was 12 or 13 because he found it boring. He earned his eighth grade diploma when he was incarcerated in a juvenile facility, but then was moved to another facility where school was not mandatory, and he stopped attending school. When Jerry was 17 and in another facility, he decided he wanted to earn his GED. GED classes were optional and not encouraged, but he began taking the classes. He found the classes uninteresting and became fidgety, just as Antonio had. He was kicked out of the prison school for disruptive behavior. When Jerry was moved to an adult prison at 18, he earned a GED but was not able to pay the fee for a certificate. Ten years later, Jerry's mother paid the fee for him and requested a copy of his certificate. She was told that there was no record of his having taken the test; apparently, the prison Jerry had taken the test in did not file the paperwork stating that he had taken and passed the test. Although Jerry did earn a GED, the disjointed nature of his education left him confused and convinced that he lacked intelligence.

Angel left school when he was 14 and joined a gang. Not long after that, he was sentenced to a juvenile facility. The juvenile facilities Angel was in at age 15 and 16 provided basic skills education. When he was 16, he was moved to a facility that offered some optional occupational courses and he took drafting classes. Released at age 18, Angel went on to earn his GED when he was 19 and not in prison. Later, when he was back in prison, he was told that he would have to take a battery of tests to check his math and communication skills unless he had a GED certificate. He had lost his copy of the certificate and so, even though he had earned a GED and there was a record of this in the county, Angel has had to retake the battery of tests every year for ten years. When Angel entered an adult facility at age 22, he was not allowed to participate in educational opportunities because of his high security rating and his long sentence (life without parole). The prison school is located in a zone of the prison that high security prisoners are not allowed to enter. In the twelve years he's been in adult prison, he has participated in one class, a drug awareness class, which was canceled after two weeks for reasons unknown to Angel.

Lorna Rios, author of *Me . . . Teach Criminals? The True Adventures of a Prison Teacher,* tells a story that illustrates well the consequences of illiteracy:

> My favorite quote is from Ira Shor: "Vocationalism economically reproduces stratification and politically retards alternative thought." I like to write this sentence on the board and ask my students what it means. They cannot even read all the "big" words, so we go over them and then I ask if this is saying that vocationalism is good or bad. They all say that it is good, which is exactly the opposite of what Ira Shor intended to say and proves his point exactly.[39]

Rios continues, "too often lawyers and counselors have spoken to my students using English from the academic culture of a university. Not only do my students not understand the 'big words,' they also do not understand the complex sentences."[40] Rios's students are not simply unable to read the "big words," they are unable to understand the "big words." They are unable to make sense of them. The prison-industrial complex clearly has a stake in keeping prisoners ignorant of Ira Shor's opinion of vocationalism. Illiteracy among prisoners means fewer grievances and appeals. It means reduced capacity for logical thought. It means prisoners are more easily manipulated.

In *The German Ideology*, Marx says "the production of ideas, of conceptions, of consciousness, is at first directly interwoven with the material activity and the material intercourse of men, the language of real life." He is referring to material activity as the real language of life. Just as Marx emphasized that workers have different relationships to the means of production from those that capitalists have, we can examine how prisoners' relationships to the means of language production are different from non-prisoners' relationships to the means of language production.

Prison slang is replete with examples of prisoners' awareness of the power of language. For example, most prisoners divide the population at their institution into two main groups: *convicts* and *inmates*. These two words are not simply synonyms for each other or for "prisoner." Linguist Bert Little found that a *convict* is a prisoner who has earned the respect of the other prisoners through his self-confidence, relative autonomy, and refusal to defer to the guards. An *inmate*, on the other hand, is not to be trusted, as he appears too eager to please the guards and play by the administration's rules. Because the connotations of these two words are so widely known among prisoners, prison staff is careful about the way they use the terms.[41] The problem is that most prisoners do not understand how to harness the power of language. They bitterly notice only how language has been used against them. Joe's feeling is representative: "I think the language used by the courts, lawyers, etc. is done with the express purpose to confuse those who are ignorant."[42]

One reason that the prison-industrial complex seeks to limit the literacy of prisoners is that literacy gives prisoners a sense of control; Red Bear feels that as long as he controls his mind and spirit, he can keep himself from becoming "the number the prison assigned me." He reads to "expand [his] mind, thought, and spirit." He reads as much as he can "to keep my mind alive, expanding, and fed with knowledge. This place can have my body, but it will never have my mind and spirit." Antonio has noticed that the more letters he writes, the better he gets at expressing himself in writing. He thinks he will soon have enough confidence in his writing to write some essays on prison life to be posted on the Internet. Jerry has found one of the benefits of his literacy to be that he is better able to defend himself against false disciplinary charges. He says he is more likely to file a grievance now when he believes his rights have been violated because he is more confident that he will be able to articulately explain himself.

The primary reason for the institutional limits on literacy, however, is simple: increased literacy leads to resistance. All but three of my correspondents have written legal documents, including grievances, appeals, and motions. Manuel recently had a disciplinary hearing in which he argued that the prison authorities had violated their own policies on drug testing of inmates. In preparing his defense, he was allowed only 30 minutes in the prison law library. When he was found guilty of the charge, he went back to his cell and wrote a letter to the local newspaper detailing how his rights had been violated. Jerry says that since he began corresponding with pen pals three years ago, he has written three grievances. He never wrote any before finding pen pals. Angel has also written legal documents off and on for a few years, and about once a month in the past year. The men that have written grievances say that becoming more literate has enabled them to do legal research more efficiently and better understand—and fight—disciplinary charges against them.

THE NOTION OF THE SUPERPREDATOR AND THE PRISON-INDUSTRIAL COMPLEX

Late stage capitalism depends on an ideology of hyper-efficiency and punitiveness to ensure hyper-profits for the ruling class. The wars on drugs, crime, and poverty in the U.S. are evidence of this ideology. Instead of seeking to treat and end drug abuse, crime, or poverty, official policy focuses on punishment. In the name of efficiency, certain drug users, outlaws, and the poor lose their freedom and their right to vote for long periods of time. Increasingly, official policy seeks not only to punish drug abuse, crime, and poverty but to enable the ruling class to profit from them as well.

Some of the results of the prison-industrial complex are economic. California, for example, requires government agencies, schools, libraries, and hospitals to buy prison-made goods. The prison-industrial complex depends on the labor of prisoners. Prison officials and politicians may claim that work is a form of rehabilitation, but while there is much research showing the benefits of education as rehabilitative, there is no data to support the idea that working in a factory improves critical thinking skills or decision making skills. Reese Ehrlich found that in California, officials "long ago stopped claiming that prison labor rehabilitates inmates. Wardens just want to keep them occupied. If prisoners refuse to work, they are moved to disciplinary housing and lose canteen privileges. Most importantly, they lose 'good time' credit that reduces their sentence."[43] Clearly prisoners are required to work because the prison-industrial complex benefits from their labor, not because prisoners benefit from the experience. This situation occurs across the country: prisoners are required to work, or penalized if they don't work, but they reap almost nothing from their labor. Wages, when there are any, are even more ridiculously low than any minimum wage. UNICOR, the federal prison industries, for example, pays prisoners between 23 cents and $1.50 an hour. Prisoners are then allowed to spend their wages only on items that have been approved by prison authorities. Most prisons require prisoners to make the majority of their purchases from the prison canteen, where a 13-inch color TV can sell for $175 and an outdated typewriter for $225.[44] The prison-industrial complex also results in the type of labor abuses that plague any enterprise driven by profit. Furthermore, since prisoners do not have the right to unionize, there is little they can do to protect themselves from such abuses. In the few instances where the working conditions of prisoners are publicized, politicians label prisoner complaints "frivolous."

Late stage capitalism depends on a slave class, and people in prisons make up part of that slave class.[45] Housing juvenile offenders in adult prisons, sentencing women who date drug dealers to 20 years in prison, and subjecting someone who is caught shoplifting three times to "three strikes and you're out" legislation, which can result in a life sentence, keeps prisons full. To get the public to support these travesties, politicians and the media refer repeatedly to "the coming crime wave" and the new generation of "superpredators," young, mostly minority, men who are supposedly lurking everywhere, looking to commit senseless violent crimes without provocation. Amnesty International asserts that "the notion of the 'super predator' and the 'teenage time bomb' has fueled irrational and short-sighted policies which ultimately strip young people of their human dignity and rob our society of untapped human potential."[46]

Crime legislation since the 1994 Crime Bill has placed authority in prosecutors' hands, rather than judges', to determine whether juveniles should be tried as adults. Children as young as 13 can now be prosecuted as adults, and children and adult prisoners can be housed together, although research shows that children housed with adults have higher recidivism rates. Many states have reduced the age at which juveniles can be sentenced to life in prison without parole, so that it is possible for a child who is sentenced at 14 or 15 never to be released from prison.

Gary L. Smith's chapter in this same volume discusses in greater detail some of the dangerous implications of legislation affecting juveniles.

In 1996, Laura Murphy, director of the ACLU's Washington National Office, addressed the scapegoating of juveniles in a speech to the Congressional Black Caucus Brain Trust on Juvenile Justice:

> In this election year, politicians have once again seized the issue of crime in America as one of the fundamental building blocks of their campaigns. But this year, the crime scapegoat is not Willie Horton—it is our children. Teenagers, and even pre-teens, are being demonized as "superpredators" and "natural born killers" which creates an atmosphere of fear and blame directed largely at inner city, minority youth.[47]

Unfortunately, the 2000 election year did not differ significantly in this area. The fact that crime among juveniles is actually down does not get mentioned in mainstream political discourse because the prison-industrial complex depends for its livelihood on the public's fear of juvenile criminals—whether they truly exist or not—and the taxpayers' continued funding of prisons.

Moving more juveniles into the prison system earlier improves the chances of illiteracy taking hold. The earlier a juvenile enters the system, the less likely it is that he or she will ever completely escape the prison-industrial complex's clutches.

RESISTANCE

Ironically, while the prison-industrial complex works to discourage literacy, imprisonment itself seems to encourage literacy for some prisoners. Ten of my correspondents say they seldom did any reading or writing of any type before coming to prison. Nine were involved in gangs before coming to prison and three were addicted to drugs as well, conditions that do not encourage literacy. Jerry says he does not remember ever having received a letter before coming to prison. Eight of my correspondents dropped out of high school and stopped reading and writing completely.

Manuel's story illustrates the typical fits and starts in education experienced by people who grow up imprisoned. Manuel left school when he was "probably ten" because "school wasn't cool." He earned a GED while incarcerated in a juvenile detention facility. It was here that he took a typing class and some job skills classes. Once in an adult prison, he took some basic electronics classes, but found them confusing. The prison did not offer him any help in understanding the concepts and he eventually became frustrated and stopped taking classes. Five years later Manuel again began taking classes, this time in Spanish and computers, but his tuition was covered by Pell grants and when that program became unavailable to prisoners, he was forced to again stop taking classes. He finally decided to advertise for a pen pal because he wanted to know about life outside prison.

Antonio quit school when he was sent to prison at 18. He never liked school anyway so he wasn't too upset about being forced to quit. While on lockdown, he earned his GED because he had "all the time in the world to study." Antonio says the best educational experience he had was a wilderness challenge course sponsored by the Texas Youth Commission. The course taught him to get along with others, which has been invaluable in his 15 years in federal prisons. When he was 18, he was in a federal facility that did not offer any educational programs. When he was 19, he was sent to a prison where he was able to earn his GED. Antonio advertised for a pen pal because his friends were doing it. He surprised himself by becoming an avid letter writer, and having to find new and interesting things to tell his pen pals has helped him begin to notice new things about his life and environment.

All twelve prisoners say that they read much more since their incarceration. Manuel reads and writes in many different genres almost daily. He reads several novels a month, including titles such as Isabel Allende's *The House of the Spirits* and Gary Jennings's *Aztec,* and last summer he read Byron's "Manfred." He reads non-fiction several times a year. Last month he read *A Brief History of Time* by Stephen Hawking. He has begun reading law books more frequently as he is working on an appeal and a grievance. Jerry reads mysteries, adventure novels, autobiographies, true crime, and love stories. He has been teaching himself Spanish and the basics of hydroponic gardening through self-study of books. He now reads a daily newspaper and many magazines. Angel says that during the first few years of his imprisonment, he read many novels, but he has stopped reading fiction altogether now in favor of non-fiction. He has become more concerned lately with self-improvement and feels that fiction is more of an escape, while non-fiction is more directly educational. He has recently been reading *The Rosicrucian Cosmo-Conception* and essays on postmodernism. Antonio recently finished *Love in the Time of Cholera* by Gabriel García Márquez. He reads history and art history books related to his Aztec heritage. Last year he began reading Confucius's *Analects*. He speaks English and Spanish and has begun studying an Aztec language. Red Bear no longer reads a newspaper as "all they bring is bad news." He has always enjoyed fantasy novels such as those by Anne Rice and J. R. R. Tolkien. Now Pete almost never reads a newspaper, but he does read two novels a month and two non-fiction books on health or medicine a month. His favorite fiction writers are Agatha Christie and Tony Hillerman.

All twelve write more now, too, reading and writing letters weekly. Jerry is working on his autobiography. In the past five years, Angel has written a poem about every two months. Since coming to prison, Pete has become a key member of the prison's peer counseling and support group. He wrote the orientation handbook for the organization, as well as various documents for use by the group, such as job duties and self-assessments. He has also done quite a bit of writing for his correspondence courses. In addition to degree-related courses, he has taken a course in legal writing. Manuel took his first correspondence course last semester and is planning to enroll for another course in the fall. Antonio will be beginning correspondence courses this fall.

All twelve of my correspondents are dramatically more literate now than when they first came to prison. Jerry says he does not particularly enjoy writing, but it is one of the only ways he can keep in contact with friends and family. Since a 15-minute call from the prison costs $12, a letter is much more practical. Jerry says writing regularly has made him pay more attention to how he phrases things. Red Bear says that now pen pals are his "ears, eyes to what life is like out there. Through their letters I can see the world." He writes more now than he did before he came to prison to pass the time. It also helps him to feel less isolated. Red Bear also does research on topics of interest to him for when he is released, such as flying planes and helicopters, hydroponic gardening, and solar heating systems. Jerry sees writing as a necessity in prison, while it was a luxury before he came to prison. Pete attributes the changes in his reading and writing habits to a change in his value system which made him appreciate reading and writing more. He says,

> Personal growth and necessity as well as education and experience [have caused me to want to read and write more]. The circumstances of being incarcerated create opportunities to spend time in ways not thought about before being limited in options. This has been a good thing for me, since it has led me to investigate avenues of enjoyment like reading which I never would have if I had never come to prison.

All cited reading and writing as effective ways to pass the time, to take their minds off of prison, and to provide an outlet for anger and bitterness.

A common thread runs through these stories. After several years of not reading and writing, these men began to see literacy as a way to find more meaning in their lives and use their time more constructively; as these men became more literate, they had a greater appreciation for literacy and began to seek it out even more actively. In these men, literacy increased literacy. Each of these men began to see literacy as empowerment and resistance. Communicating with pen pals makes these men feel connected to a community outside the prison. Being able to communicate articulately with the courts makes these men more confident in standing up for their rights.

The prison-industrial complex has done much to squelch the literacy of prisoners, but this system of oppression works only as long as prisoners have no voices. I believe that cautious optimism is justified. A very cursory search of prisoner pen pal sites on the Internet showed a minimum of 10,000 prisoners searching for correspondence. Most of them are probably not specifically seeking to improve their literacy, but if they are anything like my correspondents, their literacy will begin to improve with correspondence and as their literacy grows, so will their interest in their own literacy. Another reason for optimism is the phenomenon of prisoner produced 'zines and newsletters. One of the most successful is *Prison Legal News*, which began in 1990 with 75 subscribers. Today it is a monthly tabloid of 32 pages, reaching 3,200 subscribers. The newspaper includes reports on recent court decisions, editorials and letters to the editor on prison issues, and how-to articles on how to write effective legal motions. It is so powerful that several states have banned it from their prisons. Similar publications include *Florida Prison Legal Perspectives*, *Voices Behind the Walls*, and *Southland Prison News*.[48]

There are also many educators in the correctional system and a few brave judges working to increase the literacy of prisoners. The Changing Lives Through Literature program in Massachusetts is an example of the difference a well thought-out program can make. The privately funded program, started by Robert Waxler, a literature professor at the University of Massachusetts, combines the concept of a reading group with the concept of a literature seminar and focuses on helping prisoners understand personal responsibility and consequence through structured response and discussion of novels. Judge Robert Kane sentences many offenders to the program. After tracking 68 convicts who completed the program for two to four years, Kane found that the recidivism rate was dramatically lower than expected.[49] Another program that can be used as a model is the Writing for Our Lives program, a program that uses writing about short stories to teach cognitive skills to prisoners.[50] We need more programs like these.

We also need to make more college programs available to prisoners who are fighting to become literate. Raymond L. Jones and Peter d'Errico, both professors of legal studies at the University of Massachusetts, suggest "[higher education] can be a vehicle through which incarcerated men and women might be able to transform their lives,"[51] but few prisons provide on-site college programming, which means prisoners must rely on distance courses. With the current push away from correspondence courses and toward Internet-based courses at the college level, many prisoners are finding it more and more difficult to take college courses since few prisons grant Internet access to prisoners. Prisoners also find paying tuition difficult and some prisons do not allow prisoners to accept scholarships (when Manuel received a scholarship application in the mail, he was told that accepting a scholarship would mean "entering into a contract," which prisoners are prohibited from doing).

Educators can and should act as advocates for stable educational programming, increased access to appropriate education programming, and increased opportunities for college-level programming for incarcerated juveniles and adults. Educators can and should agitate for fewer limitations on the types and amount of reading materials prisoners have access to. Educators have a responsibility to address crises like the systematic limiting of prisoners' literacy.

NOTES

1. California has become infamous for not being able to build prisons fast enough, and California is not alone. For example, Colorado, with a population of barely four million, has found itself in a similar position. *Prison Legal News* reports that "at an average of 1.3% per month in the second quarter of 1999, [Colorado's] prison population grew at twice the rate it did during the same period in 1998." If the prison population continues to grow at this rate, Colorado will need to build a new 2,500-bed prison every two years. Bob Williams, "Colorado Prison Population Exploding," *Prison Legal News* 11 (2000), 21.

2. Michael Hedges, "Murder, Rape, Robbery Rates across U.S. Fall to Lowest Point since Early '70s, " *Denver Rocky Mountain News*, 6 May 2000, 55A.

3. Michael Tonry, quoted in Eric Schlosser, "The Prison Industrial Complex," *The Atlantic Monthly,* December 1998, 77.

4. Schlosser, 77.

5. See Joel Olsen's discussion of how prisons achieve social control and how merely labeling someone a criminal can make them so. Joel Olsen, "Gardens of the Law: The Role of Prisons in Capitalist Society," in *Criminal Injustice: Confronting the Prison Crisis*, ed. Elihu Rosenblatt (Boston: South End Press, 1996), 40-46.

6. Jamie Fellner and Marc Mauer, *Losing the Vote: The Impact of Felony Disenfranchisement Laws in the United States* (Washington, D.C.: Human Rights Watch and the Sentencing Project, 1998).

7. Alexander C. Lichtenstein and Michael A. Kroll, "The Fortress Economy: The Economic Role of the U.S. Prison System," in *Criminal Injustice: Confronting the Prison Crisis*, ed. Elihu Rosenblatt (Boston: South End Press, 1996), 20-21.

8. Eileen Poe-Yamagata and Michael A. Jones, *And Justice for Some* (Washington, D.C.: Building Blocks for Youth, April 2000).

9. David Cole, "See No Evil, Hear No Evil," *Nation*, 9 October 2000, 30.

10. Lichtenstein and Kroll describe racial discrimination in the prison-industrial complex: "Prisons illustrate how racial and economic discrimination reinforce one another. . . . prison inmates are drawn from the ranks of the economically marginalized of all races. As an institution, however, prisons have a far greater impact on communities of color because of their disproportionate representation in prison populations. . . . The official unemployment rate for African Americans and Latinos is roughly twice that of Euro-Americans. Median income for African American families is 56% that of white families. Thirty percent of Black households have no assets, surviving on what they earn week by week. . . . All of these forces have a profoundly negative effect on a community's ability to sustain family life." Lichtenstein and Kroll, 24.

Karen Hempstead of *Black World Today* points out that "Able to warehouse young people during their prime working years, and having a poorly educated and increasingly impoverished citizenry, avaricious businessmen (and women) are strategically positioning themselves to gain from an expanded prison-industrial complex" in California. Karen E. Hempstead, "The Prison Industrial Complex," *The Black World Today Home Page*, 19 April 1999, http://www.blackworldtoday.com/views/fet/feat1094.asp (8 May 2000).

11. Schlosser, 54.

12. An important component of the prison-industrial complex is the private prison boom. The concept of a privately run prison runs counter to the principle of state punishment—if crimes are seen as transgressions against society, then the society should be re-

sponsible for punishing or rehabilitating. Schlosser argues that with private prisons, "the line between the public interest and the private interests has blurred . . . fundamental choices about public safety, employee training, and the denial of personal freedoms are increasingly being made with an eye to the bottom line." Private prisons are motivated not by responsibility to society but by profit. Private prisons can only be profitable if the cells are full, thus private prisons have a vested interest in keeping prisoners longer and having more people sentenced to prison time. In addition, since private prisons are motivated by profit, they can be tempted to cut corners. Schlosser, 63. See also Julie Light's description of a typical relationship between industry and private prisons. Julie Light, "The Prison Industry: Capitalist Punishment," *Corporate Watch Home Page*, 28 October 1999, http://www.igc.org/trac/feature/prisons/editorial.html (1 May 2000). Schlosser also provides an extensive litany of ills at private prisons operated by Bobby Ross Group, U.S. Corrections Corporation, Wachenhut Corrections, and the Corrections Corporation of America.

13. Jon M. Taylor, "Post Secondary Correctional Education: An Evaluation of Effectiveness and Efficiency," *Journal of Correctional Education* 43, no. 3 (1992): 132.

14. Citizens United to Rehabilitate Errants, "Correctional Education," *CURE Home Page*, http://www.curenational.org/Position/curepo5.html (3 May 2000).

15. Lorna Rios, "Correctional Education Connections," *Correctional Education Home Page*, 18 February 1998, http://www.io.com/~elite/6.html (16 March 2000).

16. I located all of my correspondents through pen pal services, except for the two African American men. Most pen pal services allow prisoners to specify whether they are looking for friends or romantic prospects; the majority of ads placed by African Americans were for romantic prospects. I wrote to several African American men who had placed ads looking for friends, but received no responses. The two African American men who participated in my surveys were actually located by prisoners who were already participating in my surveys.

17. Karen Abbott, "ACLU Accuses State Prison System of Illegal Censorship," *Denver Rocky Mountain News*, 23 March 2000, 5A.

18. All prisoners' names have been changed, as some feared retaliation from prison authorities for participating in my study.

19. Charles Sparks, letters to author, October 1998-May 2000.

20. Lawrence Peter Medici, letter to author, 26 February 1999.

21. Dino Monzo, telephone interview with author, 28 April 2000.

22. Dirk Johnson, "E-Mail Pen Pal Sites Give Prisoners a Link to the World Outside," *New York Times*, 1 August 2000.

23. Anabel P. Newman, Warren Lewis, and Caroline Beverstock, *Prison Literacy: Implications for Program and Assessment Policy* (Bloomington, Ind.: National Center for Adult Literacy, 1993), 14.

24. Mitchell Jancic, "Does Correctional Education Have an Effect on Recidivism?" *Journal of Correctional Education* 49, no. 4 (1998).

25. Dennis J. Stevens and Charles S. Ward, "College Education and Recidivism: Educating Criminals Is Meritorious," *Journal of Correctional Education* 48, no. 3 (1997): 106-11.

26. Stevens and Ward, 108.

27. Stevens and Ward, 107.

28. Newman, 24.

29. Newman, 28.

30. Newman, 30.

31. Jimmy Santiago Baca, *Working in the Dark: Reflections of a Poet of the Barrio* (Santa Fe: Red Crane Press, 1992), 4.

32. Newman, 16.

33. Newman, 16.

34. Newman, 16.

35. Newman, 16.

36. Newman, 33.

37. Thom L. Felton, "The Learning Modes of an Incarcerated Population," *Journal of Correctional Education* 45, no. 3 (1994): 118-21.

38. Newman, 6.

39. Lorna Rios, "Correctional Education Connections," *Correctional Education Home Page*, 18 February 1998, http://www.io.com/~elite/6.html (16 March 2000).

40. Rios, http://www.io.com/~elite/6.html (16 March 2000).

41. Bert Little, "Prison Lingo: A Style of American English Slang," *Anthropological Linguistics: Exploring the Languages of the World* 24, no. 2 (1982).

42. Several men pointed out the irony that the memos and written directives produced by the prison staffs are riddled with typos, misspellings, and grammatical errors. When asked about the use of language by court officials, Pete said, "The language is not the problem. The misapplication of clear precedents and the way they can twist the meanings to fit their current agenda is something I would have vehemently denied as a reality in America only a few years ago. Many times the same case is construed as support in one incident, but as counter in another, for the same foundation and ideology, as well as application of the law."

43. Reese Ehrlich, "Prison Labor: Workin' for the Man," *Covert Action Quarterly* 54 (Fall 1995), http://www.prop1.org/legal/prisons/labor.htm (1 May 2000).

44. Monzo, telephone interview.

45. Ehrlich traces the roots of the prison labor system to slavery: "In fact, prison labor has its roots in slavery. Following reconstruction, former Confederate Democrats instituted 'convict leasing.' Inmates, mostly freed slaves convicted of petty theft, were rented out to do everything from picking cotton to building railroads," http://www.prop1.org./legal/prisons/labor.htm (1 May 2000).

46. See Ehrlich and Lichtenstein and Kroll. The "criminal class" is held up as evidence that more prisons are needed, more surveillance is needed, stricter punishments are needed, and that all this is to protect the public. Where does the money for these things come from? Ehrlich says "as programs for the poor and disadvantaged face the axe, spending for police and prisons grows rapidly" (http://www.prop1.org./legal/prisons/labor.htm [1 May 2000]). Lichtenstein and Kroll point out that "the high cost of prisons cuts into the health, education, and welfare services needed by the very people who, lacking such supports, often end up in prison. The ultimate victims of these punitive policies are the same poor communities that have the most to fear from crime" (Lichtenstein and Kroll, 24). See also Schlosser, who asserts that poor communities also suffer indirectly from these measures. Seventy-five percent of the 80,000 women in prison have children, which means many of these children grow up without their mothers. The vast majority of the mothers come from poor communities.

47. Laura Murphy, "Statement before the Congressional Black Caucus Brain Trust on Juvenile Justice," *American Civil Liberties Union Home Page*, 14 May 1996, http://aclu.org (14 November 2000).

48. Paul Wright. "The History of Prison Legal News," *Prison Legal News*, May 2000.

49. William Bole, "A Novel Approach to Sentencing Criminals," *Village Life Magazine,* 20 January 1997, http://www.villagelife.org/ (18 December 2000).

50. Cynthia Blinn, "Teaching Cognitive Skills to Effect Behavioral Change through a Writing Program, " *Journal of Correctional Education* 46, no. 4 (1995).

51. Raymond L. Jones and Peter d'Errico, "The Paradox of Higher Education in Prisons," in *Higher Education in Prisons: A Contradiction in Terms?* ed. Miriam Williford (Phoenix: Oryx Press, 1994), 14.

BIBLIOGRAPHY

Abbott, Karen. "ACLU Accuses State Prison System of Illegal Censorship," *Denver Rocky Mountain News*, 23 March 2000, 5A.

Blinn, Cynthia. "Teaching Cognitive Skills to Effect Behavioral Change through a Writing Program, " *Journal of Correctional Education* 46, no. 4 (1995): 146-55.

Bole, William. "A Novel Approach to Sentencing Criminals," *Village Life Magazine,* 20 January 1997, http://www.villagelife.org/ (18 December 2000).

Citizens United to Rehabilitate Errants, "Correctional Education," *CURE Home Page*, http://www.curenational.org/Position/curepo5.html (3 May 2000).

Cole, David. "See No Evil, Hear No Evil," *Nation*, 9 October 2000, 30.

Corporate Watch Home Page, 28 October 1999, http://www.igc.org/trac/feature/prisons/editorial.html (1 May 2000).

Ehrlich, Reese. "Prison Labor: Workin' for the Man," *Covert Action Quarterly* 54 (Fall 1995), http://www.prop1.org/legal/prisons/labor.htm (1 May 2000).

Felton, Thom L."The Learning Modes of an Incarcerated Population," *Journal of Correctional Education* 45, no. 3 (1994): 118-21.

Hedges, Michael. "Murder, Rape, Robbery Rates across U.S. Fall to Lowest Point since Early '70s," *Denver Rocky Mountain News*, 6 May 2000, 55A.

Jancic, Mitchell."Does Correctional Education Have an Effect on Recidivism?" *Journal of Correctional Education* 49, no. 4 (1998): 152-61.

Johnson, Dirk. "E-Mail Pen Pal Sites Give Prisoners a Link to the World Outside," *New York Times*, 1 August 2000.

Jones, Raymond L., and Peter d'Errico, "The Paradox of Higher Education in Prisons," in *Higher Education in Prisons: A Contradiction in Terms?* ed. Miriam Williford. Phoenix: Oryx Press, 1994, 14.

Lichtenstein, Alexander C., and Michael A. Kroll, "The Fortress Economy: The Economic Role of the U.S. Prison System," in *Criminal Injustice: Confronting the Prison Crisis*, ed. Elihu Rosenblatt. Boston: South End Press, 1996, 13-39.

Light, Julie. "The Prison Industry: Capitalist Punishment," *Corporate Watch Home Page*, 28 October 1999, http://www.igc.org/trac/feature/prisons/editorial.html (1 May 2000).

Little, Bert. "Prison Lingo: A Style of American English Slang," *Anthropological Linguistics: Exploring the Languages of the World* 24, no. 2 (1982), 206-44.

Murphy, Laura. "Statement before the Congressional Black Caucus Brain Trust on Juvenile Justice," *American Civil Liberties Union Home Page*, 14 May 1996, http://aclu.org (14 November 2000).

Newman, Anabel P., Warren Lewis, and Caroline Beverstock. *Prison Literacy: Implications for Program and Assessment Policy.* Bloomington, Ind.: National Center for Adult Literacy, 1993.

Olsen, Joel. "Gardens of the Law: The Role of Prisons in Capitalist Society," in *Criminal Injustice: Confronting the Prison Crisis*, ed. Elihu Rosenblatt. Boston: South End Press, 1996, 40-46.

Poe-Yamagata, Eileen, and Michael A. Jones. *And Justice for Some.* Washington, D.C.: Building Blocks for Youth, April 2000.

Rios, Lorna. "Correctional Education Connections," *Correctional Education Home Page*, 18 February 1998, http://www.io.com/~elite/6.html (16 March 2000).

Santiago Baca, Jimmy. *Working in the Dark: Reflections of a Poet of the Barrio.* Santa Fe: Red Crane Press, 1992.

Schlosser, Eric."The Prison Industrial Complex," *Atlantic Monthly* (December 1998), 51-77.

Stevens, Dennis J., and Charles S. Ward, "College Education and Recidivism: Educating Criminals Is Meritorious," *Journal of Correctional Education* 48, no. 3 (1997): 106-11.

Taylor, John M. "Post Secondary Correctional Education: An Evaluation of Effectiveness and Efficiency," *Journal of Correctional Education* 43, no. 3 (1992): 132-43.

Williams, Bob. " Colorado Prison Population Exploding," *Prison Legal News* 11 (2000): 21.

Wright, Paul. "The History of Prison Legal News," *Prison Legal News* (May 2000).

7
Ideology and Interpellation in the First-Person Shooter

Andrew Kurtz

> And just where do your capacities come from? Why do you always go where I want and do what I say?
>
> The AI Durandal, *Marathon 2*

> Previously, men were mere appendages to the machine, today they are appendages as such.
>
> Max Horkheimer, "The End of Reason"

In this essay I will make what I hope are some provocative comments regarding the ideological and interpellative processes at work in home computer games. Though I believe the general trajectory of my remarks may be applied across a range of gaming systems, my focus will be on the genre of games called first-person shooters, in which play is oriented from the perspective of the player. Notable games in this genre include *Marathon*, *Doom*, *Duke Nuke 'Em*, *Quake*, and *Half Life*. My reasons for concentrating on the first-person shooter should be obvious to just about anyone with a passing knowledge of these games. Without a doubt, these games have redefined the representation of violence for an industry arguably built upon the commodification of Manichaean ideologies in which the only "other" in the game is an enemy to be destroyed. While such ideologies permeate virtually all media texts, from film and television to government propaganda that encodes and reduces complex geopolitical relations as a struggle between good and evil, stable and unstable, rational and irrational, these ideologies are able to exist and become hegemonic only because they are filtered through larger discursive structures such as humanism, democracy, and globalization. This crucial philtre is precisely missing from first-person shooters. Bereft of any humanistic dimension, they are one of the "dark paths of the divine world order" condemned by Adorno and Horkheimer. They are degree zero ideology.

It is not surprising, therefore, that the first-person shooter should become the focus of universal media and government condemnation, especially in light of their perceived role in the recent school shootings at Littleton, Colorado, and West Paducah, Kentucky. Setting the tone for this very one-sided discussion is columnist John C. Dvorak, who has called these games "murder simulators," arguing with no real evidence that "if you're going to tear up a place like a maniac, you'll do a lot more damage after playing *Doom* for a year or two than if you've never played the game."[1] More astute and compelling because it alludes to the class characteristics of computer gaming is an observation from 12-year-old Danielle Shimotakahara. Invoking their arcade counterparts housed in family oriented restaurants throughout suburban America, Shimotakahara recently reminded a committee of senators convened to address the issue of violence in the media that "parents eat pizza while their kids blow somebody up."[2] The polemical tone of this discussion is no doubt informed by a mass of literature from the disciplines of sociology and psychology which has attempted to verify empirically the extent to which the violence-laden fantasies of these games seep into the everyday lives of the gamer in the form of aggressive or otherwise antisocial behavior.[3]

The discourse railing against first-person shooters, as pervasive as the games themselves, warrants further investigation if for no other reason than it represents hegemony against itself, face to face with its own internal cultural productions and inherent contradictions. This chapter, though, is more limited in scope. It seeks mainly to examine the ideological contours of first-person shooters, for I believe they highlight the ideological processes inherent to virtually all computer games by assuming a direct identification between the player and the game's protagonist through its representational apparatus. But this is only part of the story. Following the work of Katherine Hayles, I will suggest that the representational content of first-person shooters is one component in a complex circuit of ideological relationships, involving not only the gaming content but also the player's subjective response to that content as mediated through his articulation with hardware controls.[4]

My analysis is thus oriented around an Althusserian model of ideological processes, which, through the concept of interpellation, seeks to understand the reproduction of hegemony as a function of the individual's response to ideology. To summarize briefly, in his essay "Ideology and Ideological State Apparatuses" Althusser equates the process of subject formation with the workings of ideology, itself a manifestation of ruling social and cultural institutions (the "Ideological State Apparatuses"). The role of ideology (its only role) in the reproduction of hegemonic relations is to create subjects from individuals by "hailing" or "interpellating" those individuals through cultural representations. To use Althusser's famous words, "all ideology hails or interpellates concrete individuals as concrete subjects."[5] This process all but guarantees the reproduction of ruling ideas by monopolizing the terrain of subject formation. Althusser therefore sees no distinction between ideology as a discrete structure and the process of ideological reproduction/subject formation through interpellation.[6] Althusser's analysis of subject formation is certainly not without problems, most notably, as Paul Smith argues, the seeming disregard for any theory of agency within the process of subject formation, a topic to which we will return. One must also acknowledge the criticisms of Althusser leveled by Stuart Hall, Ernesto Laclau, and Chantal Mouffe, which register charges of essentialism to Althusser's unambiguous rendering of interpellation as fundamentally rooted in the class make up of society. Nevertheless, in the analysis of cultural texts and especially those which are characterized primarily by their ability to hold so powerfully the individual in a state that can only be described as hegemonic incapacity, the model of interpellation as described by Althusser is at the very least a useful starting point, one that may in turn generate a more complex understanding of ideological processes at work in cultural sites determined as much by technology per se as by the representations produced by technology in, say, film, print, or on the Internet.

Andrew Feenberg's analysis of "technical codes" is particularly relevant at this juncture. In *Critical Theory of Technology* Feenberg uses a linguistic model to discern a *cultural grammar* of technology. Feenberg employs the term "technical elements" to describe specific objects (pulleys, computer chips, fiber optics, etc.) that remain "relatively neutral" with respect to their hegemonic bearing until such a time when they are "strung together—coded—to form a variety of 'sentences' with different meanings and intentions."[7] By arranging technical elements in configurations determined by the hegemonic goals of a society at a particular historical moment, *individual technologies* (the devices resulting from this arrangement) become imbued with ideology. Feenberg, therefore, states that "the study of any specific technology can trace in it the impress of a mesh of social determinations which preconstruct a whole domain of social activity aimed at definite social goals."[8] The site of this social activity is also the site of interpellation; for within any given technology social activity and the goals associated with it are only potentialities. For example, a Lexus (a configuration of technical elements) traveling atop an 18-wheeler on a deserted highway at three in the morning does not work to reproduce hegemonic ideologies. The same car, at rest in the overdetermined solace of the new car lot, ingratiates itself and its ideologies upon every new potential customer. Indeed, "customer" is arguably its primary interpellation, the "owner" being a mere cheerleader for the circuit of exchange.

Forty years after Barthes's analysis of cultural icons, such ideas are not news to cultural studies. However there is an inherent weakness to Feenberg's transposition of the semiological model onto the sphere of technology that results in an inability to see technical elements themselves as having ideological value. This weakness stems from the notion that technical elements must be configured with other technical elements in order to realize a specific social use. A question immediately arises: at what point in the configuration process do technical elements obtain at the level of ideology? At what point do technical elements reach this critical mass? Is it simply when a "product" is produced, which is to say when something useful is placed on the market for exchange? If this were the case, then there would be no need to analyze the steps leading up to the final semiological object, except, of course, as steps in the larger process of economic production. As far as decoding the "impress of social determinations" Feenberg's model would suggest that we need not be concerned with the "technical elements"of any given technology. This is a theoretical difficulty symptomatic, I believe, of Feenberg's transposition of the semiological model onto the site of technology development. The term "element" as used by, for example, Laclau and Mouffe in *Hegemony and Socialist Strategy*, describes components of signifying systems before their concatenation or "articulation" as discursive structures (mirroring Feenberg's "individual technologies").[9] Elements do indeed have ideological value, though at any given historical moment they may be given a particular inflection, depending on the hegemonic context within which they are articulated. The same would hold true for technical elements. For even those minutia of production, capacitors in circuit boards, filaments in lightbulbs, twisted copper in telephone lines, have ideological characteristics which are finally brought to bear in the manufacture of more complex technologies.[10] Thus, I believe the special reservation placed on "technical elements" in Feenberg's discussion greatly reduces the complexity of interpellations possible at any cultural site in which technology is the primary node of ideological transmission. It is more likely the case, as we will see in our discussion of first-person shooters, that specific technologies *masquerade* as ideologically neutral, when, in fact, the interpellations they afford are more powerful than any representation coming through the cathode ray tube.

GAME THEORY

Within the small body of literature that comprises cultural studies' foray into the world of video games, the overarching theme is the experience of game play as it relates to the process of subject-production. Utilizing psychoanalytic theory, Peter Buse argues that video games are notable for their ability to negate narrative closure by virtue of their inherently participatory characteristics. What matters in the video game milieu is not story telling as such, nor, as some critics have argued, mastery over the game's narrative, but rather the pleasure afforded the player through ceaseless repetition,[11] what Buse finally calls a "teleology without telos."[12] Similarly, in his emphasis on the utopian dimension of video games, Schroeder sees a homology between Baudrillard's discussion of simulation and the hyperreal and the ideologies inherent to violent gaming content. Unlike Buse's, Schroeder's argument extends beyond a simple application of the Baudrillardian position to the representational content of video games. In an interesting turn of argumentation, Schroeder posits that the lack of critical orientation which characterizes the writings of Baudrillard finds itself played out in the violent world of gaming technology. According to Schroeder "there is no ethics of the hyperreal,"[13] and as a result, the violent parody of historical context found in the video game is lost on the player who, like Baudrillard, sees the world as only a game.

While these writings are valuable for providing a critical base from which subsequent research can begin, neither comes to terms with the actual interpellative processes at work in video game play, let alone the ménage à trois of player, hardware, and representation with which I am concerned in this paper. In his important work on the semiotics of popular culture, John Fiske stipulates that the relationship between individual and machine within arcade culture is a literal mirror of the productive processes found in late capitalism.[14] As a mirror image, relations of exploitation become counterhegemonic. Echoing Marcuse's thesis that "play is unproductive and useless precisely because it cancels the repressive and exploitative traits of labor and leisure,"[15] Fiske argues that the "pleasure" of interacting with arcade machines results from an inversion of capitalist relations of production in which the individual's orientation with the machine serves to foreground the alienating nature of work itself.[16] Purchasing time on arcade machines is one way that social subordinates (young, nonwhite males, especially) have access to a form of subjectivity in which power is not circumscribed by hegemonic ideologies.[17] Emphasizing the very masculine demographics of arcade culture, Fiske writes:

> The most noticeable common factor among the consumer/machinists appears to be that they are the masculine subordinate in a white, patriarchal, capitalist society. We may deduce from this that their subjectivities are the site of potentially disabling contractions between the socially determined subordination, with its lack of access to power in any form, and the equally, but differently, socially constructed sense of masculinity, with its ideology of dominance. Thus, in sitting down to the video game machine, the vital act is the grasp of the joystick, the touch of the firing button. In this moment "control" passes from society to self, and pleasure becomes possible. . . . What the playing subject is doing, in grasping the controls, is gaining the power to control not just the machine, but his own meanings, and these meanings are intimately connected with masculinity and its relationship to power/ subordination.[18]

Although the vital link between player and machine is the basis for his argument, Fiske's position is nonetheless a peculiar one. Without downplaying the general importance of social emasculation among nonwhite males in capitalist society, to call the reproduction of patriarchal ideologies of power and dominance in any way resistant (even if non-alienated) is simply untenable; for such ideologies can only ever serve the interests of hegemony.[19]

More related to our discussion, Simon Gottschalk contends that Fiske is able to make his argument only by ignoring the representational content of video games which "hail and re-inscribe the young male p(l)ayers as subjects of a decidedly violent, paranoid, individualist, racist, sexist, militarized, and oversaturated electronic New World Order whose trigger-happy patriotic young white male agents brutally enforce a 'zero-tolerance' policy toward drug-smugglers and a great variety of others, while keeping women 'in their place'."[20] Gottschalk goes on to argue that the resistance to hegemonic relations attributed to video games by Fiske "rest[s] on the tacit acceptance and reproduction of these assumptions."[21] Gottschalk's classification of gaming content, what he terms "videology," is a necessary corrective to Fiske's optimistic recuperation of gaming culture. Nonetheless, this analysis, like Fiske's, falls short of understanding the complex whole of subject production within the gaming environment, and is therefore reductionist. Just as Fiske's argument fails to consider the role of representational content, Gottschalk fails to account for the role hardware technology plays in enabling the production of an interpellated subject in the first place. They are two sides of the same quarter. One must then return to the site of game play and recognize precisely how each of its cultural components—the player, the machine, and the content—work in the creation of a subject and, ultimately, the reinscription of hegemonic discourse.

THE QUICK AND THE DEAD

The first-person shooter is a mongrel in the world of computer gaming, appropriating elements from a range of disparate genres and systems. In 1992, when shareware versions of the now legendary *Wolfenstein 3D*[22] became available on FTP sites around the world, it was at once immediately recognizable and yet radically different from anything that had come before. By the time *Wolfenstein 3D* became available, computer and arcade gamers were aware that most games were variations on a very limited number of themes. Thus, most familiar in *Wolfenstein 3D* would have been the game's thematic and representational logic (the two are inextricably linked in computer games). As in the most venerable of arcade games, *Space Invaders* (Atari 1978) and *Pac Man* (Bally/Midway 1980), the general thematic of *Wolfenstein 3D* (and almost all subsequent first-person shooters) was quite simply, kill or be killed, with the litmus test of expertise being based upon one's ability to withstand the onslaught of baddies coming in ever-increasing waves of speed and complexity. Players of *Wolfenstein 3D* would also have been familiar with an earlier genre of fighting games, the horizontally oriented side-scroller. Unlike previous arcade games in which the violence was abstracted through iconic representations of machines, spaceships, and cartoonish figures, side-scrollers such as *Street Fighter* (Capcom 1987) and *Altered Beast* (Sega 1988) allowed players to control the horizontal movement and attack/defense postures of a predesignated human character, most often a surrealistically muscle-bound male figure.[23] Finally, computer gaming enthusiasts booting up *Wolfenstein 3D* would also have seen elements of early computer role playing games, such as *Wizardry* (Sir-Tech 1981), which used a slide show metaphor in an attempt to produce a more immersive experience. And later, that small minority of *Marathon* (Bungie 1994) players who took time out from blasting aliens to engage the storyline would certainly have noted its connection to elements of interactive fiction and other forms of computer-based storytelling.[24] While it is possible in retrospect to point out such similarities, engaging in a session with *Wolfenstein 3D* in 1992 would have been truly mind-boggling; for in the radical shift from third-person to first-person, the game created an experiential space without previous historical reference.

Unlike all other computer and arcade games in which the player is both puppeteer and audience, first-person shooters like *Wolfenstein 3D* attempt a more realistic experience by shifting the player's perspective to that of the puppet itself. Seeing the game's world through the eyes of the protagonist, the player negotiates the gaming space as he would in any computer game, through an input control such as a keyboard, mouse, or joystick. To create an even more seamless first-person environment, the player typically sees a representation of the protagonist's hands, most often armed with a range of selectable weaponry, protruding into video space from the bottom of the player's screen, roughly at hip-level relative to the protagonist's/player's "eyes." From this perspective the player moves the protagonist through a series of environments, ranging from simple room-based mazes as in *Wolfenstein 3D* and *Pathways Into Darkness*, to more complex outdoor environments as in the *Marathon* and *Half Life* series of games. Given varying degrees of narrative complexity, the ultimate goal in the first-person shooter is to traverse from point A to point B, ridding the environment of the enemies which inhabit it.

However, in its attempt to create a virtual reality experience for the player, the first-person shooter is overwhelmingly characterized by its *inability* to generate such an environment. This inability stems mainly from the major assumption of the game—that regardless of the protagonist's masculine prowess, he is still fallible, reacts to the injuries inflicted upon him by those he is trying to kill. Thus, the player must receive information regarding the protagonist's condition, including the weaponry and ammunition he is carrying, even what he is wearing. The transmission of such meta-data obviously risks breaking the verisimilitude set up through the game's first-person orientation by creating an insurmountable gulf between player and protagonist. This tension can be seen most clearly in games such as *Quake* and *Doom*. In order to transmit data regarding the protagonist's condition, these games depart from the virtual experience altogether by inserting an information bar at the bottom of the screen, which, among other things, contains a graphic representation of the protagonist's face. Depending on the amount of blood seeping from its mouth, ears, and nose, this representation gives indication of the protagonist's "health" at any point in the game. More importantly, the iconic representation restricts the game's virtual experience to the extent that the player is always conscious of some other body within the machine, a body that due to its cartoonish parody of masculinity, is never the body at the machine.[25] In attempting to reconcile this tension, some games incorporate character information into the protagonist's point of view. For example, in *Marathon*, the protagonist wears a spacesuit within which he can access game data—the protagonist's bodily condition is, in this case, a direct function of the suit's ability to withstand attack. Unlike the out-of-character information bar, the player in this case understands performance data as part of the game's construction of reality. However, I would argue that this is little more than a plot device overdetermined by the player's knowledge of the generic conventions of the game and the need for such data. Thus, contrary to its goal of creating a more realistic environment, such devices actually widen the gap of realism between player and game by calling attention to its generic structure.

Finally, virtuality is further restricted by the user-interface, both at the hardware and software level. No game, for example, has been able to interface seamlessly with the computer's operating system, so that saving a game (the possibility of which is perhaps the greatest departure from any form of reality, virtual or otherwise) generally means leaving the gaming environment for software components operating in the background.

Such a failure to produce a virtual reality experience would seem effectively to negate the validity of both leftist and bourgeois critiques which attempt to draw a connection between the violence of the gaming environment and the transmission of that violence into "real world" contexts. Indeed, to the extent that the critics reviewed above assume a mode of interpellation which privileges the unproblematic articulation of individual with representation in order to reproduce the violent and arguably capitalist ideologies contained within these games, the failure to account for the meta-data contained within these representations suggests at the very least an incomplete picture of the ideological processes at work in computer gaming environments. For, more than anything else, the restricted realism of the most realistic gaming genre (at least from a representational standpoint) highlights its origin as computer code, the extent of user manipulation and content mutability, and the very technology which enables its transmission. It is important to point out that all other cultural texts seek to hide the technologies subtending their production, making the first-person shooter unique in this regard. Thus, in order to see our way out of this impasse and to provide a more accurate rendering of the interpellative processes involved in computer gaming, and first-person shooters in particular, one must understand the gaming environment as a complex system, ideologically encoded through a dynamic relationship between representation, individual, and technology.

POSTHUMAN INTERACTIONS

I take my cue here from N. Katherine Hayles's *How We Became Posthuman*. In her book Hayles reconceptualizes the liberal humanist subject and its concomitant appeal to individual freedom and agency through an examination of how the tensions between the liberal humanist subject and the new subject position resulting from its confrontation with communication technology are manifest within a variety of discursive structures, most notably Cybernetics and science fiction. This subject position, which she calls the posthuman, is characterized primarily by its articulation with computer technology, thus problematizing the very nature of that which we call human being. Hayles writes, "In the posthuman there are no essential differences or absolute demarcations between bodily existence and computer simulation, cybernetic mechanism and biological organism, robot teleology and human goals."[26] The phrase "in the posthuman" is multivalent. It suggests both a historical moment and a series of narratives derived mainly from the discipline of Cybernetics in which the connection between information and the body, an essential element in humanist discourse, becomes theoretically tenuous, finally disappearing altogether. The rift between the humanist and posthuman subjects is fundamental. In the posthuman there is no necessary connection between human bodies and subjectivity. The ethical and ontological questions raised by Philip K. Dick in *Do Androids Dream of Electric Sheep?* are rendered moot. To be "in the posthuman" suggests as well a recognition of the social and cultural implications of these narratives, which mandate in their wake a reorientation of one's analytical perspective. Hayles calls this new conceptual framework the "posthuman view," and stipulates four basic principles around which one organizes the production of knowledge:

> First, the posthuman view privileges informational pattern over material instantiation, so that embodiment in a biological substrate is seen as an accident of history rather than an inevitability of life. Second, the posthuman view considers concsiousness . . . as an epiphenomenon, as an evolutionary upstart trying to claim that it is the whole show when in actuality it is only a minor sideshow. Third, the posthuman view thinks of the body as the original prosthesis we all learn to manipulate, so that extending or replacing the body with other prostheses becomes a continuation of a process that began before we were born. Fourth, and most importantly, by these and other means, the posthuman view configures human being so that it can be seamlessly articulated with intelligent machines.[27]

Although Hayles suggests that the last of these, something akin to an ontology of technology, is the most important aspect of the posthuman view, it is clearly only symptomatic of her thesis emphasizing informational pattern over the locus of its embodiment. In this sense the posthuman view is profoundly antiessentialist, as much embracing a multiplicity of sites in which data becomes code as humanism embraced the consciousness of the individual as a single site of translation, interpretation, and ultimately domination. The posthuman relegates human consciousness to a level, if not secondary to, then certainly on a par with, any other site upon which information may coalesce, and it is for this reason that Hayles may understate her case that the articulation of humans with machines is a potentiality, when, in fact, it is a cultural and technological imperative—the human "must be" (seamlessly or otherwise) articulated with intelligent machines in order to fully realize its "posting."

This impulse to problematize the liberal humanist understanding of consciousness in the context of information theory, Cybernetics, and communication technologies is tempered by Hayles's recognition that historical and material relations play an important role in the embodiment of information and the deployment of technologies which enable such embodiment. For example, she is careful to acknowledge that "'human' and 'posthuman' coexist in shifting configurations that vary with historically specific contexts."[28] In other words, the transition from human to posthuman is not Foucault's epistemic shift, nor is it Lyotard's postmodern condition (though it contains elements of each). Rather, it is a mode of subjectivity whose emergence is complicated by the political, cultural, and economic structures endemic to late capitalism.

Hayles's insistence on the historical parameters of the posthuman, along with her more elusive thesis regarding the body as "the original prosthesis we all learn to manipulate," allow us to consider the possibility of the emergence of the posthuman space in the context of computer gaming environments. At one level, the first-person shooter functions as a proto-filmic space characterized by the interplay of representations and interactivity. The representations on the screen interface with the individual's capacity to manipulate those representations through the game's environment. As such, these representations reinscribe hegemonic ideologies in much the same way as other image-based texts—through the condensation of ideology upon the representation itself. Moreover, the ideologies encoded within these rep-resentations are those which resonate throughout the majority of hegemonic cultural texts, encapsulated in bell hooks's famous phrase "white supremacist capitalist pa-triarchy." At the same time, and unlike the ideological processes at work in a traditional image-based experience, the relationship between representation and subjectivity is mediated by the individual's body movements—the player's articulation with computer hardware. And thus the feedback loop generated by these systems is predicated upon both the individual player's awareness of the information produced by the game's representations and an awareness of his ability to generate a response through interaction with the machine. Within this model the computer becomes a data prosthetic, affording a direct linkage to both the game's representational environment and to the ideologies inherent to the *processes* by which information is conveyed within this environment. In this way interpellation through the individual's articulation with representations is amended by another mode of interpellation which foregrounds information transferal from the subject back to the game itself.

The contours of this process may be described by answering a fairly elementary question: what enabling processes are facilitated by hardware input controls? At a very simple level, information sent back to the computer changes the representations on the screen such as in the movement of the protagonist through the spatial configuration of the gaming environment or in the killing of those who stand in the way of the protagonist's movement through this space. Most games allow the player to configure input controls such as the mouse or the keyboard, thus providing hardware consistency across game titles. Such consistency affords the player a more seamless articulation with his hardware across time. Manipulating input controls becomes second nature, like holding a pencil or looking through glasses; the technology is both present and absent. Even more fundamentally, the disidentification with the gaming environment that is the result of the game's restricted realism and the player's position within the feedback loop means that input controls facilitate the translation of randomness into pattern. Throughout the first-person shooter the player constantly struggles to reconfigure the information sent from the computer into messages that will result in the game's environment changing to the protagonist's advantage.

Looking more closely at the role computer hardware plays in this process, we find that it is more than simply mediating or catalytic technology. Rather, the relationship between player and hardware is clearly prosthetic in nature. It is important to point out that prosthesis, as used here, does *not* reference what has become, *via* the fiction of William Gibson and others, terminology denoting cybernetic enhancement; this is not Rikki's Zeiss Ikon implants ("Burning Chrome") nor is it Johnny Mnemonic's mass storage system. Rather, the meaning of prosthesis as used in conjunction with first-person gaming systems is mundane and traditional, suggesting a replacement that by virtue of its artifice is culturally marked as a lack or absence. Bluntly put, the joystick is a hook-arm.[29] The ideological function of computer hardware, therefore, mirrors that of other cultural sites in which technology exists in a prosthetic relationship to the subject's body. For example, it could be argued that the move toward more lenient handgun laws in the United States is symptomatic of a breakdown in the hegemonically constructed ideology of personal freedom and happiness. The handgun, itself overdetermined by the ideology of personal freedom, becomes a prosthetic extension of the human body guaranteeing the reproduction of hegemony even as it calls attention to its own contradictions. In a similar fashion, the mass deployment of wireless communication devices such as cell phones and pagers reconceptualizes the importance of human contact even as it speaks to the inability of capitalism to foster a robust and productive community.

Applying this logic to first-person gaming systems we come to what I believe to be the most important theme of these games, namely the player's domination of uncharted space. Interpellation at this level occurs not through the reception of representational information from the game but rather at the moment he responds to that information via an input control, the prosthesis itself. At this point, the player articulates with the very heart of liberal humanist ideology, the impulse to counter the irrational and unforeseen with individual free will. Ideologies of masculinity and violence notwithstanding, what makes the ideological nexus of subject-hardware-freedom so compelling is its ability to translate individual subjectivity into an utterly seamless experience of agency. For while at play in this abhorrently violent world, the subject has complete control over both the body at and in the machine.

But the deck is, quite literally, stacked. The subject position resulting from the prosthetic relationship between body/individual and hardware functions only to the extent that the individual is made unaware of the contradictions inherent to the system. These contradictions are writ large in the first-person shooter. Not only does the player articulate with a representation of an ideal human body, but with one that has complete access to his world and who, by creating his own form of chaos and disturbance, becomes a singularity in an austere universe of one. This is not surprising, for it mirrors precisely the ideological contours of liberal ideology described by Theodor Adorno:

> In [liberal ideology], and beyond it, the question of freedom was the genuine question whether society permits the individual to be as free as it promises; and thus it was also the question whether society itself is as free as it promises. Temporarily, the individual looms above the blind social context, but in his windowless isolation he only helps so much more to reproduce that context.[30]

And thus, the exertion of individual free will, the reconfiguration of randomness into self-affirming pattern, is illusory in the first-person shooter, as it is within all aspects of capitalist discourse. It is illusory because the player's experience of randomness in this context is precisely the experience of predetermined code with limited variables and outcomes. In other words, randomness is only the appearance of randomness, freedom only the appearance of freedom, agency, in fact, the complete and utter denial of agency. While the player can control his environment, he cannot rewrite the code.[31]

Or can he? In his arguments against the Althusserian theory of interpellation, Paul Smith has suggested that political agency evolves precisely at the site of subject production, through, in part, an individual awareness of ideological contradiction. Interpellation, according to Smith, begs the important question of how "human agents" negotiate ideology, sometimes proffering themselves up to ideology, other times choosing to inhabit spaces of resistance.[32] While Smith construes such resistant spaces through the political discourse of Marxism and feminism, I would add that dominant ideology opens doors to other forms of agency characterized by their unpredictability and political ambivalence.

And so on April 20, 1999, Dylan Klebold and Eric Harris stole into Columbine High School armed to the teeth with semiautomatic weaponry and homemade incendiary devices. Media analysis of the subsequent massacre in Littleton, Colorado, reached a climax on December 20 when *Time* magazine published a lengthy expose after being given sole viewing rights to 5 videotapes in which Klebold and Harris documented their plan and their rationale (such as it was). On one of the tapes Klebold sits in an easy chair "with a bottle of Jack Daniels and a sawed-off shotgun in his lap."[33] At one point he references one of the most infamous of first-person shooters, staring into the video camera and saying, "It's going to be like fucking *Doom*."[34] Indeed, *Doom* is a nodal point throughout this bizarre production as Klebold constantly refers to his gun as Arlene, an allusion to a character in *Doom: Knee Deep in the Dead*, a spin-off novel from the computer game.

The rhetorical impulse motivating writers Nancy Gibbs and Timothy Roche to link Klebold's gun with the game *Doom* is transparent. More than simply a piece of trivia, a detail the likes of which journalists are always on the lookout for, to link Klebold's gun with a particularly violent video game serves to naturalize the massacre. It provides an interpretive foothold for those attempting to explain the motivations of the killers; for Klebold's explanations, the surrealistic rantings of a psychotic, will never suffice. Indeed, it would seem an all-too-easy explanation for the events at Columbine High School, especially easy because for a time that April, the halls, the classrooms, the cafeteria, and the library were literally transformed into a "level"—it was, for Klebold and Harris, Columbine *Quake*. Such an explanation is seductive, affording critics, cops, and senators the very obvious pleasure of having mastered an inexplicable set of events, a pleasure not unlike that of the gamer who masters a particularly difficult level. And of course, this connection plays into the hands of those who argue, in spite of available empirical and historical evidence, that immersion in violent representations, from media such as computer games, films, TV, and music, has a desensitizing effect on the individual, which, in turn leads to an acting out of those representations in real life.

The reality of the situation is much more complex, as can be attested to by the sheer number of explanations propounded by various media "experts" in the months following the shootings. Taking the hit here were video games, music (especially that of renegade poseur Marilyn Manson), films (*Natural Born Killers*, *Reservoir Dogs*), Goths, the Internet, trench coats, Prozac, even run-of-the-mill teenage angst —albeit, gone bad. When one considers that Klebold's and Harris's actions were not anomalous, that they were one in a series of similar events beginning in 1996, this multiplicity of explanations begins to suggest that a conceptual breakdown has occurred, that at some fundamental level dominant discourse does not have the language to understand, let alone explain, what is going on here.

At the same time, the connection between Klebold's gun and the game *Doom* is intriguing. If what I have said above has any validity whatsoever, then perhaps one of the unforeseen consequences of so fundamentally linking liberal ideologies of freedom and rationality with technology that affords the individual the powerful experience of being interpellated by these ideologies is that this cultural impulse cannot simply be contained and exercised within such a limited cultural construct as a computer game. The prosthetic imaginary bleeds forth beyond the computer screen; the control device transforms from a joystick into a shotgun gotten through channels of friendship, bespeaking a history of the subject clearly unaccounted for by the interpellative moment analyzed above.

Hayles argues that at this particular historical moment the human and the posthuman coexist unevenly at the socioeconomic level. It is not such a great leap, therefore, to further surmise an equally vexed relationship at the level of subject interpellation. Indeed, as we have seen with computer gaming, liberal humanist ideologies find purchase in posthuman sites of production. This would suggest that the subjective experience of the posthuman in everyday life should be profoundly fractured, alienating, and disorienting. I do not want to stretch this argument too far, but perhaps understanding such apparently random and irrational acts of violence as the Columbine tragedy as symptomatic of the cultural tensions which follow in the wake of the posthuman would prove enlightening. In wielding their sawed-offs and bombs, perhaps Klebold and Harris were doing more than reacting violently to the alienation that comes from years of bullying from their classmates. Perhaps they were enacting the alienation of the posthuman. Perhaps they were writing code.

NOTES

1. John C. Dvorak, "The Doom Factor," *PC Magazine* 18, no. 2 (1999): 87.

2. Danielle Shimotakahara, "Prepared Testimony of Danielle Shimotakahara before the Senate Committee on Commerce, Science, and Transportation," par. 3, 21 March 2000. *Congressional Universe*, Lexis Nexis (20 June 2000).

3. For a review of this literature, see Dill and Dill.

4. The male pronoun in this paper is neither generic nor universal. The overwhelming majority of computer gamers are male.

5. Louis Althusser, *Lenin and Philosophy* (New York: Monthly Review Press, 1971), 173.

6. Althusser, 174.

7. Andrew Feenberg, *Critical Theory of Technology* (New York: Oxford University Press, 1991), 81.

8. Feenberg, 81.

9. Ernesto Laclau and Chantal Mouffe, *Hegemony and Socialist Strategy: Towards a Radical Democratic Politics* (London: Verso, 1985), 105.

10. One of the most interesting recent examples of the ideological characteristics of technical elements is the discursive production of the Central Processing Unit (CPU), in which "mhz" and "ghz" signify speed, efficiency, and technological prowess. These abstractions are, of course, fetishistic in nature, with no real connection to actual speed and efficiency. Upon introducing their new 1.4 ghz chip, Intel came under fire from the computer press for marketing a "faster" chip that actually benchmarked slower than "slower" versions. These criticisms have been ignored by the major computer manufacturers whose marketing literature continues to stress the importance of this particular technical element, arguably to the exclusion of the overall individual technology. The technical element, in other words, becomes a nodal point around which the ideological production of individual technologies is articulated.

11. Peter Buse, "Nintendo and Telos: Will You Ever Reach the End?" *Cultural Critique* 34 (Fall 1996): 174.

12. Buse, 181.

13. Randy Schroeder, "Playspace Invaders: Huizinga, Baudrillard, and Video Game Violence," *Journal of Popular Culture* 30, no. 3 (Winter 1996): 150.

14. John Fiske, *Reading the Popular* (Boston: Unwin Hyman), 1989, 85.

15. Herbert Marcuse, *Eros and Civilization* (Boston: Beacon Press), 1966, 195.

16. Fiske, 82.

17. Fiske, 85.

18. Fiske, 85.

19. This argument, after all, informed Clarence Thomas's defense against Anita Hill.

20. Simon Gottschalk, "Videology: Video-Games as Postmodern Sites/Sights of Ideological Reproduction," *Symbolic Interaction* 18, no. 1 (1995): 14.

21. Gottschalk, 14.

22. *Wolfenstein 3D* was preceded by at least one other first-person shooter: *Catacombs 3D* was released in 1991 by ID Software, the same company that developed *Wolfenstein 3D*. However, *Wolfenstein 3D* was the first game to reach what can only be described as best-seller status. To date over a quarter million retail copies of the game have been sold. This does not include the many millions who have downloaded the shareware version of the game. After almost a decade, it continues to be one of the most popular games played by individuals around the world.

23. The side-scrolling fighter continues to be popular, especially in home console formats. Its 3D cousin, dubbed by gamers the "third-person shooter," is also noteworthy for its inclusion of female characters, the most famous of which is Lara Croft of the *Tomb Raider* series (Eidos, 1996-2000). However, in the adolescent fantasy world of video games, equal opportunity is only yet one more opportunity for exploitation, as suggested by Eidos's downloadable pin-up art of Croft and the sites that comprise the *Nude Raider* webring.

24. Unlike most computer games, the Marathon series was a Macintosh only product.

25. At one point in ID Software's *Duke Nuke'Em* the protagonist Duke enters a room with a mirror. Upon looking into the mirror, the player is confronted with a full-frontal view of Duke himself, at which point the computer blurts out a Schwarzeneggerish "Mmm, lookin' good."

26. N. Katherine Hayles, *How We Became Posthuman: Virtual Bodies in Cybernetics, Literature, and Informatics* (Chicago: University of Chicago Press, 1999), 3.

27. Hayles, 2-3.

28. Hayles, 6.

29. It is surely tempting at this point to delve into the psychoanalytic contours of this phenomenon. However, wielding psychoanalytic terminology in the context of a discussion of ideology and interpellation risks, I believe, diluting both psychoanalytic concepts and, finally, the political import of my remarks.

30. Theodor Adorno, *Negative Dialectics* (New York: Continuum, 1987), 219.

31. Ellen Ullman describes this situation from the engineer's point of view: "The computer, as the engineer sees it, makes a toddler seem brilliant. For what engineers do is create artificial smartness. Our job is to make a simulacrum of intelligence, a thing that seems to contain knowledge only because it has been programmed to behave that way"(Ellen Ullman, "Come in CQ: The Body on the Wire." In *Composing Cyberspace*, Ed. Richard Holeton. Boston: McGraw Hill, 1998, 37).

32. Paul Smith, *Discerning the Subject* (Minneapolis: University of Minnesota Press, 1988), 34-40.

33. Nancy Gibbs, "The Columbine Tapes," *Time* 154, no. 25 (20 December 1999): 40.
34. Gibbs, 42.

BIBLIOGRAPHY

Adorno, Theodor. *Negative Dialectics*. New York: Continuum, 1987.

Althusser, Louis. *Lenin and Philosophy*. New York: Monthly Review Press, 1971.

Buse, Peter. "Nintendo and Telos: Will You Ever Reach the End?" *Cultural Critique* 34 (Fall 1996): 163-84.

Dill, K. E., and Dill, J. C. "Video Game Violence: A Review of the Empirical Literature," *Aggression and Violent Behavior* 3, no.4 (Winter 1998): 407-28.

Dvorak, John C. "The *Doom* Factor," *PC Magazine* 18, no. 2 (1999): 87.

Feenberg, Andrew. *Critical Theory of Technology*. New York: Oxford University Press, 1991.

Fiske, John. *Reading the Popular*. Boston: Unwin Hyman, 1989.

Gibbs, Nancy. "The Columbine Tapes," *Time* 154, no. 25 (20 December 1999): 40-51.

Gottschalk, Simon. "Videology: Video-Games as Postmodern Sites/Sights of Ideological Reproduction," *Symbolic Interaction* 18, no. 1 (1995): 1-18.

Hayles, N. Katherine. *How We Became Posthuman: Virtual Bodies in Cybernetics, Literature, and Informatics*. Chicago: University of Chicago Press, 1999.

Kinder, Marsha. *Playing with Power in Movies, Television, and Video Games: From Muppet Babies to Teenage Mutant Ninja Turtles*. Berkeley: University of California Press, 1991.

Laclau, Ernesto, and Chantal Mouffe. *Hegemony and Socialist Strategy: Towards a Radical Democratic Politics*. London: Verso, 1985.

Marcuse, Herbert. *Eros and Civilization*. Boston: Beacon Press, 1966.

Schroeder, Randy. "Playspace Invaders: Huizinga, Baudrillard, and Video Game Violence," *Journal of Popular Culture* 30, no. 3 (Winter 1996): 143-53.

Shimotakahara, Danielle. "Prepared Testimony of Danielle Shimotakahara before the Senate Committee on Commerce, Science, and Transportation," 21 March 2000, *Congressional Universe*. Lexis Nexis (20 June 2000).

Smith, Paul. *Discerning the Subject*. Minneapolis: University of Minnesota Press, 1988.

Ullman, Ellen. "Come in CQ: The Body on the Wire," in *Composing Cyberspace*, ed. Richard Holeton. Boston: McGraw-Hill, 1998, 32-47.

8
Trouble Child: Barthes's Imagined Youth

Timothy Scheie

In June of 1989, the Corcoran Gallery of Art in Washington, D.C., cancelled a photography exhibit, *Robert Mapplethorpe: The Perfect Moment*, which had in preceding weeks drawn strident criticism from politicians and others who decried the publicly subsidized exhibition of images that many viewers found shocking or offensive. This gesture caught the national media's eye and further stirred the troubled waters of public funding for controversial art that were already churning over Andres Serrano's "Piss Christ," a photograph of a crucifix submerged in the artist's urine whose exhibition had in part been funded by the National Endowment for the Arts. Alongside Mapplethorpe's notoriously graphic photographs of well-endowed male nudes, homoeroticism, and sadomasochism, in *The Perfect Moment* two portraits of children were frequently the site of contention. One shows a seated girl exposing her genitals under her dress; in another a young boy stands staring at the camera. The unconventional nudity, the intensity of the children's gaze, and most notably the images' exhibition alongside graphic images of sexual acts led Mapplethorpe's detractors to brand the childhood images as pornographic. Others, however, defended their artistic merit and, invoking freedom of expression, the artist's right to issue a provocative statement.[1] The controversy escalated further in the months following the cancellation when grants approved for four other artists (the "NEA Four") were revoked. The "culture wars" raged over the next few years and drew many artists into the fray, but long after the Corcoran incident Mapplethorpe continued to figure at the center of the debate and the charge was mounted time and again against the *Perfect Moment* images.[2] As with the NEA Four, a vocal aversion to homosexuality also fueled the jeremiads against Mapplethorpe, even when the photos in question had no explicit gay content as in the case of the child nudes. Pornography, pederasty, and sexual "perversion," most notably homosexuality, circulated together in the anti-Mapplethorpe discourse as a block of virtually substitutable terms.[3] For his detractors, Mapplethorpe's lens assumed a hermeneutic function as the invisible interpretant of the controversial images of the children, situating the viewers to consider the nude children from the same tainted viewpoint from which they had looked with shock, fascination, curiosity, or pleasure at the other images close at hand. By metonymic contagion the alleged pornography of the childhood portraits both confirmed and derived from the "deviant" or "sick" homosexuality of the photographer.

Although the implied cause of the outrage was concern over the exploitation of children, this positioning of the gaze would explain the exceptional fierceness of the responses to these images. The viewers of *The Perfect Moment* looked on that most familiar of photographed subjects, the child, through a lens that distorted the assumptions conventionally invested in this ideologically charged figure. "The Child" is perhaps the most revered repository of values for a naturalized heterosexuality and a patriarchal regime. Lee Edelman observes that the figure of "The Child" not only "impregnates" heterosexuality with the future of humanity, but also, as the emblem of regeneration as repetition, secures the future of signification itself (the "symbolic order") in the terms of this apparently necessary and inevitable heterosexuality.[4] The photographic genre of the child portrait is, furthermore, the cherished emblem of this figure so heavily imbued with our culture's most deeply embedded values and prejudices. Nowhere is the imperative of reproductive coupling more sanctified and endlessly repeated than in those ubiquitous icons that consecrate walls, desks, wallets, and coffee tables as shrines to procreative sex—hence the jarring dissonance resulting from the exhibition of childhood portraits alongside images of very clearly nonreproductive sexual practices that inflect (even if only metonymically) desire, pleasure, and "perverse" sexuality onto such hallowed ground. The *Perfect Moment* exhibit perhaps proved so uniquely unsettling because it suggests that those children so endlessly represented in photographs can and undeniably often do fail to fulfill their reproductive promise. The visceral fear in the reactions of politicians and others would therefore spring less from the risk that these children will be the objects of an eroticized visual pleasure and victims of kiddie porn than from the incontrovertible fact that some children, this little boy perhaps, will grow up to *be* one of the men in the other images, that he might himself one day sport one of those monumental Mapplethorpian penises whose future as an instrument of procreation, as evinced in the adjacent photographs, is not guaranteed. Mapplethorpe effectively desecrated the sanctum sanctorum of the childhood portrait, and his photographs are therefore doubly abhorrent in the eyes of his inquisitors: not only are they allegedly pornographic, but they rival Serrano in sacrilege.

I open with this brief meditation on Mapplethorpe because the issues raised illuminate our consideration of another series of photographs. In the opening pages of *Roland Barthes by Roland Barthes*, the author furnishes a photo gallery of his own, including several images of himself as a child. At first glance, the provocation of these images might not be evident. None would likely be considered obscene, pornographic or, with perhaps one exception, homoerotic, and there is little chance that an exhibition of these photographs would offend the sensibilities of conservative critics. However, the crushing familiarity of the childhood portrait begs a demythification the likes of which Barthes himself executed in the 1950s, and, though it might not be immediately apparent, the later Barthes duly refused to permit the childhood portrait's heavy ideological investment to go unchallenged. Furthermore, an invisible lens of homosexuality also filters Barthes's writing, especially in his later years when he wrote *Roland Barthes* and compiled this collection of photographs. If the status of these images as the object of sexual pleasure seems unlikely—even in the case of Mapplethorpe's nudes it was contested—they would nonetheless seem unable to guarantee a future that redounds to the same when they trace subtly yet insistently the profile of a child who, like the man Barthes becomes, fails to serve as the blazon of procreative sex.

A crucial difference, of course, distinguishes Barthes from Mapplethorpe as they divest the child of its presumably inevitable heterosexual future. Barthes's figuration of homosexuality remains oblique, invisible even; unlike Mapplethorpe he offers no graphic adjacent confirmation of it, at least during his lifetime.[5] Much has been made of Barthes's virtual silence on the topic of homosexuality and the meaning of this discretion is neither immediately evident nor uncontested. While Barthes vocally assumed his class identity as bourgeois, pondered the consequences of his minority Protestant upbringing, and frequently reflected on his status as an intellectual, during his lifetime he deliberately kept his sexuality a blind spot, the jealously guarded and empty center of peripheral hints and references. He refused to let his sexuality "congeal" into a stable identity or discursive position. Homosexuality constitutes a figure of supplementarity in Barthes's work, less a secret than a carefully maintained gap in meaning and subjectivity about which one can say nothing, at once a lack and an excess: a love that has no name to speak, even if it dared. If Barthes indeed unsettles the heterosexual imperative invested in the child, he refuses his readers any powerfully visible alternative.

One might wonder if it is possible to accomplish the first gesture without the second. Clearly Barthes will disappoint a strategy grounded in the necessity of a visible and vocal oppositional identity. He eschewed militancy of any kind, and a less generous critic might consider his silence a closeted acquiescence. To do so, however, would be to ignore that this strategic elusiveness also purchases him a certain critical dint. From the non-lieu of his sexuality, Barthes can thumb his nose at the arrogance of political discourse and the ideological doxa, the commonsensical idée reçue, perhaps most pervasively exemplified in the presumed inevitability of heterosexuality and the concomitant stigmatization of a deviant homosexual identity. Unable to overthrow the political "father," unwilling to perpetuate the din of political babble to speak against him, choosing to be thus bound and gagged Barthes irreverently turns and, as he puts it, silently "shows his derrière"—a provocation (invitation?) of a decidedly nonreproductive sort in terms of both procreation and signification.[6] This marginal, supplemental position proved to be a remarkably productive theoretical figure, and the same gap in meaning and subjectivity where his invisible sexuality roams impels Barthes's prolific appreciation of music, painting, photography, and literature, among other systems of representation. An unspoken homosexuality lies at the very heart of this criticism, a pervasive inflection that might warrant the anachronistic contention that Barthes was engaged in a *queering* of Schumann's music, Eisenstein's films, Twombly's paintings, and the other objects of his critical attention in the later years of his life.[7] Barthes shares a queer suspicion of a purportedly stable gay subject and a similar desire to discredit the imaginary stability of all such positions, and invest their moment of failure with "perverse" sexual desire.

Barthes's ludic and elusive figuration of sexuality resonates with current discussions of identity and representation. While pride in an increasingly visible minority identity and the struggle for equal rights within the existing power structure have frequently been the goals of gay and lesbian activism, the liberal, tolerant society that many activists envision comes at an often hidden cost. To win a place at the table does not mean that this will be a place of honor, and having a place, *knowing* one's place, is not necessarily an empowering gesture. One needs to ask as well what new lines of inclusion and exclusion or of normativity and difference are being drawn as, for example, gays and lesbians seek civil rights and privileges such as marriage and the right to adopt. Many critics, artists, and writers have in recent years explored the transgressive power of a strategic refusal to stake a claim to a stable place within representation, and they have often done so in the name of "queer." Barthes's irreverence and his refusal to claim a "gay" place in both the sym-bolic and social orders would appear to make him a precursor to this strain of thought. However, to hail him as pre-queer or proto-queer, even cautiously, opens his work to the skepticism of other critics who are unwilling to relinquish so readily a distinctly gay or lesbian identity and a specific gay or lesbian voice. Leo Bersani, for example, cautions that when "gay" as a meaningful term, a specific sexual practice, and a minority community is challenged by a presumably more radical queer that destabilizes the binaries (homosexual/heterosexual, masculine/feminine) that shape it, this constitutes a fundamentally "de-gaying" gesture that risks once again erasing gay men (or lesbians, or bisexuals, or any other group whose distinctness is obscured under the umbrella of queer) in a universalizing discourse.[8] Addressing the already marginal status of lesbians in writings on homosexuality, queer or otherwise, Sue-Ellen Case also wonders whether the "radical evacuation" of lesbian in a queer commentary in fact represents just one more mechanism for keeping the lesbian in her historically invisible place.[9]

The plight of queer youth, another historically invisible population, would appear to amplify the worries of critics like Bersani and Case, and illustrates starkly the ambivalent terms of this debate and what specifically is at stake in an attempt to "queer" the figure of the child. Statistics show that gay, lesbian, bisexual, and transgendered youth are at greater risk than their heterosexual counterparts for a host of problems, including domestic violence, substance abuse, sexually transmitted diseases, and suicide. One well-known guide for high school counselors draws on a broad range of medical and social science research to conclude that self-identification and visibility in a "coming out" gesture as gay or lesbian is an important hedge against the disproportionate incidence of harmful behaviors that afflict this population. The language the author uses, however, is sure to generate discomfort among many readers: "Coming out is an adjusting between the real and the social self and as such, is a necessary process for healthy personality integration."[10] Clearly, the notions of "health" and "real" in this discourse cry out for interrogation, and a critical queer would make short shrift of their juridico-medical pathologizing of those who fail to obey the injunction to assimilate into the taxonomies of a naturalized epistemological regime. The same could be said of the essentialist overtones that resonate through the invocation of a "real" identity opposed to the "social self." Furthermore, intolerance of "flamboyancy," the "stereotypical," and "in-your-face" behavior also subtends the author's discussion. It could therefore be easily argued that the "coming out" envisioned here is not an act of liberation, but of assimilating constraint and conformity to the norms of a "proper" gay identity or of society at large. Even so, despite the urgency of these caveats one might nonetheless wonder what the radical discrediting of the terms "gay" or "lesbian" and a fortiori discretion à la Barthes would signify for those who are young and engaged in the fraught and often dangerous negotiation of their sexual identity. What could Barthes's silent and invisible sexuality, or a queer critique more generally, offer in the place of liberal assimilation or of gay/lesbian pride to mitigate the great risk of harm, danger, and even death whose frequently cited causes are, precisely, pervasive silence and invisibility? Would it foster the production of new and multiple possibilities for imagining a queer youth identity, however provisional, or insidiously reinforce the brutal regime of silence that prevents a queer youth identity from finding a voice at all?

The para-discursive pleasures of an aging critic pondering his lifelong discretion have, suprisingly perhaps, more to do with the isolation, exclusion, and despair of a stigmatized adolescent sexuality than one might anticipate. The convergence in Barthes's montage of a tacit homosexuality and the figure of the child produces neither the optimism that characterizes many invocations of queerness nor the eroticized textual pleasure that in the preceding years had prevailed in his writing. When Barthes brings his obliquely invoked homosexuality and this figure's richness as a cunning and even subversive interpretant to bear on the images of himself as a child in *Roland Barthes by Roland Barthes*, an acknowledged pain accompanies the anticipated *plaisir du texte*. The celebrated gap where silent pleasures circulate is also a site of anxiety and suffering akin to the melancholy that pervades his final works, *A Lover's Discourse* and *Camera Lucida*, his book on photography. Indeed, the confluence of the medium of photography, sexuality, and childhood make these images a compellingly ambivalent testament to the power, pleasures, and pain of Barthes's tacit figuration of his homosexuality. Far from denying the anguish of a sexuality condemned to silence, Barthes makes it a principal trope of his unavowed desires and pleasures.

Before examining the photographs of *Roland Barthes by Roland Barthes,* it is helpful to historicize this work by situating it within the trajectory of Barthes's lifelong interest in photography. His remarks on photography trace a map of his thought as it meanders through the successive "phases" of his career.[11] In the early *Mythologies* (written between 1953 and 1956), Barthes offers trenchant readings of Greta Garbo's face, studio portraits, tabloid photos of royalty, and other images whose banality cloaks their ideological underpinnings. The structuralist Barthes of the following years reads the photograph as a system of signification, and maintains that even an analog art like photography, despite certain "traumatic" elements that seem to defy signification (and announce his later thought), is riddled with linguistic, syntactic, and rhetorical codes that make it "the most social of institutions."[12] Around 1970, however, his thought undergoes a seismic shift as the closed systems of structural analysis break open and give way to the freely circulating signifier. He theorizes a new aspect of photography, its "obtuse meaning," where it exceeds the code as a "scandal" in signification. Barthes refers to this obtuse meaning as "lovable," or as "touching"; one can only affirm that it exists. To say what it is would be to eliminate it, to draw it into the linguistic codes that it purportedly exceeds.[13] In his most extensive discussion of photography and last book-length study, *Camera Lucida*, Barthes develops the "trauma" and the "obtuse sense" further, theorizing a distinctly individual "*punctum*," the detail where the photograph tears through language, ideology, and myth to stab a viewer's individual and inarticulate fascination with the melancholy realization that "this thing was": *cela a été*.[14] It will be his mother's body that "punctures" the codes and brings Barthes, who after her death finds an old photograph of her, to experience her radical individuality, her uniqueness, her unnamed, unnamable *cela* (Barthes even calls it her "soul"). Photography's inarticulate *cela a été* is an encounter with death, with what is no more, what cannot be repeated or reproduced.

In the introduction to *Roland Barthes,* Barthes announces that he chose only the photographs that *fascinate* him. This fascination defies reason and further predication, and recalls the obtuse meanings of the preceding years. However, the strange mix of eroticized textual pleasure and brooding melancholy that pervades Barthes's fascination effectively bridges the gap between the blissful supplements of the early 1970s and the introspective, highly personal readings of his final years. Although *Roland Barthes* predates the discussion of the "*punctum*" and the mourning of his mother in *Camera Lucida*, one can detect an early articulation of this figure. One image precedes and is set apart from the others, a blurred photo of his mother walking on a beach in which, he writes later, he sees her unnamable individuality, where the symbolic tears and he can once again apprehend this body "as such." But only he can do this. The *punctum* is an individual affair. Barthes never even shows his readers the other photo of his mother that he invokes, the "winter garden" photograph that inspires a great part of *Camera Lucida*, for they would see simply a little girl in late nineteenth-century dress.[15] In these images, Barthes apprehends the singularity of his mother's being that piques his singular desire, and in this inarticulate union he experiences both bliss and pain, both the obtuse *cela* of the mother's body and its inexorable lack in death. The blurred photograph is therefore as much a testament to his mother's being as to Barthes's own unique desire, his own *cela*, which would explain its enigmatic position as the frontispiece to the book by and about Barthes himself.

Of the forty or so photographs in the series that follows, many are of Barthes's family or of his hometown Bayonne, but several represent the young Barthes at different ages. Throughout, a figurative indeterminacy of the self's borders echoes the literal blurriness of the image on the inside cover. A startling photograph bearing the caption "the demand for love" opens the series. Barthes wraps his arms around his mother's neck, clinging to her like an infant while the length of his dangling legs betrays that he is quite a bit older, too old, perhaps, to assume with ease this infantile pose. In the short preface to the photograph section on the opposite page, Barthes deploys a familiar vocabulary:

> such imagery acts as a medium and put me in a relation with my body's ID [*cela*]; it provokes within me a kind of obtuse dream, whose units are teeth, hair, a nose, skinniness, long legs in knee-length stockings which don't belong to me, though to no one else: here I am henceforth in a state of disturbing familiarity: I *see* the fissure in the subject (the very thing about which he can say nothing).[16]

Barthes looks in mute fascination on the *cela* of his own body, as he had done elsewhere to that of his mother—indeed, his body is not fully distinguishable from his mother's. A sort of chronically incomplete mirror stage continues to a perversely, even grotesquely advanced age in the "demand for love" image, and the mother's body remains a part of a Barthes whose discrete selfhood fails to separate and "congeal" into a tidy imaginary whole.

The Lacanian reference becomes explicit near the middle of the photograph section in a picture of a baby in its mother's arms, staring intently at the camera, that echoes the pose of the "demand for love" photograph.[17] This is in fact a photograph of Barthes's infant mother in his grandmother's arms, but nowhere is this indicated and, given the context, one would more likely assume that it is baby Roland in the picture. The possible confusion of son and mother is not without resonance. In case one missed the visual cue, a caption culled from the closing passages of Lacan's article on the mirror stage reads: "Tu es cela."[18] This simple statement announces what would normally be the end of the mirror stage, the imaginary formation of the child's "I," but Barthes chafes under this imperative and the greater project of *Roland Barthes* is to resist such imaginary totality, to shatter the "mask" of the self into fragments, into a dynamic subjectivity that generates meaning without producing *a* meaning, *a* subject, or even *a* body. Barthes resists the baby's normal movement through the vicissitudes of the *tu* and the future subject's formation and lingers instead in mute fascination over the *cela*, the "thing itself" here and elsewhere represented by his mother's body.

On the following page, a photo of baby Barthes toddling on a beach might have appeared innocent enough, had not the prior invocation of psychoanalysis stripped the infant of its Edenic innocence and refigured it as a conflicted bundle of fears, fantasies, and libidinal desires. Already considered through a lens colored by a troubled negotiation of the Lacanian mirror stage, this baby's promise as a future person-to-be taking its first steps down a familiar narrative path that will culminate in the reproduction of subjecthood is further compromised by the caption: "Contemporaries? I was starting to walk, Proust was still living, and was finishing *la Recherche*." The specter of Proust looms over all of *Barthes by Barthes,* and this often explicit invocation draws attention to the similarity of their projects. Both authors try to imagine a novel yet to be, and ruminate over how to write a subject and his life. Both also ponder at length the intrusion of the past into the present, Proust through his involuntary memories and Barthes in figures such as the *punctum* and its predecessors. However, Proust's narrator has the celebrated epiphany in the Prince de Guermantes's library that enables him to envision a means of expressing his timeless vrai moi, "true self," by linking present sensations and past memories on an "essential" plane that transcends time. In contrast to Proust's narrator's desire to create a work of art whose originality captures a "reality" in a new and presumably truer manner—a wish that might loosely define the modernist esthetic—Barthes's literary work, his narrative self, and his life's story remain fragmented and resolutely inchoate. Proust's cathedral of a novel is replaced by a mass of building blocks with no apparent architecture other than an arbitrary alphabetical ordering, and if Barthes instructs us propadeutically that the work should be read as if narrated by a character in a novel, this voice, unlike that of Proust's narrator, never "congeals" into a discrete and consistent subject, a *vrai moi.* Throughout the text Barthes refers to himself as both "I" and "you," as "RB," or simply as "he," but there is no unified character, any more than there is the consistency and causal logic of a narrative whole that one might call a novel. Barthes seeks to produce "novelishness" freed of a novel's organizing structure, "subjectness" liberated from subjectivity's demand for consistency, a text with no clear boundaries, in short, a "Barthesiness" with no pretension of erecting a unified subject following a single life's trajectory in any recognizable narrative or biographical form. Barthes occasionally hinted at an autobiographical novel that he might write, his own *Vita*

Nuova, but this remains a future dream, a future that cannot be guaranteed, that might never arrive (and indeed, that never does).[19] The little baby, Proust's "heir," represents less the promise of a future subject and a future novel than of their uncertainty.

Likewise, at first glance one might not immediately see how the sad cuteness of the photograph on the facing page, showing Barthes at age two (or so), participates in a radical dissolution of the child subject. A caption, once again with Proustian overtones, reads:

> Of the past, it is my childhood that fascinates me the most; it alone, when I look at it, does not make me regret the time that has passed. Because it is not the irreversible that I see in it, but the irreducible: all that is still in me, by fits and starts; in the child I read the dark reverse side of myself, boredom, vulnerability, prone to despairs (fortunately in the plural), internal emotions, cut off by its misfortune from any expression.[20]

Under all the predication that one might heap on this photograph there is something more, an irreducible quality, an individuality that cannot be articulated, or as Barthes writes, expressed: the "dark reverse side" of himself. Barthes has a face he will never show, one on which no beam of enlightenment can shine, whose truth no novel can recount: his cela. Barthes establishes a gap that represents the failure of the signifier, of iteration, of the subject, in short, the site of the jouissance he had theorized in the previous years—yet this little boy is not a happy child wallowing in the euphoric bliss of fragmentary subjectivity. The dizzying pleasures of jouissance are here accompanied or even supplanted by a brooding and even painful ennui, and where an earlier Barthes invested this moment of failure with pleasure here he invokes a disturbing consequence of his failed mirror stage. The body's *cela* is no longer a playful term of subversion. Proust's narrator's sensation upon discovering the secret "essence" of his identity through the involuntary memory is one of joy and fulfillment, hence another difference from the narrator of *Barthes by Barthes*: the "dark side" linking a past body to his present one no less fascinates Barthes, but far from provoking a beatific revelation and inspiration it incites if not regret then profound feelings of anxiety, boredom, and neediness—and silence. For Barthes it remains precisely that about which he can say nothing other than, simply, *it is.*

Significantly, it is in this same mute gap that Barthes's elusive sexuality and desire also circulate. Barthes refigures this silent gap often throughout his later career—the punctum is one instance, also the tel (the "as such") of the *Lover's Discourse*, among others. This theoretical figure is often articulated through a language of sexuality and desire, unsettling the binaries of both gender (masculine/feminine) and, less explicitly, of sexuality (heterosexual/homosexual). A fascination with le neutre, "neuter" in both a grammatical and a sexual sense, pervades these later writings, but finds its perhaps most memorable articulation at the advent of Barthes's final "phases" in the figure of La Zambinella, the castrato of Balzac's novella “Sarrasine” that Barthes shatters into fragments in *S/Z*. La Zambinella is represented in the novella on several occasions: on stage in a female role, as a boy giving a recital, then as the ideal feminine figure in a sculpture, which is in turn copied by a painter, and then again by Girodet as an effeminate but unquestionably male Endymion, which is then admired by the narrator’s companion (“Can anyone be so beautiful?” she asks), and it is finally revealed that a ghastly old man, described in detail, is none other than the aged castrato himself. Throughout the novella the castrato is repeatedly painted, sculpted, and narrated as both male and female; this body effectively acts as a shifter in the gender binary, and always demands further rewriting. There is no stable “truth” about the castrato’s gender, no language in which to express it definitively. La Zambinella’s body is the perfect metaphor for textual pleasure, not only for Barthes but for the broad range of voyeurs, listeners, artists, authors, spectators, and readers (including ourselves) who all create this body anew, according to their own desires. Although Barthes muses on an ideal “neuter/neutral” exempt from the imposition of gendered meaning, the castrato’s body represents less what cannot be thought or written than that which *must* be rewritten. The figure of the castrato is therefore not sterile, indeed it is very productive, but it fails to be reproductive, quite literally and also as the figure of the elusive “third term” that disrupts the faithful reinscription of the male/female binary. In terms of both the species and of gender categories it cannot secure the future as an iteration of the terms of the present.

In the series of photos Barthes craftily situates his childhood body to function also as a figure of indeterminate excess, although instead of gender, as with La Zambinella, here he imbues the “dark side” with a veiled sexuality and desire that likewise demand further writing by the reader. To look upon the boy of 10 years or so in shorts and kneesocks, smiling at the camera with his hands behind his back, as the object of a perverse sexuality would be in many people’s minds to harbor criminal thoughts worthy of censure. Barthes, however, demands that we do so: “The large garden formed a rather foreign territory. It could be said that it served mainly to bury the excess litters of small cats. In the background, a dark alley and two hollow balls of boxwood: several episodes of childhood sexuality took place there.”[21] The yard in Bayonne, with its suggestive shrubbery, is no Garden of Eden, and this demure boy is a sexually active one. Barthes refuses us the image of a sexually innocent youth and raises the question of this boy’s young, and so by many standards already perverse, desire. The image of another little park in Bayonne also belies an erotic charge: “Coming home in the evening, a frequent detour along the Adour, the Allées marines: tall trees, abandoned boats, unspecified strollers, boredom’s drift: here floated the sexuality of public gardens, or parks.”[22] Once again, Barthes hints at a precocious consciousness of sexuality. “Unspecified strollers,” “sexuality of public gardens”: what does he mean? Prostitutes? A more likely answer might be a dockside cruising area for men that fascinated the young boy Barthes, though he gives no indication that this is the case. In both photos, he infuses the image with an otherwise invisible sexuality, the nature of which remains unarticulated.

Lawrence Schehr refers to Barthes's elusiveness as a game of veils and masks, a metaphor Barthes encourages with a pair of photographs that appear later in the series.[23] One shows the author as a young man, masked and playing in a Greek tragedy in the courtyard of the Sorbonne. The caption reads:

> Darius, a part that had always given me terrible stage fright, had two long declamations in which I was likely to forget my lines: I was fascinated by the temptation of thinking about something else. Through the tiny holes of the mask, I could see only very high up, and very far away; while I delivered the dead king's prophecies, my eyes came to rest on inert—free—objects and books, a window, a cornice, a piece of the sky: they at least weren't afraid. I excoriated myself for getting caught in this uncomfortable trap—while my voice continued its smooth delivery, resisting the expressions I should have given it. (33)

It is not hard to imagine why Barthes chose to comment on this image, for it evokes many recurring motifs in his writing: the mask as an arbitrary and exterior sign of identity, desire that both generates and subverts signification, the lack of a coherent subject or agent that exercises authority over a text, the mixture of pleasure and fear in the vertiginous breakdown of meaning, representation, and "literature." It is interesting for the present discussion because it offers a glimpse at what might lie under the façade of the subject, of the character Darius, of mimesis and its narratives, and more generally of the "great" Western cultural tradition and even signification itself. Barthes here invokes the dark side of the mask, the hidden face, whose fragmented visual field, wandering mind, and transgressive desires and impulses threaten to disrupt the faithful rendering of the ancient text. The "dark side" is not, however, a space of freedom and bliss; if it fosters fascination and desire, it is also riddled with constraint, discomfort, and anxiety. This unease behind the mask and its implications for his tacit sexuality are reinforced in the photo on the following page. Barthes, as a young man, and a woman sit on a lawn (a date?) in clothing that seems unduly formal for the occasion. The caption reads: "Where does that look come from? Nature? The Code?"[24] Here Barthes otherwise writerly body has been rewritten as heterosexual; it wears the mask of a code, the false nature that is conventional and, to judge by his ironic questions and the stiffness of his pose, stultifying.[25]

Compare this to another photograph of a pensive adolescent sprawled bare-shouldered and barefoot on a beach, wearing a trace of a smile and lounging in the ethereal haze of the camera's soft focus. The resemblance of the adolescent Barthes to Girodet's alleged copy of La Zambinella—languid pose, heavy eyelids, gender ambiguity—is striking, both visually and textually. It is no coincidence that this same image inspired Pierre St. Amand to recognize his own love for Barthes, a photo whose sensuality is "full of intentions but keeps its secret . . . caught in a voluptuous suspension."[26] Barthes cultivates this suspension when he provides no caption other than an enigmatic "us, still us."[27] Who is this "We"? Is it he and his mother (the picture appears to have been taken the same day as the one of his mother that opens the book)? Is it the reader complicit with the boy in the image? Or someone else? Is it the plural Barthes himself? Or is there no truth, no answer, only a purely deictic pronoun that refers to whomever the reader might desire? The relaxed pose contrasts with the "coded" body of the uncomfortable heterosexual picnic, yet to seek the truth about this boy's sexuality is futile. If Barthes removes the coded mask of heterosexuality, the face underneath only offers an enigmatic half smile. The boy invites the reader to *write* the meaning of his body or, even more perversely, to leave it unwritten.

The carefully maintained and eroticized indeterminacy permits a new understanding of what Barthes saw in the sad young eyes of the little boy. Barthes's picture gallery does not reproduce the privileged imperative of heterosexual coupling, nor does it establish the "deviant" homosexual identity that is a function of it. As with his adult "productive self in the written text that follows, the photographed child ultimately fails to produce the iterable signifiers of sexuality that secure the future both of signification by reproducing a homosexual/heterosexual binary, and very literally of the human species: in the photo section he writes of an acute awareness that he is the end of the family line. There will be no more Barthes after he dies.[28] Barthes effectively realizes, avant la lettre, what Edelman calls the "impossible project" of imagining a position exempt from a repetition of signifiers and their ideological investment that, through the child, justifies and perpetuates a politics of reproduction. This gesture issues a compelling retort to anyone who might too quickly condemn the discreet Barthes as a craven closet case. Barthes is even worthy of the outrage of Mapplethorpe's critics, likely more than they would ever guess. To recognize the desire implicated in "reading/rewriting" these photographs, and the sexuality that Barthes so deliberately infused into this act, is to acknowledge that one has gazed upon the child's body with a textual pleasure. To put it bluntly Barthes invites and even coerces his reader to participate in an act of textual pedophilia, and by situating the textuality of the child's body in the same gap where sexuality and *jouissance* roam he trespasses one of the most aggressively policed boundaries in our society.

Barthes's incitement to transgression, however, remains under an injunction to silence. If he craftily situates his reader to consider these photographs through a homosexual hermeneutics, this interpretive lens is either transparent or else so subtly tinted that the reader is free to ignore it. Could anyone expect the exhibition of these images to provoke a scandal, or even to disturb the ideology of reproduction invested in the figure of The Child? Would not the images of the toddler or the sad little boy far more likely elicit the cries of "isn't he adorable" that the childhood photograph conventionally inspires? Abstention from an oppressive discourse, even a cunning, voluptuous, and informed silence, does not guarantee exemption from its effects. Barthes was never sanguine enough about the transformative power of his politics or sexuality to warrant a reconciliation of his thought with the optimism that underlies many invocations of queerness. An in-your-face brand of activism or visibility would have undoubtedly drawn Barthes's trenchant disapproval, and his silence would have made a poor model for the resistant resignification of the injurious terms of patriarchy implied in the word "queer" itself.[29] From his eroticized non-lieu of subjectivity, Barthes cannot sustain a viable political or activist discourse on any topic, in particular homosexuality. Barthes's queer subject, like his political one, must remain, in his words, "sensitive, avid, and silent."[30] If by showing his derrière Barthes wishes to remain the joker in the deck of the epistemological regime, what, one might wonder, would compel the "political father" to pay this irreverent gesture any heed, or to refrain from filling the gap Barthes so perversely offers with its own arrogant discourse?

Moreover, Barthes's playful, irreverent, and silent sexual subject does not inhabit a blissful queer utopia. As his writing becomes more autobiographical and personal, trauma and ennui characterize the silent, indeterminate subject far more than the abstract and theoretical delights of *jouissance. Roland Barthes by Roland Barthes* clearly revises the vertiginous ecstasies of *The Pleasure of the Text.* The tone of celebration vanishes, and even the languid boy on the beach, in St. Amand's estimation an apparent holdover from the more heady days of jouissance and textual pleasure in the early 1970s, gives pause when we consider the lived experience of the character he so closely resembles. La Zambinella might be the emblem of the neutral, the textual, whose gender and trajectory of desire must always be rewritten, but s/he is also the jittery and frightened plaything of more powerful men, manipulated, exploited, held prisoner, kidnapped, and very nearly killed, who ends up a frightening and pathetic specter shunned by society and kept hidden in the secret chambers of a Parisian mansion. While decidedly lacking in such Balzacian drama, Barthes's own queer childhood is presented as bored and lonely, anxious and despairing, the emblem of the disquieting "dark side" of himself that is "cut off from expression." No more than La Zambinella does Barthes's childhood in *Roland Barthes by Roland Barthes* provide a model that queers—adolescent, critical, or otherwise—would likely want to follow.

Perhaps if we consider "impossible" the operative term here, the "impossible" project of staking out an oppositional political position, only then can we think of Barthes's photographs as participating in a queer politics. One could even imagine Barthes chiding Edelman who, in his vehement refusal of the future as the child's alibi of inevitability, nevertheless invokes a "we" that loosely coalesces into an oppositional collective, and who, though he qualifies it as impossible, restores a temporal trajectory and hopefully envisions a future of his own by laying out the preconditions for imagining the unimaginable, impossible political position cited above. Edelman writes:

> For to escape both the constrictions of a sexuality that is silenced and the dangers of a sexuality inscribed as essential, we must construct retroactively out of the various accidents that constitute "our" history a difference from the heterosexual logic of identity—propped up as it is by the notion of a disavowed and projected sexual difference—in order to deconstruct the repressive ideology of similitude or identity itself.[31]

Although this project resolutely resists erecting a triumphant oppositional identity of its own or providing a rigid blueprint for a utopian future, a measure of both a new identity and a better tomorrow motivates it nonetheless: it is worth remarking in this passage how the first person plural moves in and out of inverted commas, and that deconstruction leads to a future "escape." It is precisely this strategic "we" and this goal that lend such discourse the activist dimension and political clout that Barthes forsakes. This gives rise to a vexing conundrum: how can one reject the future without invoking a postfuture future? Barthes was ever mindful that staking a claim to a visible and vocal identity, no matter how provisional, is a precarious tightrope walk between a calculated if impotent silence and recuperation/reproduction as part of the *doxa*, and he seemed to think, at least at the time he was writing, that one will inevitably fall to one side or the other. On the question of homosexuality, he knowingly assumed the role of a spectator in the political arena who, relegated to the sidelines, abstains from the fray and relinquishes the possibility of active intervention. Committed critic-activists of today, visible and vocal, queer or otherwise, have compelling reasons to reject his decision and even to judge it harshly, but must also weigh the measure of self-implication in such a verdict. Barthes's tacit politico-sexual subject resembles, in some instances closely, many of the provisional and unstable figurations of homosexuality that proliferate in the wake of deconstruction. He might, paradoxically perhaps, even realize their ideals more fully by unremittingly enacting the necessary impossibility of the project. The discreet Barthes acts as their silent shadow, their cautionary flip side, their anxious double, their passive twin: the "dark, reverse side" of queer itself.

NOTES

1. Judith Reisman of the conservative American Family Association, for example, contended that the photograph of the girl "advertises the availability of this vulnerable child for photographic assault and rape. It would be purchased by child sex abusers as child pornography, which is what it is." "Promoting Child Abuse as Art," *Washington Times,* July 7, 1989, in *Culture Wars: Documents from the Recent Controversies in the Arts,* ed. Richard Bolton (New York: New Press, 1992), 57. C. Carr countered in the *Village Voice* that these images "don't reinforce fantasy, which is porn's job. They confront fantasy, which is art's job." "War on Art," *Village Voice,* June 5, 1990, in *Culture Wars*, 230.

2. The Mapplethorpe affair reached what was perhaps its dramatic climax in 1990

when the director of Cincinnati's Contemporary Arts Center, Dennis Barrie, was arrested on obscenity charges for exhibiting the photographs.

3. The first of the three restrictions on NEA funding in the Helms Amendment (eventually defeated) reads "none of the funds authorized to be appropriated pursuant to this Act may be used to promote, disseminate, or produce obscene or indecent materials, including but not limited to depictions of sadomasochism, homo-eroticism, the exploitation of children, or individuals engaged in sex acts" ("Debate in Senate over Helms Amendment," in *Culture Wars*, 73). When enumerating the more incendiary photographs in a mailing to the members of the Christian Coalition, Pat Robertson mentions "a photo of young pre-school girl with her genitals exposed" between "a photo of a man's arm (up to the forearm) in another man's rectum" and "a photo of naked children in bed with a naked man." "Christian Coalition direct mail," *Culture Wars*, 125.

4. Lee Edelman, "The Future Is Kid Stuff: Queer Theory, Disidentification, and the Death Drive" (paper delivered as the Craig Owens Memorial Lecture, University of Rochester, November 1998).

5. I am here bracketing off the texts collected in the posthumous *Incidents* (1987). It is important to note that during his lifetime Barthes chose *not* to publish these texts, and the autobiographical fragments that he did authorize to appear, some written at the same time as "Soirées de Paris," make no mention of his sexual exploits. D. A. Miller offers, with post-*Incidents* hindsight, a reading of Barthes's numerous oblique references to his sexuality. Miller views Barthes's figuration provocative but deficient, and sees the need to "develop a gay muscle" for him. D. A. Miller, *Bringing Out Roland Barthes* (Berkeley: University of California Press, 1992). For a discussion of the circumstances through which *Incidents* appeared, see the sections on Barthes's posthumous publications in Louis-Jean Calvet's biography *Roland Barthes* (Paris: Flammarion, 1990).

6. The short fragment in *The Pleasure of the Text* entitled "politique" reads as follows: "The text is (should be) that inhibited person who shows his behind [*derrière*] to the *Political Father*." Roland Barthes, *The Pleasure of the Text* (1973), trans. Richard Miller (New York: Hill and Wang, 1975), 53.

7. Lawrence Schehr offers a pithy discussion of Barthes's homosexuality as an interpretant, "a secret formula, a theory of observation and understanding that can function only if he does not fully let on what the secret is." Lawrence Schehr, *The Shock of Men: Homosexual Hermeneutics in French Writing* (Stanford, Calif.: Stanford University Press, 1995), 122. It is interesting to note that, even though Schehr does not specifically undertake a critique of the ideological investment in procreation, he deploys a vocabulary similar to that of Edelman's deconstruction of The Child: "To take a militant stand is to move homosexuality from the realm of the *productive* into that of the *reproductive*, to take it away from the neuter and force it into an opposition with doxological heterosexuality" (122, emphasis added).

8. Leo Bersani, *Homos* (Cambridge, Mass.: Harvard University Press, 1995), 71.

9. Sue-Ellen Case, "Performing Lesbian in the Space of Technology: Part I," *Theatre Journal* 47 (1995): 1-18.

10. Robert E. Owens Jr., *Queer Kids: The Challenges and Promise for Lesbian, Gay, and Bisexual Youth* (New York: Haworth Press, 1998), 36.

11. In *Roland Barthes,* Barthes offers a schema of his career, dividing into four distinct "phases." While these are somewhat arbitrary and do not reflect the more organic development of some of his thought (Barthes himself offers a litany of qualifications), they serve as useful

milestones for following the trajectory of his career. See Roland Barthes, *Roland Barthes*, trans. Richard Howard (New York: Hill and Wang, 1977), 145.

12. Roland Barthes, "The Photographic Message" (1961), in *Image Music Text*, trans. Stephen Heath (New York: Noonday Press, 1977), 31.

13. Roland Barthes, "The Third Meaning: Research Notes on Eisenstein Stills," in *Image Music Text*, 56-65, passim.

14. Roland Barthes, *Camera Lucida* (1980), trans. Richard Howard (New York: Hill and Wang), passim.

15. One critic even doubts the photo even exists. See Diana Knight, "Roland Barthes, or the Woman without a Shadow," in *Writing the Image after Roland Barthes,* ed. Jean-Michel Rabaté (Philadelphia: University of Pennsylvania Press, 1997), 138.

16. *Camera Lucida*, 7.

17. Barthes, *Roland Barthes*, 21.

18. Jacques Lacan, "Le stade du miroir comme formateur de la fonction du Je," in *Ecrits* (Paris: Seuil, 1966), 100.

19. The *Œuvres complètes* include the outline of this *Vita Nuova* in photoreproduction—it is brief, scrawled on eight sheets of paper, and so schematic that it is virtually impossible to imagine what this text would have looked like if written; Barthes's novel will always remain an emblem of an impossible future that fails to secure the reproduction of the present or the past. Murray Pratt offers a reading of Barthes's autobiographical writings, specifically the figuration of an oblique homosexuality, as "belonging to a deferred future" (Murray Pratt, "From 'Incident' to 'Texte': Homosexuality and Autobiography in Barthes' Late Writing. *French Forum* 22, no. 2 [May 1997]: 228) that permits them to evade the reviled *doxa* of the present and its will to secure the subject within its terms. Pratt disqualifies the posthumous *Incidents* as "Barthes' gay autobiography" on the ground that it fails, when considered apart from his greater œuvre, to enact the more characteristic deferral of autobiography into the future.

20. Barthes, *Roland Barthes,* 22.

21. *Roland Barthes*, 10.

22. *Roland Barthes*, 17.

23. Schehr, 122.

24. *Roland Barthes*, 34.

25. It is worth pointing out that "nature" and "code" act as epithets in Barthes's vocabulary.

26. Pierre St. Amand, "The Secretive Body: Roland Barthes' Gay Erotics," *Yale French Studies* 90 (1996): 171.

27. St. Amand, 28.

28. Several of the other images betray Barthes's preoccupation with the end of his family line, including a childhood picture of his sole aunt who, the caption informs us, died unmarried and childless.

29. I am thinking here in particular of Judith Butler's much discussed "critical queer." See the concluding chapter of Judith Butler, *Bodies That Matter: On the Discursive Limits of "Sex"* (New York: Routledge, 1993), 223-42.

30. *Roland Barthes*, 53.

31. Lee Edelman, *Homographesis* (New York: Routledge, 1994), 23.

BIBLIOGRAPHY

Barthes, Roland. *Camera Lucida*. Trans. Richard Howard. New York: Hill and Wang, 1981 (1980).

———. *Image Music Text*. Trans. Stephen Heath. New York: Noonday Press, 1977.

———. *Incidents*. Trans. Richard Howard. Berkeley: University of California Press, 1987.

———. *The Pleasure of the Text*. Trans. Richard Miller. New York: Hill and Wang, 1975 (1973).

———. *Roland Barthes*. Trans. Richard Howard. New York: Hill and Wang, 1977 (1975).

———. *S/Z*. Trans. Richard Miller. New York: Hill and Wang, 1974 (1970).

Bersani, Leo. *Homos*. Cambridge, Mass.: Harvard University Press, 1995.

Butler, Judith. *Bodies That Matter: On the Discursive Limits of "Sex."* New York: Routledge, 1993.

Calvet, Louis-Jean. *Roland Barthes*. Paris: Flammarion, 1990.

Case, Sue-Ellen. "Performing Lesbian in the Space of Technology: Part I." *Theatre Journal* 47 (1995): 1-18.

Culture Wars: Documents from the Recent Controversies in the Arts. Ed. Richard Bolton. New York: New Press, 1992.

Edelman, Lee. "The Future Is Kid Stuff: Queer Theory, Disidentification, and the Death Drive." Paper delivered as the Craig Owens Memorial Lecture, University of Rochester, November 1998.

———. *Homographesis*. New York: Routledge, 1994.

Knight, Diana. "Roland Barthes, or the Woman without a Shadow." In *Writing the Image after Roland Barthes*. Ed. Jean-Michel Rabaté. Philadelphia: University of Pennsylvania Press, 1997, 132-43.

Lacan, Jacques. *Ecrits*. Paris: Seuil, 1966.

Miller, D. A. *Bringing Out Roland Barthes*. Berkeley: University of California Press, 1992.

Owens, Robert E., Jr. *Queer Kids: The Challenges and Promise for Lesbian, Gay, and Bisexual Youth*. New York: Haworth Press, 1998.

Pratt, Murray. "From 'Incident' to '*Texte*': Homosexuality and Autobiography in Barthes' Late Writing." *French Forum* 22, no. 2 (May 1997): 217-33.

Schehr, Lawrence. *The Shock of Men: Homosexual Hermeneutics in French Writing*. Stanford, Calif.: Stanford University Press, 1995.

St. Amand, Pierre. "The Secretive Body: Roland Barthes' Gay Erotics." *Yale French Studies* 90 (1996):153-71.

9

The Big Business of Surfing's Oceanic Feeling: Thirty Years of *Tracks* Magazine

Margaret Henderson

A distinguishing feature of the American counterculture of the 1960s was the importance accorded to cultural politics in bringing about fundamental social and individual transformation, hence the proliferation of distinctively countercultural texts in the form of newspapers, brochures, manifestoes, street theatre, and magazines, such as *Rolling Stone*.[1] The Australian counterculture shared this emphasis on cultural politics, yet with local variations.[2] Given the centrality of sport and leisure to the dominant Australian culture and *mythoi*, it is not surprising that one specifically Australian countercultural text appeared in the form of *Tracks* surfing magazine. Since the first issue in October 1970 at the height of surfboard riding's counterculture phase, *Tracks* magazine has been central to the formation of Australian surfing's subcultural identity,[3] and prototypical for a number of surfing magazines.[4] With its open embrace of the counterculture, idiosyncratic format, and self-proclaimed role as chronicle of an authentic surfing lifestyle, *Tracks* was a vanguard text in defining surfing not as a sport, but as radical "play," an art form, and an expression of the Australian counterculture without parallel in any other surfing nation.[5] After thirty years *Tracks* remains metonymic of Australian surfing, but in a very different shape and form: glossy, commercialized, rebelliously adolescent, and hypermasculine.[6] This essay traces how *Tracks* transformed from counterculture text into shop counter text, given the specific sociohistorical contexts of consumer capitalism and second-wave feminism, and their conflicting rearrangement of a patriarchal capitalist gender order.[7]

The surfing media's crucial role in constructing a surfing subculture, and *Tracks*'s aim of "presenting a current account of what's happening in surfing as it passes along," means that my feminist textual analysis of *Tracks* locates not only the magazine's permutations, but suggests changes in surfing more generally.[8] A diachronic reading of *Tracks* allows the fate of a countercultural leisure form (with its implicit critique of modernity)[9] to be traced through a period when consumer capitalism (and its related cultural and aesthetic movements/moment termed postmodernism) impacts most fully upon Australian sport and leisure.[10] Further, given that sports media are "prime sites for playing out struggles for dominance and legitimation," *Tracks* is an interesting case of the ways in which a leisure form's gender codings and symbolic identities respond to the forces of consumer capitalism and the modern women's movement.[11] Thus my reading of *Tracks* is a tale of how the oceanic pleasures of surfing became a big business, and remain big business for masculine identity.[12]

I examine both form and content because, as Margaret Carlisle Duncan suggests, "we must examine the medium itself, and the cultural and historical contexts in which that specific text is embedded, to discover how patriarchal ideology operates—which particular structures produce and reproduce the mechanisms that oppress sporting women."[13] Hence I read *Tracks* through categories of subcultural identity; format, style, and discourse; and recurrent issues of politics, masculinities, and the role of women in surfing. Thus five phases or paradigms of *Tracks* emerge: Country Soul (1970-late 1973); Transition 1: Changing Currents (late 1973-late 1977); Pro Surfing's King Tide (late 1977-1980); Transition 2: Postmodern Surfing Takes Shape (1981-late 1994); and Hardcore Men and Wild Boys (late 1994 to the present).[14]

An historical reading of *Tracks* uncovers, as the magazine's subtitle states, a "continuous line, series of marks, left by a person, animal, or thing in passing along"[15] surfing and its forms of self-representation.[16] The marks uncovered outline two related problems of commodification and the place of women in surfing, problems that have troubled the magazine since its inception. I argue that *Tracks* has attempted to reconcile surfing's widening contradiction between oppositional or alternative subculture and profitable commodified lifestyle available to all, and the increasing demands by women for a place in the surfing line up, by "hardening" its patriarchal ideology and masculine symbolic identities. Simultaneously, it attempts to create a "necessary illusion" of some openness to women's advancement in surfing and wider society.[17] Consequently, *Tracks* is indeed a textualization of the pleasures and pains of growing up postmodern, in specifically gendered and sporting terms.

COUNTRY SOUL

Unlike American surfing's World War II roots and influence from Beat culture, factors which encouraged a more radical form of subcultural identity,[18] modern (that is, post-World War II) Australian surfing did not begin as a countercultural practice. Generally it functioned as just another form of sport or leisure, carrying only minor antisocial connotations.[19] In the mid-1960s, however, the meanings and practices associated with Australian surfing start to change and to be influenced by the rise of the counterculture.[20] The early spread of countercultural ideas and practices into surfing was aided by the then major Australian surf magazine, *Surfing World*,[21] a role which *Tracks* was to take over from its first issue in October 1970. To compare the two magazines in their countercultural phase is to understand why *Tracks* was so unique and transgressive. *Surfing World* may indeed have championed a "new era" in surfing from 1966,[22] but it maintained a standard sports/surf magazine format: A4 size, not much text, plenty of photos, and relatively high production values. *Tracks*, though, was an entirely different creature, as befitting a magazine arising out of the Australian counterculture, and exemplifying the countercultural mode of surfing known as Country Soul.[23]

Country Soul is a descriptor used in surfing to denote a specific ideology and form of surfing. Namely, surfing is the foundation of an oppositional or alternative lifestyle that rejects the competitiveness of life symbolized by the city, sport, and capitalism, and instead embraces nature by "dropping out," moving to the country, and living to surf. Country Soul is thus surfing's utopian and Romantic mode, and its adherents are known as soul surfers. In order to represent this emergent culture and dream, *Tracks* needed to clearly mark its difference from the dominant culture and sports of society, and from conventional surfing magazines such as the American publication, *Surfer* (disparaged as the "glossies"), which it did most visibly through its format and layout, and then its content.[24] *Tracks* was tabloid sized, used non-glossy paper, had a maximum of two colors throughout, began its lead story on the cover, had fairly rough production values of offset printing,[25] relied heavily on text rather than photographs, and was edited collectively.[26] Consequently, it had the "look" of an underground newspaper, which is how it saw itself: "an Australian surfing news magazine" for countercultural surfing.[27]

This distinctive countercultural look was reinforced in the style and type of contents. The tone is gentle, reflective, philosophical, at times apocalyptic and revolutionary, as exemplified in the first editorial: "Each one of us must care enough to alter the nature and direction of the life that we lead, and the environment in which it should be led. Otherwise, quite simply we will not survive as a species."[28] The consistent presence of poetry is significant, marking an aesthetic and artistic approach to surfing, and reinscribes the basic themes of Country Soul: the beauty of nature and surfing, the dehumanizing effects of technocratic society, and the individual's (read "male") philosophical and mystical quest. Correspondingly, advertising is a small and non-intrusive presence. As befitting an alternative lifestyle cottage industry, only a limited range of products (mainly boards or wet suits) feature, while the advertisements are unsophisticated and often humorous.

The Country Soul dream/lifestyle is also constructed through the numerous articles on drugs, meditation, vegetarian food, India, philosophy, mysticism, particular rock bands, ecology, antitechnocracy, literature, and cinema, with only a minor focus on competitive surfing. This wide-ranging philosophico-intellectual subject matter, and *Tracks*'s emphasis on text rather than photographs, denotes Country Soul as an intellectualization of surfing.

Complementing this trait is the other distinctive marker of this phase: political issues form a major presence, and there is a politicized approach to surfing more generally. Like the broader counterculture, Country Soul's politics are a mix of anarchism, anticapitalism, individualism, antidevelopment, and ecology, underwritten by the above-mentioned revolutionary and apocalyptic tone.[29] Australia and the world seemed poised on the edge of destruction, and Country Soul was one path out of the chaos. But Country Soul was also a politics of surfing, and its major opponent was surf lifesaving, the epitome of the male athleticism of dominant Australian culture: conformist, beer-swilling, competitive, ocker, and all that Country Soul sought to escape.[30] This dominant masculine (sporting) culture was satirized in the "Captain Goodvibes" comic strip that mixed countercultural politics, underground humor, hedonism, Robert Crumb stylistics, and surfing, and which began towards the end of this first phase.[31]

Captain Goodvibes, the beer-swilling "clubbie,"[32] was the antithesis of Country Soul masculinity that was influenced by hippy culture and its "feminization" of aspects of Australian masculinity. Given the sexism of the counterculture, *Tracks*'s iconic soul surfer was, not surprisingly, male, but a bearded, longhaired, nonaggressive, philosophical type who wore scruffy no-brand clothing and who could discuss or participate in pottery, new wave cinema, or surfing.[33] Hence the soul surfer was (as in the case of the counterculture more generally) an updating and reembodiment of the bohemian or Romantic hero. He was also, it seems, heterosexual, as the idyllic images and narratives of Country Soul living revolved around your "chick/lady," a few animals, your friends, maybe a couple of children, sitting around on the verandah of a shack near the beach. So although women are a part of the dream, they have a very limited presence in the pages, and usually as passive objects of male fantasy. They are not allowed the identity of surfers (even though from early issues onwards women write letters to the editors demanding to be respected as surfers, or complaining about the sexism of male surfers).

This circumscription of women in early *Tracks* needs to be interpreted in relation to the lack of overt sexism, misogyny, or homophobia (except for the occasional outburst in the letters pages). Is this lack a marker of a kinder, gentler masculine subculture, or is it made possible only by the near invisibility of women? This is a question to which we return below, but at this point it is obvious that Country Soul, like *Rolling Stone* magazine, for example, and the wider Australian counterculture,[34] was very much a boys' own adventure, an Oedipal rebellion against the fathers of modernity but with only a superficial engagement with the repressed feminine/oppressed women of modernity. This phase indeed marked a bold experiment in conceptualizing how leisure might function as a political strategy to change the lifeworld, and how such leisure might be represented in the magazine form, yet this potentially revolutionary physical culture remained resolutely male dominated.[35]

TRANSITION 1: CHANGING CURRENTS

The Country Soul mix of paradise and apocalypse was only a brief, though influential phase, fuelled as it was by a radicalism inspired by the Vietnam War protests and the early optimism inspired by the reformist Whitlam government, and supported by economic prosperity.[36] While these conditions came to an end, surfing and *Tracks* grew in popularity.[37] From late 1973 to late 1977 *Tracks* moves into a transitional period in which the counterculture heritage which defined it and made it popular, struggles with emergent discourses of an increasingly successful leisure form that requires and constructs a material base, whether from professionalization or commercialization.

It should be noted, however, that the seeds of professional competition and commodification were inherent even in surfing's Country Soul phase. Competitive surfing didn't die out during Country Soul, rather it was moved from center stage. Surfing also needs to be understood as a "commodity oriented youth subculture" in that the member seeks self-realization through a particular commodity form, in this case, the surfboard.[38] Jon Stratton argues that "[c]ommodity oriented youth subcultures are much more closely tied to generalised fundamental aspects of the capitalist social order such as consumerism and individualism than are spectacular youth cultures [such as Mods or Teds]."[39] We can observe this orientation occurring embryonically in *Tracks*'s most anticapitalist phase; namely, in the advertisements for the products required by surfers to sustain their individual and collective identity, products that were in turn manufactured by other surfers of varying entrepreneurial shades. Moreover, Thomas Frank's analysis of the American counterculture notes an uncanny alignment between countercultural values and perfect consumer behavior, such as the stress on individual self-realization, a desire for instant gratification, and a restless search for new experiences and sensations.[40] This alignment should be remembered as we observe surfing's commodification. So the first transitional phase of *Tracks* shows the attractiveness of countercultural surfing to commercial interests, the attractiveness of the professional sport approach to surfing, and *Tracks*'s first overt engagement with the problem of women.

A subtle though significant shift occurs towards the end of the Country Soul era when the first group of editors changed *Tracks*'s layout. In effect, this reduced the space allocated for specifically countercultural articles, and made it easier for the gradual dilution of Country Soul by the transition phase's editors, John Grissim (an American and ex-*Rolling Stone* editor) followed by Phil Jarratt (early contributor to *Tracks* and later editor of *Australian Playboy*).[41] While the counterculture remained a strong and identifying presence in terms of issues covered,[42] the articles were less frequent, and generally disconnected from either a revolutionary lifestyle or a politics. Not one story on political issues was published for over two years and, more importantly, the apocalyptic and revolutionary tone had dissipated.[43]

This dissociation of the counterculture from an overt political framework allowed business interests to cash in on the frisson generated by *Tracks*'s countercultural origins and the growing popularity of surfing. As Dick Hebdige notes in relation to subcultures more generally, Country Soul begins to experience both ideological and commodity based forms of incorporation.[44] The soul surfer now had a wide range of products, both surfing and non-surfing, to fill the political lack: for example, a special version of the Ford panel van, the *Tracks* Travel company, a *Tracks* bag, dope leaf shaped pendants, *Simply Living* magazine, and a range of clothes for surfers.[45] Such incorporation is paralleled by changes in the advertisements. The first Coca-Cola advertisement appeared in May 1975, signalling the attractiveness of *Tracks*'s youth readership and the iconography of surfing, and *Tracks*'s nondiscriminatory approach to multinational corporations. Significantly, the only full color glossy centerfolds are advertisements for Crystal Cylinders clothing (August 1975) and Golden Breed clothing (November 1975). Surfers finally had their own clothing range.

Country Soul was also challenged by the leading surfers' move towards a better organized and resourced professional surfing circuit throughout this period.[46] Clearly, the professionalization of surfing places more emphasis upon competitive surfing in general, and upon the cash nexus, while it also necessitates the setting up of formal structures and institutions (contest directors, a circuit, sponsors, judging, professional associations, and so on) that in turn introduce "corporate logic" into surfing. Furthermore, the heroes of surfing culture are transformed from Romantic outsiders to (semi)professional athletes. Thus professional surfing's version of modernity's instrumental rationality undermines core values of soul surfing.[47] *Tracks* did not hesitate to give ample coverage to the developing pro scene, although not without some reservations.[48] For example, the blatant commodification of personality and surfing that characterized the Bronzed Aussies (the first Australian professional surf team) met with ongoing criticism in the pages of *Tracks,* suggesting that this version of pro surfing was too advanced for Australian surfing.

The ebb tide of Country Soul is also apparent in changes to the format, language, and content. Production values slowly improved; for example, the cover increased from two to four colors in March 1974, and then went full color in December 1976. November 1974 features a sensationalist cover, a typical marketing ploy of mainstream magazines, and a technique that *Tracks* had not used before. The letters to the editor section was expanded, which in turn increased the coarse and sexist language and vindictiveness. The dreamy and gentle raves by readers had virtually disappeared. Such a shift in language also occurred in the feature articles,[49] and in the advertisements, which were now increasingly futuristic and aggressive.[50]

In terms of gender codings, ominous signs appeared for future versions of *Tracks*'s masculinities and femininities. First, the image and voice of hegemonic Australian masculinity, namely, the ocker, emerged, whether in Phil Jarratt's editorial approach ("It's yer all Aussie issue mate"),[51] satirical characters ("Clyde Strange" and "Ozzie Bonzer"—both archetypal yobbo surfers), letters from readers, or some of the surfers profiled. Homosexuality remained taboo, except for rare occasions in the letter pages. The dominant form of Australian masculinity thus begins to move into surfing and competes (along with the pro surfer) against the Romantic soul surfer for the position of central surfing icon. This impacts upon not only codings of femininity, but also on what surfing can potentially signify. As we see in later phases, the infiltration of surfing by the dominant discourse of Australian masculinity "frees up" the signification of surfing. That is, surfing can be nationalistic, jingoistic, misogynistic, moralistic, interested in rugby league, drink (to excess) at the RSL,[52] and so on, a far cry from Country Soul's rejection of mainstream Australian society.

Corresponding with a shift in masculinities is the increased presence of women, but also a related acceleration of sexism in articles, tone, photographs, and editorials. "Woman" becomes significant in *Tracks* discourse, but in a highly circumscribed way. From this point onwards, the category and positioning of Woman is set up as overwhelmingly visual, decorative, and in many cases, fetishized. Females are overwhelmingly represented in photographs as passive object of male desire, in various states of undress, and rarely surfing, while the female body is fetishized by the repetitive and gratuitous use of body parts throughout the magazine. This visual dismemberment of Woman has obvious resonances with soft-core pornography magazines, and which *Tracks* attempts to exploit so as to increase readership. Such an emphasis on Woman as erotic object, and on the inscription of hegemonic masculinity into surfing, also defuses the homoeroticism inherent in men gazing at men's semi-naked or neoprene-clad bodies, a scopophilia that is "hedged about with taboo, and has to be mystified and camouflaged."[53] One result is that the pleasures of surfing are now positioned as synonymous with male heterosexual pleasures and fantasies.

Women do gain limited recognition as surfers, with a number of champion surfers interviewed and a couple of articles on women and surfing being published, yet these are short and infrequent pieces that often stress the feminine appearance of the surfer. More importantly is the strategy that *Tracks* uses to deal with the ongoing complaints of sexism and neglect of women surfers, a technique I term "discipline and punish." This refers to the method where *Tracks* publishes a generally supportive article on women's surfing accompanied by a sexist graphic, or in the same issue or the following issue, publishes an absolutely misogynist article or particularly sexist photograph(s).[54] Such a strategy refutes accusations of neglect but also contains the representation of women surfers. Women are, in effect, disciplined and punished for seeking textual and material space and a voice as surfers. Hence, the positioning of Woman in *Tracks* signifies a symbolic form of male dominance specific to the production and reading of sports magazines, as Carlisle Duncan explains: "[Men] exercise their power *not* with real women, but with the sign or concept of Woman, which is objectified, commodified, and looked at illicitly at the formal level."[55]

In this first transition phase it is not only the counterculture and surfing which have been commodified, but also women's bodies. Although its appropriation of the iconography of soft-core pornography was meant to signal ongoing transgressiveness, *Tracks* was clearly paddling towards the mainstream. In its "Commercialism" issue of April 1977, *Tracks* confronted any residual anxieties about surfing's direction head-on, and unambiguously and pragmatically defended itself. As Jarratt said, "the age of commercialism in surfing has arrived. And it's the most important surfing development of the decade. . . . Keep surfing is what we've all been telling ourselves, and the economy dictates that the best way to do that is to get paid for it."[56]

PRO SURFING'S KING TIDE

Pro surfing is emblematic of *Tracks*'s third phase (late 1977-1980) in terms of the amount of coverage it receives, and in how it influences the representation of, and reduces space available for, other aspects of surfing.[57] Only one editor, Paul Holmes (who also was the contest director for the 2SM Surfabout competition for a few years), oversees this stage. Given the editor's orientation and the consolidation of international pro surfing, it is predictable that *Tracks* moves further away from its earlier countercultural alignments, and into the form of a subcultural sports magazine. To maintain its distinctiveness and credibility, *Tracks* relies on various signifiers of transgressiveness: coarse language and humor, drug references, soft-core porn imagery, and relatively rough production values.[58] *Tracks* has thus become the schizoid voice of what it originally disavowed: part surfing larrikin, part professional sport, residing in a rapidly thinning countercultural skin.

Residual traces of Country Soul remain in a few articles, advertisements for various alternative lifestyle products, or a generalized rebellious tone. The elements which have managed to cross over to this emergent surf subculture are those revolving around drugs (typically marijuana), individualism, hedonism, various forms of pantheistic inflected spiritualism, a related quasi-philosophical interpretation of surfing, and a fantasy of dropping out from society to surf. These are important in preserving some connection to *Tracks*'s origins, and also contribute to its present transgressive character. However, these nature-centered elements and the shift to surfing as a professionalized sporting code mean that politics becomes limited to the coverage of environmental issues.[59]

More important is the impact of pro surfing on the language and tone used in *Tracks*, most noticeably in the proliferation of discourses surrounding competition, and by an interrelated increase in an aggressive tone. The growing number of competition reports and accompanying photographs, contest previews, overall surfers' rankings, and the significant presence of pro surfers in advertisements alter the perspective in which surfing is represented. While this phase is marked by an approximately equal emphasis on feature articles which cover the noncompetitive surfing lifestyle (at least in quantitative terms), a presence which preserves *Tracks*'s earlier countercultural orientation, pro surfing and its ideologies become integrated and normalized. This ability to deal with subcultural contradictions is a large factor in *Tracks*'s longevity, and the importance of maintaining the underground "look" and feel of the magazine should not be underestimated. To read a *Tracks* from this period is to read pages and pages of competition stories, yet the reader still feels that she is in touch with a distinct and seemingly radical lifestyle, not a rapidly professionalizing and commercializing sport.[60]

The image of the pro surfer and the nature of pro surfing are also critical factors in disguising surfing's modernization. This era's Australian pro surfers can be categorized into two groups: the overtly commercial types, namely the Bronzed Aussies, and the more acceptable "blokes," like Wayne "Rabbit" Bartholomew. The overtly commercial types were the controversial face of pro surfing, while the majority of pros shared a family resemblance with the countercultural soul surfer, appearing as natural, slightly scruffy, unaffected, and gifted *individuals* who were lucky enough to make a living from surfing. The majority of pros were regular Aussie men, who spoke and behaved like the average surfer. And according to accounts in *Tracks*, the pro circuit was not the typical smoothly run professional sport. Rather, it seemed to attract flamboyant organizers, contests were often unpredictable, and so far the pro circuit had not required the athletes to conform to the norms of mainstream professional sport. This anarchic, hedonistic, and idiosyncratic image of pro surfing helped it to appear less threatening and more as an organic outgrowth of surfing.

Tracks also maintained a grassroots connection with the mass of surfers by an increase in the more accessible language and values of dominant Australian masculinity, or, blokiness.[61] For example, the 100th issue published the "Gourmet Chunder Guide."[62] This incorporation of dominant masculine discourse and behavior was generally done via parody, so that *Tracks* could simultaneously distance itself from and reinforce those traits. The result was that surfing appeared both unique and like any other sport an Australian male might like to watch or play.

The surfer didn't have to change or question anything much about society or himself to be a surfer. Rather, *Tracks* represented surfing and itself as the realm of freedom for repressed masculine values, under threat by resurgent Australian feminism and its rejection of patriarchal Australia.[63] These values could be expressed in *Tracks* because they were often parodied, and they were enacted through surfing because the surfer was, by virtue of earlier countercultural alignments, a rebel and an individual.

This, of course, has ramifications for women. While pro surfing meant a slight improvement in the status and organization of women's surfing, hence a minor increase in articles on women's surfing,[64] their decorative role continued unabated, if not increased. Pro surfing positioned women as spoils for the victor, and as an aesthetic dimension to the lifestyle.[65] The various nude or semi-nude body part photographs continued to mark *Tracks*'s transgressive (yet staunchly heterosexual) status, as did the discipline-and-punish strategy. Consequently, all these containment devices for women contribute to an emergent surfing version of hegemonic Australian masculinity.[66] In fact, this period is notable for its overt misogyny, which I suggest can be attributed to anxieties generated by both men's and women's pro surfing, and the increased visibility of, and advances made by, the women's movement through the 1970s.[67] Two outbreaks exemplify these anxieties: the December 1979 issue published a highly critical review of the adolescent feminist surfing novel, *Puberty Blues*, and an offensive satire on a surf groupie-nymphomaniac.[68] Then the October 1980 issue contains a semi-scientific article on why women can't surf as well as men because of their physiological characteristics. Women are being clearly told their place: the men, whether soul surfer or pro, are king.

Just how far *Tracks* had moved from its early beginnings is signified by the following events. First, it publishes a profile of superstar lifesaver Grant Kenny.[69] What would Captain Goodvibes have thought of this clubbie/butch/clean-cut conformist penetrating deep into the heart of the subculture? Second, two surfing magazines, *Sea Notes* and *Breakway*, begin publication in 1977. They are very similar in appearance to *Tracks* in terms of layout, contents, and graphics, though *Sea Notes* is a far more political magazine.[70] While neither magazine lasted long, their appearance suggests the allure of the *Tracks* formula.

TRANSITION 2: POSTMODERN SURFING

Although this second transition covers fourteen years (1981-94) and five editors, it is crucial in the final rearrangement of the various elements that makes *Tracks* into its current version of Hardcore Men and Wild Boys. This period is formative to *Tracks*'s and surfing's postmodern state, being a time when the surfing subculture becomes more stridently masculinist and commodified into a fashion-lifestyle industry; surfing functions as a fully professional sport; and there is an interrelated aestheticization of the surfing image in *Tracks*, particularly in terms of advertising and improved production methods.[71]

Changes in layout and discourse are suggestive of changes in other categories of *Tracks*, and it is here that we can observe surfing's incorporation into the regime of consumer capitalism/culture with its key emphasis on the consumer's stylization of life via the consumption of goods as signs.[72] David Harvey explains the significance of lifestyle to consumer capitalism thus: "[t]he mobilization of fashion in mass (as opposed to elite) markets provided a means to accelerate the pace of consumption not only in clothing, ornament, and decoration but also across a wide swathe of life-styles and recreational activities (leisure and sporting habits, pop music styles, video and children's games, and the like)."[73] Surfing was to be part of this accelerated and expanded field of consumption. For instance, the amount and range of advertising in *Tracks* increased dramatically in the mid-1980s, which not only signifies the commercial aspect of surfing and its packaging into lifestyle, but also changes the look and feel of the magazine.[74] The voice of *Tracks* is often indistinct or submerged in the plethora of advertisements for a huge range of products that are now positioned as crucial to adopting the surfing lifestyle. Consequently, it is difficult to discern a separation of the spheres of consumption and an authentic (that is, noncommercial) subcultural experience.

Further, until the mid-1980s, advertisements in *Tracks* generally lagged behind the magazine's overt sexism. In the mid-1980s, however, advertisements were increasingly sexist and sexually aggressive, paralleling *Tracks*'*s* own trajectory. From the late 1980s on, advertisements became sleek, often full page, full color, and sophisticated in appearance and content. Gone are the days of amateur advertising for a cottage industry that relied on name surfers and the occasional topless female. Instead, women are now sexual predators, surfing is a form of sexual or violent conquest, the humor is coarse and sexualized and, from the early 1990s on, the surfer becomes a macho, brooding figure of menace. The image(ry) of surfing, and the surf industry itself, were now big business and, predictably, had little interest in representing politically subversive or alternative ideologies. *Tracks* and the surfing industry upon which it was now reliant purveyed similar dreams: glossy, hedonistic, sexualized, and slightly threatening.

Note also a shift in the role of the pro surfer, which signals a further commodification of subcultural identity. The pro now functions as fashion model (with its feminine inflections) as well as athlete: slickly and heavily packaged in his surfwear, whether in advertisements, photo spreads, contest reports, or features. Gone is the unkempt no-brand appearance, replaced by neat haircuts, fluoro wet suits, and surfclothing labels from head to foot. His body is now disciplined by both the instrumental techniques of professional sport and by the demands of surfing as commodity form.[75] As compensation, and to mark his difference from mainstream society, the pro assumes increasingly macho poses in advertisements from the early 1990s on.

This commodification of surfing into lifestyle in the 1980s meant two things: the diffusion of its practices and signifiers into a broader section of the population (including females and non-surfers); and a changed, even estranged relationship between the surfer and the signifiers of a surfing identity. Mike Featherstone provides an explanation of the interrelation between these two effects: "the problems of inflation produced by an oversupply and rapid circulation of symbolic goods and consumer commodities have the danger of threatening the readability of goods used as signs of social status."[76] If anyone can buy the signs of being a surfer, then how was one to know who was the real thing? What was to be surfing's Other against which it could define itself? As we shall see in the final phase, the answer was Woman (and to a lesser extent, gay men).

Such changes to the image of surfing did not occur unchallenged, as exemplified in early 1980s debates over the direction of surfing. Although the editor may have tried to consign Country Soul to the dustbin of surfing history in the 150th issue, describing its adherents as "those who are remnants of by-gone hippy days,"[77] the complications caused by pro surfing and the commercial appeal of surfing remained. Some argued that it was time for surfing to improve its public image so it could gain access to government funding like other sporting organizations,[78] while the perennial debate over whether surfing has sold out to commercialism periodically erupts.[79] One editor, Kirk Willcox, was forced to justify *Tracks*'s emphasis on pro surfing, and argued that surfing was now a pluralistic subculture: "Today there are basically three categories of surfers: those who do it for love; those who do it for money"; and the above mentioned hippy leftovers.[80] Whether one surfs for money or is anticompetitive is presented as a simple lifestyle choice. This pluralism is supposed to contain surfing's ongoing tensions of being both competitive sport and anticompetitive leisure form, and the dominance of pro surfing's identity.[81] In this revisioning of the subculture, women continue as a notable absence.

As if to balance the shift in identity, the depoliticization of *Tracks* is briefly reversed through the 1980s. This reemphasis on political issues helped to maintain *Tracks*'s difference from new competitors such as *Australian Waves* and *Australia's Surfing Life* by harking back to its countercultural origins.[82] Willcox instituted a regular environmental column that dealt with more than just coastal development, while articles on South Africa and pro surfing, unemployment (given Australia's recession), Sydney's ocean outfalls, and nuclear weapons were also published. During Tim Baker's editorship, however, politics disappeared, to return in only a minor form in the early 1990s.

Tracks's brief return to politics, however, was not informed by any notion of sexual politics, for this second transition is marked by the hardening and stridency of the range and types of masculinities on display. That is, the foundations are laid for a fully formed hypermasculinity in the final stage. Hypermasculinity refers to a specifically postmodern form of symbolic masculinity that is "an exaggerated version of the traditional hegemonic model,"[83] with two characteristics being "enforcement" of the traditional gender order, and "a more brutal violence [symbolic, potential, or otherwise] than that in which their forefathers indulged."[84] This form needs to be linked to the explosive nexus of the increased commodification of the male body,[85] the advances made by feminism, a shift in the modus operandi of capitalism,[86] and the omnipresence of the capitalist image culture industries (of which sport is an integral part).

The *Tracks* prototype of hypermasculinity is comprised by a number of elements. First, the icons of the yobbo/larrikin and the pro surfer are joined by the figure of the rebel via three new comic strips: "Lash," "Private Pigdog," and "Grubb." The difference between these comics and their ancestor, "Captain Goodvibes," is highly significant. These latest emanations are fairly juvenile and non-subversive. Whichever hero it is, the narratives are the same: a violent, sexist quest for the gratification of male pleasure. Social satire is secondary in these distillations of the adolescent fantasies increasingly offered by *Tracks* to the lucrative youth market.[87]

Second, the yobbo/larrikin surfer gains an increased presence by three new regular columns: the chauvinist R. J. Kegg, "Sutho's Backside" (a backyard philosopher surfer), and Kev 'Gubby' Ironmonger's "Pub Talk: A Working Man's View of Pro Surfing." These columnists function as the voice of common sense, misogyny, and as tribal elders. In their criticisms of pro surfing and commercialization they suggest that *Tracks* is open to dissent, and that it is still the magazine for grassroots surfers. Finally, with the 1980s being the era of the HIV/AIDS pandemic, *Tracks* and its readers quickly used AIDS panic as a justification for homophobia, whether in an increased prevalence of homophobic letters to editor (some of which are extremely violent), or in using gay males as sources of humor.[88] Like other mainstream sports, *Tracks* indulged in the "symbolic annhiliation" of homosexuality.[89]

Surprisingly, this period was almost a "golden age" for women surfers, until Gary Dunne becomes editor in March 1991. The number of sexist photographs declined significantly, and all editors published the infrequent, but supportive articles on women pro surfers, without using the containment strategies of previous stages. *Tracks* had finally caught the second wave of feminism. Woman, however, was still being taught her place through language. The signifiers for Woman had diversified from "chick," "lady," "sheilas," and "broads" into "scrubber," "bushpig," "birds," and "wenches," while the above-mentioned yobbo/larrikin columnists became primary sites where reactionary conceptions of Woman were placed into discourse.

The final editor in this stage, Gary Dunne, was particularly reactionary, as if trying to recoup any gains made by women through the 1980s. Consequently, he sets the scene for the containment of women in *Tracks*'s final phase. Under Dunne, tit shots and misogyny are rampant, as exemplified by the short story, "The Bitch," with its plot about a female pro surfer who surfs as well as the men, but who turns out to be a robot.[90] What clearer expression does one need of deep masculine anxieties around the current generation of competent female surfers (such as Lisa Andersen and Pam Burridge)? Further, *Tracks*'s hypersensitivity to feminist criticisms became clear when it published a number of shots of g-strings "just to get up the feminists' noses,"[91] and in the columnist Sutho's angry response to a *Bulletin* article on sexism in surf magazines.[92]

This second transitional period is significant in that it demonstrates that the current state of *Tracks* has not been achieved by the simple onward march of a patriarchal capitalism. For a major part, *Tracks* regained some degree of political conscience, and did attempt to improve the coverage of women's surfing. Yet these progressive moments were always framed by an archetypal Australian larrikinism, an emphasis only on the elite of women surfers, the pressures of an increasingly competitive market for surfing magazines,[93] and a continuing commodification and professionalization of surfing which threatened its self-identity.

HARDCORE MEN AND WILD BOYS

To read a copy of *Tracks* today is to read a very different text from its first incarnation as voice of the Australian surfing subculture. First and most noticeable is the physical difference. From January 1995 *Tracks* has a full color glossy cover; some color pages are added in August 1997; *Tracks* goes into cybersurf with its website (October 1997); and the most important change is the shift to A4, full color glossy pages in March 2000.[94] *Tracks* appears to be as slick and glossy as any of the other surfing or sports magazines on a crowded newsstand. The major theme in this final phase, therefore, is the story of how *Tracks* attempts to maintain a distinctive surfing identity, mainly through an inscription of a hypermasculinity. This hypermasculinity is required to serve a number of purposes: ideally it should accommodate the yobbo, athlete, and rebel versions of masculinity; ease the tensions of a split subculture; and meet the fantasy needs of its largely teenage male audience.[95] By its "symbolic annihilation" of women and gay men, and its "symbolic glorification" of heterosexual males, *Tracks*'s hardcore men and wild boys can thus contain the twin problems besetting surfing: namely, commodification/professionalism and women.[96]

Tracks continues to publish the typical range of articles with countercultural origins, and it actively tries to maintain its links with this particular heritage in the regular column, "X-Files," which reprints photographs from early issues. Considering the recent wave of surfing nostalgia symbolized by the return of the Malibu board and the appearance of magazines like the *Australian Surfer's Journal*, and the aging of influential sections of the surfing fraternity, this is not particularly surprising. Yet it is a selective nostalgia. *Tracks* is overtly critical and moralistic about a number of aspects of the Country Soul legacy, publishing articles critical about Nimbin (once countercultural Mecca) and ferals (postmodern hippies),[97] and a number of antidrug stories.[98] When anxieties about the selling out of surfing[99] are occasionally voiced by readers or contributors, *Tracks* is particularly blunt:

> This was the day that the mail brought a truckload of letters decrying the loss of the "soul surfer." The mangy, feral, ratty-jumper-wearing, bearded, unemployed "soul surfer" of surf-societies, [*sic*] collective dreams. I can't believe that in this so-called "enlightened age" we surfers cling so heavily to visions of days gone by and only connote "soul" with that image, with that time. . . . Yeah, yeah, we've lost it here for making a living out of surfing and bringing images of far off (and not so far) waves to the stoked flatday masses.[100]

This is the typical *Tracks* apologia for its role as purveyor of pro surfing: a defensive tone, an implied elitism of soul surfing, and an appeal to respectable workerist and capitalist notions of earning a living and making money, respectively.

The mainstreaming of the subculture is further reflected in how politics is reconstituted. Politics is a regular presence in terms of occasional interviews or features on the environment or nuclear issues, and from December 1995 onwards "The Fly's" monthly column reports from Canberra on issues that affect surfers. "The Fly" is quite scathing about federal government policies on education and welfare, for instance, and he encourages surfers to vote. So politics is now made equivalent to youth issues, and activism is located in both the existing parliamentary system and single issue politics. And, as usual, there is a repression of feminism and sexual politics.

Such a disavowal seems a symptom of changes in gender relations within surfing and wider Australian society, whether that more women are surfing, or feminist challenges to patriarchal privilege. *Tracks*, therefore, introduces the latest enforcer of the traditional gender order: hypermasculinity. The hypermasculinity characteristic of this period is comprised by a blend of the icon of the pro surfer as macho hero, surfing as masculine form of sexualized physical conquest, and in the columnist-character of Gull Allder, the latest and most extreme emanation from the *Tracks* pantheon of yobbos who generally express its purest forms of misogyny and homophobia. A story titled "Ballistic Surfing" provides a quintessential description of hardcore surfing: "No softcocking here, just fast, hard, and out of the water."[101] In a more relaxed register, Gull Allder writes on the pre-Oedipal pleasures of shitting, pissing, drinking excessively, testicles, flashing his buttocks, and the horrors of accidentally visiting a gay bar. Thus *Tracks*'s ideal masculinity is composed along a spectrum that encompasses physical courage, skill, aggression and perfection at one end; and larrikin and chauvinistic behavior and humor at the other end. Hence, it reinscribes the dominant form of Australian masculinity in a pseudo-rebellious shape, and thus exemplifies Arthur Brittan's observation that "hegemonic masculinity is able to defuse crisis tendencies in the gender order by using counter and oppositional discourses for its own purposes."[102]

This pseudo-rebel figure also functions as a bridge between the contradictions of surfing as valuable commodity and as an authentic youth subculture. Frank notes the importance of the rebel to both public culture and the advertising industry since the 1960s in energizing consumer capitalism.[103] He argues that "rebellion is the high- and mass-cultural motif of the age; Order is its great bogeyman," and youth culture continues to replenish "hip consumerism."[104] This is a perfect description for how *Tracks* has enlisted an updated figure of the male rebel to reenergize its subculture, thus increasing surfing's attractiveness to adolescent males and business interests. As a result, however, surfing as art form and potentially oppositional lifestyle is submerged in the aggressive terminology used to describe the practice and lifestyle, the macho image of its best practitioners, and the continuing disavowal and containment of femininity and homosexuality.[105] *Tracks* offers readers a similar subjective and ideological orientation to that contained in conventional sports, which Brian Pronger describes as "an apprenticeship in orthodox masculinity."[106]

While the men and boys have become hardcore in their masculinity and passion for the lifestyle, women have regressed to being soft-core. This phase marks the worst space and time for women in *Tracks* even though, if not because, more women surf better than ever. The representation of women has now lurched back into the consistent use of the discipline-and-punish strategy, and the proliferation of soft-core body part photographs. Although *Tracks* institutes a regular women's page (predictably titled "G-Spot") and covers the growing women's pro scene, this coverage is undercut by the juvenile fascination with women's bodies as source of pleasure or humor (for example, the "show us your tits and win a surfboard competition" or the "pin the hands on Pamela Anderson" game).[107] How telling is it when the May 1997 issue sees an advertisement for the film *Blackrock*, which deals with the gang rape and murder of a young woman in a coastal town; a surf travel story, "Pedro and the House of Whores"; and an article on a women's surf team, Team Wahini?[108] The editor, however, ignores the contradictions or the connections among these texts, and justifies the decorative role of women by arguing that "[b]eautiful women have always played a role in the life of the surfer,"[109] at least in *Tracks*'s imaginings and longings.

Alby Falzon, surf photographer and member of the first editorial group, makes one of the strongest criticisms of the current direction of *Tracks*. In a recent interview, Falzon criticized the "overt consumerism" of surfing and the big surfing corporations: "They're out of control now and I don't think all those guys who started 20 years ago realised they would get to this point." But the surf media is also a target: "Magazines have got the responsibility to pass the truth on. . . . If you're not going to make some statement or try and give some guidance or direction through the magazine, get out of there, forget it."[110] The problem is not only *Tracks*'s selective amnesia about its origins, but also the type of guidance that it's giving to surfing. *Tracks*'s subjugation of women and championing of professionalism and commodification in a potentially oppositional lifestyle in effect, like many other contemporary sports, reproduces the (post)modern world.[111]

TRAJECTORIES OF *TRACKS*

The thirty-year history of *Tracks* is comprised by a number of trajectories where the relationship between modernity (as a particular form of instrumental rationality) and postmodernism (as a specific regime of commodification and symbolization) is played out. In terms of surfing ideology and organization, *Tracks* moves from a Romantic, antimodern phase to the professionalized mode of surfing that is marked by modern forms of rationality and structures (coaches, professional associations, objective forms of evaluation in competition, and so on). A parallel development occurs in the ideal role of the surfer, shifting from artist figure to professional athlete.[112] These forms of modernity affect not only the elite of the subculture but, as I have shown, fundamentally alter the consciousness, emphases and direction of the leisure form, hence preparing the ground for postmodernism to fully profit from surfing. Postmodernism thus needs to be seen as both an extension and internal condition of modernity, rather than simply a break.

The postmodern form of capitalism is a crucial factor in a number of *Tracks*'s trajectories, particularly in the transformation of the surfing lifestyle, image, and industry into glossy spectacle and big business,[113] and in the shift in symbolic masculinities—from a putatively antimodern figure to the highly commodified yobbo/athlete/rebel. The position of women, however, follows a rather idiosyncratic path. Women move from near invisibility to minor subjecthood but major object status as surfing modernizes, to a slightly improved presence as surfers while experiencing the most extreme forms of objectification in surfing's postmodernity. The potentially emancipatory effects of modern rationality and efficiency, or postmodernism's indiscriminate quest for consumers, have had only a minor effect on women surfers' progress.

One could interpret *Tracks*'s recalcitrance in two ways. First, the modern and postmodern colonization of the traditionally masculine lifeworld of surfing has contributed to this reaction against women's quest to participate. The containment of women is compensation for the containment of surfing. For, as Teresa Ebert notes, "[t]he differentiation between masculine and feminine increasingly collapse under the pressure of capitalism, yet patriarchy finds new ways to perpetuate male privilege."[114] Second (and related to the former), perhaps surfing and/in its texts has been made to function as such a deep repository of masculine pleasures, needs, identities, and fantasies that it cannot bear to have its symbolic and bodily integrity challenged or violated by advances made possible by second wave feminism. Having so far escaped the capitalist (or to a lesser extent, feminist) inspired "domestication" of other male-dominated sports such as rugby league or cricket, postmodern surfing thus becomes a fantasized last frontier for increasingly anxious men and youths. And like the rebel culture or "hip consumerism" that exemplifies it, postmodern surfing reenergizes its parent culture and its associated regimes of (sexual) oppression and instrumentality, by seductive, but limited, pleasures and freedoms.

Many thanks to the assistant editor of *Tracks*, Sean Doherty, for allowing me to work in the *Tracks* archives.

NOTES

1. Julie Stephens, *Anti-Disciplinary Protest: Sixties Radicalism and Postmodernism* (Cambridge: Cambridge University Press, 1998), 96.

2. See Michael Denholm, *Small Press Publishing in Australia* (North Sydney: Second Back Row, 1979) for a full account of alternative publishing in this period.

3. Surfing here refers to surfboard riding, not body surfing or bodyboards, and will be the terminology used throughout this essay.

4. Early examples include *Sea Notes* and *Backdoor*, which borrowed the *Tracks* look. Later examples are *Underground Surf* and *Australia's Surfing Life* that incorporated *Tracks*'s radical image and rebellious adolescent tone.

5. Ricky J. Farmer categorizes recreational surfing as a form of play or game, as in Roger Caillois's sense of the terms, in "Surfing: Motivations, Values, and Culture," *Journal of Sport Behavior* 15, no. 3 (1992): 243.

6. Throughout the 1970s and 1980s, *Tracks* consistently outsold its closest competitor, *Surfing World*. It has remained the second largest selling surfing magazine in the 1980s and 1990s, and its circulation figures have remained between 35,000-37,000 copies per issue. Source: *Press, Radio and TV Guide* (Sydney: Country Press), and *Margaret Gee's Australian Media Guide* (Melbourne: Information Australia-Margaret Gee Media).

7. I define consumer capitalism as a more descriptive term for Ernest Mandel's "late capitalism," a stage marked by the prioritization of consumption over production, with a concomitant rise in the aestheticization of everyday life. See Mike Featherstone, *Consumer Culture and Postmodernism* (London: Sage, 1991) for a full account.

8. John Irwin's pioneering ethnographic study of surfers argued that surfing was not a true subculture, but rather a scene, in "Surfing: The Natural History of an Urban Scene," *Urban Life and Culture* 2, no. 2 (1973): 132. While he is accurate in social terms, I agree with the distinction made by Kent Pearson between social and cultural forms of a subculture. See

Pearson's *Surfing Subcultures of Australia and New Zealand* (St. Lucia: University of Queensland Press, 1979) for a full discussion. Thus Leanne Steadman is correct when she argues that the surfing subculture only exists in and through the surf media, in "From Gidget to Gonad Man: Surfers, Feminists, and Postmodernization," *Australian and New Zealand Journal of Sociology* 33, no. 1 (1997): 76.

9. Luis Britto-Garcia, "Critiques of Modernity: Avant-Garde, Counterculture, Revolution," *South Atlantic Quarterly* 92, no. 3 (1993): 516.

10. Jim McKay and Toby Miller identify three main factors in the rapid professionalization and commodification of Australian sport in the late 1970s and 1980s: World Series Cricket in 1977; the 1983 America's Cup victory; and "the integration of sport, leisure, and recreation into strategies for managing the fiscal and hegemonic crises of the state," in "From Old Boys to Men and Women of the Corporation: The Americanization and Commodification of Australian Sport," *Sociology of Sport Journal* 8, no. 1 (1991): 88.

11. Donald Sabo and Sue Curry Jansen, "Images of Men in Sport Media: The Social Reproduction of Gender Order," *Men, Masculinity, and the Media*, ed. Steve Craig (Newbury Park, Calif.: Sage, 1992), 184.

12. Freud defines the oceanic feeling as "the notion of limitless extension and oneness with the universe," where the ego does not feel itself to be separated from the world, in *Civilization and Its Discontents*, trans. Joan Riviere (1930; London: Hogarth, 1957), 14. Mark Stranger explores surfing's oceanic feeling in surfing, in "The Aesthetics of Risk: A Study of Surfing," *International Review for the Sociology of Sport* 34, no. 3 (1999): 265-76.

13. Margaret Carlisle Duncan, "Beyond Analyses of Sport Media Texts: An Argument of Formal Analyses of Institutional Structures," *Sociology of Sport Journal* 10, no. 4 (1993): 354.

14. Exact cut-off dates are not provided for the phases because the shifts between stages cannot necessarily be attributed to a single magazine issue, a particular event that "caused" a new stage to emerge, or change of editor. Each phase is thus constructed from general and dominant tendencies consistently observable across a period of time.

15. In the first issue *Tracks* explained its title by referring to the *Concise Oxford Dictionary* definition of a track: a "continuous line, series of marks, left by person, animal, or thing in passing," which is how the magazine saw its role in relation to surfing. "*Tracks* is an Australian surfing news magazine aimed at presenting a current account of what's happening in surfing as it passes along," John Witzig, editorial, *Tracks* October 1970, 3. This definition formed the magazine's first subtitle until April 1972.

16. Longtime surf journalist, Phil Jarratt, notes that "It's no longer about teenage rebellion, it's a family sport," in Mike Safe, "Chairman of the Board," *Australian Magazine,* 18-19 April 1996, 27.

17. In her analysis of the Australian general sports magazine, *Inside Sport*, Helen Jefferson Lenskyj uses the Chomskyan concept of "necessary illusions" to explain the magazine's strategies of being resolutely sexist while seemingly open to covering women's sport and to reader dissent, in "'Inside Sport' or 'On the Margins'?: Australian Women and the Sport Media," *International Review for the Sociology of Sport* 33, no. 1 (1998): 30.

18. Irwin, 131. R. L. Rutsky notes that this early American surfing subculture borrowed quite heavily from Beat culture, in "Surfing the Other: Ideology on the Beach," *Film Quarterly* 52, no. 4 (1999): 13.

19. Modern surfing was made possible by a number of factors, most notably consumer capitalism's postwar boom and valorization of leisure, and by developments in board design.

Other factors include the construction of a "youth" identity, the availability of the motor car, and the role of the mass media in spreading Californian surf culture either through films or music. See either Douglas Booth, "Surfing 60s: A Case Study in the History of Pleasure and Discipline," *Australian Historical Studies* 10, no. 3 (1994) or Pearson for good accounts of modern Australian surfing's beginnings. Board riding in Australia actually has much earlier origins, namely, in the use of rescue boards by the Surf Life Saving Association, although surfboard riding as we understand it today is not practiced on a widespread basis until the 1950s (Pearson, 57).

20. Booth, 275.

21. Booth, 275.

22. See *Surfing World* 8, no. 1 (1966) for an announcement of a new era in surfing. For example, Nat Young proclaims that "we have moved into a completely new dynamic attitude towards our surfing. Surfing is in the mind, more so than in the body," in "A New Era! McTavish and Young Discuss," *Surfing World* 8, no. 1 (1966): 23.

23. In a perceptive analysis of Australian sport, Bob Stewart links the emergence of surfing to a changing cultural mood in the late 1960s that he denotes as Romantic: non-competitive, naturalistic, and unregulated; in "Leisure and the Changing Patterns of Sport and Exercise," *Sport and Leisure: Trends in Australian Popular Culture*, ed. David Rowe and Geoff Lawrence (Sydney: Harcourt, Brace, Jovanovich, 1990), 183.

24. Witzig, 3.

25. *Tracks* chose an offset printing method to shorten production times for more up-to-date coverage of contests and the general movement of surfing so that it was "what's happening now," Witzig, 3.

26. From October 1970 to July 1974 *Tracks* was edited by a nucleus of three: David Elfick, John Witzig, and Albert Falzon, who were joined by other personnel at various times, for example, Rusty Miller and Mick Eyre.

27. Witzig, 3.

28. Witzig, 3.

29. For example, "Good old spaceship earth is careering through space with madmen at the helm," Paul Witzig, "Paul's Thing," *Tracks,* December 1970, 5.

30. Ocker refers to the uncouth, chauvinistic, philistine qualities that comprise a stereotypical dominant form of Australian masculinity. "Yobbo" is a recent synonym for an ocker.

31. "Captain Goodvibes" by Tony Edwards first appears in May 1973.

32. "Clubbie" is surfer slang for a surf lifesaver. Throughout surfing history, the clubbie has functioned as folk devil or "other" because of surf lifesavers' supposed conformism, competitiveness, semi-militarism, and conventional form of masculinity. See Pearson for a full account, and Ed Jaggard for an alternative but not entirely convincing reading of the "clubbie-surfer" dichotomy, in "Chameleons in the Surf," *Journal of Australian Studies* 53 (1997): 183-91.

33. See, for example, *Tracks,* June 1972, 4, for champion surfer Mark Warren's article on pottery.

34. See Robert Draper, *Rolling Stone Magazine: The Uncensored History* (New York: Doubleday, 1990) and Ellen Willis's perceptive review of Draper, "Getting a Lock on Rock," *Columbia Journalism Review* 29 (November/December 1990): 59-62, for an account of *Rolling Stone*'s history and uneasy relationship with feminism.

35. See Marilyn Lake, *Getting Equal: The History of Australian Feminism* (St. Leonards: Allen and Unwin, 1999), 220, for a brief discussion of the sexism of the Australian New Left.

36. Booth, 277.

37. *Tracks,* August 1973, 3, announces that *Tracks* has achieved its highest circulation figures yet.

38. Jon Stratton, "Youth Subcultures and Their Cultural Contexts," *Australian and New Zealand Journal of Sociology* 21, no. 2 (1985): 194.

39. Stratton, 194.

40. Thomas Frank, *The Conquest of Cool: Business Culture, Counterculture, and the Rise of Hip Consumerism* (Chicago: University of Chicago Press, 1997), 119.

41. This change occurred in the August 1973 issue. The space allocated was reduced from three pages to one page.

42. The political issues covered included the battle to legalize drugs, antinuclear campaigns, woodchipping, alternative energy, and a debate on surfing in South Africa.

43. Further, *Tracks* published only nine political stories in over forty-eight months.

44. Dick Hebdige, *Subculture: The Meaning of Style* (London: Methuen, 1979), 94.

45. *Simply Living* is an Australian alternative lifestyle magazine.

46. 1974 is an important year for the Australian professional surfing circuit, for the first time staging two major international events: the first professional Bells Beach competition and the 2SM Coke Classic. In 1975 the first association for Australian professional surfers was organized so as to give riders some input into the burgeoning international circuit, and in 1976 the first professional team of surfers, the Bronzed Aussies (Ian Cairns, Peter Townend, Mark Richardson, and later Cheyne Horan), was started.

47. Jim McKay, *No Pain, No Gain? Sport and Australian Culture* (New York: Prentice Hall, 1991), 42. McKay argues that such a form of logic changes sport in the following way: "Sports have gradually changed from local, spontaneous, rule-of-thumb, informal activities into regional, national, and international bureaucracies that mirror all the formal, impersonal and alienating characteristics of bureaucratic life in general," 49. Surfing's particularly anti- or non-sport past means that the shifts are even more pronounced and painful for its adherents.

48. Compare the zero pages of coverage of pro or competitive surfing in September 1971 with the eight pages (or 22 percent of the magazine) of pro surfing in September 1977.

49. See "Cindy and Brad," a misogynistic satire on the surf romance, in the June 1975 issue.

50. For example, in this advertisement for O'Neill wet suits: "Radicalman! [sic] Shaun Thomson is all speed, power, and aggression," *Tracks* July 1976, 40.

51. Cover headline, *Tracks* February. 1975, 1.

52. The RSL is the acronym for the Returned Services League, a right-wing association of ex-servicemen. Many towns and suburbs have an RSL club, where members go to indulge in homosocial rituals, particularly drinking alcohol.

53. Roger Horrocks, *Male Myths and Icons: Masculinity in Popular Culture* (Basingstoke: Macmillan, 1995), 55.

54. This strategy first appears in September 1974, when a reader complains about sexual double standard. The editor requests that "girls" send in photographs of themselves for the readers' pleasure. In March 1976 an article is published on what surfing means to women. In the same issue is a section called "Sheila of the Month" with a photograph of a supposedly ugly old woman. The strategy is repeated at least four times in this phase alone.

55. Carlisle Duncan, 368.

56. Phil Jarratt, "Is Surfing Selling Out?" *Tracks,* April 1977, 11.

57. For example, 17.5 percent of the magazine in September 1980 is devoted to pro or competitive surfing compared to virtually negligible coverage in September 1974.

58. In this phase the only change in layout is that some of the advertisements go full color.

59. Only three political stories were published in the three years of this phase.

60. This feeling of radicalism should also be seen in relation to the conservatism of orthodox Australian sporting culture of the time, dominated by traditionally Australian sports such as cricket, various codes of football, and horse racing.

61. "Blokiness" is derived from bloke, an informal Australian term for an average type of male.

62. Brian Bile, "Gourmet Chunder Guide," *Tracks,* January 1979, 42-43. See also Hugh Hamilton on the increasing aggression in surfing, in "Aggression: In Search of World War III," *Tracks* Jan. 1979, 47. "Chunder" is Australian slang for vomit.

63.Gisela Kaplan describes the early to mid-1970s as the highpoint of the Australian women's movement. The movement continued throughout the late 1970s and onwards, but in an altered, more bureaucratised form (34-35). See Kaplan's *The Meagre Harvest: The Australian Women's Movement 1950s-1990s* (St Leonards: Allen and Unwin, 1996) for a full account.

64. On average, coverage increases from an article every six months, to an article every five months.

65. For example, any contest report from the French leg of the circuit will, without fail, include photographs of topless French women.

66. R. W. Connell defines hegemonic masculinity as "the masculinity that occupies the hegemonic position in a given pattern of gender relations, a position always contestable," in *Masculinities* (St. Leonards: Allen and Unwin, 1995), 76. The importance of physical prowess and courage, the repression of emotion, the subordination of women, and a distrust of creativity and the intellect are major hallmarks of Australian masculinity.

67. This increased feminist visibility was symbolised by events like International Women's Year in 1975. The conservative Fraser government was in power during this period; however, the activism and institutionalization of Australian feminism continued under these difficult circumstances, as noted by Lake, 253-76.

68. *Puberty Blues* gave a teenage girl's perspective on the sexism of the Sydney surf scene; Gabrielle Carey and Kathy Lette, *Puberty Blues* (Carlton, Vic.: McPhee Gribble, 1979). It was later made into a feature film.

69. Phil Abrahams, "So You Think You're Tough," *Tracks,* December 1980, 13.

70. The similarities with *Tracks* are not surprising. The first editor of *Sea Notes*, John Witzig, was also in the first group of editors for *Tracks*.

71. *Tracks* introduced stapling and the hot press production method in November 1990, which involved using better quality paper and improved quality of photographic reproduction.

72. Featherstone, 85-86.

73. David Harvey, *The Condition of Postmodernity: An Enquiry into the Origins of Cultural Change* (Oxford: Basil Blackwell, 1989), 285.

74. From *Tracks*'s inception, advertising had remained at approximately 35 percent of the total contents. In September 1985, however, advertising increased to 57.5 percent. It remained at this level till the late 1990s when it increased again, to 60 percent.

75. Lindsay Fitzclarence argues that the commodification of the athletic body is made possible by the connection between the marketplace and instrumental rationality in "The Body as Commodity," *Sport and Leisure: Trends in Australia's Popular Culture*, ed. David Rowe and Geoff Lawrence (Sydney: Harcourt, Brace, Jovanovich, 1990), 106.

76. Featherstone, 19.

77. Kirk Willcox, editorial, *Tracks,* March 1983, 3.

78. Geoff Booth, "Thoughts for the '80s . . . and Beyond," *Tracks,* August 1981, 29.

79. See the two articles in March 1983: Geoffrey Wren, "Surfing: Sub-culture or Cultural Hype?" (42) and Kirk Willcox, "The Act Remains the Same," (43) debate whether surfing had sold out to commercialism.

80. Kirk Willcox, editorial, *Tracks,* March 1983, 3.

81. *Tracks* restates the ideal of a plural subculture in April 1986, "Lifestyles: Six Faces of Surfing" where various types of surfers are categorized (including the Country Soul surfer and the competitor). "Lifestyles," *Tracks,* April 1986, 35.

82. *Australian Waves* is first published in 1980 as a glossy, visually orientated text that emphasized surfing as lifestyle, not sport. A second competitor is *Australia's Surfing Life* that starts in 1985. It also is a glossy with an emphasis on photographs, but not as alternative in philosophy as *Australian Waves*.

83. Steadman, 81.

84. Fred Pfeil, *White Guys: Studies in Postmodern Domination and Difference* (London: Verso, 1995), 149.

85. Edisol Dotson traces the mainstreaming of the male body and male beauty into contemporary culture in *Behold the Man: The Hype and Selling of Male Beauty in Media and Culture* (New York: Haworth, 1999).

86. Pfeil, 236.

87. This target audience is also suggested by the amount of space devoted to grommets (young surfers) from the early 1990s on.

88. See, for example, R. J. Kegg, "A Gay Excursion," *Tracks,* January 1985, 21; and A. P. Riphool, "Shock Survey Shows Surfers Turning Gay!!!" *Tracks,* April 1991, 18.

89. McKay, 98.

90. Richard Thomas, "The Bitch," (part one), *Tracks,* March 1992, 93, 95; and "The Bitch," (part two) *Tracks,* April 1992, 83-84.

91. Editorial, *Tracks,* July 1994, 3.

92. "Sutho's Backside," *Tracks,* October 1994, 147.

93. By the early 1990s, *Australia's Surfing Life* is Australia's biggest selling surfing magazine (at 38,000 copies per month), while *Tracks* trails behind in second place (at 32,500 copies per month). Source: *Press, Radio and TV Guide* (Sydney: Country Press), and *Margaret Gee's Australian Media Guide* (Melbourne: Information Australia-Margaret Gee Media, 1970-2001).

94. Such a radical change in layout required the editor to reassure his readers that, in essence, *Tracks* was still the same: "Inside is still packed with the same old *Tracks* larrikin humour, with the usual balls-to-the-wall shots from the best sessions that have been going down all over this wonderful planet, only now on this new slick paper they look 50 times better," editorial, *Tracks,* March 2000, 4.

95. See my article, "Some Tales of Two Mags: Sports Magazines as Glossy Reservoirs of Male Fantasies," *Journal of Australian Studies* 62 (1999): 64-75, for a detailed account of the male fantasies offered by *Tracks* in its postmodern phase.

96. "Symbolic annihilation" and "symbolic glorification" are phrases Jim McKay uses to describe how the sports media maintains hegemonic forms of masculinity, "Men, the Media, and Sporting Heroes." *XY: Men Sex, Politics* 6, no. 2 (1996): 16.

97. For example, Monty Webber, "What Tribe?" *Tracks,* January 1997, 66-71.

98. See, for example, the antidrug editorial in *Tracks,* January 1996, 3; and Sarge, "Drug Fucked or Dead," *Tracks,* December 1998, 128-29.

99. Alby Falzon, "Morning of the Earth 2000: Alby Falzon's Wake Up Call," with Brad Farmer, *Tracks,* October 1999, 88-91; and Monty Webber, "The Reverse Effect," *Tracks,* February 1997, 73.

100. Editorial, *Tracks,* July 1997, 3.

101. "Ballistic Surfing," *Tracks,* January 1995, 104.

102. Arthur Brittan, *Masculinity and Power* (Oxford: Blackwell, 1989), 187.

103. Frank, 227.

104. Frank, 235.

105. The editorial in *Tracks* March 1997 provides a classic statement of the postmodern Aussie surfer and surfing style: "slowly but surely a new hybrid has emerged: an animal, which, if need be, can pull out the tricks, but would rather belt the shit out of the lip than tenderfoot over and around it any day. Yes, the pig is back in the boys (at last) and they'll be grunting their way all over everything in sight this summer. Go sick, you monsters," 3.

106. Brian Pronger, *The Arena of Masculinity: Sports, Homosexuality, and the Meaning of Sex* (New York: St Martin's, 1990), 10.

107. *Tracks* October 1996 and *Tracks,* March 1995, respectively.

108. The film *Blackrock* was based on a play by Nick Enright. Interestingly, one of the first editors of *Tracks*, David Elfick, was the film's producer (*Blackrock,* dir. Steven Vidler, Palm Beach Pictures, 1996).

109. "X-Files," *Tracks* July 1996, 94.

110. Farmer, 91.

111. John L. Stewart gives a full account of how the commodification of sport helps to reproduce the modern world in "The Commodification of Sport," *Media, Audience, and Social Structure*, ed. Sandra J. Ball-Rokeach and Muriel G. Cantor (Newbury Park, Calif.: Sage, 1986), 174-88.

112. Juha Heikkela describes the trajectory of the professional athlete thus: "in a career ascending to international top-level, the athlete is moving from the spontaneous, self-regulated and communal activities of the backyard's sporting 'Gemeinschaft' to the 'Gesellschaft' of rationalized, standardized, specialized and global action-system sports markets," "Modernity, Morality, and the Logic of Competing," *International Review for the Sociology of Sport* 28, no. 4 (1993): 359. We can see this alienation expressed in the pro surfer's boredom with the routine of travel and competition, most clearly exemplified by the early (first) retirement of Mark Occhilupo.

113. The global surfing apparel industry has an estimated value of $5.5 billion dollars per year; see Jane-Anne Lee, "Riding the Globalization Wave," *Bulletin,* 5 May 1998, 81. Domestic sales of clothing in Australia were worth $230 million in 1993-94, compared to surfboard sales worth $38.8 million in the same year, in Arthur Konstad, "Riding a Wave of Success," *Australian Leisure Management* December 1998-January 1999, 41. Further evidence of surfing's big business orientation is the recent announcement that Billabong, an Australian surfwear manufacturer, is to be floated on the stock market. See Tony Grant-Taylor, "Billabong in the Take-Off Zone for Public Float," *Courier Mail,* 15 June 2000, 25-

26.

114. Teresa Ebert, "The Romance of Patriarchy: Ideology, Subjectivity, and Postmodern Feminist Cultural Theory," *Cultural Critique* 10 (1988): 21.

BIBLIOGRAPHY

Abrahams, Phil. "So You Think You're Tough," *Tracks,* December 1980, 13.

Bile, Brian. "Gourmet Chunder Guide," *Tracks,* January 1979, 42-43.

Booth, Douglas. "Surfing '60s: A Case Study in the History of Pleasure and Discipline," *Australian Historical Studies* 10, no. 3 (1994): 262-79.

Booth, Geoff. "Thoughts for the '80s . . . and Beyond," *Tracks,* August 1981, 29.

Brittan, Arthur. *Masculinity and Power.* Oxford: Blackwell, 1989.

Britto-Garcia, Luis. "Critiques of Modernity: Avant-Garde, Counterculture, Revolution," *South Atlantic Quarterly* 92, no. 3 (1993): 515-27.

Carey, Gabrielle, and Kathy Lette. *Puberty Blues*. Carlton, Victoria: McPhee Gribble, 1979.

Connell, R. W. *Masculinities.* St. Leonards: Allen and Unwin, 1995.

Denholm, Michael. *Small Press Publishing in Australia.* North Sydney: Second Back Row, 1979.

Dotson, Edisol. *Behold the Man: The Hype and Selling of Male Beauty in Media and Culture*. New York: Haworth, 1999.

Draper, Robert. *Rolling Stone Magazine: The Uncensored History.* New York: Doubleday, 1990.

Duncan, Margaret Carlisle. "Beyond Analyses of Sport Media Texts: An Argument of Formal Analyses of Institutional Structures," *Sociology of Sport Journal* 10, no. 4 (1993): 353-72.

Ebert, Theresa. "The Romance of Patriarchy: Ideology, Subjectivity, and Postmodern Feminist Cultural Theory," *Cultural Critique* 10 (1988): 19-57.

Falzon, Alby, with Brad Farmer. "Morning of the Earth 2000: Alby Falzon's Wake Up Call," *Tracks,* October 1999, 88-91.

Farmer, Ricky J. "Surfing: Motivations, Values and Culture," *Journal of Sport Behavior* 15, no. 3 (1992): 241-57.

Featherstone, Mike. *Consumer Culture and Postmodernism.* London: Sage, 1991.

Fitzclarence, Lindsey. *Sport and Leisure: Trends in Australia's Popular Culture*, ed. David Rowe and Geoff Lawrence. Sydney: Harcourt, Brace, Jovanovich, 1990.

Frank, Thomas. *The Conquest of Cool: Business Culture, Counterculture, and the Rise of Hip Consumerism*. Chicago: University of Chicago Press, 1997.

Freud, Sigmund. *Civilization and Its Discontents*, trans. Joan Riviere. London: Hogarth, 1957 (1930).

Hamilton, Hugh. "Aggression: In Search of World War III," *Tracks,* January 1979, 47.

Harvey, David. *The Condition of Postmodernity: An Enquiry into the Origins of Cultural Change.* Oxford: Basil Blackwell, 1989.

Hebdige, Dick. *Subculture: The Meaning of Style.* London: Methuen, 1979.

Heikkela, Juha. "Modernity, Morality, and the Logic of Competing," *International Review for the Sociology of Sport* 28, no. 4 (1993): 355-72.

Henderson, Margaret. "Some Tales of Two Mags: Sports Magazines as Glossy Reservoirs of Male Fantasies," *Journal of Australian Studies* 62 (1999): 64-75.

Horrocks, Roger. *Male Myths and Icons: Masculinity in Popular Culture* (Basingstoke: Macmillan, 1995), 55.

Irwin, John. "Surfing: The Natural History of an Urban Scene," *Urban Life and Culture* 2, no. 2 (1973): 131-60.

Jarratt, Phil. "Is Surfing Selling Out?" *Tracks,* April 1977, 11.

Kaplan, Gisela. *The Meagre Harvest: The Australian Women's Movement, 1950s-1990s.* St. Leonards: Allen and Unwin, 1996.

Kegg, R. J. "A Gay Excursion," *Tracks,* Jan. 1985, 21.

Lake, Marilyn. *Getting Equal: The History of Australian Feminism.* St. Leonards: Allen and Unwin, 1999.

Lee, Jane-Anne. "Riding the Globalization Wave," *Bulletin,* 5 May 1998.

Lenskyj, Helen Jefferson. "'Inside Sport' or 'On the Margins'?: Australian Women and the Sport Media," *International Review for the Sociology of Sport* 33, no. 1 (1998): 19-32.

McKay, Jim. *No Pain, No Gain? Sport and Australian Culture* (New York: Prentice Hall, 1991.

———. "Men, the Media and Sporting Heroes." *XY: Men Sex, Politics* 6, no. 2 (1996).

———, and Toby Miller. "From Old Boys to Men and Women of the Corporation: The Americanization and Commodification of Australian Sport," *Sociology of Sport Journal* 8, no. 1 (1991): 86-94.

Margaret Gee's Australian Media Guide. Melbourne: Information Australia-Margaret Gee Media, 1970-2001.

Pearson, Kent. *Surfing Subcultures of Australia and New Zealand.* St. Lucia: University of Queensland Press, 1979.

Pfeil, Fred. *White Guys: Studies in Postmodern Domination and Difference.* London: Verso, 1995.

Pronger, Brian. *The Arena of Masculinity: Sports, Homosexuality, and the Meaning of Sex.* New York: St. Martin's, 1990.

Riphool, A. P. "Shock Survey Shows Surfers Turning Gay!!!" *Tracks,* April 1991, 18.

Rutsky, R. L. "Surfing the Other: Ideology on the Beach," *Film Quarterly* 52, no. 4 (1999): 12-23.

Sabo, Donald, and Sue Curry Jansen. "Images of Men in Sport Media: The Social Reproduction of Gender Order," in *Men, Masculinity, and the Media*, ed. Steve Craig. Newbury Park: Sage, 1992, 169-84.

Safe, Mike. "Chairman of the Board," *Australian Magazine,* 18-19 April 1996, 27.

Steadman, Leanne. "From Gidget to Gonad Man: Surfers, Feminists, and Postmodernization," *Australian and New Zealand Journal of Sociology* 33, no. 1 (1997): 75-90.

Stephens, Julie. *Anti-Disciplinary Protest: Sixties Radicalism and Postmodernism.* Cambridge: Cambridge University Press, 1998.

Stewart, Bob. "Leisure and the Changing Patterns of Sport and Exercise," in *Sport and Leisure: Trends in Australian Popular Culture*, ed. David Rowe and Geoff Lawrence. Sydney: Harcourt, Brace, Jovanovich, 1990, 174-88.

Stewart, John L. "The Commodification of Sport," in *Media, Audience, and Social Structure*, ed. Sandra J. Ball-Rokeach and Muriel G. Cantor. Newbury Park, Calif.: Sage, 1986, 174-88.

Stratton, Jon. "Youth Subcultures and Their Cultural Contexts," *Australian and New Zealand Journal of Sociology* 21, no. 2 (1985), 194-218.

Thomas, Richard. "The Bitch," (part one), *Tracks,* March 1992, 93, 95.

———. "The Bitch," (part two), *Tracks,* April 1992, 83-84.

Webber, Monty. "The Reverse Effect," *Tracks,* February 1997, 73.

Willcox, Kirk. "The Act Remains the Same," *Tracks,* March 1983, 43.

———. Editorial, *Tracks,* March 1983, 3.

Willis, Ellen. "Getting a Lock on Rock," *Columbia Journalism Review* 29 (November/December 1990): 59-62.

Witzig, John. Editorial, *Tracks,* October 1970, 3.

Witzig, Paul. "Paul's Thing," *Tracks,* December 1970, 5.

Wren, Geoffrey. "Surfing: Subculture or Cultural Hype?" *Tracks,* March 1983, 42.

Young, Nat. "A New Era! McTavish and Young Discuss," *Surfing World* 8, no. 1 (1966): 23.

10
Female Adolescence and Its Discontents

Angela E. Hubler

A significant body of literature has recently been published on female adolescence, highlighting the crisis it constitutes for girls. The most influential of these texts are the American Association of University Women's *Shortchanging Girls, Shortchanging America*; Mary Pipher's *Reviving Ophelia: Saving the Selves of Adolescent Girls*; and the work of Carol Gilligan.[1] Because each of these works has garnered significant media, popular, and academic attention, it is important to give them credit for focusing attention on the difficulties experienced by adolescent girls. These works have defined the conversation about female adolescence, that is, the problems, their origins, and potential solutions. However, they have done so in a critically limited way because their common perspective is narrowly psychological. They focus on how gender is experienced by individuals. But they do not adequately analyze the economic, social, political, and historical factors that construct and institutionalize those gendered, individual experiences. Thus, while they offer short-term, therapeutic, individual remedies for the maladies experienced by adolescent girls, they do not adequately identify the source of these problems. Because they offer only a superficial understanding of the origin of the problems they address, they do not identify the collective and political transformations that would be necessary to eliminate them.

Ironically, a work of fiction by Chickasaw writer Linda Hogan, *Solar Storms*, offers a much more thoroughgoing analysis of the problems of female adolescence and suggests solutions much more adequate to them than the texts which explicitly set out to do so. Because Hogan's teenage, female protagonist is Native American, the problems that she experiences overlap with those described by the texts I identify above, though they are not identical to them. Yet, as I argue below, analyzing gender in relation to race as well as class is vitally important. Indeed, those most marginalized by white, male-dominated, capitalist society may have a privileged perspective from which to understand society as a totality. Their intensified experience of domination may yield a superior understanding of what is necessary to overcome it. In fact, I argue this is the power and usefulness of Hogan's novel. In it, she traces not only the individual experience of oppression but the social and historical totality responsible for it.

THE CONTEMPORARY DISCUSSION

Much of the recent discussion about female adolescence has been initiated by Carol Gilligan, who identifies a loss of voice as definitive of female adolescence, a thematic focus that reveals the continuity between her recent work on female adolescence and her earlier landmark *In a Different Voice*.[2] Valerie Hey credits *In a Different Voice* and the works which follow it with the "social-psychological 'discovery' of girls as moral agents."[3] In contrast to Lawrence Kohlberg, who had found that women scored lower than men on scales of moral development, Gilligan argued that women express moral concerns "in a different voice," one not of abstract rights and justice but of interrelationships and care. Subsequently, in a number of different texts, some coauthored with her students, Gilligan describes middle-school-aged girls as engaged in "authentic" relationships, unintimidated by conflict, and confident in "the strength of their voices and the depths of their knowing and the intensity of their desire for honest relationships."[4] At adolescence, however, girls are pressured to silence this voice and to relinquish authenticity in order to conform to an idealized image of femininity: "the model of the pure or perfectly good woman: the woman whom everyone will promote and value and want to be with"("Women's Psychological Development," 24). Gilligan sees this as a crisis point in female development, equivalent in significance to the Oedipal complex in boys: "this is the time when girls' desire for relationships and for knowledge comes up against the wall of Western culture and a resistance breaks out which is, I will claim, potentially of great human value."[5] To foster this resistance, Gilligan suggests that girls should keep journals, "to amplify their voices for themselves."[6] She argues that if girls' "insistence on knowing what one knows and a willingness to be outspoken" can be preserved through the crisis of adolescence they can, "by remaining political, work to bring a new order of living into the world" ("Joining the Resistance," 502, 533). Gilligan doesn't explicitly detail what that "new order" of living would be; however, she refers both to Aristophanes' *Lysistrata* (411 B.C.), and Woolf's *Three Guineas* (1938), texts which Gilligan says ask whether there "is . . . a way in which women can help men prevent rather than wage what has historically been the male act of war" ("Joining the Resistance," 508). Thus, Gilligan posits a transhistorical, peaceful, and nurturant femininity by which Western society might be rescued from violent masculinity.

Gilligan's work with adolescent girls has been widely reviewed and reported upon in popular and academic venues. It was, for example, the subject of a *New York Times Magazine* article in 1990. As the result of such publicity, perhaps, her work seems even to have influenced fiction written for adolescent girls. The editor of the best-selling Dear America series books, for example, says that "A large mission . . . of the Dear America series as a whole, is to give voice to those who historically were denied it—namely girls be they white, Native American, African American, etc."[7] Moreover, the loss of female voice at adolescence is a central theme in several of the titles in the series. To illustrate the influence of Gilligan's work in another arena, subscribers to WMST-L, the largest, international list-serve for faculty and administrators in Women's Studies, frequently recommend *Meeting at the Crossroads*, coauthored by Gilligan with Lyn Brown, and *Between Voice and Silence: Women and Girls, Race and Relationships*, coauthored with Jill Taylor and Amy Sullivan, for introductory Women's Studies classes, and for courses on "Growing up Female." (Pipher's *Reviving Ophelia* is also frequently recommended for both such courses on the same discussion list.)

Soon after Gilligan's early publications on female adolescence, in 1991, the American Association of University Women published the results of a study of "three thousand children between grades four and ten."[8] The most widely reported finding in that study concerned self-esteem: while boys' self-esteem is higher than that of girls even in elementary school, the gap increases as they get older. While in elementary school, 67 percent of boys, as compared to 60 percent of girls, say they are "happy the way I am": by high school, 46 percent of boys, and 29 percent of girls feel this way (AAUW, Graph A).[9] The study interprets the significance of these findings in relation to career aspirations: "Adolescence, the period of transition from childhood to adulthood, is a critical time for the development of self-identity. It is one of the stages of a person's life where changes in biology and psychology are dramatic. It is a critical moment of a person's life to make a broad set of choices and decisions. . . . The higher self-esteem of young men translates into bigger career dreams" (2, 8). Thus, feelings about the self are understood to determine the future economic decisions and status of boys and girls.

Pipher's work has been less controversial than that of Gilligan or the AAUW, but has generated as much media attention. *Reviving Ophelia* was number one on the *New York Times* best-seller list. By 1996, 500,000 copies of the book were in print, and it had been featured in *Time*, *Newsweek*, *USA Today*, and Hillary Clinton's syndicated newspaper column.[10] More recently, a video version of the book has been released. The book also inspired the publication of *Ophelia Speaks*, a book of first-person narratives by adolescent girls edited by seventeen-year-old Sara Shandler.

Pipher, a clinical psychologist, understands the problems of the girls she sees in her private practice not as originating in individual or family pathology but as symptomatic of a sick culture that teaches girls that their value lies in their appearance and sexuality, insofar as it can please men, rather than in their "autonomous," "authentic selves."[11] Pipher sees the consequences of the "girl-poisoning," "junk" culture in girls who are brought in to see her because of eating disorders, depression, multiple unplanned pregnancies, substance abuse, self-mutilation, suicide attempts, running away, and so on (12, 13). Pipher engages in a kind of consciousness-raising with these girls, teaching them to evaluate critically the media's representation of women, and to develop sources of self-esteem and meaning in their lives other than their looks. She encourages them to keep journals, to keep track of sexist remarks, to talk to friends or parents about their pain, to get involved in volunteer work, and to engage in other activities designed to get them to "understand the effects of the culture on their lives. . . . They learn that they have conscious choices to make and ultimate responsibility for those choices" (44).

Pipher concludes the book with a discussion of cultural changes that would enable adolescent girls to manifest their "true selves" (22). She suggests the formation of school groups "organized around talents, interests and needs, rather than cliques" (290). Schools should also formulate sexual and physical harassment policies and awareness training in "lookism, racism and sexism" (290). Such structures could provide the framework and training for better decision making about sexuality and drug and alcohol use. She calls for a redefinition of manhood, especially in terms of the male relationship to violence, "places for kids to go," "wholesome rituals for coming of age," and a national debate on media violence and sex (290-91).

Pipher follows her case studies of girls she saw in therapy with the stories of five strong girls. She remarks, "It's not accidental that two of the young women are black, one is Hispanic and three are poor. Properly faced, adversity builds character" (281). But since Pipher has not discussed the problems of poor or minority girls throughout the text, her use of these concluding case studies is problematic. With the exception of two American Indian girls (one of whom had been adopted by a middle-class, white family), she does not deal with the particular challenges faced by girls of minority race or those who live in poverty. The structural character of racism and poverty escapes notice: "adversity" serves as a character-building challenge in Pipher's use of these girls to support the aphorism "when life gives you lemons, make lemonade." Had Pipher followed the suggestion of bell hooks, that theorists and activists move the lives of people of color "from margin to center," rather than offering these case studies as inspirational stories of individual fortitude, she would have written a very different book. If Pipher had considered race and class in relation to gender, it would have been clear that her suggestions—making the right choices, taking responsibility, and facing hardship with the right attitude—cannot address the problems of many adolescent girls.

Pipher does not recognize this, however, because she does not closely analyze the lives of those poor and minority girls most damaged by social hierarchy. Moreover, although she departs from much psychological literature in that she argues that girls' problems result not from dysfunctional families but from a dysfunctional culture, as with the discipline of psychology in general, her focus remains on individuals and on providing them with strategies for dealing with this culture. As her case studies indicate, these coping strategies are desperately needed and she provides an invaluable service to girls and their parents in suggesting them. However, while they may provide relief for individuals, these strategies don't address the source of the problems from which girls suffer. As with Gilligan's insistence that girls speak in their own voices, the changes that Pipher calls for are important and necessary, but they cannot eliminate the problems that she discusses.

Neither Gilligan nor Pipher frames her discussion of adolescent girls in terms of the overall changes necessary for full female equality within society. For example, in her video encapsulation of *Reviving Ophelia*, Pipher does not explain the violence suffered by the girls she treats in terms of the male domination of society. She does not talk about the wage gap between men and women, or the fact that women still make up only 12 percent of Congress. When she calls for cultural change she does not identify feminism as engaged in an ongoing project of such change. Tellingly, Pipher does not call for social, but "cultural" change, a choice of words that implies that overall, structural changes are either unnecessary or impractical (Pipher, 293). Gilligan does suggest the need for political resistance, which she distinguishes from psychological resistance. Psychological resistance, says Gilligan, is "a reluctance to know what one knows and a fear that such knowledge, if spoken, will endanger relationships and threaten survival" ("Joining the Resistance," 502). In contrast to this she offers an example of political resistance in the following situation: Anna "voices conflict in relationship" when she goes shopping for clothes with her mother, and "honestly" expresses "her opinion" (513). While the female self-expression that Gilligan wants to encourage is valuable, it does not automatically translate into collective, political activity designed to alter the economic and political organization of society.

Yet, economic and political change is necessary to eliminate the kinds of problems discussed by these writers. The mass media's sexual objectification of girls and women discussed by Pipher, for example, is inextricably linked to the continuing economic subordination of women to men, and to the gendered separation of the productive and reproductive spheres of life. Women continue to be primarily responsible for child rearing and housework because U.S. culture is not organized such that women and men can easily combine work and family. This reality accounts for the male-identification and sexualization of adolescent girls, and the continuing conflict between femininity and achievement. Pipher and Gilligan fail to point out that the ideologies they challenge stem from these material realities and to call for major economic reforms, along the lines of those implemented in Western social democracies, that would begin to address them. For example, paid parental leave, universal health insurance, subsidized child care, a shortened work week, and four to six weeks paid vacation yearly, at the least, would provide relief from some of the conditions most damaging to women and girls. The analyses of Gilligan, Pipher, and the AAUW, because they do not contextualize the problems they discuss within this broad, social context, are, finally, insufficiently political.

Their analyses locate the origin of the problems experienced by adolescent girls in the process of subject formation rather than in social stratification. While they have, admirably, raised awareness about many critical problems, they suggest that the problem is girls and the way they feel about themselves rather than institutional sexism. The AAUW, for example, articulates the significance of their finding of lower self-esteem in girls in terms of their future careers. But do the lower career aspirations of girls really derive from the way they feel about themselves? Couldn't the differing career dreams of girls and boys originate instead in a realistic recognition of social hierarchy? A sociological perspective insists that rather than internal qualities like self-esteem, external factors shape behavior: "achievement ambitions . . . are, directly related to one's chances of succeeding."[12]

According to sociologist R. W. Connell, the individualistic focus of such an approach to gender results in an insufficient attention to social structures as a whole. As stated by Connell and his coauthors: "Talking about gender relations in terms of roles, internalized expectations, attitudes and traits directs attention away from larger structures and focuses explanations of inequality on what is going on inside the heads of the subordinated group. It is a classic case of blaming the victim."[13] M. Brinton Lykes makes a similar point specifically about Gilligan (and Jean Baker Miller):

> by focusing on interpersonal relations, they fail to clarify how structural forces of gender, race, ethnicity, class, and culture constrain and influence the development of one's sense of self. Thus the role of power inequities in the development of a psychological sense of self and identity is ignored.[14]

Gilligan's work exhibits just such an inadequate understanding of the relationship between the individual and society, tellingly revealed by her ahistorical conceptions of masculinity and femininity. Ideas about gender are not self-sufficient, self-perpetuating images, but ideological constructs developed within divisions of power structuring society as a whole.

Herein lies the problem with the analyses of the AAUW, Pipher, and Gilligan—and perhaps, the secret of their success. In simplifying, psychologizing, and individualizing the effects of capitalist patriarchy on adolescent girls, these texts present a palatable and manageable version of the "crisis of female adolescence" to parents, teachers, academics, and even to the critics and authors of fiction for adolescent girls. Clearly, changes in the organization of work, health care, and leisure time are much more thoroughgoing than the changes called for by the AAUW, Gilligan, or Pipher. Consequently, the magnitude of the social transformation needed to significantly alter the experience of female adolescence may be one factor accounting for its absence in most discussions of its problems. However, the character of such changes must also be considered as a factor. Because these changes are structural in character and would consequently require major concessions from government and business (and so would likely be labeled as communistic, socialistic, or un-American) they are much less likely to be embraced by a wide spectrum of the population than the changes suggested by these psychologically oriented texts that fit comfortably with the ideology of American individualism.

In part, the limitations of these texts derive from their disciplinary origin. Psychology, as a discipline, because it is founded upon the analysis of the individual, is poorly equipped to analyze problems that manifest themselves in individuals but whose origins lie in the totality of social relations. Social totality is, however, susceptible to analysis and representation—as classically demonstrated in the novel. The novel, as a form, is able to represent and connect subjectivity and the social. As Georg Lukacs argues, the novel "not only expresses what today may be seen upon the surface of life and is consciously known, but can delve into the real origins both of the oppression and degeneration and of the path to liberation. It creates *models* which *accelerate* the consciousness and resoluteness of the longing for liberation."[15]

SOLAR STORMS

The novelistic treatment of female adolescence in Linda Hogan's *Solar Storms* does just this, narrating the struggles of its American Indian adolescent female protagonist as the result of the historical and social catastrophe largely constitutive of modernity. The novel begins with seventeen-year-old Angela Jensen's reunion with her paternal great-grandmother, Agnes. Angela has grown up in foster homes, after being removed from the custody of her mother, Hannah Wing, because of her abuse. Angela is scarred, physically and emotionally, by the abuse and displays many of the self-destructive symptoms described by Pipher. Angela says of herself:

> I was the girl who ran away, the girl who never cried, the girl who was strong enough to tattoo her own arm and hand. An ink-blue cross on one knuckle, the initials of Lonnie Faro on my upper left arm. A cross on my thigh. And no one had ever wanted me for good.
>
> In my life this far, there had been two places, two things that shaped and moved me. . . . They were like rooms I inhabited. . . . One, the darkest, was a room of fear, a fear of everything—silence, closeness, motionlessness and how it made me think and feel. . . . And there was the fire red room of anger I inhabited permanently.[16]

After reestablishing contact with Agnes, her grandfather's wife, Bush, and her great-great-grandmother, Dora Rouge, Angela begins a process of healing and rebirth. She learns, from her grandmothers' stories, that her mother was mentally ill: "the old people said it was soul loss, an old sickness" (98). And, she learns that although her grandmothers tried to protect her from her mother, Angela was taken from them when she was five years old and returned to Hannah by "the county" and then lost to her grandmothers in foster care. In an interview, Hogan explains how common is the removal of Indian children from their families and homes, and says, "I began to think that it was really important to write the story of what happens to children when they go home and try to search out their families, or when they are taken away from family and brought up in another culture."[17] In depicting Angela's healing return to Native American traditions, Hogan addresses a theme common in Native American literature. Angela says, "It was an old world in which I began to bloom. Their stories called me home" (48).

But Angela is not cured just by returning to find that her family, though not her mother, had always loved her and welcomes her return, for her personal healing leaves the conditions that wounded her unchanged: individual, psychological healing is incomplete. Indeed, Angela looks around her and sees the magnitude of the malady that had crippled her:

> The young children drank alcohol and sniffed glue and paint. They staggered about and lay down on the streets. Some of them had children of their own, infants who were left untouched, untended by their child-parents. Sometimes they were given beer when they cried. It was the only medicine left for all that pain. Even the healing plants had been destroyed. Those without alcohol were even worse off, and the people wept without end, and tried to cut and burn their own bodies. The older people tied their hands with rope and held them tight hoping the desire to die would pass. . . . The devastation and ruin that had fallen over the land fell over the people, too. Most were too broken to fight . . . and that perhaps had been the intention all along. (226)

Angela understands the common origin of the cultural disintegration she witnesses and her own abuse in the stories told her by her grandmothers and other old people. They tell Angela that her mother too had been scarred and abused by her mother, Loretta. Agnes explains, "What happened to you started long ago. It began around the time of the killing of the wolves. When people were starving. There wasn't a single beaver that year. They'd killed them all. And they'd just logged the last of the pine forests" (37). Thus, the violence that wounded Angela originated in the incursions of whites into the lands of the Cree and Inuit peoples around the Hudson Bay. Loretta, Hannah's mother, Agnes says, was from

> the Elk Islanders, the people who became so hungry they ate the poisoned carcasses of deer that the settlers left out for the wolves. . . . The curse on that poor

> girl's life came from watching the desperate people of her tribe die . . . after that, when she was still a girl, she'd been taken and used by men who fed her and beat her and forced her. That was how one day she became the one who hurt others. It was passed down. (38-39)

Hogan also connects the personal and the political in dealing with appearance, a topic also extensively treated by Pipher. Angela's face has been severely scarred by her mother, and she says that "my ugliness, as I called it, had ruled my life. My need for love had been so great I would offer myself to any boy or man who would take me" (54). When she goes to live with Bush, however, she finds there are no mirrors in her house "because as Bush said, mirrors had cost us our lives" (69). With this, Bush refers to the fur trade, fueled by the fashion for beaver hats, that had, by the turn of the seventeenth century, already disrupted traditional Native American "farming, hunting, gathering" in what is now the northeastern United States and southeastern part of Canada.[18] One of the characters in the novel, Husk, explains that in trapping for fur rather than for meat, the Indians had broken a contract with animals: "There had once been a covenant between animals and men. . . . They would care for one another. . . . This pact . . . had been broken, forced by need and hunger" (35).

Ultimately, Angela and her grandmothers realize that, in order to stop the historical cycle of poverty, alcoholism, abuse, and family disintegration that nearly destroyed Angela, they must resist colonization and the loss of the self-determination of native people. They do so by protesting the building of a major hydroelectric project, modeled on the James Bay project, which would have "dammed and diverted five rivers that flow into the Hudson Bay."[19] The project would have flooded more than 2,000 square miles in northern Quebec, threatening the land and livelihood of the Cree Indians.

Dora Rouge, Angela's great-great-grandmother, believes that only with such resistance can "conquered people get back their lives. . . . She and others knew the protests against the dams and river diversions was their only hope. Those who protested were the ones who could still believe they might survive as a people" (226). This belief reflects Hogan's conviction, stated in an interview, that "Once people are victims, they have to struggle hard to politicize themselves and to be able to break the cycle, to be able somehow . . . to empower themselves once again, to get back their health and their wholeness."[20]

The process of politicization depicted in *Solar Storms* is rooted in an analysis of oppression enabled by a knowledge of history. The stories told to Angela by the old people in the novel, like the novel itself, draw a cognitive map, a representation of the relationship between subjectivity and its structural determinants—between appearance and essence—that is not available in their "immediate, lived experience and . . . often not even conceptualizable for most people."[21] This cognitive map of social totality makes it clear that without a structural transformation of society, liberation for girls, especially those oppressed not only upon the basis of their sex, but also on that of their race and class, is not possible. The interventions suggested by Gilligan, Pipher, and the AAUW might enable girls privileged by virtue of their race and class to transcend social oppression as individuals. For example, legislation banning sex-based discrimination, like Title IX, which made discrimination based on sex in education illegal, enables some girls to compete equally with boys. Yet, as Orenstein reports, "socioeconomic status remains the best predictor of educational outcome."[22] Thus, Joanna Brenner argues that feminism must go beyond a gender-only approach, focused on eliminating discrimination, to embrace new forms of collective challenge to "corporate capital's political and economic power."[23] So, while the protests against the dam in *Solar Storms* may seem only peripherally connected to the issues confronting adolescent girls, Hogan shows the structural connections between them. Her socially and historically complex narrative goes beyond the superficial, individually focused analyses that have become so popular through the work of Gilligan, the AAUW, and Pipher to show readers the kind of collective struggle necessary for feminism today.

I am very grateful to Tim Dayton, Carol Franko, Suzanne Franks, and Ron Strickland for reading and commenting on earlier drafts of this manuscript.

NOTES

1. Additional, particularly useful, texts include those by Orenstein, Brumberg, and Sidel.

2. This book has been both enormously influential and very controversial. Many of the criticisms of the work and Gilligan's reply are articulated in a valuable, early discussion of it: Linda K. Kerber, Catherine G. Greeno and Eleanor E. Maccoby, Zella Luria, Carol B. Stack, and Carol Gilligan "On *In a Different Voice:* An Interdisciplinary Forum," *Signs* 11, no. 2 (1985): 304-333.

3. Valerie Hey, *The Company She Keeps* (Buckingham: Open University Press, 1997), 10.

4. Lyn Mikel Brown and Carol Gilligan, *Meeting at the Crossroads: Women's Psychology and Girls' Development* (Cambridge, Mass.: Harvard University Press, 1992), 43; Carol Gilligan, "Women's Psychological Development: Implications for Psychotherapy, *Women and Therapy* 11, nos. 3-4 (1991): 15.

5. Carol Gilligan, "Joining the Resistance: Psychology, Politics, Girls, and Women," *Michigan Quarterly Review* 19, no. 4 (1990): 502.

6. Francine Prose, "Confident at 11, Confused at 16," *New York Times,* 7 January 1990, sec. 6, 22, LEXIS-NEXIS Academic Universe.

7. Quoted in John Mason, "Dear America—The Publisher's Response," http://www.scils.rutgers.edu/childlit/apr99/0217.html (23 April 1999).

8. American Association of University Women, *Shortchanging Girls, Shortchanging*

America, 1991, ERIC, ED 340657. Interestingly, one of the individuals thanked in the AAUW report for helping to develop the questionnaire and to interpret the poll data is Dr. Nancy Goldberger, a psychologist and coauthor of *Women's Ways of Knowing: The Development of Self, Voice, and Mind.* Goldberger and her coauthors dedicate their book to Gilligan.

9. Of course, the fact that the self-esteem of *both* boys and girls drops dramatically is, or should be, of concern. However, the reasons for the greater decrease in girls should be investigated.

10. Daisy Maryles, "Happy Birthday, Ophelia!" *Publishers Weekly*, 15 April 1996, 24.

11. Mary Pipher, *Reviving Ophelia* (New York: Ballantine, 1994), 21-22.

12. Carol Tavris and Carole Wade, *The Longest War: Sex Differences in Perspective* (San Diego: Harcourt, Brace, Jovanovich, 1984), 256.

13. S. Kessler, D. J. Ashenden, R. W. Connell, and G. W. Dowsett, "Gender Relations in Secondary Schooling," *Sociology of Education* (1985): 35.

14. M. Brinton Lykes, "Whose Meeting at Which Crossroads? A Response to Brown and Gilligan," *Feminism and Psychology* 4, no. 3 (1994): 346. Lykes's article appeared as a part of a special feature in volume four of *Feminism and Psychology* consisting of responses to an article by Carol Gilligan and Lyn Mikel Brown published in volume three of the journal. (The article is essentially the first chapter of their book, *Meeting at the Crossroads*.) Gilligan, Brown, and another of Gilligan's coauthors, Annie Rogers, also reply to criticisms raised in the articles.

15. Georg Lukacs, *The Historical Novel*, trans. Hannah Mitchell and Stanley Mitchell (Boston: Beacon Press, 1963), 340.

16. Linda Hogan, *Solar Storms* (New York: Scribner, 1995), 26-27.

17. Interview. *Conversations with American Novelists: The Best Interviews from the Missouri Review and the American Prose Library*, ed. Kay Bonetti et al. (Columbia: University of Missouri Press, 1997), 198.

18. David Thomas et al. *The Native American: An Illustrated History* (Atlanta: Turner Publishing, 1993), 163.

19. Amy Wilson, "Victory over Hydro-Quebec at James Bay," *The Planet,* December/January 1995, http://www.mv.com/dan/nhsc/planet/planet1294/ftr-canada.html.

20. Interview with Laura Coltelli. *Winged Words: American Indian Writers Speak* (Lincoln: University of Nebraska Press, 1990), 81.

21. Fredric Jameson, "Cognitive Mapping," in *Marxism and the Interpretation of Culture* ed. Cary Nelson and Lawrence Grossberg (Urbana: University of Illinois Press, 1988), 349.

22. Peggy Orenstein, *Schoolgirls: Young Women, Self-Esteem, and the Confidence Gap* (New York: Doubleday, 1994), 301.

23. Joanna Brenner, *Women and the Politics of Class* (New York: Monthly Review Press), 6.

BIBLIOGRAPHY

American Association of University Women. *Shortchanging Girls, Shortchanging America.* 1991.

Brenner, Joanna. *Women and the Politics of Class*. New York: Monthly Review Press, 2000.

Brown, Lyn Mikel, and Carol Gilligan. *Meeting at the Crossroads: Women's Psychology and Girls' Development*. Cambridge, Massachusetts: Harvard University Press, 1992.
Brumberg, Joan Jacobs. *The Body Project: An Intimate History of American Girls*. New York: Vintage Books, 1997.
Gilligan, Carol. "Joining the Resistance: Psychology, Politics, Girls, and Women." *Michigan Quarterly Review* 19, no. 4 (1990): 501-36.
———. *In a Different Voice*. Cambridge, Mass.: Harvard University Press, 1982.
———. "Women's Psychological Development: Implications for Psychotherapy." *Women and Therapy* 11, no. 3-4 (1991): 5-27.
Hey, Valerie. *The Company She Keeps*. Buckingham, UK: Open University Press, 1997.
Hogan, Linda. Interview with Laura Coltelli. *Winged Words: American Indian Writers Speak*. Lincoln: University of Nebraska Press, 1990.
———. Interview. *Conversations with American Novelists: The Best Interviews from the Missouri Review and the American Audio Prose Library*. Ed. Kay Bonetti et al. Columbia: University of Missouri Press, 1997.
———. *Solar Storms*. New York: Scribner, 1995.
hooks, bell. *Feminist Theory: From Margin to Center*. Boston: South End Press, 1984.
Jameson, Fredric. "Cognitive Mapping." In *Marxism and the Interpretation of Culture*. Ed. Cary Nelson and Lawrence Grossberg. Urbana: University of Illinois Press, 1988, 347-357.
Kerber, Linda K., Catherine G. Greeno and Eleanor E. Maccoby, Zella Luria, Carol B. Stack, and Carol Gilligan. "On *In a Different Voice*: An Interdisciplinary Forum." *Signs* 11, no. 2 (1985): 304-33.
Kessler, S., D. J. Ashenden, R. W. Connell, and G. W. Dowsett. "Gender Relations in Secondary Schooling." *Sociology of Education* 58 (1985): 34-48.
Lykes, M. Brinton. "Whose Meeting at Which Crossroads? A Response to Brown and Gilligan." *Feminism and Psychology* 4, no. 3 (1994): 345-49.
Lukacs, George. *The Historical Novel*. Translated by Hannah and Stanley Mitchell. Boston: Beacon Press, 1963.
Maryles, Daisy. "Happy Birthday, Ophelia!" *Publisher's Weekly* 15 April 1996, 24. Online. Infotrac/Expanded Academic ASAP.
Mason, John. "Dear America—The Publisher's Response." Online posting. 23 April 1999. Child-lit., http://www.scils.rutgers.edu/childlit/april99/0217.html (26 April 1999).
Orenstein, Peggy. *Schoolgirls: Young Women, Self-Esteem, and the Confidence Gap*. New York: Doubleday, 1994.
Pipher, Mary. *Reviving Ophelia*. New York: Ballantine, 1994.
Prose, Francine. "Confident at 11, Confused at 16." *New York Times*, 7 January 1990, sect. 6, 22.
Sidel, Ruth. *On Her Own: Growing Up in the Shadow of the American Dream*. New York: Penguin, 1990.
Tavris, Carol, and Carole Wade. *The Longest War: Sex Differences in Perspective*. San Diego: Harcourt, Brace, Jovanovich, 1984.
Thomas, David, et al. *The Native American: An Illustrated History*. Atlanta: Turner Publishing, 1993.
Wilson, Amy. "Victory over Hydro-Quebec at James Bay." *The Planet*. December/January 1995, http://www.mv.com/dan/nhsc/planet/planet1294/ftr-canada.html.

11
The Mis/Education of Righteous Babes: Popular Culture and Third-Wave Feminism

Jennifer Drake

Growing up in the 1970s, during feminism's second wave, I took many of the movement's accomplishments for granted even as I benefitted from the opportunities opening up to girls and women. And like many young women basking in the warm sun of entitlement, I thought feminism had done its job and could go away, until in my late teens I decided that I needed feminism's powers and pleasures, its critical and creative and cacaphonous work, how it helped me to historicize my own sense of power and possibility, as well as to name the limits of that power and to narrate the silences shaping my family, my education, and my neighborhoods. For those of us who came to feminism after 1980, however, our introduction to feminist thought and action would be as strongly shaped by the critiques of the movement by women of color as it would be shaped by this kind of "aha" experience. Reading Elizabeth Cady Stanton, Margaret Sanger, Betty Friedan, Gloria Steinem, Adrienne Rich, and Luce Irigaray alongside Gloria Anzaldua's and Cherrie Moraga's *This Bridge Called My Back: Writings by Radical Women of Color*, Barbara Smith's *Home Girls: A Black Feminist Anthology*, and Alice Walker's *In Search of Our Mother's Gardens*, we understood that the personal was political even as we learned always to ask "which personal?" and "whose political?" In the sometimes contentious relationships between feminist texts and perspectives, and within the writing of U.S. third world feminists in particular, we found "languages and images that account(ed) for multiplicity and difference, that negotiate(d) contradiction in affirmative ways, and that (gave) voice to a politics of hybridity and coalition."[1] To many of us, these nuanced models of self and community made sense, looked like the complexities of real life, articulated why we could taste possibility and limitation, hope and fear, all at the same time.

Certainly backlash has also had a hand in shaping feminism's third wave. It's been almost a decade since Susan Faludi's book of that title appeared, and a little longer since the term "political correctness," once an in-joke among lefties, was appropriated to bludgeon anyone who attempts to speak critically and creatively about the various "isms" that shape our individual and collective lives. If anything, backlash grew more vitriolic during the 1990s, fueling welfare reform debates, dismantling affirmative action programs, threatening our right to safe and legal abortion, and contributing to the rise in racist and homophobic hate crimes. Third-wave journalist Farai Chideya describes the effects of backlash like this:

> The individuals in my generation—the Backlash Babies—find it difficult to stand up for what we believe in, because if we do, we are immediately branded angry, irrational, anti-free-speech and un-American. We kids of the Backlash, who are not just female and non-white but from across the spectrum of identity, must be very careful how we assert ourselves. The slightest indication that we care passionately about anything will be used against us. . . . [But] I *am* angry, *we*—the Backlash babies labeled irrational for merely wanting honest debate about (equality)—are angry. In a world where all the talk about race and gender has become doublespeak, the keepers of the status quo assume the guise of martyrs while those who fight the status quo fight with their hands tied behind their backs.[2]

Negotiating these kinds of contradictions, already contradictory ourselves, living lives marked by multicultural exchange and multicultural conflict, lives that combine male-identification and female-identification, the desire for middle-class status and the reality of staggering debt, lives shaped by our participation in and critiques of competitive individualism and a voracious consumer culture, we mistrust labels while sometimes embracing them strategically. We make homes as we go, or we bring change home to rest for a while, even though we know that home is not necessarily a safe space. We try to keep our hands untied long enough to fight the good fight, and we use a variety of trickster tactics to slip the knots.

There's a postcard by third-wave artist Stella Mars that proclaims "Redefine feminism so it includes you," and that's what this third-wave feminist generation is up to. Orthodoxy is out, if it was ever in. It is no coincidence, then, that third-wave feminists, despite and because of our differences, seem to agree that contradiction, as well as multiplicity and coalition, define third-wave feminist desires and strategies. The wave metaphor captures this ethos. It emphasizes continuities within feminist thought and action even as it acknowledges differences within the feminist movement. If there's anything that we've learned over the past 150 years or so, it's that the feminist movement has always been informed by specific struggles and circumstances, and this is where third-wavers site their hopes. Often focusing on the self and the community—in other words, the local—as places where change might actually take root, third-wave feminists both dialogue with feminism's grassroots traditions and resist feminism understood as a master narrative. Remember, we never had the luxury of believing that a 1960s style movement could be sustained , but add up all the work we do all over the country and see if you don't see movement being made.

On the road towards individual and collective redefinitions of feminism, third-wave women and men talk a lot about pleasure. Could be because we're young, or because we're such well-trained consumers, or because we're into some kind of playful postmodern aesthetic, or because we watched too much TV growing up, but I can't dismiss this, it's such a hunger and a joy in third-wave talk and work. Clearly, the pleasure-seeking impulse makes its unruly way through this generation's personal and political play with sex and sexuality, practices particularly informed by the intersections between third-wave feminism and queer culture and politics, but the pleasure-seeking impulse also consistently informs third-wave claims to feminism itself. In an essay about the Rodeo Caldonia High-Fidelity Performance Theater, a third-wave Black feminist/womanist performance group, artist and cultural critic Lisa Jones makes this clear:

> We are smart-ass girls with a sense of entitlement, who avail ourselves of the goods of two continents, delight in our sexual bravura, and live womanism as pleasure, not academic mandate. . . . We didn't come together around a rigid ideology or fixed notions of black identity. We came simply to break bread and share our yearnings. . . . Outside of debates on employment rights, abortion, child care, and whether feminism serves women of color—and the other big politics of the movement—what has kept me interested in feminism and *identifying* is the pleasure.[3]

Yearning shows up too, sister to pleasure, cousin to entitlement. As bell hooks writes, "All too often our political desire for change is seen as separate from longings and passions that consume lots of time and energy in daily life. . . . [But] surely our desire for radical social change is intimately linked with the desire to experience pleasure, erotic fulfillment, and a host of other passions."[4] Feminism's third wave draws upon this kind of faith, in and of the everyday, unruly and full of possibility, a faith descended from Audre Lorde's formulations of the erotic and creative anger.[5]

However, in the most conservative and most visible versions of third-wave feminism, represented by Naomi Wolf, Katie Roiphe, and Rene Denfeld, authors of, respectively, *Fire with Fire: The New Female Power and How to Use It*; *The Morning After: Sex, Fear, and Feminism*; and *The New Victorians: A Young Woman's Challenge to the Old Feminist Order*, the strong kinship between passion and social change is exploited, the link between them broken, so that only a self-indulgent pleasure is left. But these versions of third-wave feminism, variously called "power feminism," "capitalist feminism" and "do-me feminism," have strong appeal to third-wave women and men as well as to an eclectic cross section of the general public. As third-wave writer Danzy Senna explains in "To Be Real":

> Glamorous young women are congratulated at having outdone their mothers, on having won women's liberation without breaking a nail. And unavoidably I feel a certain identification with this "new feminism." . . . It is a feminism no longer on the defensive, with a fun, playful aesthetic that acknowledges the erotic and narcissistic pleasure women receive from beautifying themselves, a pleasure not to be denied.[6]

In this scenario, "power feminists" are sexy feminists, and "power feminists" have won the battle of the sexes by embracing strategies their bad feminist foremothers refused: don't beat 'em, join 'em! You can be one of the guys and a pretty girl too! Therefore, "power feminists" get to be the girls with the most cake, while all the rest of us are "victim feminists," old or just old before our time, always ready to kill the fun by making some irritating point about how oppression still exists. But as Senna observes in her critique of "power feminism," "[T]he power feminists are not necessarily the same women who were locked out of the power structure in the first place. . . . Feminism isn't necessarily on the side of the dispossessed. . . . [W]ithout the recognition of power in all its different forms, and of the unexpected places power can come from, we are only fooling ourselves."[7] So, in sisterhood with Senna, let me kill the fun: Just because things have changed for some of us, doesn't mean they've changed. Say "token." Say "glass ceiling." Say "look outside your life, to where the neighborhood changes." If I say, "Don't be stupid enough to believe that you earned your success all by yourself" and "Success is not always what it seems," will I be starting a catfight?

Within the dominant culture, then, "power feminism" has been privileged as the "new" feminism because it shores up competitive individualism, meritocracy, consumerism, and catfighting, its motto being "work, buy, and/or claw your way to the top." And as third-wave feminist theorist Catherine Orr argues, these privileged versions of feminism refuse to navigate contradiction, like other third-wave feminisms; rather, "these authors deny that feminism necessarily and inevitably holds contradictions. They imagine there is some pure outside where women can stand free of both gendered oppression and other forms of exploitation."[8] To make their feminist visions work, these writers deny the differences among women, making that old mistake of assuming that the Euro-American middle-class college-educated woman can stand in for all women. But "power feminism" has also attracted young women and men, not all of whom are Euro-American, middle-class, and college-educated, because "power feminism" offers success stories rather than victim or survival narratives. It is precisely because so many young people continue to feel simultaneously disempowered and hopeful in their personal and political lives that they resist what they perceive to be victim-talk. They want solutions and new worlds, not more diagnosis and analysis of the same old depressing problems.

To feed this hunger, and to counter the conservative feminism of daddy's good daughters, third-wavers must provide models for living feminism that also clarify the connections between different forms of yearning, including the yearning to live in a more just world. Further, these alternative feminisms need to be disseminated in the mass media, where this "sisterly" drama is already playing out and where we third-wavers are used to finding and making and critiquing our cultural histories. It's no mistake, then, that many third-wave feminists bring their emphases on self-empowerment and grassroots activism to bear on their engagements with popular culture, both as creators and consumers of cultural texts, and it's no mistake that any number of third-wave voices and images *are* currently being heard and seen in the mass media. As second-wave feminist cultural critic Susan Douglas reminds us, "The media, simultaneously, love and hate women. . . . The war that has been raging in the media is not a simplistic war against women but a complex struggle between feminism and antifeminism that has reflected, reinforced, and exaggerated our culture's ambivalence about women's roles for over thirty-five years."[9] And despite the media's derision of feminism and feminists as (you know the rant) loud hairy man-hating bitches, or its affirmation of certain kinds of feminisms and feminists, or its perpetual focus on cute-thin-blond-poreless-wrinkle-free women, the media also sometimes makes other feminist ideas and images available for girls and women to use. These contradictory images of women in the media both shape and reflect our shattered, seeking, powerfully multiple selves. What is more, Douglas argues, growing up with these contradictory mass media images has helped to make millions of women into feminists of whatever wave, whether or not they ever claim that word.

And now contradictory girls are everywhere, "girl" being the newly rescued referent for all things female. We've all seen the Girl Power baby tees and the Xena magnets and the girly-girl bands and the many faces of Courtney Love. If we've been looking, we've also found Websites like Nrrdgrrrl, magazines like *HUES* and *Bust* and *Bitch*, books like *Listen Up*, *To Be Real*, *Third Wave Agenda*, and *Manifesta*. Looking harder, we've discovered the 'zine scene and many other forms of third-wave feminist grassroots activism. From the mainstream to the underground girls are shaping the public eye, even as they continue to be shaped by it.

As cultural critic Ann Powers notes in *Spin* magazine's November 1997 Girl Issue, the terms "Girl Culture" and "Girl Power" have been manufactured to sell things to this assertive and increasingly visible audience of young women. At the same time, Powers argues, the linkage of "culture" and "power" to the diminutive "girl" also signifies an important shift in what it means to grow up female at the turn of the century. She's right on both counts, which is, as I've been suggesting, one way to talk about the predicament that shapes contemporary girls' lives as well as feminism's third wave. According to Powers:

> Unlike conventional feminism, which focused on women's socially imposed weaknesses, Girl Culture assumes that women are free agents in the world, that they start out strong, and that the odds are in their favor. . . . Girl Culture insists that

> being strong doesn't single you out; on the contrary, it recasts sisterhood in the image of a girl gang expanding its turf. . . . While feminism tried to imagine what women could become, Girl Culture urges them to enjoy what they have—muscles, guile, sex appeal—and to go ahead and use it. . . . "Being a girl" means taking pride in the very qualities denigrated by both sexists and doctrinaire feminists.[10]

Powers's description of Girl Culture might sound like third-wave power feminism pitted against a second-wave victim feminism, until you think about how second-wave feminism and other liberation movements created a context in which today's young women might experience themselves as strong and free agents in the world; until you think about how Girl Culture deploys the second-wave concept of sisterhood in playful and serious ways, understanding from jump that sisters have differences and will fight but had also better know how to kiss and make up fast so as to have each other's backs; until you think about how Girl Culture reclaims and revalues ways of acting and being associated with femininity, even as it makes fun of (and has fun with) traditional gender scripts.

Girl Culture dialogues directly, if not always respectfully, with second-wave feminism, and it challenges backlash against feminism even as it is marked by it. Ann Powers traces the emergence of Girl Culture to the publication of Faludi's *Backlash*, a text in which the second and the third wave came together as subject and audience:

> The mood was one of vengeance, the same spirit cultivated by Susan Faludi's best-selling . . . book *Backlash*, which detailed contemporary sexism in terms that called for a war against it. Young women took that directive to heart, publishing zines with titles like *Chainsaw* and forming defiantly dirty bands like 7 Year Bitch. Turning up the volume, they began to play with sexual personae that neither feminism nor conventional femininity could accommodate: goddess and whore, genius and tart, dominatrix and masochist.[11]

As girls around the country turned up the volume, asserting visibility by starting bands and by writing 'zines that recalled the personal and political writing of New Left underground rags, the energy and creativity emerging from various locations began to draw national attention and Girl Culture went pop. While this pop culture appropriation of grassroots girl culture was strongly critiqued in the mid-1990s by the Riot Grrrls, a loosely organized movement of punk rock feminists who rightly saw that their overtly feminist focus would be diluted, the move of girl-driven creativity from youth subcultures to mainstream pop culture brought third-wave feminists and feminisms into national view, making these images and discourses accessible to young women and men all over the country.

But all this, you say, is so . . . pop, so consumer oriented, so, well, youthful? And where are the *women*? And where are the *politics*? Certainly a focus on the most visible—consumable—aspects of Girl Culture can flatten its grassroots energy, its constant in(ter)ventions. Part of the problem here is that when we talk about "Girl Culture" we're navigating the complex borderlands between folk culture and mass culture. Grassroots cultural activity feeds new data into the consumer machine, and this data gets processed into the latest fad; in turn, the latest fads shape grassroots cultural practices. On the one hand, then, young women's activisms and pleasures and yearnings *are* being blowdried, fluffed, and sold back to them, which, as we know, is nothing new. Since the Baby Boom hit, youth cultures have fueled the capitalist money-making machine. But on the other hand, the advent of mass-market Girl Culture suggests that "feminism has become, to many girls, a discourse as powerful and pervasive as pop music or romance novels."[12] If, as Powers reminds us, "girls are more than just shoppers, and the effects of the culture we embrace go deeper than the pocketbook,"[13] then the popularization of Girl Culture signifies a repositioning of girls as cultural actors and a girl-driven backlash against backlash.

In "Charting the Currents of the Third Wave," third-wave feminist Catherine Orr argues that "the fact that the third wave is taking place outside more traditional feminist institutions is cause for optimism. Besides allowing for alternative venues and forms of institution building, this newest wave is returning to popular culture, the medium through which feminism captured the popular imagination—and thus political clout—in the late 1960s and early 1970s."[14] Deborah Seigel, also a third-wave feminist, shares Orr's optimism, writing that "the activity of the third wave . . . is quite possibly beginning to resemble that of an earlier period, in which links between feminism, the academy, and grassroots activism were visible and viable."[15] If Orr and Seigel are right, and I think and I hope that they are, then it is very important for feminist teachers to familiarize ourselves with the ways contemporary Girl Culture signifies *on* feminist issues and *for* young women and men. As the third wave knows, cultural production is a powerful educational tool and a possible activist site.

In the 1990s and into the twenty-first century, popular music has proven to be the most important cultural form for expressing and disseminating third-wave feminist perspectives. As cultural critic Andrew Ross has argued:

> The level of attention and meaning invested in music by youth is still unmatched by almost any other organized activity in society, including religion. As a daily companion, social bible, commercial guide and spiritual source, youth music is still *the* place of faith, hope, and refuge. In the forty-odd years since "youth culture" was created as a consumer category, music remains the medium for the most creative and powerful stories about those things that often seem to count the most in our daily lives.[16]

Listening to P. J. Harvey, Tori Amos, Queen Latifah, Courtney Love, Erykah Badu, Team Dresch, Bikini Kill, Liz Phair, Sleater Kinney, Missy Elliot, Melissa Etheridge, Kristen Hersh, Lauryn Hill, and Ani DiFranco, it becomes especially clear that this music undoes the power/victim divide, building on second-wave insights and strategies in third-wave ways. Recent women in music sing and rap and taunt and spit and growl and scream and whisper and speak out about rape, harassment, racism, economic inequity, and their own desires, shouting with voices and guitars and bass beats about and against their "victimization," not playing the passive victim role at all. And while women in country music might sound more conservative than their rock and rap sisters, performers like Terri Clark, Kathy Mattea, the Dixie Chicks, and Lucinda Williams play with their genre's gender scripts by singing women's road songs; their characters take to the road because they love to fix and drive hot cars, or because they're seeking the freedom of wide open spaces, or because they're leaving an abusive partner, or all three of these. And clearly, women and men are listening to this girl music. It's selling like mad, it's winning all the big awards, and it's disseminating a variety of feminist voices and women's perspectives.

The title of this essay is taken from rap-soul artist Lauryn Hill's debut solo album, *The Miseducation of Lauryn Hill*, and the name of folk-punk artist Ani DiFranco's girl-founded-and-owned indie record label, Righteous Babe Records, because their songs are particularly good examples of how to craft a dynamic feminism out of the tension between agency and victimization, entitlement and backlash. Both Lauryn and Ani have received critical acclaim and have made a good living from their work; both their music and their perspectives are available and accessible to mainstream audiences through record stores, music magazines, and the Internet; and they express third-wave feminist points of view by using the sonic and lyric force of their music to reeducate themselves and their peers, and by mixing musical forms so as to speak to multiple communities and acknowledge their musical debts. Their music brings news about how to combat oppression in contemporary terms, information which young people can use towards making change in their own lives and communities. It's also damn fun to listen to.[17]

Words and guitar and vocalized sounds make conversation in Ani's songs, kinda doing different things together: the lyrics don't hide behind a wall of sound, the guitar doesn't always drive the lyrics, the voice is an instrument not restricted to words. Songs clash, change tune and tempo from one to the next—lullaby to fury, folk to punk. (Tension, contradiction that doesn't contradict. She listens to everything, a self-proclaimed musical slut.) Using wood and skin to make different kinds of loud—fat loud, picking loud, listening loud—her acoustic guitar percolates, skitters, hiccups, hammers. She plays so hard, she tells *Guitar Player* magazine, that she knocks the braces out of her guitars' insides, and wears Nailine double-thick fashion nails secured with electric tape to keep up the assault.[18] And you thought press-on nails impeded hard work and feminist progress.

Ani's music works to sound out the third wave. It gives sonic expression to the struggle for conversation, community, collective voice when we sometimes feel isolated, differences drawn so deep and wide we don't know how to begin, difference acting as a wedge rather than a way to mark particularities and sites of productive conflict. She says, "You can bridge a lot of space by just turning up your amp. But there are other ways of bridging the gap—by making someone strain to meet you and then by meeting them halfway. Then you can talk."[19] Doing her best work as a live performer, Ani uses sounds of all kinds to create spaces where community, and therefore collective action, can be imagined and made. Part of this strategy is an overt alignment with the "subcorporate music" of the folk and punk scenes, past and present.[20] The folk scene appeals to the down-to-earth geeky Ani. Punk appeals to the loud-in-your-face Ani. Both appeal to the anticorporate do-it-yourself Ani, the community-based Ani, the social protestor Ani, the artist-activist Ani. Of course, shaking up folk music's earnestness with all-over-the-place passion, and substituting "righteous rage for punk's nihilism"[21] means that, as she puts it, "I'm never quite sure if I'm a freak at the folk festival or some chick with an acoustic guitar at a rock club."[22]

One thing is clear: coming from the folk and punk scenes, Ani and her fans experience her shows as intimately inclusive public conversations, and they understand music as a powerful form of social activity. Lauryn Hill, true to her hip-hop roots, also understands the role of music in developing community and calling for social change. In a recent *Rolling Stone* interview, she tells writer Touré that "We're in this war. . . . There's always a constant spiritual war, but there's a battle for the souls of black folk, and just folks in general, and the music has a lot to do with it."[23] Rap music expresses this war in a number of ways. It can call out racism and economic oppression. It can dismantle stereotypes and speak complex yearnings. It can critically and creatively represent issues within black communities. And it can be severely marked (and marketed) by war's scars and miseducation's blindnesses. *The Miseducation of Lauryn Hill* is an assertively autobiographical album named after Carter G. Woodson's 1933 book *The Miseducation of the Negro*, and Lauryn clearly intends to exploit the call-and-response tension between autobiography understood as representing one young African American woman's voice and life and autobiography understood in communal terms. By moving among different black musical styles, and by reconstructing her speaking/singing voice in and through these styles, Hill makes "a talking book that tells the history of soul, R&B, reggae, and hip-hop."[24] This brilliant critical and creative move rewrites Woodson's book with a young African American audience in mind, builds bridges between generations within the community, describes her own coming-of-age as an African American woman and new mother, and gets its messages out to diverse audiences based on its literate pop appeal. Like Ani, Lauryn sounds out the third wave's struggle for conversation, community, and collective voice while valuing difference and multiplicity, and creates spaces where various incarnations of "we" can come together.

Lyrically, Ani and Lauryn offer unabashed talk about the miseducation of girls, and they use their words to offer alternatives. Engaging different histories and voices but crafting and expressing a similarly strong sense of self, Ani and Lauryn show how we are "shattered into multiple pieces, some of them imprinted by femininity, others by feminism," some of them imprinted by our pride and our privilege, others imprinted by sexism and racism, some of them imprinted by our desires for capitalist versions of success, others imprinted by our critique of these power structures.[25] Ani's words give voice to an inclusive, bisexual, sex-positive feminist politics predicated on a hunger for humor, justice, honesty, and other possible worlds. In her songs injustice sucks, so let's say that and then do something about it. Hair matters because bodies mark the passage of time; bodies make history. Ani's "Not A Pretty Girl," the title track of her seventh CD, has become the anthem for all those pro-active (anti)fairy tale princesses out there.[26] The appeal is in the way Ani translates "pretty," refusing the social role of prettiness as the measure of a girl's value without altogether throwing out the body and the concept of beauty. In her songs she gathers the shattered pieces of self and doesn't bother hiding the scars. She still sometimes reads from the girl-script she meant to rip up, then she remembers another map and drives out of range. Claiming Woody Guthrie as her ancestor and strangers as her progeny, Ani takes feminism on the road, makes her borrowed, breakable body a home. Highways for stretchmarks, Ani shows how the third wave does feminism dynamically, every day, and how we try to make a living while we're at it.

If Ani's lyrics take feminism on the road in order to forge and unsettle herself, Lauryn Hill's womanist lyrics bring her whole complex self back home. Written and recorded when Lauryn was pregnant with her first child, *Miseducation* expresses Hill's emotional and spiritual journey from girl to woman. This journey is not linear, for Hill or the rest of us. It can be a journey towards reclaiming a lost version of oneself, a journey through choices made and consequences faced, through failed relationships and lost faith, through the pleasures and dangers of career-related success. Individually, the songs on *Miseducation* can be read as love songs, break-up songs, boastful songs, nostalgic songs, pissed-off songs, and listen-up songs, but taken together, the songs form a third-wave narrative reminiscent of Ntozake Shange's important second-wave choreopoem *For Colored Girls Who Have Considered Suicide When the Rainbow is Enuf*. In the second to last song on the CD, "Everything is Everything," Lauryn lays her hand on the table. Asserting the connectedness of everything in the chorus, and offering her words to other young people struggling with and against and through their mis/educations, Lauryn maps a strong womanist consciousness rooted in black diaspora history and culture. She also lays claim to hip-hop spirituality, a generationally specific way to site self that takes up African traditions of creating individual and collective selves through musical forms. Clearly, Ani's and Lauryn's songs—girl talk, talking back—craft a dynamic feminism out of the tension *between* agency and victimization, *between* entitlement and backlash, suggesting that self becomes something women must *do*, preferably in dialogue with other women, as well as with our other selves, communities, ancestors.

This kind of girl-talk also shapes girl 'zines, self-published mags filled with confessional poetry, record and concert reviews, informational articles about breast cancer, contraception, women's history, or how to come out to your parents, and critical commentary on local, national, and international women's issues. Positioning themselves as an alternative to commercial girl's and women's magazines, the 'zines often ironically appropriate retro images of women and deliberately employ a diary-like tone and low-budget look, for intimacy's sake. Some of these 'zines have grown up into more glossy and better-funded mags while still remaining indie. *HUES* magazine, for example, began as a 'zine produced by Dyann Logwood and Tali and Ophira Edut in 1992 while they were students at the University of Michigan, and became the first and only national, multicultural magazine for young women, delivering what they call "a special brand of media activism—intelligence and information with a long-overdue dose of color and flavor." *Bust* magazine, founded by Marcelle Karp and Debbie Stoller, is aimed at the older end of the third wave and provides smart and irreverent feminist commentary on chick culture past and present.[27]

Part of what gets confusing, though, for all of us, is the slippery slope between real righteous babes and constructed righteous babes, which is a really complicated theoretical conversation that I won't get into here, but something weird is going on when a *TV character* is chosen by *Time* magazine to represent third-wave feminists. The cover of the June 29, 1998, issue, perhaps intended to "commemorate" the 150th anniversary of the Seneca Falls Convention, depicts Susan B. Anthony, Betty Friedan, Gloria Steinem, and Calista Flockhart, who plays Ally McBeal, a spazzy Boston lawyer whose life story plays on the Fox channel Monday nights. All four of the women are disembodied. Their heads float on a black background. Susan, Betty, and Gloria are shot in black and white, looking frumpy and dead, while Ally, shot in color, looks pretty but sort of doe-eyed spacey. Her picture is positioned above the red-letter caption, "Is feminism dead?" While the story's writer, Ginia Bellafante, makes the important point that while "the women's movement changed our individual lives and expectations . . . that doesn't mean that American society is supporting [us] much in our choices"[28]—on this, she's clearly writing out of the same contradictory space between entitlement and backlash that I have been naming as formative for the third wave—she also trashes contemporary feminism across the board, dismissing it as "silly," using Ally, Camille Paglia, Lisa Palac, Elizabeth Wurtzel, Deborah Garrison, Katie Roiphe, Naomi Wolf, the Spice Girls, *The Vagina Monologues*, and *Bust* magazine's sex issue as her representatives and her evidence. As *Ms.* editor Marcia Gillespie observes of the piece,

> Young women's activism was totally ignored, as if the Spice Girls were the epitome of "girl power." No mention of Nomy Lamm, or Ani DiFranco, organizations like the Third Wave, or interviews with any of the many women of that generation who are doing righteous work. Feminists of color didn't even make *Time*'s radar screen—but then we never do. Nor did all the ongoing, change-making work of

feminists of all ages, classes, and ethnicities.[29]

Bellafante doesn't look carefully enough even in mass culture, let alone in the culture at large, for signs of the third wave voicing and naming our contradictory selves. TV gives us Buffy, Xena, and the Dark Angel. The literary world offers Edwidge Danticat, Erika Lopez, Alix Olson, Lois-Ann Yamanaka, and the recent third-wave anthologies *Adios, Barbie*, *To Be Real*, and *Listen Up*. Music offers a zillion voices in lieu of, or in dialogue with, the Spice Girls, as I argue above. Feminist cultural productions like *The Vagina Monologues* and *Bust* might be understood in their broader context, which includes Heather Findley's *Girlfriends* magazine, Christy Haubegger's *Latina* magazine, Lisa Miya-Jervis's *Bitch: Feminist Response to Pop Culture*, Carla Williams's and Lorna Simpson's photography, and any number of feminist performance art pieces. These are, of course, very short lists.

Perhaps where the third wave has failed so far is in not extending its use of the mass media as a pedagogical tool far enough, so that the less sexy activist projects engaged by the third wave get ample P.R. and can be seen and heard alongside the 'zines and the music.[30] So, towards this end, just a few, just so you know: The Third Wave is the name of an activist network with an emphasis on politicizing and organizing young feminists from diverse cultural and economic backgrounds on a variety of issues. Their first project was Freedom Ride 1992, a three-week bus tour to register voters in poor communities of color across the country. The Young Women's Project is a national and multicultural organization that supports young women leaders and organizations by offering them information and leadership training. Its community-based actions include sexual assault workshops, antiracism workshops, and training in STD/AIDS information and prevention. Lauryn Hill's Refugee Project assists at-risk youth by supporting local projects that focus on personal growth, community service, education, cultural awareness, and interpersonal skills. Third-wave feminist Rinku Sen codirects the California-based Center for Third World Organizing, which trains young women and men of color to be student, labor, and community organizers. Melissa Bradley founded and directs The Entrepreneurial Development Institute, which works in public housing projects, inner-city schools, and juvenile detention facilities to teach young people how to start their own socially-responsible businesses. Brigitte M. Moore created Black Grrrl Revolution, an organization that provides street and inner-city based pro-black grrrl feminist programs and services. Jody Blyele, member of the all-lesbian rock band Team Dresch, created and marketed a workbook and a CD about self-defense for young women, and the band incorporated self-defense workshops into its 1995 shows. There are also the countless examples of third-wave feminists working in domestic violence shelters, rape crisis hotlines, and literacy programs, or choosing to teach or practice medicine or law in underserved communities, or breaking new ground for women in their communities, whatever that means where they live.

Third-wave feminists know that messing with pop culture is a dangerous thing. We're not really at the helm, at least not always and not yet, and the currents of consumption and erasure run strong. Just because we get the way we're riffing among and between Ally McBeal, Buffy the Vampire Slayer, Edwidge Danticat, Ani DiFranco, Lauryn Hill, our own selves and our best friends and all of the other characters and cultural workers and activists I have named to get at the big picture of the third wave, doesn't mean that our various audiences will get the connections and contradictions we're engaging. This is why, in our feminist travels, we come back home to ourselves and our communities to touch base, to get the work done, to root the changes. I want to bring this chapter home, to the third wave here at Indiana State University, in Terre Haute, Indiana, where I live and teach. I want to offer you the voices of some young women and men as they variously engage the invitation to "Redefine feminism so it includes you."

This was my invitation to the students who took my course on women writers of the United States during the 1996-1997 academic year, and the excerpts below are taken from response papers they wrote. Some of the responses refer to readings assigned in the course, which included the following: Barbara Findlen, *Listen Up: Voices from the Next Feminist Generation*; Leslie Marmon Silko, *Ceremony*; Maxine Hong Kingston, *The Woman Warrior: Memoirs of a Girlhood among Ghosts*; Cherrie Moraga, *Loving in the War Years*; Jane Smiley, *A Thousand Acres*; Dorothy Allison, *Skin: Talking about Sex, Class and Literature*; Susan Douglas, *Where the Girls Are: Growing Up Female with the Mass Media*; Audre Lorde, *Sister Outsider*; Ntozake Shange, *A Daughter's Geography*; and Lisa Jones, *Bulletproof Diva: Tales of Race, Sex, and Hair*. I have excerpted from the students' papers, I have used the spell-checker even when they did not, I have deleted names, and I have added titles. Nothing else has been changed.

When I performed the students' words as part of a paper I gave a few years ago at the National Women's Studies Association annual conference, someone in the audience commented, "Thank you for reading that; now I know what we're up against." But this speaker had missed my point. She hadn't *listened* to the students as they struggled with feminism and backlash and their own multiple positionings. As performance artist Anna Deavere Smith suggests, "American character lives not in . . . what has been fully articulated, but in what is in the process of being articulated, not in the smooth-sounding words, but in the very moment when the smooth-sounding words fail us. It is alive right now. We might not like what we see, but in order to change it, we have to see clearly."[31] Smith's attempt to find American character on the road, in process, in the juxtapositions between many speaker's words, in *how* people speak and stutter and struggle with language as well as in *what* they say, shows me one way to take my students and my peers and my foremothers *at* their word. I am reminded that feminism is renewed and remade at the margins, and in America's heartland, through imperfect words like these.

Resisting Junk

We don't have bodies, we are body. When we change our bodies we are changing our minds about what femininity means to us. We all resist different things in our everyday life. We resist against disrespect, and violence for example. I resist dieting by eating when I am hungry. Sound simple? I think that all the junk society has created for us to eat is just JUNK! I make long-term decisions about the food I eat, this is my biggest form of resistance. I am a vegetarian.

Nair America

Commercialization and media influences were almost non-existing on tribal ground. What exposure we did receive was only through television, which we didn't watch except for on Saturday mornings and occasionally a news brief. I didn't recognize any large differences in gender roles in those days, or at least they were not so pronounced. But later I realized how different things actually were when we moved off the reservation into mainstream America. I began to actualize on my family values to redirect the changes that were beginning to affect me. Instead of becoming worried or cautious of what the effects of gender imaging would have on me, I became more aware of what society wanted to create as a *desired* image. I began to see these images sculpting the social trends that my fellow students used and adopted as consumers. Like *Nair*: no more razor cuts! Women were strutting their legs all over the country which brought attention from whistling men!

Who Wouldn't?

I teach step and water aerobics, as well as train people in Nautilus at a YMCA. After reading Alisa Valdes' essay in Barbara Findlen's *Listen Up*, I do not know if I should feel guilty for encouraging women's obsessions with their bodies or not. I like to think that I am training people to think more in terms of personal health rather than achieving society's bodily standards. But am I also encouraging women to obsess about their appearance? This is still an unresolved struggle for me. I don't think young people are striving for long-term benefits, but rather striving to fulfill the bodily standards set by society. For the most part, I am exercising and eating right to feel better and also for the long-term benefits, but I also like being accepted by society—who wouldn't?

White Towels

I was guilty of playing the game with white towels wrapped around my head, pretending I had long luxurious hair. I did these things to myself and against my culture, due to the mentally engraved myth of what it is to be beautiful.

Hair Is Just Like a Ritual

African hair is defined by most Africans as being a way to demonstrate their talents and it's an expression of their culture, life, and the way they feel. It is the concept of one's beauty, which also deals with the smile and the body. Like *Ceremony* written by Silko, hair is just like a ritual because it is a way of life. The environment I grew up in has made it that way.

Believe That Sisterhood Is a Feminist Issue

Dear Sherry: I know you do not get into feminism. You say you don't trust it. I want you to know more about it, and maybe if you learn how it helped me, you will see that maybe you need a piece of it too, if only a tiny one. Mother in her own way is very much a feminist. She raised four children on her own and did a wonderful job. Sherry, you oftentimes say that you don't remember much of your childhood, and sometimes I help you remember it. Mom worked in a job where she was surrounded by men. She had to get up every day for nearly ten years and work as a carpenter where she was not wanted by many. Mom gained empowerment from knowing her job and doing it well in spite of what others had to say. Mom would come home and tell us the stories of what men would say and do to her on the job. She would complain if it got too bad, but nothing was ever done. She oftentimes stayed silent, like many women do.

As Maxine Hong Kingston writes, "This is a terrible ghost country, where a human being works her life away." Working is something that mother taught us was essential to living.

The Fear That I May Be Heard

Why do I speak my mind? In the most base explanation, I have the need to be seen by others. I have the need to be seen because I seek validation for myself as a person through the way others view me and my opinions. I seek validation because if others don't see me, then I am nobody. If I am nobody (in the eyes of others) then I have no purpose, and therefore may as well speak the ultimate silence. But in so much as I feel this way, the fear that I *may* be heard is as terrifying as the prior. To be heard means to hold a certain power. With people listening to you comes a reponsibility for people's feelings and lives.

Guys I Know That I Could Beat Up

I have not really played the part of a victim in my eyes because I have been dealing with being raped without help from anyone for the past six years. I really don't want anyone's sympathy. I would just like to help stop it from happening to other women.

I think part of why I blamed myself was because women have been programmed to think it is their fault when a man violates them in some way. I think that I also place the blame on myself because I did not want to be a victim. You have to help yourself before anyone can help you.

I am slowly dealing with this in my own way. For example, since this occurred I have always dated guys I know that I could beat up if I had to. I have a very loving and caring family and I have a bright future. You need to look at the good things in your life and get up and make the rest of it better.

Joyful Walkway or Warzone?
Whitney Walker, author of "Why I Fight Back" in Barbara Findlen's *Listen Up*, has an excellent point when she suggests that she must be ready and willing to fight back. I do however think that her reliance on movie-glorified martial arts is not very realistic nor useful. I believe that the use of firearms is a much better idea and I am not a member of the NRA. The street can be either a joyful walkway or a warzone, a place where you want to survive in the best possible way. Run if you can, it IS the best option, but if you have to resist, please leave the Bruce Lee garbage at home.

Men That Excite
I think that Cherrie Moraga and Jane Smiley don't show men in a very good light and that they are just making the stereotype problem worse. If they don't want men to take control of their lives and run everything, then they shouldn't write about men like this. We all know that men like that excite, but the real male, the one we can be equals with, is the person I'm not sure is out there. I think that is the character they should be writing about. The man that understands that he is given certain rights because of his protruding sex organs, that is willing to give up some of his own privileges so we can be equal. I know the monsters like Larry (in *A Thousand Acres*) are out there, but by writing about them the way these authors do, it seems that they are the only type of men that excite, that in fact they are telling men that in order to be real men you have to act like Larry or Moraga's brother. These authors should look to Leslie Silko for an idea of how to write a male character. In Leslie Silko's *Ceremony* we at least got to see the good, bad, and normal male characteristics and see that a man can be softer without being a coward or gay.

We Are All Victims
This is not just a feminist battle. We all suffer at the hands of the patriarch. Men also have the problem in trying to fulfill the role that has been handed down to them. We are all victims of not being able to stomach who we see in the mirror but it is usually because of not being able to handle the standards put forth to us by our society. These are often the same feelings that keep races, cultures, and other backgrounds from crossing the borders to each other.

> We don't know if we will be welcomed
> We don't know what to say

This Is Where Men Start Evolving
It is very true that women were and still are at a disadvantage to men when it comes to certain situations. However, just as a woman's frame of mind has evolved to a point of feeling comfortable with her freedom of choices and right to success, a man has to have the chance to evolve also. Men have to break the mold of generations of being taught that if they are not the breadwinner, then they're really not a man.

Indirectly, I Was Born a Feminist
Feminism in the sense of liberation was not a household word when I was growing up. At school and at home I learned that to be feminine was to behave like a lady, feet crossed and hands folded. However, while growing up I did learn a very valuable lesson on being independent. Indirectly, then, I was born a feminist. As an African-American growing up in a single-parent household, this meant survival. Veronica Chambers writes that "To be strong, smart, independent, and unashamed were necessary elements for survival."[32] These same tactics must be used within the feminist movement so that all women will have a voice and place in liberation. One woman can't speak for all of us.

Reprogramming the World
Just as Dorothy Allison said, "Let me make clear how much has changed in the short span of my life. Although there are few people who think of themselves as revolutionaries any more, the world has been remade. Look around you." I want to add to her statement that the world will continue to be remade or re-programmed as long as there are people willing to fight for their rights. Women especially need to keep standing up and fighting for their rights. These changes will not come about all at once or even, perhaps, in the near future. The change needs to begin with one person or a small group then move to the community and then eventually to Washington.

Class, Capitalistic Style
Class inequity is an issue that I think the feminist movement hasn't really helped. With the capitalistic style of America, it is very hard for one to move out of the class they were born in. It seems that birth is a lottery, and if you're rich you got the right numbers. Competition has driven us to a race that makes us be paranoid and fearful of who or what might be plotting to steal what we have right from under our feet.

Fed Up
Women need to stick up for and help other women out whether they are old, young, or a different race to end this discrimination against us. We need to do what the small Chinese and Korean businesses do when banks will not lend them the money to open their own businesses. When this happens they arrange a loan from a fellow businessman of the same ethnicity in order to start their business. I have heard of women doing just this. They help each other out. If we could all just do this in all aspects of our lives then the feminist movement would be on the right track again. Right now I feel that it is just a bunch of crap as did some of the authors that we read this semester. I think that right now it consists of a certain race and class of women that are out to get all they can and that do not care about other women.

No Perfect Way
In trying to be a true feminist based on how society paints it or outlines it women

forget to be true to themselves. Feminism is about being who you really are and not trying to become this "ideal" society wants you to be. It is about being in control of yourself and your life and having the courage to speak your mind. There is no perfect way to define yourself as a feminist.

Not Out of Touch with Her Femininity
Sexuality is more than just sex. It is the empowerment of the soul. It is the way a woman carries herself, speaks, and even thinks. It is how a woman expresses herself and her right to make choices that no one should be able to make for her. Choices that should not be condemned, should she choose to spend her life with a man or a woman. Which brings us to the question of sexuality being an expression of femininity. I feel that most women would answer with an affirmation. So then reality is that a lesbian or bisexual woman is not out of touch with her femininity, but that her gender role in life is different from a heterosexual woman.

Using My Sexuality
I think that a lot of my struggle is the same as these writers. But I am different in that I am not interested in radically trying to change the views of society. I will settle for becoming the kind of woman I want to be. What I think I try to do that probably would piss these women off is that I try to gain power by using my sexuality. As much as my sexuality is a part of me, it is also a tool for me to use to gain position. My field of choice is a boy's club, and rather than try and be butch and show the guys I can do everything, I sometimes let them do things for me. I don't think that makes me less of a woman.

Redefining Feminism So It Includes You
I see the statement "I'm not a feminist but" as a way of redefining feminism without actually using the word "feminism." I see the statement as a way of supporting the ideas of feminism, but not at the expense of femininity. This is a way to integrate the traditional femininity (wearing makeup and being a nurturing mother) with the traditional feminism (being a powerful career woman). Just like women of color seek to integrate their feminism with their culture and tradition, so do young white women.

Our Constitution
To be quite honest, I am still quite skeptical of the idea that because one has used the phrase "I'm not a feminist but . . ." that it makes the individual, in fact, a feminist (according to Susan Douglas anyway). I disagree. The fact is, all the information I have gathered so far about feminists from the readings is that they just do not seem to be thankful for all the rights and privileges they do have. Please do not misunderstand me—I think any individual should be paid equal pay for equal work (all races, all creeds)—but that does not strike me as a "feminist" issue. That is just a matter of what is written in our Constitution.

Breaking away from the Theory That "All Men Are Created Equal," We Have to See What Exactly Applies to Whom

It is clear that we were not all created equal. Women have the power to bring children into this world, but they do not possess the power to make everyone love these children and accept them for who or what they are. Life is not a series of simple steps, but rather a complex structure that can be debated every step of the way. Therefore it cannot be broken down into equality.

From the Second Wave to the Third

When the feminists first started coming out in large numbers and into the public spotlight it seemed that they wanted everything right now. These women didn't seem to have the language that is necessary to get the reaction that would be helpful to their cause and this led to the negative image that many people see. However, when we read Audre Lorde and Ntozake Shange, and finally Lisa Jones, I began to appreciate some of their views. Their approach was more directed at observing situations from more angles than just one. They seem to have been able to find a language that can make their points come across easier, the sort of writing that lets you feel your way through it and lets you find the meaning for yourself. I feel that this style has helped feminists overcome somewhat the image that the media has portrayed of them. This evolution is one that will help the third-wave generation see more into the feminist idea.

Balance

My life is scored primarily with two words: fear and hope. It's a delicate balance between the two, and lately, one that is being acted on with Paxil medication tablets. The "third wave" among us really stimulates the hopes within me, as they are the bold, defiant, and *numerous* "troops of tomorrow." The struggle is raging on and if it goes on (as it should) the right wing will transform, through constant shifts to the left—where *freedom* is. Critical tools: exposure (lectures, seminars, pamphlets, *the Web*, *bands* . . .) provided to the unexposed ones.

I Had Accepted Her As One of My Closest Friends and a Sister

Many African-American women feel betrayed by the feminist movement, and I feel betrayed because of some of the events that have occurred in my life in the past few years in college. We were at the apartment one night and my white roommate had some friends over. One of her guy friends and I were joking around. I called him "Buzz Light-year" from *Toy Story* and he called me "Aunt Jemima." I stopped and look at him. And I said to him "don't ever say that to another Black woman as long as you live, because she might turn around and knock the hell out of you." His reply to me was "yeah, yeah, yeah, whatever." And for some reason I could hear my mother saying to me, where is your roommate now? Is she going to take your side or his? While we do share that common ground as women we don't know enough about each other, and what's more important is that we don't understand each other.

Success Story
I always took for granted that my teenage pregnancy would not ruin my life and it didn't, but why? Why am I in college and married and not single and on welfare? Why have I "succeeded" when so many other women in my place have "failed"? I, of course, would like to attribute it to my own determination and ability, but this would be a lie. Upon closer inspection, I must admit that the main reason for my "success" is the fact that I am a white, middle class woman who came from a "nice family." Society allowed, even encouraged me to succeed and overcome my mistake, but judged and punished non-middle class and/or non-white girls in the same situation so that they had little, if any, chance to succeed.

The question I must now ask myself is "what am I going to do about it?" Yet, I am afraid of what I may discover if I look more intensely at the "little world" I live in and what it costs me and others to maintain it. I only know that I now see with clearer, more critical eyes, and somehow I will use this knowledge to make a difference, somehow, on some level.

Multiplicity
We (as a country) have created fear, and this has promoted out silence. This has affected the expression of feminism by creating the multiplicity of our identities, and creating the fear that expressing our identities will cause judgments from others that we do not "have it together." We live in silence, instead of as ourselves: fragmented and multiplistic. When our multiplicity has helped us to free ourselves. It is what has allowed us to become feminists, and mothers, and wives, and all at the same time. Multiplicity has helped to shed us of the fear of expressing ourselves and is an identity in itself.

Fighting for a Utopia That Does Not Exist
I think that it is important to reflect upon not what each woman said this semester, but what they say together. Alone each woman is fighting for her own cause, but together they are fighting for a Utopia that does not exist. However, the fight should not end, it should grow, become stronger, and look to others of different lives for answers so that we can all be more educated and understanding of pain, no matter who it is affecting.

NOTES

1. Leslie Heywood and Jennifer Drake, *Third-Wave Agenda: Being Feminist, Doing Feminism* (Minneapolis: University of Minnesota Press, 1997), 9.

2. Farai Chideya, "Confessions of a Backlash Baby: Race and Gender Doublespeak."

http://www.popandpolitics.com/essays/backlash.html (February 19, 1999), 3.

3. Lisa Jones, *Bulletproof Diva: Tales of Race, Sex, and Hair* (New York: Doubleday, 1994), 256, 253.

4. bell hooks, *Yearning: Race, Gender, and Cultural Politics* (Boston: South End Press, 1990), 12-13.

5. See Audre Lorde's essay collection *Sister Outsider*.

6. Danzy Senna, "To Be Real." In Rebecca Walker, *To Be Real: Telling the Truth and Changing the Face of Feminism* (New York: Doubleday, 1995), 16.

7. Senna, 17-18.

8. Catherine Orr, "Charting the Currents of the Third Wave." *Hypatia* 12, no. 3 (Summer 1997): 5.

9. Susan Douglas, *Where the Girls Are: Growing Up Female with the Mass Media* (New York: Random House, 1995), 12-13.

10. Ann Powers, "Everything and the Girl." *Spin* (November 1997): 76-77.

11. Powers, 77.

12. Orr, "Charting the Currents of the Third Wave," 42.

13. Powers, 80.

14. Orr, 41, 42.

15. Deborah Siegel, "Reading between the Waves: Feminist Historiography in a 'Postfeminist' Moment." In Heywood and Drake, 70.

16. Andrew Ross and Tricia Rose, *Microphone Fiends: Youth Music and Youth Culture* (New York: Routledge, 1994), 3.

17. Ani's CDs, all available from Righteous Babe Records, include *Ani DiFranco* (1990); *Not So Soft* (1991); *Imperfectly* (1990); *Like I Said: Songs 1990-1991* (1993); *Puddle Dive* (1993); *Out of Range* (1994); *Not a Pretty Girl* (1995); *Dilate*; *The Past Didn't Go Anywhere* with Utah Phillips (1996); *Living in Clip* (1997); *Little Plastic Castle* (1998); *Up Up Up Up Up Up* (1999); *Fellow Workers* with Utah Phillips (1999); *To the Teeth* (2000); and *Revelling/Reckoning* (2001). Lauryn Hill's *The Miseducation of Lauryn Hill* (1998) is available from Columbia Records.

18. Interview with James Rotondi, "Ani DiFranco's Ferocious Folk." *Guitar Player* (December 1994), http://world.std.com/~megazone/Ani/guitplay.html (October 20, 1997).

19. Susan G. Cole, "Folk-Punk Phenom Unleashes Songs and Real-Life Passions." *NOW Magazine* (Toronto), March 1995, http://world.std.com/~megazone/Ani/now.html (October 20, 1997).

20. Evelyn McDonnell, "On the Edge '95: Ani DiFranco." *Rolling Stone* 16 November 1995. http://www.cc.columbia.edu/~marg/ani/articles/rolling_stone.html (20 October 1997).

21. Cole, "Folk-Punk Phenom."

22. Jason Cherkis, "The New Folk Renegades." *Option Magazine*, May/June 1994, http://world.std.com/~megazone/Ani/option.html (October 20, 1997).

23. Touré, "Lady Soul." *Rolling Stone,* 18 February 1999, 46.

24. Touré, 48.

25. Douglas, 293-94.

26. Lois Maffeo uses the "pro-active fairy tale princess" phrase in relation to Ani in "How I Learned to Stop Worrying and Love Ani DiFranco," in Lois Maffeo, "How I Learned to Stop Worrying and Love Ani DiFranco" *CMJ* (March 1997): http://www.geocities.com/SunsetStrip/Towers/2626/ani2.html (20 October 1997).

27. For information on third-wave cultural production, including 'zines, see Melissa

Klein, "Duality and Redefinition: Young Feminism and the Alternative Music Community"; Jen Smith, "Doin' It for the Ladies—Youth Feminism: Cultural Productions/Cultural Activism"; and Tali Edut, with Dyann Logwood and Ophira Edut, "*HUES* Magazine: The Making of a Movement" in Heywood and Drake, *Third-Wave Agenda: Being Feminist, Doing Feminism*. The publication of *HUES* ended with the March/April 1999 Action and Adventure issue due to lack of revenue.

28. Ginia Bellafante, "Feminism: It's All about Me!" *Time* 151, no. 25 (29 June 1998): 58.

29. Marcia Gillespie, "Equal Time." *Ms.* 9, no. 2 (September/October 1998): 1.

30. For profiles of third-wave activists and artists, including some of those mentioned here, see "21 for the 21st," *Ms.* 7, no. 2 (September/October 1997): 102-11, and Deborah Siegel, "The Legacy of the Personal: Generating Theory in Feminism's Third Wave," 70 n. 3, in *Hypatia* 12, no. 3 (Summer 1997), 46-75. Jennifer Baumgardner and Amy Richards include useful appendices of young women's political organizations, cultural groups, publications, and Websites in *Manifesta: Young Women, Feminism, and the Future*, New York: Farrar, Strauss and Giroux, 2000.

31. Anna Deavere Smith, *Fires in the Mirror*. New York: Anchor/Doubleday, 1993, xli.

32. Veronica Chambers, "Betrayal of Feminism," in Barbara Findlen, *Listen Up: Voices from the Next Feminist Generation* (Seattle: Seal Press, 1995), 23.

BIBLIOGRAPHY

"21 for the 21st." *Ms.* 7, no. 2 (September/October 1997): 102-11.

Allison, Dorothy. *Skin: Talking About Sex, Class, and Literature*. Ithaca, N.Y.: Firebrand Books, 1994.

Baumgardner, Jennifer, and Amy Richards. *Manifesta: Young Women, Feminism, and the Future*. New York: Farrar, Straus and Giroux, 2000.

Bellafante, Ginia. "Feminism: It's All about Me!" *Time* 151, no. 25 (29 June 1998): 54-60.

Cherkis, Jason. "The New Folk Renegades." *Option Magazine*, May/June 1994. http://world.std.com/~megazone/Ani/option.html (20 October 1997).

Chideya, Farai. "Confessions of a Backlash Baby: Race and Gender Doublespeak." http://www.popandpolitics.com/essays/backlash.html (19 February 1999).

Cole, Susan G. "Folk-Punk Phenom Unleashes Songs and Real-Life Passions." *NOW Magazine* (Toronto), March 1995. http://world.std.com/~megazone/Ani/now.html (20 October 1997).

Douglas, Susan. *Where the Girls Are: Growing Up Female with the Mass Media*. New York: Random House, 1995.

Edut, Ophira, ed. *Adios, Barbie: Young Women Write About Body Image and Indentity*. Seattle: Seal Press, 1998.

Findlen, Barbara. *Listen Up: Voices from the Next Feminist Generation*. Seattle: Seal Press, 1995.

Gillespie, Marcia. "Equal Time." *Ms.* 9, no. 2 (September/October 1998): 1.

Heywood, Leslie, and Jennifer Drake. *Third-Wave Agenda: Being Feminist, Doing Feminism*. Minneapolis: University of Minnesota Press, 1997.

hooks, bell. *Yearning: Race, Gender, and Cultural Politics*. Boston: South End Press, 1990.

Jones, Lisa. *Bulletproof Diva: Tales of Race, Sex, and Hair*. New York: Doubleday, 1994.

Kingston, Maxine Hong. *The Woman Warrior: Memoirs of a Girlhood among Ghosts*. New York: Knopf, 1976.

Lorde, Audre. *Sister Outsider*. Freedom, Calif.: Crossing Press, 1984.

Maffeo, Lois. "How I Learned to Stop Worrying and Love Ani DiFranco." *CMJ* (March 1997). http://www.geocities.com/SunsetStrip/Towers/2626/ani2.html (20 October 1997).

McDonnell, Evelyn. "On the Edge '95: Ani DiFranco." *Rolling Stone,* 16 November 1995. http://www.cc.columbia.edu/~marg/ani/articles/rolling_stone.html (20 October 1997).

Moraga, Cherrie. *Loving in the War Years*. Boston: South End Press, 1983.

Orr, Catherine. "Charting the Currents of the Third Wave." *Hypatia* 12, no. 3 (Summer 1997): 29-45.

Powers, Ann. "Everything and the Girl." *Spin*, November 1997, 74-80.

Ross, Andrew, and Tricia Rose. *Microphone Fiends: Youth Music and Youth Culture*. New York: Routledge, 1994.

Rotondi, James. "Ani DiFranco's Ferocious Folk." *Guitar Player* (December 1994). http://world.std.com/~megazone/Ani/guitplay.html (20 October 1997).

Senna, Danzy. "To Be Real." In Rebecca Walker, *To Be Real: Telling the Truth and Changing the Face of Feminism*. New York: Doubleday, 1995, 5-20.

Shange, Ntozake. *A Daughter's Geography*. New York: St. Martin's Press, 1983.

Siegel, Deborah. "Reading between the Waves: Feminist Historiography in a 'Postfeminist' Moment." In Heywood and Drake, *Third-Wave Agenda: Being Feminist, Doing Feminism*. Minneapolis: University of Minnesota Press, 1997, 55-82.

———. "The Legacy of the Personal: Generating Theory in Feminism's Third Wave." *Hypatia* 12, no. 3 (Summer 1997): 46-75.

Silko, Leslie Marmon. *Ceremony*. New York: Penguin, 1992.

Smiley, Jane. *A Thousand Acres*. New York: Fawcett, 1992.

Smith, Anna Deavere. *Fires in the Mirror*. New York: Anchor/Doubleday, 1993.

Touré. "Lady Soul." *Rolling Stone,* 18 February 1999, 46-50.

12
Post- '68: Theory Is in the Streets

Astra Taylor

It was November 1999 and just a couple of months into my first semester of graduate school in New York City when photographs of protesters and riot cops in Seattle hit the front pages of newspapers internationally. In a seminar the afternoon the news broke, my fellow students and I discussed the events that had taken place on the opposite coast. Many of us had received word that an action against the World Trade Organization (WTO) was being planned; however, few of us anticipated it would be the object of global attention or paused to consider that it may be the first major indication that something resembling a "movement" had started. The following April I traveled to Washington, D.C. to witness the massive demonstration against the International Monetary Fund (IMF) and the World Bank. The sheer number of activists was stunning. Young people were everywhere, discussing politics and global finance in the streets. For these protesters, the process of decision-making on hot intersections and along police blockades held great significance—they were participating in the development of a new form of movement organizing: an attempt to reclaim student activism and reinvent it for a generation that has grown up postmodern.

Since the event in D.C., the 2000 Democratic and Republican National Conventions have also been targets of the recent surge of activism. These events have demanded attention, as did the thousands of demonstrators in Seattle. Related protests have taken place worldwide, from Canada to Italy. The media's response has been ambivalent, somehow simultaneously intrigued and dismissive. In general, the overwhelmingly anticapitalist sentiment of the protests has not sat well with journalists. In the minds of many these political outbursts are baffling due to the simple fact that protesting capitalism seems downright irrational: the protests coincided with a period of substantial growth for the American economy and a sudden abundance of dot com millionaires under the age of thirty. In the words of

Marc Cooper, the demonstrations took place at a moment when "everybody thought college kids were more interested in IPOs than in WTOs."[1] Just when young people were supposed to be rushing to cash in on the new economy, thousands converged to accuse established financial institutions of burdening poor third world countries with crushing debts, impoverishing peasants, destroying the environment, and supporting sweatshop labor. Passing unnoticed by the mainstream media, numerous student actions in the form of sit-ins, protests, and teach-ins have taken place at over one hundred campuses nationwide in the span of the last few years.[2] Though many of these actions were successful on a local level, they did not enjoy national attention until after the events in Seattle. Once the student activists leading these events became the object of media scrutiny journalists were quick to pick up on the seeming ironies of the burgeoning movement, primarily that many of the more politically active campuses include the most elite private schools in the country. It is precisely the future graduates of these institutions who stand to benefit from the expanding global economy, and yet they are choosing to call attention to the injustices associated with the economic dominance of their own country. What could these kids be thinking?

Many of the key players in this new movement, which may broadly be defined as one for "economic justice," belong to the generation following "Generation X." Their predecessors came to enjoy iconic status within popular culture: narcissistic and dejected twenty-somethings who appeared appealingly disinterested in anything beyond consumerism. These "slackers" were frequently admonished by the media for their apathy and yet glorified on prime-time television and in fiction. Thus, it is no wonder that people were shocked when they suddenly realized a movement resisting consumerism and the corporatization of cities and schools had been brewing for quite some time. Many have speculated as to what caused this apparent shift in the psychic life of young people in this country. Some have pointed to summer programs sponsored by AFL-CIO over the last three years, which opened the eyes of over two thousand students from privileged schools to issues involving organized labor and the complexities of NAFTA. The growth of student groups such as United Students Against Sweatshops has played a pivotal role in giving members experience organizing and then disseminating information. However, the spread of information about social injustices is only part of the picture. Some participants in the new movement have pointed simply to the fact that young people feel a lack of substance in their lives. One prominent young activist was quoted in the *New Yorker* on why she took a pay cut to work in the nonprofit sector and devote her life to organizing: "I think a lot of people in my generation—not a majority, maybe, but a lot—feel this void. We feel like capitalism and buying things are just not fulfilling, period."[3]

Speculating as to what constitutes the void described above falls beyond the scope of this chapter and would most likely prove fruitless. While it is apparent that among a strong minority of young people apathy has fallen out of style, it is uncertain what caused this dramatic shift. The *New York Times* has stated that the recent demonstrations are part of the largest student movement since the anti-apartheid protests of the 1980s, and many participants believe the movement has only begun to gain momentum. Something drastic has certainly occurred, and considering the social advantages many student leaders enjoy and the cause they have chosen to champion, it is not so obvious why. I won't attempt to locate the spark that ignited the mounting global concern of my generation. Instead, I would like to analyze the cultural and educational milieu that surrounds many young people today, myself included, and relate it to the increasing visibility of student dissent. While I must pause to acknowledge that members of this new movement vary greatly in age and background—and that the diversity of participants is only increasing—a majority of participants are students, and for these individuals the nexus of their organizations and the center of their intellectual lives are universities. For this reason, I would specifically like to consider the role of the university in the new movement: how does the contemporary intellectual experience of the university factor into the sudden profusion of radicalism among students?

Many of these new activists have appropriated methods of resistance their parents and teachers may have used when they themselves were students in the 1960s protesting against the war in Vietnam—sit-ins, teach-ins, nonviolent training, and grassroots organizing, even the occasional traveling road show. Overall, the carnivalesque atmosphere of the large demonstrations over the last year echoes the playfulness of 1960s counterculture, as does the emphasis on the interplay between art and revolution. Recent demonstrations have served as venues for political performance and puppetry. One journalist who witnessed the demonstration against the WTO recalls, "In Seattle last November I watched a hundred sea turtles face down riot cops, a gang of Santas stumble through a cloud of tear gas, and a burly teamster march shoulder to shoulder with a pair of lesbian avengers naked to the waist except a strip of black electrical tape across each nipple."[4] A couple of generations ago, the Students for a Democratic Society advocated the nomination of a pig for president outside of the 1968 Democratic National Convention. Earlier this spring, in Washington, D.C., the protesters had a pig of their own: a giant puppet pig proudly labeled IMF who held an Earth in its jaw like an apple. 1960s-style slogans have also been appropriated. "LBJ" has been replaced in an old favorite: "Hey-hey! Ho-ho! WTO has got to go!" was a popular chant in Seattle.

And there are other parallels, beyond those outlined above, between the counterculture movement of the 1960s and recent actions for economic justice. While the events that took place over three decades ago now serve as a model of social resistance and have inspired a certain spirit of creative rebellion, I believe that the significance of the 1960s to contemporary activism, particularly the events of 1968, goes beyond the superficial resemblance of the methods and philosophies employed. The year Students for a Democratic Society led their most memorable demonstration outside the Democratic National Convention in Chicago students were restless beyond the United States. In France, a revolution was taking place. Students and workers joined forces to shut down the city of Paris, taking over universities and factories alike. The city was held joyfully captive, though for only a brief period: the workers and factories came to a compromise and the students left Paris for the summer. The shortcomings of the revolution, and in particular the prominent role of the university in the events that took place, prompted a reassessment of the intellectual's role in society. Though short-lived, the breakdown of social structures experienced by Parisian students provided compelling insights into the potential of irrationalism in social reinvention. These insights remained with many who eventually entered academia.

Many prominent figures in the development of postmodernism participated in the events in Paris. For these individuals, the experience of May 1968 played a pivotal role in their intellectual and political development. Granted, for most American students a mention of activism in the 1960s probably evokes images of the antiwar protests in Berkeley or Kent State. However, within the academy, images of the student rebellion in Paris are becoming increasingly common wherever postmodern discourses flourish; for example, in departments that incorporate such fields as cultural studies, gender studies, postcolonial studies, media studies, and psychoanalysis. I believe that postmodernism's recent rise to prominence in college curriculums, particularly at institutions that have a history of being more progressive, has left its mark on the growing number of student activists. It is this mark in particular that I would like to explore in closer detail.

As students began seriously to examine postmodern questions—questions of power, hegemony, globalization, truth, disciplinarity, performativity—it seems logical that social activism and political engagement would have become increasingly visible. Yet, the years during which postmodern thought gained acceptance within the academy were some of the most politically inactive years in decades. In considering the recent protests, many writers have concluded that the absence of student organizing and mass demonstrations was due, at least in part, to the hegemony of identity politics as opposed to broader political movements. Identity politics has certainly fostered student concern for questions relating to racial and sexual oppression. However, in the past there has been little solidarity among groups comprising the movement, and, in fact, little space for it: in many ways an implicit requirement of this form of politics is that one has to speak from the experience of specific forms of oppression to participate. This demand leaves little room for building coalitions and forming bonds between various groups, making it difficult to create a strong national front. While I believe that the actions of many socially conscious students have been dominated by concerns for issues relating to identity politics, this description does not represent the limit of political engagement within the university. Students have been extremely interested in revolutionary political ideas in ways not always apparent to those outside of the academy—political ideas have been enacted in the discursive realm. This is true on a rather abstract level; postmodernism has been used to interrogate social concerns such as race, genocide, power, gender, and labor through discourse instead of protests. While I think these theoretical interventions should be classified as political engagements, they have not been socially revolutionary in ways that are immediately obvious. With this in mind, I would like to examine the place that more traditional modes of social activism occupy in relation to my generation, which is very much a postmodern one.

Before I go further, I must pause to clarify my definition of postmodernism in order to clearly differentiate its double sense. Postmodernism may be considered: (1) As a discourse. This is the sense in which I have invoked postmodernism thus far; as a specific method of inquiry in the academy, a discourse that is taught and has a history, however diverse and expansive it may be. Here I am referring to the postmodernism that is presented in the classroom through professor summaries and textbooks. Notions of decentered truth, contingency, reflexivity, the politics of excess and pleasure, performative subjectivity, and a distrust of metanarratives characterize this postmodernism. (2) What has been described as postmodernity: this social and historical moment, and the context my generation was raised in, may be described as postmodern—regardless of whether an individual has critically engaged Derrida, for example. The critical point is that some elements of the postmodern experience are unavoidable. With these overlapping definitions in mind, the implications of postmodernism for traditional modes of political engagement become even less obvious. The effect of the hyper-reflexivity demanded by various strains of postmodern thinking on organizing and mobilizing large bodies of people seems to me, at best, problematic. Transforming technologies such as the Internet contribute to the shifting forms of activism, in addition to other conditions of postmodernity: the contraction of space and time, fracturing of culture, atomization of individuals, weakened social bonds, mediation of information, technological innovations, and the dissolution of categories such as high and low art. Working under the assumption that these factors are indeed part of contemporary social reality and constitute something that may be described as a postmodern experience, I am curious about what the repercussions are for a generation raised in such a context who hope to organize some form of social resistance.

Despite the absence of riots in the streets, students and scholars have been busy performing various political interventions through postmodern discourse: by deconstructing narratives, interrogating subjectivity, destabilizing culture, liberating the subject, and reformulating lack. The absence of any direct social unrest seems to me to bear a direct relation to the events in France during May 1968. With the example of the 1968 protests invoked in countless classrooms to contextualize postmodern philosophy, students became acutely aware of the potential failures of revolutions. For example, 1968 is hailed as a decisive moment in the now common reference *Literary Theory: An Anthology*. The editors, Julie Rivkin and Michael Ryan, introduce poststructuralism, deconstruction, and postmodernism under the heading "The Class of 1968—Post-Structuralism *par lui-même*."[5] If students know only one fact of postmodernism, they know that it is related to the events of 1968. Similarly, in the now classic overview of literary studies, *Literary Theory: An Introduction*, Terry Eagleton states:

> Post-structuralism was a product of that blend of euphoria and disillusionment, liberation and dissipation, carnival and catastrophe, which was 1968. Unable to break the structures of state power, post-structuralism found it possible instead to subvert the structures of language. Nobody, at least, was likely to beat you over the head for doing so. The student movement was flushed off the streets and driven underground into discourse.[6]

The political fervor of 1968, the passion that led students and workers to the streets in protest, was transferred by some into discursive realms when it became clear their revolution was unsuccessful. Until recently, this is where it has stayed. Considering the critical role of May of '68 in historically situating postmodern thought I would like, for the purposes of this chapter, to redefine my generation as one that is in general postmodern, but in particular, post-May '68. The questions that I have been pressing can now be summarized: How is a generation that is post-May 1968 to engage in socially revolutionary practices?

The near mythological status of May 1968 in contemporary theory provides a rather loaded foundation for a method of inquiry. Over time, the history of the student movement and rebellion in Paris has come to function as a sort of origin-story for postmodern philosophy; the experience of the student revolt is hailed as the primary cause of a fluorescence of revolutionary modes of thought even though the material revolution itself failed. This makes May 1968 a complicated symbol in addition to being a powerful one. Its most important service is that it reminds students that postmodern discussions are always implicitly political discussions. But this is a double-edged sword. On the one hand, it fosters a concern for the political among students. On the other hand, the myth of '68 supports a superficial radicalism for discursive projects that actually possess very few political implications.

In an interview centering on structuralism and poststructuralism French theorist Michel Foucault calls attention to this tendency to collapse distinctions between the discursive and the political:

> It has been said, but you have to understand when I read—and I know it has been attributed to me—the thesis "knowledge is power" or "power is knowledge," I begin to laugh, since studying their *relation* is precisely my problem. If they were identical, I would not have to study them and I would be spared a lot of fatigue as a result. The very fact that I pose the question of their relation proves clearly that I do not *identify* them.[7]

The phrases to which Foucault refers are familiar to any of my peers who have studied postmodern theory, and the tendency to equate knowledge and power represents a desire many students have had to believe that discourse alone is enough; that is, that performing postmodern critiques is identical to dismantling systems of domination. But I think Foucault's comments on the relationship between knowledge and power strive to articulate a more complex connection in which *conflict* plays a key role. Academic discussions of postmodern theory commonly sacrifice materiality or render it subordinate to discourse. This diminishes some of the most challenging potentials of postmodern thought and the possibility of combining postmodern theory and real political action.

I employ this example of a common misreading of Foucault to suggest that a more nuanced analysis of the possibility of postmodern political engagement for my generation is needed. I do not believe that either of these catchphrases, or slogans, as Foucault regards the equivalency "knowledge is power," results from close readings or deep analyses of what are often very difficult texts. Rather, they result from an attempt to convey an incredibly varied mode of inquiry in a way that is precise and palatable. In effect, it is a problem of pedagogy. Since the locus of poststructuralist and postmodern theory is in the university, the question of how to teach a discourse that has the potential to subvert many things people take for granted in a classroom—the division between teacher and student, the existence of truth, the possibility of history, the sovereignty of science—is no doubt a complicated one. However, the recent outburst of student activism, in ways I will more fully explain, illustrates that there exists an enormous potential for young people to influence social relations outside of the university through radical concepts and that postmodern criticism should be taught with this in mind. I am not making the case that all teachers present an oversimplified and pacified version of postmodernism. Texts that reflect postmodern standpoints are often difficult and as a result these texts are frequently paraphrased at the expense of some of the radical implications. A far more challenging problem arises when the texts are read with care. The question of how to interface postmodernism and traditional political action to provoke social transformation is nothing short of overwhelming.

I am astonished by the recent swell of student activism; it appears certain members of my generation are beginning to overcome the difficulty of formulating a political method that may, at least in part, be described as postmodern. In the past, the challenge of incorporating postmodern theory and traditional tools of social resistance hindered political activity among privileged students who were enthusiastic about revolutionary politics, at least in a broad sense. Reconciling an investment in postmodern theory with participation in revolutionary action is no simple task, as developing a plan of group action that is able to negotiate postmodern sensibilities requires original aims and organizational frameworks that avoid the traps revealed by postmodern critiques of previous social movements. Messianic forms of Marxism, utopian projects of the 1960s, cultural feminism, and, of course, May 1968 have all been the objects of postmodern scrutiny. Though illuminating analyses have been the result, few foundations proper to a new movement have been established. That is, until recently.

What I am referring to as "postmodern sensibilities" may be clarified with an example. The tenets of one incarnation of postmodern thought are articulated unambiguously in Foucault's introduction to Gilles Deleuze and Felix Guattari's *Anti-Oedipus: Capitalism and Schizophrenia*. Here Foucault summarizes the principles that he believes would represent the book if it were condensed into a manual or guide, some of which follow:

> Free political action from all unitary and totalizing paranoia.
>
> Develop action, thought, and desires by proliferation, juxtaposition, and disjunction, and not by subdivision and pyramidal hierarchization.
>
> Prefer what is positive and multiple, difference over uniformity, flows over unities, mobile arrangements over systems.
>
> Do not think that one has to be sad in order to be militant, even though the thing one is fighting is abominable.
>
> Do not use thought to ground political action in Truth; nor political action to discredit, as mere speculation, a line of thought.
>
> Do not become enamored of power.[8]

This particular passage clearly articulates the demands of a distinct and influential version of postmodernism for political action. Additionally, this text has perhaps been the most influential text in my education thus far, introducing me to the immense difficulties and intriguing possibilities of a postmodern politics. While I find these tenets inspiring, I am haunted by the looming question of how one is to engage such complicated demands. As if these principles are not difficult enough to synthesize, innumerable insights from other theorists also must be taken into consideration. The complexity of trying to navigate the fluid territory of contemporary theory is coupled with the challenge of organizing in this era of postmodernity; the challenge of developing a postmodern organizational philosophy is inseparable from the challenge of formulating a group movement in a cultural space that is often referred to as fractured, in which the atomization of individuals may serve as yet another obstacle to social action.

Yet, despite these difficulties, there has been an explosion of student activism. Is it legitimate to relate these incidents to postmodernism? Are the mass demonstrations that have occurred over the last year proper to a generation that has "grown up postmodern"? I have pointed out that, at least superficially, there are many striking resemblances between protests in the 1960s and the new activism. However, as we move beyond the similarities in style and towards a closer examination of the relation of the two generations of activists it becomes apparent that the new movement represents a true innovation in organization. The abundance of press surrounding the proceedings in Seattle and the following events emphasized three attributes of the demonstrations that I would like to examine more closely: (1) There is no single group or organization to which all the protesters are connected. Instead, the individuals participating are associated with "affinity" groups, distinct groups with different focuses and agendas that join forces for a common cause. (2) The structure of the growing movement is nonhierarchical: there are no "leaders" in a conventional sense. (3) The essential role online communication played in the dissemination of information and planning of events: the movement is able to be decentralized and yet remain strong and strategically connected largely because of the Internet. I am not arguing that these new modes of coordinating social resistance are a direct repercussion of the popularity of postmodern discourse, as I recognize that postmodern theory is not something every member of the movement has been exposed to. Instead, I contend that they are the product of an intersection of postmodern education and the experience of growing up in this era of postmodernity. Certain elements of the new movement correlate in many respects to the academic discourse of postmodernism: the ability of the participants to elude hierarchical power structures within their groups, the ability to perform a sort of micro-politics through affinity groups, the ability to perform interventions while lacking a theoretical or organizational center, and the social critiques presented by organizers, which tend to reject messianic ideologies or a single utopian vision. The central role of the Internet as a medium for communication and organization relates to postmodernity's place as a legitimate factor of social reality, as does the prominence of issues such as globalization and capitalism.

Coverage of the new movement in the *New York Times* repeatedly attempts to convey the movement's lack of an organizational center through the term "diffuse."[9] The term is employed under the assumption that what it signifies is negative; that diffuseness and weakness are synonyms. However, this lack of an organizational center is no accident. Young organizers have self-consciously worked to create a movement that lacks overarching organization and leaders in the traditional sense, describing their ranks as full of lieutenants, no generals. Emphasis is instead placed on affinity groups: small, semi-independent units that are committed to coalition principles but free to determine their own agendas and actions. These groups keep a degree of autonomy, while coming together to protest the same or overlapping causes. The movement has yielded an unlikely coalition of protesters and interest groups united in their desire to alert others to the dangers of globalization: "The call to temper the capitalism around the globe comes from parties as diverse as the Catholic church and a cell of anarchists, and many people and organizations in between."[10] Some participants have made the joke that 501-C-3's (a reference to the IRS form that independent, nonprofit groups must file each year) outnumber individuals at the recent protests. The presence of organized labor in Seattle next to environmental activists still stands out in the minds of many in contrast to previous movements: "The image of Teamsters and Turtles together was light-years away from those days when the hardhats would come out to clobber the anti-war demonstrators."[11]

Many participants in the new movement are well versed in reasons for having a model of diffuseness as an organizational ideal. This quality of self-awareness or reflexivity pervades the new activism, and may be linked to postmodernism. At recent demonstrations what would have been called the headquarters in years past was referred to as the "convergence center," acknowledging that it served as a space for disparate groups to meet and form alliances instead of a point of centralized authority: "The new movement has no use for centralized authority. Instead, it cherishes the word convergence, leaving ample room for lefties, libertarians, and synthesizers of every stripe."[12] In lieu of a hierarchy of power, manifestos, or platforms, organizers have attempted to determine the movement's actions through consensus processes, depending on shared values and overlapping goals to determine action. Recognizing that consensus is an alternative to detached top-down decision making, the hope is that consensus will empower individuals through participation in decision-making processes: "The democratic process utilized during demonstrations decentralizes power even as it offers tangible solidarity; for example, affinity groups afford greater and more diverse numbers of people a real share in decision making."[13] Hopefully, it is this mixture of autonomy and empowerment that will help the movement keep momentum.

Without a definite source of authority to defer to, each participant is partly responsible for the course the actions take; at least this is the idea. Compulsory unity has been abandoned in favor of a more fluid form of coalition building: "Activism is nether singular nor unitary. It is the combined effort of small and independent groups, rooted in many different communities. It is not a single coalition but a spectrum of self-determined movements who are finding each other and figuring out how to collaborate."[14] Recognizing that the emerging movement remains viable because of the autonomy of agitators, there is noticeable resistance to the concept of forming an umbrella organization: "There neither is nor will be a single organization—be it a political party or a movement group like the 1960s Students for a Democratic Society—that can remotely claim to represent the many strains of action."[15] This lack of central authority resists at least one of the dangers of leadership: if a participant organization happens to disband or withdraw, the movement will not crumble as a result. The potential power of diffuseness should not be underestimated. A recent article in the *New York Times* provides a warning:

> A Rand Corporation study for the Pentagon detailed how Mexico's Zapatista rebel movement in 1994 used publicity tactics . . . to generate support abroad for its campaign against the North American Free Trade Agreement. The study said swarms of independent citizens groups can prove far more effective than hierarchical movements when combating established institutions because they can't easily be "decapitated."[16]

It appears decentralized models have already proven their effectiveness, in some contexts.

This mode of decentralization is a viable form of organization only because of the Internet. Like the successful capitalists of their generation, these new activists are not afraid of technological innovation; the difference being that they view the Web as a networking and publicity tool instead of a potential source of revenue. In a sense, the World Wide Web has served as a model for connections between the various affinity groups, which are linked in a way that does not follow a pyramidal model. Taking full advantage of the democratic potentials of the Internet, activists have set up independent media centers at protest locations, broadcasting their take on the events. The numerous Websites published by activists are not simply a source of news and updates, but are forums for discussion and evaluation of the movement as it progresses. These Websites were a crucial resource for this essay, allowing me to witness the ongoing process of creating a movement and gain access to the thoughtful reflections of activists on their own strengths and weaknesses.

In conjunction with the Internet, the other vital force behind the emerging movement is direct action, a broad category of civil disobedience that "encompasses everything from blockades and banner hangs to strikes and pickets: the whole panoply of pressure tactics that are not mediated by the political or legal system."[17] One of the major organizations in the new movement is the Direct Action Network (DAN), which itself is organized by the affinity group model. Though every affinity group involved in recent protests does not adhere to DAN's theories and methods, DAN has been pivotal in preparing agitators for recent interventions. A selection of their Principles of Unity follows:

> A confrontational attitude toward undemocratic organizations in which capital is the only real policy maker.
>
> A call to nonviolent direct action and civil disobedience and the construction of local alternatives by local people as answers to the actions of governments and corporations.
>
> An organizational philosophy based on decentralization, direct democracy, and local autonomy.
>
> A rejection of all forms of oppression and exploitation such as patriarchy, white supremacy and imperialism.[18]

With these principles in mind, I would like to return to the discussion of postmodern theory. I do not invoke DAN's principles to provide a philosophic foundation for the entire movement; there is not one. Rather, I quote them to reiterate the fact that many features of the new movement have been clearly articulated by activists and are rooted in a thoughtful consideration of the forms organizing has taken and could take. These principles, in addition to concerns voiced by members of the new movement, reflect what I take to be an understanding of what is at stake in postmodernism.

In an article published in the *Nation* following the protests against the Democratic National Convention in Los Angeles Naomi Klein comments on the interplay of postmodernism and the new activism : "Protest, in very short order, has gone postmodern: less about the issues than the tactics, the permits, the police response, the trials afterward—protesting about protesting itself."[19] Klein is correct in pointing out that protesters have had to fight for their right to assembly and have, unfortunately, been kept busy denouncing police brutality; however, I do not see the fact that these obstacles have detracted from the focus on economic justice as a reflection of the postmodern nature of contemporary activism. I am more interested in the traces of postmodern influence to be found below the surface of the actions themselves, in statements made by activists and in their organizational theories and democratic ideals. In other words, the postmodern element of the new activism is not something trivial to be dismissed as Klein does. The intents of the activists often coincide with postmodern insights, leaving me to believe that protest going postmodern is what has made their efforts both interesting and effective.

Returning to the tenets outlined by Foucault regarding a strain of postmodern theory, I see striking overlaps between these principles and some of the ideals of the new movement. These tenets demand that action, thought, and desires be developed in a way that evades subdivision and pyramidal hierarchization. Flows are preferred over unities, mobile arrangements over systems. Both these statements relate to the self-conscious subversion of hierarchy in organizing and the privileging of the affinity group model; one activist writes that the new movement should "Forget stifling calls for 'unity'."[20] The stress placed on the absence of leaders in the new movement reflects Foucault's warning against becoming enamored of power. The playful atmosphere, in the face of serious issues, resonates with the observation that being militant does not always mean being sad. In relation to a more general version of postmodernism, within the movement there is "emphasis on action over ideology," or on process as opposed to predetermined methods. As activists respond to contingencies, new political alliances and creative collaborations are possible. Yet, these relationships develop while activists keep in mind that the "strength of contemporary activism lies in the autonomy of agitators."[21] Changes in the social landscape, such as the fracturing of cultural groups and atomization of individuals, relate to the autonomy of affinity groups. Like these factors, many facets of social reality in this era of postmodernity have been incorporated into the new movement and reinforce it. For example, in their critique of globalization and capitalism, the activists call attention to the faults of NAFTA without recourse to protectionism: the sentiment of many activists is support of globalization, but a more localized and nonexploitative form than that which is being practiced. Finally, the convergence of creative art and creative politics points towards the postmodern aesthetic of juxtaposition and transgressing of boundaries. One activist says, "What we need is a new culture. A whole new culture."[22] It seems these activists believe that a new culture is theirs to invent.

I must acknowledge that the new movement has not been without its critics, and that I myself am not without my own criticisms. In addition to the apparent contradiction of student affluence and their critiques of global capitalism, the movement has other deficiencies. As many baby boomer activists learned, the consensus process, though in concept an attractive way to practice democracy, is often agonizing in reality. Witnessing a meeting at which activists are trying to come to a unanimous decision Cooper testifies:

> To the eyes of an old '60s veteran, this meeting is almost painfully democratic and politely orderly. There are even agreed-upon silent hand signals by which one can express support or disagreement with whoever is speaking. It's all part of the new movement's treasured principles of "consensus decision making," a cumbersome process that requires that everyone in the room eventually agree to whatever action is decided.[23]

In regard to decentralization, the affinity model has proven quite effective thus far, though some doubt whether it will be able to function as well on a larger scale. Still another criticism concedes that while the movement as a whole is skeptical of leaders, it may be time for the activists to stop criticizing systems of power and try to gain some of their own.

Rather than serious flaws, I see many of these shortcomings as problematic attempts to negotiate the difficulties surfacing as activists turn revolutionary concepts into revolutionary action. Circumventing what have come to be regarded as the downfalls of previous social movements is a challenge that faces these new activists, and though their efforts have not been faultless, the recent protests have certainly been innovative and promising. For instance, the consensus decision-making process is based on the idea that everyone should speak and be heard; the basis of a politics and community building that resists exclusion and censorship. Unfortunately, the process is both awkward and, in a way, naïve. Ultimately, however, what I am most concerned with is the fact that consensus processes are being explored at all, in ways that both resemble and deepen the attempts made in the 1960s, regardless of whether this mode of determining action may eventually be forsaken for another.

I am certain that postmodernism and the proliferation of student-initiated protests do not have a relationship that is causal; however, I am equally convinced they do have some sort of connection. My generation has come to age in a period during which the forms and goals of civil disobedience in the 1960s had to be re-evaluated. In other words, a new philosophy of social resistance had to be developed for it to be effective in the present day. Here I define effective as capturing the imagination of a generation by establishing an objective and a method proper to their specific historical moment. I am not sure if this movement has or will ever reach this point, though it is unquestionably closer than anything has been in many years. Enunciating the points of convergence between postmodern theory and the methods and philosophies of contemporary activists was not an attempt to prove that theory has inspired the new movement, only that they reflect on one another, and, in a sense, that both are inseparable from postmodernity as it relates to the structure of social relations particular to this era. As the new activists create a movement based on situated action, nonhierarchical associations, and contingent tactics, it seems that the time has come to question domination and systems of power beyond the realm of discourse and outside the walls of the university. With any luck, there will be much more to come from this generation, one that is acutely aware of what is at stake in political activism as they grow up in a period that is post-May '68.

NOTES

1. Marc Cooper, "After Seattle: Free-Trade Protests Coming to a City Near You." *LA Weekly,* 24 March 2000. http://www.laweekly.com/ink/00/18/cover-cooper.html (22 July 2001).

2. Tara Zahra, "Sweating the Big Stuff." *Salon,* 6 April 1999. http://www.salon. com/ books/it/1999/08/06/sweatshop/index2.html (22 July 2001).

3. William Finnegan, "After Seattle: Anarchists Get Organized." *New Yorker,* 17 April 2000, 41.

4. Andrew Boyd, "Extreme Costume Ball." *Village Voice,* 25 July 2000, 46.

5. Julie Rivkin and Michael Ryan. *Literary Theory: An Anthology* (London: Blackwell, 1998), 333.

6. Terry Eagleton, *Literary Theory: An Introduction* (Minnesota: University of Minnesota, 1996), 123.

7. Michel Foucault, *Aesthetics, Method, and Epistemology*. Ed. James Faubion (New York: New Press, 1998), 455.

8. Michel Foucault, Introduction, in Gilles Deleuze and Felix Guattari, *Anti-Oedipus: Capitalism and Schizophrenia* (Minneapolis: University of Minnesota Press, 1998), xiii-xiv.

9. John Kifner and David Sanger, "Financial Leaders Meet as Protests Clog Washington." *New York Times* 17 April 2000, A1.

10. Joseph Kahn, "Globalization Unifies its Many-Striped Foes." *New York Times,* 15 April 2000, A7.

11. Cooper, "After Seattle."

12. Richard Goldstein. "The Birth of a Movement." *Village Voice,* 25 July 2000, 37.

13. Cindy Milstein, "Reclaim the Cities." *Alternet.* http://www.alternet.org (13 August 2000).

14. L. A. Kauffman, "Free Radical: Whose Movement?" *Alternet.* http://www.alternet.org (27 April 2000).

15. Kauffman.

16. Kahn, A7.

17. Kauffman.

18. Direct Action Network, *DAN's Principles of Unity*. http://agitprop.org/artand revolution/missionprinciples.htm (12 July 2001).

19. Naomi Klein, "Cries in the Streets in LA." *Nation,* 4 September 2000, 7.

20. Kauffman.

21. Kauffman.

22. Tamara Straus, "Baby Steps to a Global Revolution?: Barbara Ehrenreich and Juliette Beck Discuss the New Activism." *Alternet.* http://www.alternet.org (27 April 2000).

23. Cooper, "After Seattle."

BIBLIOGRAPHY

Boyd, Andrew. "Extreme Costume Ball." *Village Voice,* 25 July 2000, 46-47.

Cooper, Marc. "After Seattle: Free-Trade Protests Coming to a City Near You." *LA Weekly,* 24 March 2000. http://www.laweekly.com/ink/00/18/cover-cooper.shtml (22 July 2001).

Deleuze, Gilles, and Felix Guattari. *Anti-Oedipus: Capitalism and Schizophrenia.* Minneapolis: University of Minnesota Press, 1998.

Direct Action Network. *DAN's Principles of Unity.* http://agitprop.org/artandrevolution/missionprinciples.htm.

Eagleton, Terry. *Literary Theory: An Introduction.* Minnesota: University of Minnesota, 1996.

Featherstone, Liza. "The New Student Movement." *Nation,* 15 May 2000.

Finnegan, William. "After Seattle: Anarchists Get Organized." *New Yorker,* 17 April 2000, 40-51.

Foucault, M. *Aesthetics, Method, and Epistemology.* Ed. James Faubion. New York: New Press, 1998.

Goldstein, Richard. "The Birth of a Movement." *Village Voice,* 25 July 2000, 37-39.

Kahn, Joseph. "Globalization Unites Its Many-Striped Foes." *New York Times,* 15 April 2000.

Kauffman, L. A. "Free Radical: Whose Movement?" *Alternet.* http://www.alternet.org (27 April 2000).

Kifner, John, and David Sanger. "Protesters Try to Shut Down World Bank and IMF Meetings," *New York Times* 17 April 2000, A1.

Klein, Naomi. "Cries in the Streets in LA," *Nation* 4 September 2000, 6-7.

Milstein, Cindy. "Reclaim the Cities," *Alternet.* http://www.alternet.org (27 April 2000).

Rivkin, Julie, and Michael Ryan. *Literary Theory: An Anthology.* London: Blackwell, 1998.

Straus, Tamara. "Baby Steps to a Global Revolution?: Barbara Ehrenreich and Juliette Beck Discuss the New Activism," *Alternet.* http://www.alternet.org (27 April 2000).

Zahra, Tara. "Sweating the Big Stuff." *Salon.* http://www.salon. com/books/it/1999/08/06/sweatshop/index2.html (22 July 2001).

13
To Be Young, Countercultural, and Black: Racial Pluralism, Countercultures, and African American Activism of the 1960s

David M. Jones

> At this point, the [counterculture] I speak of embraces only a strict minority of the youth and a handful of their adult mentors. It excludes our more conservative young, for whom a bit less Social Security and a bit more of that old-time religion (plus more police on the beat) would be sufficient to make the Great Society a thing of beauty. It excludes our more liberal youth, for whom the alpha and omega of politics is no doubt still that Kennedy style. It excludes the scattering of old-line Marxist youth groups whose members, like their fathers before them, continue to tend the ashes of the proletarian revolution, watching for a spark to leap forth. More importantly, it excludes in large measure the militant black young, whose political project has become so narrowly defined in ethnic terms that, despite its urgency, it has become as culturally old-fashioned as the nationalist mythopoesis of the nineteenth century.[1]

In his 1969 text *The Making of a Counter Culture*, which provided a name for several emerging resistance movements,[2] Theodore Roczak suggested that the 1960s countercultures had only a peripheral relationship to African American activism of the same period. Roczak's analysis appears true in that few African American activists of the 1960s are publicly identified with the period's countercultures. It is also the case that black militant organizations of the 1960s often opposed racially integrated strategies for social change, arguing that whites within black-identified organizations represented a counterrevolutionary force and African Americans would be better off organizing themselves, free from the influence of white liberals.[3] Repudiation of both whiteness and integration is often described by historians as a pervasive political stance among black revolutionary nationalists, even though prominent proponents of Black Power such as Angela Davis, Huey Newton, and Malcolm X favored multiracial political action during part or all of their public careers during the 1960s.[4]

This essay provides a more careful examination of public and private ties between African American activists and 1960s countercultures. Analysis and definitions of countercultural activism and close readings of small-circulation magazines, memoirs, and anthologized essays commenting on the period show that the goals of social justice, personal freedom, and noncorporate cultural production were pursued by cross-racial coalitions of grassroots activists. Reexamining the history of 1960s countercultures in relation to African American political and cultural activism also reveals the influence of racial pluralism over the period's identity politics.

The title of this essay makes a dual reference—first, to countercultural movements of the 1960s that were marked by African American influence, and secondly, to playwright Lorraine Hansberry. Countercultural movements influenced by African American activism include the New Left, the sexual revolution, and the folk music revival; among these movements, this essay will focus primarily on racial pluralism in the New Left and shifts in racial/sexual politics during the sexual revolutions of the 1960s. Efforts by the New Left to recognize and to promote Black Power ideology illustrate a shared sense of purpose among organizations that were led by white and African American activists. Many African American public figures of the period became heroes for youth of all races who were engaged in countercultural activism. In this context, interracial sexuality became a distinctive but controversial site of political struggle, just as the civil rights movement peaked and began to wane in influence and visibility. Despite many ties between African American justice movements and countercultures, however, retrospective scholarship on the period more often highlights differences and conflicts rather than similarities of purpose, proximity, and mutual influence.

My title also alludes to Lorraine Hansberry, a playwright and political radical who articulated critical views of black racial, sexual, and national identity, though she was not a public supporter of (or a known participant in) 1960s countercultures. Hansberry's career does provide a case study for examining the relationships between postmodern black identities and 1960s countercultures, since her life and works are poised between an Old Left favoring structural Marxism, union activism, and other economic strategies for social change, and an emerging New Left favoring additional forms of activism rooted in racial, gender, and sexual identity. Hansberry's personal struggles exemplify a dilemma faced by numerous African American activists who favored neither a separatist black revolutionary nationalism nor an approach to change focused primarily on "personal politics." I will show further that Hansberry's work would probably have supported goals and strategies of the emerging countercultures had her life not ended tragically in 1965.

Surprisingly, even African American artists with obvious ties to 1960s countercultures (such as musician Jimi Hendrix and poets Ted Joans and Bob Kaufman) have not altered the public image of countercultures as a white youth phenomenon.[5] The work of these artists and many additional historical facts illustrate multiracial participation in countercultures. Folk societies made historic recordings of black rural blues musicians such as Brownie McGhee and Lightnin' Hopkins.[6] The Black Panthers favored a Marxist, racially pluralist ideology in their peak years, and many members partook in the pleasure-oriented pastimes of the counterculture: drug use, sexual promiscuity, and music festivals. Within the peace movement, there were integrated efforts to resist draft registration (inspired in part by the Berkeley Free Speech Movement of the early 1960s, which participated in direct actions to help desegregate public accommodations in the Bay Area),[7] among other instances of cooperative work. African American activists and intellectuals born after 1960 are clearly influenced by this history of racially pluralist activism, since curricular reform and the institutionalization of Black Studies, wider availability of blues and jazz recordings, and even an increased range of sexual choices are the longer-term results of countercultural resistance and black militant activism. With this essay, I would like to encourage a more thorough examination of African American participation in countercultural movements, to inspire a present and future move toward a pluralist politics of resistance.

COUNTERCULTURALISM AND THE NEW LEFT: AFRICAN AMERICAN INFLUENCE

In the broadest sense, social movements are "organized, nongovernmental efforts of large numbers of people to attain significant social and personal change."[8] Countercultural movements are distinguished from other social movements because they favor "a set of norms and values . . . that contradict the dominant norms and values of the society of which that group is a part."[9] The "nongovernmental" orientation indicated by Burns and the contradiction of mainstream values discussed by Yinger were especially pronounced in 1960s countercultural movements, as I will show, indicating that a generation gap extended into politics.

In his text, *The American Left in the Twentieth Century*, John Diggins posits several clarifying distinctions between the Old Left and the New Left in American politics. According to Diggins, an interest in "economic democracy"[10] linked various incarnations of the Old Left, including union activists, socialists, and structural Marxists. Some of that interest in economic inequality was reflected in the New Left as well, but Diggins adds that generational differences led to distinctions in social philosophy: "A radical nucleus of a generation is formed when some young intellectuals or students, as a result of common 'destabilizing' experiences, begin to feel, articulate, and defend the identity of certain values and ideals of a society that is indifferent or hostile."[11] For the Old Left, destabilizing experiences included the Depression, the rise of fascism, the Spanish Civil War, and Stalinism, while "for the New Left they were the domestic racial crisis, the wars in Southeast Asia, Cuba, and China, and the politics of confrontation with the resultant fear of oppression."[12] The Old Left's strong interest in electoral politics and economics can be contrasted with the stronger interest in cultural change within the New Left, expressed by sexual rebellion, women's liberation, and the folk revival. Generally, 1960s countercultural movements favored the goals of expanding personal freedom, advancing social justice, opposing consumerism, and achieving ecological sustainability, all of which contradicted sharply the programmatically moral and military concerns familiar in a lingering Cold War culture,[13] and also revised the Old Left's narrower range of economic and political concerns.

One could choose from a dizzying range of cultural artifacts to illustrate countercultural ideology in practice during the post-World War II period in the United States. One could move backwards to the 1950s or even to the 1940s as moments when pockets of resistance to political and cultural orders coalesced in a process culminating in the mass resistance of the 1960s. Cultural historians usually identify Beat Generation writers, jazz and rock musicians, hippies, folkniks, and peace protesters as emblems of both 1950s and 1960s counterculturalism.[14] Countercultural movements of both decades articulated a collective response to suburbanization, consumerism, the Vietnam War, lingering racism and sexism, and failures in political leadership. This notion of principled rebellion links the legacies of SDS (Students for a Democratic Society), the Weathermen, the Youth International Party, et al., with the efforts of African American activists to bring about racial justice through the civil rights and Black Power movements. In his 1995 text *The Movement and the Sixties*, historical and cultural critic Terry Anderson argues further that less formal activism within 1960s youth cultures (blues, folk, and soul music, sexual experimentation, hallucinogenics, communal living, and even Kerouacian physical and spiritual quests) also functioned as forms of personal and group liberation.[15] The countercultural movements I discuss in detail as examples—the New Left and the sexual revolution—illustrate the range of concerns raised by the disparate groups that resisted mainstream social mores and institutions.

Counterculturalism is best understood as a pluralist construct, because a large number of distinct strategies for work and life were advocated by individuals and organizations that described themselves as countercultural. However, the term countercultural is weighted down with meanings articulated by public figures such as Jerry Rubin, Ken Kesey, Abbie Hoffman, and Timothy Leary, and by pop culture images of drug-using, free-loving, work-resisting hippies. A closer look at countercultural activism of the period reveals a prevailing pluralism, a continuum of ideologies that are commonly skeptical of dogma but revere human justice, respect tradition, and celebrate difference. In the words of Rebecca Klatch, 1960s countercultures "encompassed both an urge toward individual self-expression and self-gratification, and an urge toward collectivism and community. It is, indeed, this diversity of beliefs and practices that allowed people of varying backgrounds and ideologies to commonly identify with an oppositional [counter] culture."[16] Collectively then, the countercultural ethos encompasses not simply Timothy Leary's endorsements of LSD and Abbie Hoffman's call for "revolution for the hell of it,"[17] but also a broader push for a transformation of social structures through many different forms of self-discovery and political action.

In contrast to the Old Left, which privileged economic class conflict and was largely unsuccessful in theorizing race within models for social change and in organizing African American communities en masse,[18] the New Left voices within 1960s countercultures expressed a stronger interest in black radical ideology, an interest rooted in a general concern for "personal politics." A 1969 article by Paul Piccone, "From Youth Culture to Political Praxis," published in *Radical America*, provides a prototypical illustration of New Left political ideology. In this article, Piccone argued that the New Left's interest in the personal was not an evasion of familiar forms of political change. Instead, Piccone suggested that political change had to move beyond established institutional and intellectual models to become relevant for the new masses. Anticipating a new era of multiracial, cross-gendered, multigenerational activism, counterculturalists sought ways of becoming immediately engaged in "real" political change, as Piccone implies:

> The major thrust of the counter culture is precisely the search for the authentic which today appears all around us as having been visited into the "phony" and the "artificial." It is not accidental that the most viable categories of the counter culture are "sincerity" and "naturalness." But what the counter culture has also realized is that *mere* intellectual or theoretical therapy of these problems simply reproduces the old ruts in different forms; the way out of it is not through another more elaborate or "better" ideology or theory, but through an activity that will allow the subject to find himself and his fellow human beings, not by manipulating or being manipulated by the abstract categories of bourgeois culture but by creating a new social order free of the hang-ups of the old one.[19]

Within the countercultures, a strong interest in African American cultural life illustrated this desire for sincerity and naturalness in everyday life that could positively influence the world of politics. In the cultural arena, a folk music revival that had begun in the 1950s continued to inspire a generation of white musicians and music fans, supporting the early careers of Bob Dylan, Joan Baez, Phil Ochs, and many others. Many folksingers appeared at music festivals with classic African American blues performers, providing further inspiration for young musicians and expanding the audience for blues.[20] In his 1971 text *Freakshow*, rock critic and biographer Albert Goldman quotes singer Janis Joplin, who claimed that imitations of black music "will make me a better white."[21] Goldman used this comment as the basis for a larger observation about white youth interest in black music:

> As I pondered her [Joplin's] answer, it struck me that she had articulated this generation's great secret. They are *not* trying to pass. They are trying to save their souls. Adopting as a tentative identity the firmly set, powerfully expressive mask of the black man, the confused, conflicted, and frequently self-doubting and self-loathing offspring of Mr. and Mrs. America are released into an emotional and spiritual freedom denied them by their own inherited culture.[22]

While it is generally problematic to identify African American performance with primitive release and freedom, as white hipsters and minstrel performers have commonly done,[23] Goldman's comments compellingly characterize the intense countercultural interest in black music. The contrast between a Cold War culture obsessed with military power, economic gain, and conformity, and indigenous African American music steeped in religious spirit, pleasure, and political commitment could not have been starker. During the 1960s, amid the increasing prominence of countercultural movements, blues and soul music became a soundtrack as compelling as jazz had been for a previous coterie of 1950s white "hipsters."

In the political arena, the civil rights movement provided a proving ground for many young white activists seeking to embrace a morally forthright cause and to participate in grassroots political organizing. White student participation during the Mississippi "Freedom Summer" voting rights campaign of 1964 has been documented widely,[24] when the presence of white students led to greater national visibility for the movement. There are many additional indications of common ground between white and black activists. The Port Huron Statement, authored in 1962 by the SDS (Students for a Democratic Society), expressed support for the civil rights movement as a fight "for social welfare for all Americans; for free speech and the right to protest; for the shield of economic independence and bargaining power; for reduction of the arms race which takes national attention and resources away from the problems of domestic injustices."[25] Martin Luther King's declaration of opposition to the Vietnam War in 1965 demonstrated a cross-racial interest in pacifism that was shared widely within the New Left and African American justice movements, although support for King's antiwar stance was not universal among civil rights movement leaders,[26] and black militants of the same period would often criticize pacifism as a do-nothing response to the atrocities committed by white racists.[27]

In the late 1960s, as more and more African Americans expressed support for revolutionary nationalism and self-determination, relationships between the New Left and African American activists became strained in some cases, but significant cross-racial support for issues related to racial and economic justice was still evident. Proto-Marxist strategies for economic change were shared among black militant groups such as the Panthers, black trade union organizations such as DRUM

(Dodge Revolutionary Union Movement), SNCC (Student Non-Violent Coordinating Committee), and white-led New Left organizations such as the Progressive Labor faction within the SDS and the Young Socialist Alliance.[28] Collectively, these organizations sought to revolutionize economic, political, and cultural institutions by advocating wage increases for workers, greater freedom of expression, and increased political participation. Periodical literature produced within countercultures interspersed articles on Black Power, open sexuality, and local music scenes, illustrating a widely held assumption that personal freedom was not a condition of luxury that might usefully be delayed until issues of justice and inequality were addressed. Instead, personal freedom was widely considered to be an essential condition of a just society.

Among the publications that illustrate ties in political ideology between the New Left and 1960s black militants, SDS's *New Left Notes* was among the most prominent. According to cultural critic and period activist Todd Gitlin, this publication coined the term "pigs" as a synonym for police officers, and of course the term became a popular one in black nationalist discourse.[29] Throughout the middle and late 1960s, SDS maintained a continuing conversation with SNCC over questions of movement ideology and strategy, although the conversation was not always harmonious. In 1966, however, *New Left Notes* published a defense of Black Power that discussed in detail some of the ideological foundations of black self-determination:

> Black Power marks the beginning of a new stage in the struggle of a people toward social liberation, a stage as important today as was the Civil War and Reconstruction a century ago. For the Negro in America, the American heritage has meant centuries of slavery, transformed at last into corporate "free enterprise" slavery, poverty, and physical terror. But beyond even the lynchings and poverty, the blood and hunger, has been the systematic attempt not only to crush the Negro but to make him accept his degradation as his just due. History and tradition weaved a blanket of social lies that smothered the Negro in his own supposed inhumanity, his fitness only for manual labor, his awareness of social and even physical dependence on the power and wealth of White America, his incapability of running his own life.[30]

Landy and Cooper describe Black Power as both a political movement, concerned with the distribution of power and resources, and a cultural movement, concerned with the interplay between social meaning and artistic production. Their view of Black Power is consistent with sentiments expressed by many Black Power activists themselves, whose ideologies for change ranged from black cultural nationalism, which sought to celebrate and to theorize aesthetics, patterns of worship, family life, and other cultural practices, to black revolutionary nationalism, which sought to intervene (by violent revolution or other means) against global capitalism, colonialism, and racial discrimination in the United States. Landy and Cooper endorsed an idea also supported by SNCC under Stokely Carmichael, that a black-led nationalist movement was a necessary precursor to a pluralist mass revolution:

> Given the difficulty of the Negro's revolution and, at the same time, his minority position in American society, the problem of alliances is more difficult, but crucially important. Before one can even talk about alliances, however, it is important to understand the absolute necessity for building an internationally unified, strong, and self-respecting Negro movement. Only then, when Negroes have something strong enough that other groups can ally with it and not simply dominate it, can one consider the problem of alliances. The central problem with the Negro movement has been that there has not really been one capable of digging roots into Black communities and responding to the socio-psychological and political needs of the Negro masses. Black power . . . is a radical response to that radical need.[31]

Not surprisingly, the white-led New Left encountered a similar problem to that of the "Negro" movement: influencing politics of the larger American community proved increasingly difficult as polarizing crises—the Vietnam War, selective service, racial segregation, and Cold War confrontation—produced both youth rebellion and white backlash. However, Landy and Cooper did suggest that racially integrated organizations be the eventual goal of the period's political and cultural activism, even if time might elapse before multiracial movements could be sustained over the longer term. Landy and Cooper's article shows once again the depth of New Left interest in African American activism.

AFRICAN AMERICAN TEXTUAL/SEXUAL REBELLIONS AND COUNTERCULTURES

1960s countercultures have long been identified with an emerging sexual revolution. Most memoirs and documentaries focused on the 1960s, such as *Making Sense of the Sixties* (a series directed by David Hoffman) and the landmark *Woodstock* documentary (directed by Michael Wadleigh), discuss liberalized sexuality very centrally as an influence over the lives of youth within the counterculture. Hedonistic messages in the still-emerging musical genre of rock and roll (often presented in the form of live concerts and festivals that collected thousands of young people seeking new experiences), expanded availability of birth control, and extended time spent on the road in political organizing can be counted among many social factors that contributed to a sexual revolution among youth of the period. Todd Gitlin's description of sexual politics within SDS illustrates a widely held sentiment among period activists:

> My first year in Ann Arbor [where SDS formed], a member of the Old Guard, fresh from one of the quickie entanglements that "campus traveling" made pos-

> sible, said to me half-ironically: "The movement hangs together on the head of a penis" . . . The sexual intensity matched the political and intellectual, or was it the other way round [*sic*]? Each national meeting was not only a reconnection among people who, after all, lived scattered across the country; it was also an enclave in time where the normal social rules were suspended. No national meeting took place without its sexual liaisons—and integral to them, the protracted, anguished, frequently all-night discussions about where the new and old relationships should go from there.[32]

Other period documents and memoirs further illustrate the ties between liberated sexuality and political activism within the New Left and within the black-identified resistance movements. The November 25, 1966, issue of the *Berkeley Barb* included headline articles on Stokely Carmichael's call for a boycott of the *Oakland Tribune* (because of the unjust imprisonment of a local black leader) and on the Campus Sexual Rights Forum, which was sponsoring both a Thursday open house discussion of sexual alterity and a Saturday night "nude party for single women, homosexuals and heterosexual couples."[33] Former Panther leader Elaine Brown also comments on the period's sexual permissiveness. She describes her early years with the Panthers in her memoir *A Taste of Power*, when she worked briefly with John Floyd, a party organizer in Los Angeles:

> John Floyd and I wrote copy together, pasted up storyboards, and typed and turned out, in six weeks, the first issue of the Black Congress newspaper. It was called *Harambee*—Swahili for "Let's Pull Together." We also slept together, once. After that, however, John ignored me on a personal level, which I took personally, even though the times had changed and making love had become a thing akin to drinking water.[34]

Brown's memoir treats sexual politics specifically in the context of the Black Power movement, showing that in an era of countercultural activism, African American youth were influenced by shifts in sexual norms and practices. While the topic of sexual liberation is usually discussed as a central element of countercultural politics, this topic is commonly discussed as either peripheral to African American activist efforts or as an expression of sexism among black males. On the issue of sexism and black masculinity, it seems clear that new patterns of sexuality among African American youth created (or at minimum, revealed) deep schisms between male and female activists, probably in part because, as Alice Echols suggests, "men's desires for sexual relationships without emotional commitment certainly created a groundswell of resentment," in a way similar to tensions over issues of sex and commitment that exist more widely between heterosexual men and women in United States society.[35] Concerns about sexual violence and other physical assaults against African American women also contributed to the tensions during the period. The subject of sexual violence is treated widely in memoirs and texts of cultural criticism published in the 1980s and 1990s, such as Elaine Brown's aforementioned text and bell hooks's *Ain't I a Woman: Black Women and Feminism* (1981). I will argue here, however, that the influence of a permissive sexual ideology expressed widely within the counterculture challenged race-specific sexual taboos and widened the range of acceptable sexualities for subsequent generations of African American youth.

Countercultural movements of the 1960s invited behavioral challenges to long-standing taboos against interracial sexuality in a way similar to the movements' effects on other taboos regulating premarital sex, lesbian and gay sex, and promiscuity. The close proximity of young African American and white activists during political organizing[36] and the sexualizing of black male bodies in the discourse of youth culture (James Brown, Muhammed Ali, and Jimi Hendrix are three examples) have been cited as particular causes for a demystification of interracial sexuality. While much as been written on the idealizing of black women as politically correct sexual partners in African American literature from the period and demands for male supremacy by black male militants of the era, historic challenges to black/white sexual taboos have been observed less often as an enduring consequence of the period's sexual politics.[37] There was never a consensus among African American activists of the period that a wider range of sexual choices—particularly interracial sexuality—represented a form of liberation. However, few would argue from a contemporary perspective that a continuation of race/sex taboos would be consistent with the larger goal of a full and meaningful liberty for all. Within 1960s African American activist movements—and in the three decades following those movements—the topic of sexual liberation was not debated widely or openly enough for the relationship between countercultural ideology and African American sexuality to become common knowledge.

A close reading of period texts indicates a polarization of opinion on the question of whether sexuality represents a relevant site for political struggle, and the related question of whether demystifying interracial sexuality represents a progressive politics. Writing by black male authors often endorsed the general view of sexuality expressed widely in countercultural texts, favoring promiscuity within political movements as a form of liberation. Several notable literary texts by black male authors offered a minimum of critical commentary on sexuality, but included descriptions of sexual liaisons—interracial and otherwise—in a manner suggesting that sexual conquest is a characteristic practice among liberated black males. Cecil Brown's *The Life and Loves of Mr. Jiveass Nigger* (1969) and Clarence Major's *All Night Visitors* (1969) are two texts that depict sexual promiscuity in this way—as a familiar element of "hipster" culture, with an implied critique of race/sex taboos. The male protagonists of these novels have an irresistible sexual allure that seems to echo the encounters with the "forbidden fruit" of interracial sexuality that occurred during protest campaigns in Mississippi and elsewhere.[38]

Two of the period's most prominent nonfiction texts by black male authors treat interracial sexuality more critically, but are otherwise marred by militant posturing and suspect social science. Eldridge Cleaver's 1968 text, *Soul on Ice*, is a notable example of the earnestness and the flaws within the black nationalist discourse on interracial sexuality. In a fictionalized essay, "The Allegory of the Black Eunuchs," Cleaver declared, in the words of an imprisoned character named Lazarus, that "every time I embrace a black woman I'm embracing slavery, and when I put my arms around a white woman, well, I'm hugging freedom."[39] Cleaver's crude argument for a greater sexual freedom is framed as both a resistance to white authority and an endorsement of patriarchy, evoked as well by his infamous description of rape as an insurrectionary act.[40] *Soul on Ice* advocated black male conquest of white women at a moment when interracial liaisons, even when consensual, were considered by many to be counterrevolutionary. However, while the text is marred by its misogynistic ideology (as noted by Michele Wallace, bell hooks, and other black feminist cultural critics),[41] the text does engage with the question of what role personal sexuality should play in the militant black movement, breaking the silence on a subject that the civil rights movement and previous periods of African American radical activism had generally avoided.

A second nonfiction text, *Sex and Racism in America* by Calvin Hernton, combines personal reflections and the language of social science to identify the "hang-ups" that stand in the way of a freer sexuality in the United States. Heavy uses of humor and irony and intentional appeals to racial and sexual myths are combined to challenge and to reinforce the divisions between "black" and "white" sexuality. A passage from the introduction demonstrates the text's approach to race and sex typologies:

> The white man's self-esteem is in a constant state of sexual anxiety in all matters dealing with race relations. So is the Negro's, because his life, too, is enmeshed in the absurd system of racial hatred in America. Since racism is centered in and revolves around sex, the Negro cannot help but see himself as at once sexually affirmed and negated. While the Negro is portrayed as a great "walking phallus" with satyr-like potency, he is denied the execution of that potency, he is denied the most precious sexual image which surrounds him—the white woman. The myth of the sanctity of "white womanhood" is nothing more than a myth, but because this myth is acted upon *as if* it were real both by blacks and whites alike, then it *becomes* real as far as the behavior and sensitivities of those who must encounter it are concerned.[42]

This passage addresses critically the politicization of sexuality between African Americans and whites due to the ideology and everyday enforcement of white supremacy, a subject that was not treated widely within the mainstream civil rights movement. As Hernton suggests, white supremacist discourse has often focused centrally on African American sexuality, particularly black male sexuality ("would you want your sister to marry one?" was a popularization of white supremacist sentiment), and consequently, it would have been highly divisive to discuss publicly any relationship between integration and a widening practice of interracial sexuality. Emerging feminist, gay, and lesbian activism, however, made it clearer that the freedom to engage in consensual adult sex and to choose marriage partners is a human right, and in hindsight, many African American activists would agree that sexual choice should not be dictated by nationalist dogma. Hernton's typologies in *Sex and Racism in America* can be reductive, his reliability questionable, and his rhetoric simplistic: "In the mind of the white woman, the Negro is a superior sexual animal,"[43] but the book discusses subconscious dimensions of sex and race in some detail, and critically examines even underground practices of interracial sexuality that predate the activist movements of the 1960s.[44] This text, like Cleaver's, contains methodological flaws and idealizes black male sexuality in certain ways, but both texts invited a critical examination of race/sex taboos that never fully coalesced during the period.

As a whole, the discourses on sexuality produced by African American writers of the 1960s provide several stark stances: idealizations of black female sexuality by black male authors, a few critical examinations of interracial sexuality, endorsements of promiscuity by black male authors, and assertions of sexual humanity by black female authors. Among the prominent texts by black female authors of the period, the influence of a countercultural ethos appears restrained, though still present. A 1970 anthology entitled *The Black Woman*, edited by Toni Cade (Bambara), provides a sample of commentary on questions of race and sexuality from the standpoints of black women. The collection includes a widely anthologized and influential piece by Frances Beale, "Double Jeopardy: To Be Black and Female," an essay that inspired many later cultural critics to examine the simultaneous impact of race, class, and gender oppression. Three of the collected texts, including the essays "Who Will Revere the Black Woman" by Abbey Lincoln and "On the Issue of Roles" by Toni Cade Bambara, as well as "Woman Poem" by Nikki Giovanni, express a black feminist sentiment on sexuality, challenging the view of race and sex favored by Cleaver and Hernton by asserting the unrecognized humanity of African American women. For differing reasons, each of these black feminist texts suggests that during this period, African American women had not been liberated from the restrictions and harms stemming from both sex roles and racial inequality. Bambara questions the foundations of gender difference most centrally, echoing some sentiments within the wider youth counterculture that a fundamental rethinking of how women and men relate was a necessity before meaningful liberation might proceed.

As do Cleaver and Hernton, Abbey Lincoln describes black women and men in typological terms, generalizing widely about the social behavior and range of interests identified with black women and black men. Using this typological approach, however, Lincoln writes movingly about the need for a social force to protect the humanity of black women, since in her view, black men have abdicated their responsibility to provide protection:

> Raped and denied the right to cry out in her pain, she has been named the culprit and called "loose," "hot-blooded," "wanton," "sultry," and "amoral." She has been used as the white man's sexual outhouse and shamefully encouraged by her own ego-less man to persist in this function. Wanting, too, to be carried away by her "Prince Charming," she must, in all honesty, admit that he has been robbed of this crown by the very assaulter and assassin who has raped her. Still, she looks upon her man as God's gift to Black womanhood and is further diminished and humiliated and outraged when the feeling is not mutual.[45]

Lincoln is highly critical of interracial sexuality in her essay, speaking specifically on a heightened sexual interest between black men and black women that both racism historically and then-current activist movements had highlighted. According to Lincoln, black male interest in white women represented a key example of the abdication of responsibility among black men, as black women continued to face catastrophic social conditions and suffered for lack of romantic love:

> We are the women who dwell in the hell-hole ghettos all over the land. We are the women whose bodies are sacrificed, as living cadavers, to experimental surgery in the white man's hospitals for the sake of white medicine. We are the women who are invisible on the television and movie screens, on the Broadway stage. We are the women who are lusted after, sneered at, leered at, hissed at, yelled at, grabbed at, tracked down by white degenerates in our own pitiable, poverty-stricken, and prideless neighborhood . . . We are the women whose bars and recreation halls are invaded by flagrantly disrespectful, bigoted, simpering, amoral, emotionally unstable, outcast, maladjusted, nymphomaniacal, condescending white women . . . in desperate and untiring search of the "frothing-at-the-mouth-for-a-white-woman, strongbacked, sixty-minute hot black." Our men. We are the women who, upon protesting this invasion of our privacy and sanctity and sanity, are called "jealous," and "evil," and "small-minded," and "prejudiced."[46]

In Lincoln's view, sex between black men and white women during this period of "liberated" sexuality represented an expression of male privilege, a trivializing of the movement for racial equality, and a denial of black women's humanity. Her argument implies that black women and black men once had an essential and naturalized relationship to one another as sexual and racial partners, and that the relationship had been disrupted by the atrocities suffered by all African Americans due to racism and by a less than genuine liberation of American sexuality during the 1960s. Her analysis also centers on the salient point that historically (and in the present), black femininity had never been idealized and protected in the way that white femininity had been. However, Lincoln's essay does not argue centrally that African American women are or should be responsible for their own liberation and that their liberation should not depend on restoring a collectively stable relationship with black men. The latter view was expressed more typically among black women writers who identify explicitly as feminists. The authors of the landmark "Black Feminist Statement" by the Combahee River Collective exemplify this interest in black female self-determination, reflecting on their experiences in building a grassroots black feminist organization: "our liberation is a necessity not as an adjunct to someone else's but because of our need as human persons for autonomy . . . we realize that the only people who care enough about us to work consistently for our liberation is us."[47]

Several of the texts in *The Black Woman* anthology argued for a general re-examination of sex and gender in African American communities rather than an idealizing of black femininity that would parallel familiar idealizations of white male/white female relations within a patriarchal and capitalist state of social relations. As Toni Cade Bambara argues in "On the Issue of Roles":

> I have always, I think, opposed the stereotypic definitions of "masculine" and "feminine," not only because I thought it was a lot of merchandising nonsense, but rather because I always found the either/or implicit in those definitions antithetical to what I was all about—and what revolution for self is all about—the whole person. And I am beginning to see, especially lately, that the usual notions of sexual differentation in roles is an obstacle to political consciousness, that the way those terms are generally defined and acted upon in this part of the world is a hindrance to full development.[48]

Bambara, like Lincoln, is aware of the particular dilemmas faced by African American women due to the combination of racial and sexual oppression; her concern is evident in her work in this text and throughout her nonfiction writing. However, Bambara is closely attentive to the conventional understandings of sex and gender even in a black militant context, where black men often expected to occupy leadership roles while black women "stood behind" their men. Energized by the emergence of countercultures and multiple interrogations of race and gender norms, Bambara encourages African American activists to avoid romantic language about the restoration of black male providers and black female caregivers as a solution to the crisis faced by black women and men in a racist society.

Nikki Giovanni's "Woman Poem" strikes a middle ground between Lincoln's appeals to idealized domesticity and Bambara's call for a wholesale reexamination of gender roles. Giovanni's poem alludes to the invisibility of black female sexuality as Lincoln does in her essay, and the poem also implies that no black nationalist appeals to domesticity could serve black women's interests, a sentiment expressed in Bambara's essay. The poem is presented as the opening piece in the collection, perhaps because it boldly articulates the paradoxes of race and sex bias faced by many African American women during this period:

it's a sex object if you're pretty
and no love
or love and no sex if you're fat
get back fat black woman be a mother
grandmother strong thing but not woman
gameswoman romantic woman love needer
man seeker dick eater sweat getter
fuck needing love seeking woman.[49]

In the closing stanza, the speaker describes herself as one "whose whole life/is tied/up to unhappiness/cause it's the only/for real thing/i/know."[50] The poem endorsed neither countercultural sexual liberation nor dating within one's race as the genuine solutions to the dilemmas faced specifically by black women. Instead, the poem illustrates the deep frustrations inherent in the search for sexual liberation among both black males and black females in a society clinging to patriarchal traditions.

More recently, many African American cultural critics have noted that a more liberated sexuality is a positive outcome of 1960s social activism. Recent texts, including June Jordan's essay, "Where Is the Love" (1978) and "A New Politics of Sexuality" (1992) and bell hooks's *Outlaw Culture* (1994), have earnestly discussed the relationships between personal sexual histories, political change, and a new sexual pluralism. Jordan herself became increasingly committed to political work on a sexual front as her career proceeded. Writing on the topics of race and feminism in "Where Is the Love," Jordan argued for sexual tolerance but also held that sexuality was not essentially a public issue:

> When I speak of Black feminism, then, I am not speaking of sexuality. I am not speaking of heterosexuality or lesbianism or homosexuality or bisexuality; whatever sexuality anyone elects for his or her pursuit is not my business, nor the business of the state. And furthermore, I cannot be persuaded that one kind of sexuality, as against another, will necessarily provide for the greater happiness of the two people involved.[51]

Jordan's comments in this essay seem to distinguish her view of a liberating black feminism from a close consideration of sexual pluralism and deeply set biases under patriarchy. Several years later, however, in "A New Politics of Sexuality," Jordan argues for a broader examination of plural sexualities, expanding her earlier views. She was struck by the low levels of support expressed across communities for issues of gay and lesbian liberation:

> Freedom is indivisible or it is nothing at all besides sloganeering and temporary, short-sighted, and short-lived advancement for a few. Freedom is indivisible, and either we are working for freedom or you are working for the sake of your self-interests, and I am working for mine. If you can finally go to the bathroom

> wherever you find one, if you can finally order a cup of coffee and drink it wherever coffee is available, but you cannot follow your heart—you cannot respect the response of your own honest body in the world—then how much of what kind of freedom does any one of us possess? Or, conversely, if your heart and your honest body can be controlled by the state, or controlled by community taboo, are you not then, and in that case, no more than a slave ruled by an outside force?[52]

Jordan's later essay describes sexuality wholeheartedly as a site for political struggle, with oppressive social forces such as homophobia and sexism being "deeper and more pervasive than any other oppression."[53] Jordan participated extensively in civil rights and Black Power activism, but emerged from that experience with a willingness to rethink the issues of sexuality and human freedom that proved so contentious during the years of those movements.

Bell hooks, in "Talking Sex: Beyond the Patriarchal Phallic Imaginary," discusses experiences within a political but pleasure-oriented student resistance to illustrate the influence of a larger countercultural movement for sexual liberation:

> The feminist movement I embraced as a young coed at Stanford University highlighted the body. Refusing to shave, we let hair grow long on our legs and under our armpits. We chose whether or not to wear panties. We gave up bras, girdles, and slips. We had all-girl parties, grown-up sleepovers. We slept together. We had sex. We did it with girls and boys. We did it across race, class, nationality. We did it in groups. We watched each other doing it. We did it with the men in our lives differently. We let them celebrate with us the discovery of female sexual agency. We let them know the joys and ecstasy of mutual sexual choice. We embraced nakedness. We reclaimed the female body as a site of power and possibility.[54]

Later texts by scholars writing in the wake of the sixties include "The New Black Aesthetic" by Trey Ellis (1989), *Are We Not Men* by Phillip Bryan Harper (1996), and *When Chickenheads Come Home to Roost* by Joan Morgan (1999). Each text reexamines the politics of race and sex from the standpoint of scholars who are critical of the dogmatic nationalist identities that are commonly represented as a primary image of 1960s black militancy. Also, each text acknowledges that due to the combined efforts of activists supporting causes of civil rights, feminism, and gay and lesbian liberation, younger African American activists have a wider range of sexual choices, and having these choices provides for a fuller humanity. These cultural critics move beyond the focus on promiscuity and nudity often favored within countercultures and the appeals to African American domesticity that are common in black militant writing. By and large, the younger critics no longer idealize sexual adventure for its own sake in an age of AIDS and continued tensions and schisms within African American families. However, the overt and pluralist discourses on sexuality in recent texts indicate that sexuality was a necessary and appropriate site of struggle for 1960s black activists, whose work as a whole attests to their interest in and attention to countercultural shifts in sexual ideology and practices.

LORRAINE HANSBERRY: SEXUAL POLITICS AND COUNTERCULTURALISM

This essay's essential inspiration comes from the career of Lorraine Hansberry, who was both a supporter of and a dissenter from black militant politics of the 1950s and 1960s. Admittedly, it is risky to make another ideological claim on the legacy of this brilliant dramatist and political activist. Already, black feminist writers, lesbian writers, and Americanist literary critics have argued that Hansberry's work is best suited for their critical projects (see Giovanni [1979], Rich, and Parks). Also, the lack of a comprehensive biography hampers any effort to ascertain her views on a topic such as 1960s countercultural movements, even though these movements were emerging during her life span and, judging by geography alone, she probably knew participants in these countercultures. Hansberry has commented on the validity of civil rights activism and integration, criticizing the Black Muslim movement as "a pot-luck nationalism that looks backwards."[55] However, to claim, as I do, that Hansberry was a supporter, in fact and in spirit, of countercultural activism requires some degree of speculative analysis and even contradicts a few of her public statements. In an article entitled "The Negro Writer and His Roots: Toward a New Romanticism," Hansberry discussed her disdain for Beat writers, whose work and lives contributed significantly to the foundations of 1960s countercultural thought:

> In pursuit of the defeat of illusions it is important that we black writers not get lost in the various revolts of the merely revolted. I refer now to that small segment of the literati who have broken away to form their own vague, non-inspirational rebellion of rejection and nothingism: the Beat. They are a failure. They disturb no one because they attack everything and nothing. They are a source of amusement and confused misunderstanding to the very people who should feel most indicted by their emergence. They serve no significant purpose, neither to art nor society. Perhaps they are angry young men, but insofar as they do not make it clear with whom or *at what* are they angry, they can be said only to add bedlam to this already chaotic house.[56]

Hansberry's desire for an engaged aesthetic activism underlies her assessment of Beat writing, a body of work that she criticized in this article without naming any specific targets. With this criticism of the Beats, Hansberry sought to undermine "the all-important illusion in America that there exists an inexhaustible period of time during which we as a nation may leisurely resurrect the promise of our Constitution and begin to institute the equality of man within the frontiers of this land."[57] Hansberry criticized the Beat-identified spectacle of "brilliant and thoughtful young people searching actively for a way out of what they perceive as the human condition—without commitment to anything."[58]

Hansberry was far from alone in describing counterculturalism—personified in this case by the Beats—as irrelevant to the struggle toward a greater justice in American society. Quite often in contemporary narrative histories and cultural criticism, a distinction is made between a politically active New Left, which sought to end the Vietnam War and to address domestic justice issues, and an apathetic alternative youth counterculture that, according to many, was concerned mainly with self-discovery and sensual gratifications. In his narrative history *The Sixties: Years of Hope, Days of Rage,* Todd Gitlin (who was a former member of SDS) criticized 1960s countercultures because they pursued "the transcendentalist fantasy of the wholly, abstractedly free individual, finally released from the pains and distortions of society's traps, liberated to the embrace of nature and the wonder of essential things in an America capable of starting the world again."[59] Also writing on the escapist image of countercultures, George Lipsitz has written that "it is not surprising that a sizeable part of the counterculture felt itself drawn to the appeal of Eastern religions with their emphasis on avoiding authority, to the lure of the rural commune severed from the modern world, and to the seductiveness of hallucinogenic drugs that could block out the ugliness of ghettoes aflame and peasants' bodies scorched by napalm."[60] Commenting on 1960s rock and roll music, Lipsitz added that "the reckless hedonism of a Janis Joplin or a Jim Morrison"[61] was emblematic of a personally obsessed and politically naïve counterculture in practice.

A fuller understanding of counterculturalism should both recognize the diversity among countercultural movements and should interrogate mass media imagery and other conventional representations of 1960s countercultures. Lipsitz, in his comments, reinforces a stereotypical image of countercultures that is evoked by the popularizing slogan of "sex, drugs, and rock 'n' roll." His comments also imply, quite unfairly, that an interest in Eastern religion may be equated with "avoiding authority." African American political and cultural activism of the period suggests differently, in that a revival of mysticism contributed to a renewed interest in African cosmologies, influenced attempts to build independent and indigenous African American activist organizations, and even inspired the sublime musical art of John Coltrane, Miles Davis, and the Art Ensemble of Chicago. Within the white-identified counterculture, the formation of Utopian communities (a legacy revived by contemporary "green" politics), efforts to end the war in the name of a more spirited humanity, and a reverence for the traditions and rituals of earth religions and aboriginal peoples clearly expressed an engaged political ideology.

In response to Hansberry's comments on the Beats, one might argue further—as many did within 1960s countercultures—that personal rebellion is the substance of political rebellion, as demonstrated even within Hansberry's own life. Hansberry did not recognize—in the "Negro Writer" essay at least—that a personal journey toward an imagined but unnameable state of fulfillment might have a wider social significance. Privately, however, Hansberry's life included personal quests for intellectual and sexual fulfillment, though she did not live long enough to witness the wider embracing of personal politics as a means of social transformation. In the years following her death, collective efforts to "re-write the bill of rights in precise language, detailing ten thousand areas of freedom in *our own language*"(emphasis in original) by proponents of the feminist, gay liberation, and other activist movements would leave an enduring stamp on both public and personal life in the United States.[62]

The career of Lorraine Hansberry touched on the borders between the Old Left, which favored Marxist analysis, legal reform, and electoral politics as methods of resistance, and the New Left, which favored a wider range of economic, cultural, and sexual rebellions, as I have argued earlier. Adrienne Rich and Margaret Wilkerson have suggested that Hansberry's own efforts to articulate a political and aesthetic vision as a writer of conscience might have benefited from an immersion in the more personal politics of second-wave feminism and gay liberation. In an article titled "The Dark Vision of Lorraine Hansberry," Margaret Wilkerson states that:

> Her own contradictions were enormous. Her intellect made her formidable as an adversary in debate. "She did not tolerate fools," remarked one old friend. She trusted the intellect and looked to it for the solutions to humankind's most intransigent problems—oppression, war, and greed. Yet privately she found herself gripped by nameless fears and emotional whirlwinds that did not yield to the cold precision of rationality. Publicly "married," she was in reality separated and later divorced. Publicly forthright and convincing about humankind's potential, privately she sometimes doubted man's capacity to overcome bestial tendencies. Creator of some of the most memorable male characters in modern American plays, she was deeply "womanist" in her outlook and would at times curse supremacist males for their ignorance.[63]

In *Hansberry's Drama: Commitment and Complexity*, Steven Carter writes of Hansberry's lesbianism as a dilemma during "the pre-civil rights, pre-Gay Liberation Movement era when a community of her peers in sexual preference did not exist."[64] She did not write often in support of an overt feminism or lesbianism, although she did write anonymous letters to *One* and *The Ladder*, pro-gay and pro-lesbian publications, during the late 1950s. In the early 1960s, as feminist, gay, and lesbian liberation movements were becoming more public, Hansberry did not join the chorus of voices in the arts supporting sexual liberation. Meanwhile, homophobia continued to affect other political movements—including the civil rights and Black Power movements, as demonstrated by criticism inveighed at James Baldwin because of his sexual orientation.[65]

The roots of Hansberry's commitment to issues of justice and political resistance are contained in Hansberry's early experiences, as a child of middle-class, activist parents in Chicago. Even as a child, she met prominent African American activists such as Paul Robeson (a relationship that would be revived during her adulthood). Her childhood was also marked by a form of class alterity due to her family's success in business. Her father, Carl Augustus Hansberry, was successful as a real estate broker during his daughter's girlhood, which coincided with the Great Depression of the 1930s. In 1940, Carl Hansberry formalized his dissent from New Deal politics by running for Congress unsuccessfully on the Republican ticket, supporting a self-help, "bootstrap" ethos,[66] as Hansberry described in *To Be Young, Gifted, and Black*:

> I recall being the only child in my class who did not come from the Rooseveltian atmosphere of the homes of the Thirties. Father ran for Congress as a Republican. He believed in American private enterprise and, among other things which he had done by the time I was old enough to be aware of him, amassed—in the terms of his community—a "fortune" (though he had done absolutely nothing of the kind; relative to American society of the Nineteen Thirties and Forties, Carl A. Hansberry had simply become a reasonably successful businessman of the middle class). But we are all shaped, are we not, by that particular rim of the soup-bowl where we swim, and I have remained throughout the balance of my life a creature formed in a community atmosphere where I was known as—a "rich" girl.[67]

Hansberry reported going "to kindergarten in white fur in the middle of the depression; the kids beat me up; and I think it was from that moment I became—a rebel."[68]

To Be Young, Gifted, and Black includes several of Hansberry's reflections on her status as a racial inferior in a segregated nation and her relatively privileged economic status as the child of a real estate entrepreneur. Remembering her adolescence as her peers might have seen it, she described herself as:

> a serious odd-talking kid who could neither jump double dutch nor understand their games, but, who—classically—envied them. And their costumes. And the things that, somehow, gave them joy: quarters, fights, and their fascination to come into the carpeted quiet of our apartment.[69]

In later years, Hansberry's interests in the social currents of her childhood, the larger history of her family, and successive phases of African American activism informed her analyses of the continuing struggle for progressive social change. In a letter to the editor of the *New York Times* published in 1964, Hansberry demonstrated this familiarity with, and understanding of, both the conservative seeming (by then) strategies for civil rights protest and the more militant strategies for change favored by Black Power militants:

> My father was typical of a generation of Negroes who believed that the "Ameri-

> can way" could successfully be made to work to democratize the United States. Thus, twenty-five years ago, he spent a small personal fortune, his considerable talents, and many years of his life fighting, in association with NAACP attorneys, Chicago's "restrictive covenants" in one of this nation's ugliest ghettoes. That fight also required that our family occupy the disputed property in a hellishly hostile "white neighborhood" in which, literally, howling mobs surrounded our house. One of their missiles almost took the life of the then eight-year-old signer of this letter. My memories of this "correct" way of fighting white supremacy in America included being spit at, cursed and pummeled in the daily trek to and from school. And I also remember my desperate and courageous mother, patrolling our house all night with a loaded German luger, doggedly guarding her four children, while my father fought the respectable part of the battle in the Washington court.[70]

Hansberry's recollection emphasizes the distinct roles, related to gender, that her mother and her father occupied during this struggle. She recognized as well that neither integrationist nor militant strategy represented an unproblematic solution to racial inequality, with each strategy riddled with contradictions and requiring continual personal sacrifices on the part of activists. According to Hansberry, the effort to remain in the "white" neighborhood during her childhood "led to my father's early death as a permanently embittered exile in a foreign country when he saw that after such sacrificial efforts the Negroes of Chicago were as ghetto-locked as ever."[71]

Carl Hansbery's flight from the America he had once revered paralleled the travels of his daughter from Chicago to Madison, Wisconsin, and eventually to Greenwich Village, where her career as a playwright began in earnest in the early 1950s. In the spirit of countercultural movements of her time and after, Hansberry had conducted her own search for a location and for peers that would sustain her, financially and spiritually, as she worked. Much of her later life was spent in Greenwich Village, an epicenter among countercultural movements during the entire twentieth century in the United States.

Hansberry explored broad questions of sexual politics and the relationships between revolutionary action and personal life in her dramatic works. In her best-known play, *A Raisin in the Sun*, characters in the Younger family discussed topics in African American family life that were once thought to be too intimate and risky for public discussion—family conflicts, abortion, and struggles for personal meaning within a segregated social structure in Chicago and in the United States generally. This play provided a look behind the heroic veneer of civil rights, feminism, and black nationalism, asking probing questions about the longer-term and intimate consequences of such social change on individuals and families.

The play, however, has been mistakenly identified by some critics as a triumphalist depiction of the promise of neighborhood integration,[72] which is clearly not the case. The Younger family's deliberations on whether to move into an all-white neighborhood or to invest in a liquor store exemplify dilemmas faced by

African Americans who seek racial uplift by any number of means. Hansberry's characters illustrate conflicts between idealism and everyday struggle, from Mama's traditional Christianity and efforts to revive a "feeble little plant growing doggedly . . . on the window sill" of their ghetto apartment,[73] to her daughter Beneatha's belief that medical practice "was the one concrete thing in the world that a human being can do,"[74] to the nationalist character Asagai's future plans to participate in liberation movements on the African continent. When the family's insurance money is lost by Beneatha's brother Walter due to a swindle, Beneatha's idealist dream of becoming a doctor is imperiled, but Asagai's determination to make a difference in the world foreshadows the family's decision to defy racist hostility and move into the new home they have purchased in a middle-class neighborhood. The following passage illustrates Asagai's nationalist idealism, which is tempered by a recognition that there are limits to what one human can accomplish:

> In my village at home it is the exceptional man who can even read a newspaper . . . or who ever sees a book at all . . . But I will teach and work and things will happen, slowly and swiftly . . . And perhaps . . . perhaps I will be a great man . . . I mean perhaps I will hold on to the substance of truth and find my way always with the right course . . . and perhaps for it I will be butchered in my bed some night by the servants of the empire.[75]

The characters' personal dreams—the possible marriage of Asagai and Beneatha, the home purchase, Walter's liquor store—become at times the center of the action and other times are relegated to the periphery. Skillfully, Hansberry insures that the human fallibility of the characters remains a consideration even as the characters argue the case for particular ideological positions and strategies for change. This concern for both life stories and ideas shows that Hansberry weighed very carefully the interest in political praxis identified with the Old Left and the demand for cultural interrogation and personal transformation expressed by the New Left as she developed this drama.

Later works, including *The Sign in Sidney Brustein's Window* (1964) and *Les Blancs* (1966), also feature characters that seek effective strategies for social change despite intellectual alienation and uncertain family lives. Toward the end of her career, in her notes on an unfinished play that was inspired by the life of Toussaint L'Ouverture, she discussed the relationship between revolutionary heroism and human fallibility in the following way:

> I intended to depart from the traditional canonization of historical heroes, and try, with all my heart, to write a man—and yet, at the same time, not to lose the wonder of his magnitude, his telling affirmation. L'Ouverture was not a god; he was a man. And by the will of one man in union with a multitude Santo Domingo was transformed; aye—the French empire, the western hemisphere, the history of the United States: therefore, the world.[76]

Hansberry's observations about personal and political dimensions of revolutionary action invoke the essence of countercultural thought, as articulated during several resistance movements of her adult years and during the decade following her death. Countercultural ideologies, as I have shown, often argued that revolutionary politics and personal politics are inextricably linked. Among these countercultural ideologies, various forms of self-exploration through creative expression, sexuality, travel, and other means functioned as challenges to social inequality and moral dogma. Hansberry, while critical of the Beats as a primary representation of countercultural ideology, was a spiritual foremother of other 1960s countercultural rebellions. Indeed, it is true that some of Hansberry's public statements suggest that individual needs for personal freedom were outweighted by collective needs for concentrated political action, an assumption common within the Old Left. Ultimately, however, Hansberry recognized, at least through her dramatic characters, that individuals should examine their own lives carefully to prepare themselves to work for progressive political change. A public recognition that "the personal is political" might well have been the next step in her development as an artist and activist.

AFRICAN AMERICAN IDENTITY AND THE COUNTERCULTURAL LEGACY

To be young, black, and countercultural is a composite identity that is reflected occasionally, but not often, in characteristic constructions of black identity during the 1980s, the 1990s, and at present. In one acknowledgment of this composite identity, a well-circulated essay, "The New Black Aesthetic" (1989), Trey Ellis described himself and his cohorts as "alienated (junior) intellectuals," being "some of the only blacks who admit liking both Jim and Toni Morrison."[77] A few years later, Nelson George, in a 1992 collection of *Village Voice* essays, *Buppies, Bohos, B-Boys, and Baps: Notes on Post-Soul Black Culture*, used the term "bohos" to describe "black bohemians" in the New York cultural scene. Jake Lamar's 1998 novel, *Close to the Bone*, features a biracial protagonist who identifies as African American and follows a proto-countercultural life course that includes leaving college, travels in Europe, sexual promiscuity, dreadlocks, heavy marijuana use, and a personal quest for meaning. There are, of course, other references in African American cultural criticism to varied kinds of cultural rebellion, but not even the assertive social criticism and the calls for free gangsta love and ganja preached by hip-hop artists such as Snoop Doggy Dogg, Li'l Kim, and Cyprus Hill are described as "countercultural" constructions of black identity by critics or by the artists themselves.

Since the 1980s, African American cultural critics have written critically about the racial essentialism that affects black political and cultural activism, noting that the most widely circulated images of African Americans continue to privilege urban, often inner-city landscapes, while a small number of national figures (Jesse Jackson, Louis Farrakahn, Al Sharpton, and even Malcolm X) are commonly depicted as representatives of, and spokespersons for, African American political interests and personal character. Rap musicians have served a similar function with respect to "the postindustrial masculine culture of rap artists, popular filmmakers, and their critical fans," having been described as the mouthpieces for African Americans who are disenfranchised economically and even musically.[78] Consequently, aggressive and generally masculinist responses to economic and political disenfranchisement remain central in recent popular constructions of African American identity, reinvoking, sometimes intentionally, black nationalist sentiments of the 1960s.

Recent African American cultural critics usually recognize that the new urban imagery can reinforce stereotypes, but are less likely to call for radical reimaginings of African American identity in light of the ideological, economic, gender, and sexual pluralism that is present in African American communities. Joan Morgan, for instance, describes the influence of the women's liberation movement in her 1999 text, *When Chickenheads Come Home to Roost*, but insists that a functional feminism must "acknowledge that black folks in nineties America are living and trying to love in a war zone,"[79] and with that sentiment in mind, "my decision to expose myself to the sexism of Dr. Dre, Ice Cube, Snoop Dogg, or the Notorious B.I.G. is really my plea to my brothers to tell me who they are."[80] By Morgan's reasoning, consuming hip-hop, despite any degree of sexism and racial essentialism, is a necessity for understanding contemporary black identity. Tricia Rose, in *Black Noise: Rap Music and Black Culture in Contemporary America*, discusses a similar paradox, that rap music reinforces stereotypes but also is a highly compelling expression of recent urban black identities. Rose states, for instance, that "the return of the ghetto as a central black popular narrative has also fulfilled national fantasies about the violence and danger that purportedly consume the economically fragile communities of color."[81] However, most of her text is focused on hip- hop music as it is practiced in these same "ghetto" settings, reinforcing the centrality of the "ghetto" as an overarching image of African American experience. By comparison, investigating the relationship between recent African American identity politics and the legacies of counterculturalism invites attention to a wider variety of musical forms (blues, soul, and gospel as well as hip-hop), sites of cultural production (the South and the Midwest as well as the coasts), sexualities (lesbian, gay, bisexual, and celibate as well as heterosexual), and political ideologies (from assimilationist to internationalist and separatist) in African American culture.

If African American intellectuals are to move further from the deterministic politics of racial essentialism that have been so widely criticized in contemporary cultural criticism, investigations of "black countercultural consciousness" are needed, expanding the notion of an "oppositional" African American cultural criticism that Michael Dyson called for in *Reflecting Black: African-American Cultural Criticism.*[82] A countercultural consciousness should encourage principled rebellions against multiple forms of oppression, inviting greater personal freedom and collective social action, as Dyson suggests: "oppositional African American cultural criticism must . . . acknowledge the broad range of American experiences that influence its makeup, shape its expression, and challenge its existence."[83] Similarly, a black countercultural consciousness must move beyond the race-centered and utilitarian boundaries that legitimize some forms of African American activism and marginalize other forms.

Ultimately, however, a black countercultural consciousness must challenge the notion that personal searches for meaning, fulfillment, and pleasure are irrelevant to the lives of African American youth. A black countercultural consciousness must, when necessary, continue to contest conventional assumptions that social change can be understood strictly as a collective phenomenon, and that personal fulfillment can be distinguished from a progressive struggle for justice. During the 1960s, countercultural challenges to cultural dogma in the areas of race, sexuality, and politics spearheaded a close critical examination of African American identity, influencing cultural production as well as grassroots political activism in African American communities. This legacy of counterculturalism and assertive black politics can help future activists develop cross-racial movements for progressive change in the twenty-first century.

NOTES

1. Theodore Roczak, *The Making of a Counter Culture*. Garden City, N.Y.: Anchor, 1969, xii.

2. David Chalmers, *And the Crooked Places Made Straight: The Struggle for Social Change in the 1960s*. Baltimore, Md.: Johns Hopkins University Press, 1991, 89.

3. Stokely Carmichael and Charles Hamilton, *Black Power: The Politics of Liberation in America*. New York: Vintage, 1967, 55.

4. During most of her activist career in the 1960s and 1970s, Angela Davis was a supporter of Communism and a multiracial approach to political organizing, even though for a wider public she came to symbolize black revolutionary nationalism and racial separatism. Similarly, during their peak years, the Black Panthers' official positions favored Marxist models for social change as well as coalition building with white organizations. As is widely known, Malcolm X repudiated the Nation of Islam's "white devil" rhetoric after his pilgrimage to Mecca. For more information on these topics, see the texts by Davis, Newton, and Malcolm X cited in the bibliography.

5. Jimi Hendrix performed at two of the best-known rock music festivals of the era, the Monterey Pop Festival in 1967 and Woodstock in 1969, securing the recognition and admiration of many within the counterculture and challenging narrow constructions of black nationalist identity. Poets Ted Joans and Bob Kaufman were influential figures within the Beat movement, contemporaries of Jack Kerouac and Allen Ginsberg. Their poetry is an-

thologized widely, but few scholars have explored in detail the connection between these figures and the counterculture.

6. Samuel Charters, *The Country Blues*. London: M. Joseph, 1960, 177.

7. The film *Berkeley in the Sixties*, directed by Mark Kitchell (New York: First Run Features, 1990) documents well the history of direct actions in the Bay Area in support of several radical causes, and includes a discussion of cooperative work between whites and African Americans during these actions.

8. Stewart Burns, *Social Movements of the 1960s: Searching for Democracy*. Boston: Twayne Publishers, 1990, xii.

9. Milton Yinger, *Countercultures: The Promise of a World Turned Upside Down*. New York: Free Press, 1982, 3.

10. John Diggins, *The American Left in the Twentieth Century*. New York: Harbrace, 1973, 9.

11. Diggins, 19.

12. Diggins, 20.

13. Terry Anderson, *The Movement and the Sixties*. New York: Oxford University Press, 1995, 241.

14. David Burner, *Making Peace with the 60s*. Princeton, N.J.: Princeton University Press, 1996, 127-28.

15. Anderson, 242-43.

16. Rebecca Klatch, *A Generation Divided: The New Left, the New Right, and the 1960s*. Berkeley: University of California Press, 1999, 135-36.

17. Abbie Hoffman, in Judith Albert and Stewart Albert, eds. *The Sixties Papers: Documents of a Rebellious Decade*. New York: Praeger, 1984, 417.

18. In his text of narrative history, *The Negro in the Making of America* (New York: Collier, 1964), Benjamin Quarles discusses the difficulties Old Left activists had in organizing within African American communities. Quarles reports that Communists and Socialists of the 1920s challenged instances of racial discrimination in the courts, tried to increase African American participation in the labor movement, and sought to appoint African Americans in positions of authority within party structures. However, Quarles continues, "despite their strenuous efforts, the Communists made few Negro converts; by 1928 there were, estimates Wilson Record, not more than 200 Negro party members in the United States" (205). The American Communist Party even adopted for a time a black nationalist position that a separate land mass for African Americans become the 49th state, but African Americans still did not join the party in large numbers. Quarles concludes that "typically American, the Negro was individualistic, not likely to submerge his personality in conformity to a party line from which there could be no deviation" (207). See also Richard Wright's discussion of his experience working with the Communist Party in *Black Boy* (New York: Harper Perennial, 1993).

19. Paul Piccone, "From Youth Culture to Political Praxis." *Radical America* 3, no. 6 (November 1969): 18.

20. Robert Cantwell, *When We Were Good: The Folk Revival*. Cambridge, Mass.: Harvard University Press, 1996, 298.

21. Albert Goldman, *Freakshow; The Rocksoulbluesjazzsickjewblackhumorsexpoppsychgig and OtherScenes from the Counter-Culture*. New York: Atheneum, 1971, 113.

22. Goldman, 113-4.

23. W. T. Lhamon, "Ebery Time I Wheel about I Jump Jim Crow: Cycles of Minstrel

Transgression from Cool White to Vanilla Ice." In *Inside the Minstrel Mask: Readings in Nineteenth-Century Blackface Minstrelsy*, eds. Annemarie Bean, James Hatch, and Brooks McNamara. Hanover, N.H.: Wesleyan Press, 1996, 175; Norman Mailer, *Advertisements for Myself*. New York: Putnam, 1959, 272.

24. Burns, 30.

25. Albert and Albert, 193.

26. Michael Dyson, *I May Not Get There with You: The True Martin Luther King, Jr.* New York: Free Press, 2000, 52; Stephen Oates, *Let the Trumpet Sound: The Life of Martin Luther King, Jr.* New York: Harper and Row, 1982, 376.

27. In his text *Negroes with Guns* (reprinted in *The Black Power Revolt* edited by Floyd Barbour, New York: Collier, 1968), Robert F. Williams describes the case for African American self-defense in opposition to the practices of nonviolent direct action and pacifism represented by civil rights groups such as the NAACP and the Southern Christian Leadership Conference, Martin Luther King's organization. In Williams' words, the Afro-American "does not *introduce* violence into a racist social system—the violence is already there, and has always been there. It is precisely this unchallenged violence that allows a racist social system to perpetuate itself" (177). Williams is also directly critical of the motivations of African American leaders who support nonviolence and pacifism: "Nor should we forget that [these] same deceiving pacifist-preaching, well-to-do southern blacks profit from the struggle, living lives of luxury while most Afro-Americans continue to suffer" (178). This sentiment was shared widely among African Americans who supported both self-defense and revolutionary nationalism, such as Malcolm X, Nathan Hare, and Stokely Carmichael.

28. Edward Bacciocco, *The New Left in America: Reform to Revolution, 1956-1970.* Stanford, CA: Hoover Institution Press, 1974, 199-200.

29. Todd Gitlin, *The Sixties: Years of Hope, Days of Rage*. New York: Bantam, 1993, 246.

30. Sy Landy and Charles Cooper, "In Defense of Black Power." *New Left Notes*, 9 September 1966, 4. Available in *Underground Newspaper Collection*. Pro. Micro Photo Division, Bell and Howell Co., and the Underground Newspaper Syndicate. Wooster, OH: The Division, 1970-1986.

31. Landy and Cooper, 4.

32. Gitlin, 108-9.

33. *Berkeley Barb* 3, no. 21 (25 November 1966): 1. "Stokeley in Action as Oakland Blacks Act" and "Nationwide Sexual Freedom Meet on Here." Available in *Underground Newspaper Collection*. Pro. Micro Photo Division, Bell and Howell Co., and the Underground Newspaper Syndicate. Wooster, OH: The Division, 1970-1986.

34. Cecil Brown, *The Life and Loves of Mr. Jiveass Nigger*. New York: Farrar, Straus, and Giroux, 1969, 107.

35. Alice Echols, *Daring to Be Bad: Radical Feminism in America, 1967-1975.* Minneapolis: University of Minnesota Press, 1989, 43.

36. Chalmers, 98.

37. Mary Helen Washington, "Black Women Image Makers." *Black World*, August 1974, 18.

38. Anderson, 77.

39. Eldridge Cleaver, *Soul on Ice*. New York: Dell, 1968, 160.

40. Cleaver, 14.

41. Among the primary texts that illustrate the influence of sexism and misogyny on

black male nationalist discourse, Ron Karenga's *The Quotable Karenga* (Los Angeles: US Organization, 1967), Elijah Muhammed's *Message to the Blackman in America* (Philadelphia: House of Knowledge Publications, 1965), and, of course, Eldridge Cleaver's *Soul On Ice* have been cited often. Black feminist analysis of these patterns of sexism and misogyny include Michele Wallace's *Black Macho and the Myth of the Superwoman* (New York: Dial, 1979), bell hooks's *Ain't I A Woman: Black Women and Feminism* (Boston: South End Press, 1981), and Barbara Smith's "Toward a Black Feminist Criticism" (collected in *Within the Circle: An Anthology of African-American Literary Criticism from the Harlem Renaissance to the Present*. Durham, N.C.: Duke University Press, 1994).

42. Calvin Hernton, *Sex and Racism in America*. New York: Grove Press, 1966, 7.

43. Hernton, 26.

44. Hernton integrated an explicit male feminist standpoint into his commentaries on sex and race in a 1987 text, *The Sexual Mountain and Black Women Writers* (see bibliography). This text features a foreword by Gloria Wade-Gayles, a prominent black feminist literary critic, and the overriding purpose of the text, according to the author, is to fulfill "the burning need for a black male writer to speak out against the red bricks of slander and bigotry that are hurled at black women and the literature they produce" (xxv). The text repudiates earlier and continuing attempts by black men to discredit black women writers who criticize sexism: "when the women tell the truth about men and refuse to accept the blame for what men have done to them, the men get mad as hell. They get 'hurt.' They try to discredit and invalidate the women" (46). The text might have gone further than it does to recognize the pluralist standpoints of African American men and women even in the context of 1960s masculinist activism, but an interest in a future pluralist politics is clearly evident.

45. Lincoln, in Toni Cade (Bambara), "On the Issue of Roles." *The Black Woman: An Anthology*. New York: New American Library, 1970, 82.

46. Cade (Bambara), 84.

47. Combahee River Collective, "A Black Feminist Statement." In *Words of Fire: an Anthology of African-American Feminist Thought*. Ed. Beverly Guy-Sheftall. New York: New Press, 1995, 234.

48. Cade (Bambara), 101.

49. Nikki Giovanni, "Woman Poem." *The Black Woman: An Anthology*. Ed. Toni Cade (Bambara). New York: New American Library, 1970, 3.

50. Giovanni, 14-15.

51. June Jordan, "Where Is the Love." *Civil Wars: Observations from the Front Lines of America*. New York: Simon and Schuster, 1995, 144.

52. June Jordan, "A New Politics of Sexuality." *Technical Difficulties*. New York: Vintage, 1992, 190.

53. Jordan, "A New Politics of Sexuality," 188.

54. bell hooks, "Talking Sex: Beyond the Patriarchal Phallic Imaginary." *Outlaw Culture*. New York: Routledge, 1994, 74.

55. Hansberry, *The Movement: Documentary of a Struggle for Equality.* New York: Simon and Schuster, 1964, 48.

56. Lorraine Hansberry, "The Negro Writer and His Roots: Toward a New Romanticism." *The Black Scholar*, March/April 1981, 6-7.

57. Hansberry, "The Negro Writer," 6.

58. Hansberry, "The Negro Writer," 7.

59. Gitlin, 201.

60. George Lipsitz, "Who'll Stop the Rain: Youth Culture, Rock and Roll, and Social Crisis." *The Sixties, From Memory to History*, ed. David Farber. Chapel Hill: University of North Carolina Press, 1991, 206-34.

61. Lipsitz, 61.

62. Sanders in Albert and Albert 429.

63. Margaret Wilkerson, "The Dark Vision of Lorraine Hansberry: Excerpts from a Literary Biography." *Massachusetts Review* 28, no. 4 (Winter 1987), 645.

64. Stephen Carter, *Hansberry's Drama: Commitment and Complexity*. Urbana: University of Illinois Press, 1991, 5.

65. Cleaver, 97; Julian Mayfield, "And Then Came Baldwin." *Freedomways* 3, no. 2 (Spring 1963), 143.

66. Margaret Wilkerson, "Lorraine Hansberry." In *African-American Writers*. Eds. Valerie Smith, Lea Baechler, and A. Walton Litz. New York: Charles Scribner's Sons, 1991, 147.

67. Lorraine Hansberry, *To Be Young, Gifted, and Black*. Englewood Cliffs, N.J.: Prentice Hall, 1969, 63.

68. Hansberry, *To Be Young*, 63.

69. Hansberry, *To Be Young* , 66.

70. Hansberry, *To Be Young,* 51.

71. Hansberry, *To Be Young,* 51.

72. Harold Cruse, *The Crisis of the Negro Intellectual*. New York: William Morrow, 1967, 278.

73. Lorraine Hansberry, *A Raisin in the Sun*. New York: Random House, 1959, 22.

74. Hansberry, *A Raisin in the Sun,* 125.

75. Hansberry, *A Raisin in the Sun,* 128.

76. Hansberry, *To Be Young,* 138.

77. Trey Ellis, "The New Black Aesthetic." *Callaloo* 12, no. 1 (Winter 1989), 234.

78. Paula Ebron, "Enchanted Memories of Regional Difference in African American Culture."*American Anthropologist* 100, no. 1 (March 1998): 94-108.

79. Joan Morgan, *When Chickenheads Come Home To Roost: My Life as a Hip-Hop Feminist*. New York: Simon and Schuster, 1999, 72.

80. Morgan, 72.

81. Tricia Rose, *Black Noise: Rap Music and Black Culture in Contemporary America*. Hanover, NH: Wesleyan University Press/University Press of New England, 1994, 11.

82. Michael Dyson, *Reflecting Black: African-American Cultural Criticism*. Minneapolis: University of Minnesota Press, 1993, xxi.

83. Dyson, xxi.

BIBLIOGRAPHY

Albert, Judith, and Stewart Albert. *The Sixties Papers: Documents of a Rebellious Decade*. New York: Praeger, 1984.

Anderson, Terry. *The Movement and the Sixties*. New York: Oxford University Press, 1995.

"At the Point of Production." *Radical America* 5, no. 2 (March-April 1971), 63-81.

Bacciocco, Edward. *The New Left in America: Reform to Revolution, 1956-1970*. Stanford, CA: Hoover Institution Press, 1974.

(Bambara), Toni Cade. "On the Issue of Roles." *The Black Woman: An Anthology*. New York: New American Library, 1970.

Berkeley Barb 3, no. 21 (November 25, 1966): "Stokeley in Action as Oakland Blacks Act" and "Nationwide Sexual Freedom Meet on Here" 1. Available in *Underground Newspaper Collection*. Pro. Micro Photo Division, Bell and Howell Co., and the Underground Newspaper Syndicate. Wooster, Ohio: The Division, 1970-1986.

Brown, Cecil. *The Life and Loves of Mr. Jiveass Nigger*. New York: Farrar, Straus, and Giroux, 1969.

Brown, Elaine. *A Taste of Power*. New York: Pantheon, 1992.

Burner, David. *Making Peace with the 60s*. Princeton: Princeton University Press, 1996.

Burns, Stewart. *Social Movements of the 1960s: Searching for Democracy*. Boston: Twayne Publishers, 1990.

Cantwell, Robert. *When We Were Good: The Folk Revival*. Cambridge, Mass.: Harvard University Press, 1996.

Carmichael, Stokely, and Charles Hamilton. *Black Power: The Politics of Liberation in America*. New York: Vintage, 1967.

Carter, Steven. *Hansberry's Drama: Commitment and Complexity*. Urbana: University of Illinois Press, 1991.

Chalmers, David. *And the Crooked Places Made Straight: The Struggle for Social Change in the 1960s*. Baltimore, Md.: Johns Hopkins University Press, 1991.

Charters, Samuel. *The Country Blues*. London: M. Joseph, 1960.

Cleaver, Eldridge. *Soul on Ice*. New York: Dell, 1968.

Combahee River Collective. "A Black Feminist Statement." *Words of Fire: An Anthology of African-American Feminist Thought*. Ed. Beverly Guy-Sheftall. New York: New Press, 1995, 232-240.

Cruse, Harold. *The Crisis of the Negro Intellectual*. New York: William Morrow, 1967.

Davis, Angela. *Angela Davis: An Autobiography*. New York: Random House, 1974.

DeBenedetti, Charles. *American Ordeal: The Anti-War Movement of the Vietnam Era*. Syracuse, N.Y.: Syracuse University Press, 1990.

Diggins, John. *The American Left in the Twentieth Century*. New York: Harbrace, 1973.

Dyson, Michael. *I May Not Get There with You: The True Martin Luther King, Jr.* New York: Free Press, 2000.

———. *Reflecting Black: African-American Cultural Criticism*. Minneapolis: University of Minnesota Press, 1993.

Ebron, Paulla. "Enchanted Memories of Regional Difference in African American Culture."*American Anthropologist* 100, no. 1 (March 1998): 94-108. Available on Wilson Web Online.

Echols, Alice. *Daring to be Bad: Radical Feminism in America, 1967-1975*. Minneapolis: University of Minnesota Press, 1989.

Ellis, Trey. "The New Black Aesthetic." *Callaloo* 12, no. 1 (Winter 1989): 233-251.

Flowers, Sandra. *African-American Nationalist Literature of the 1960s: Pens of Fire*. New York: Garland, 1996.

Friedman, Sharon. "Feminism as Theme in Twentieth-Century American Women's Drama." *American Studies* 25, no. 1 (Spring 1984): 69-89.

George, Nelson. *Buppies, B-Boys, Baps and Bohos: Notes on Post-Soul Black Culture*. New York: Harper, 1992.

Giovanni, Nikki. "Woman Poem." *The Black Woman: An Anthology*. Ed. Toni Cade (Bambara).

New York: New American Library, 1970, 3.

———. "An Emotional View of Lorraine Hansberry." *Freedomways* 19 (1979), 81-84.

Gitlin, Todd. *The Sixties: Years of Hope, Days of Rage*. New York: Bantam, 1993.

Goldman, Albert. *Freakshow; The Rocksoulbluesjazzsickjewblackhumorsexpoppsychgig and OtherSscenes from the Counter-Culture.* New York: Atheneum, 1971.

Hansberry, Lorraine. *Les Blancs: The Collected Last Plays of Lorraine Hansberry*. New York: Random House, 1972.

———. "The Negro Writer and His Roots: Toward a New Romanticism." *The Black Scholar*, March/April 1981, 2-12.

———. *A Raisin in the Sun*. New York: Random House, 1959.

———. *To Be Young, Gifted, and Black.* Englewood Cliffs, N.J.: Prentice Hall, 1969.

Harper, Phillip Bryan. *Are We Not Men: Masculine Anxiety and the Problem of African American Identity*. New York: Oxford University Press, 1996.

Hernton, Calvin. *Sex and Racism in America*. New York: Grove Press, 1966.

———. *The Sexual Mountain and Black Women Writers*. New York: Anchor Doubleday, 1987.

Hoffman, David, Dir. *Making Sense of the Sixties*. Videorecording. Pro. WETA in Boston. Alexandria, VA: PBS Video, 1991.

hooks, bell. "Talking Sex: Beyond the Patriarchal Phallic Imaginary." *Outlaw Culture*. New York: Routledge, 1994, 73-81.

Jordan, June. "Where Is the Love." *Civil Wars: Observations from the Front Lines of America*. New York: Simon and Schuster, 1995, 140-46.

Jordan, June. "A New Politics of Sexuality." *Technical Difficulties*. New York: Vintage, 1992, 187-93.

Klatch, Rebecca. *A Generation Divided: The New Left, the New Right, and the 1960s.* Berkeley: University of California Press, 1999.

Lamar, Jake. *Close to the Bone*. New York: Crown Publishers, 1998.

Landy, Sy, and Charles Cooper. "In Defense of Black Power." *New Left Notes*, September 9, 1966, 4-5. Available in *Underground Newspaper Collection*. Pro. Micro Photo Division, Bell and Howell Co., and the Underground Newspaper Syndicate. Wooster, Ohio: The Division, 1970-1986.

Lipsitz, George. "Who'll Stop the Rain: Youth Culture, Rock and Roll, and Social Crisis." *The Sixties, From Memory to History*, ed. David Farber. Chapel Hill: University of North Carolina Press, 1991, 206-34.

Lhamon, W. T. "Ebery Time I Wheel about I Jump Jim Crow: Cycles of Minstrel Transgression from Cool White to Vanilla Ice." *Inside the Minstrel Mask: Readings in Nineteenth-Century Blackface Minstrelsy*. Eds. Annemarie Bean, James Hatch, and Brooks McNamara. Hanover, N.H.: Wesleyan University Press, 1996.

Lincoln, Abbey. "Who Will Revere the Black Woman?" *The Black Woman: An Anthology*. Ed. Toni Cade (Bambara). New York: New American Library, 1970.

Mailer, Norman. *Advertisements for Myself.* New York: Putnam, 1959.

Majors, Clarence. *All-Night Visitors*. Boston: Northeastern University Press, 1998.

X, Malcolm and Alex Haley. *Autobiography of Malcolm X*. New York: Grove Press, 1965.

Mayfield, Julian. "And Then Came Baldwin." *Freedomways* 3, no. 2 (Spring 1963): 143-55.

Mead, Margaret. *Culture and Commitment: A Study of the Generation Gap*. New York: Columbia University Press, 1978.

Mora, Dennis, David Samas, and James Johnson. "The Ford Hood Three: The Case of the Three GI's Who Said 'No' to the War in Vietnam—Three Speeches." *The Sixties Papers*. New York: Praeger, 1984, 301-9.

Morgan, Joan. *When Chickenheads Come Home to Roost: My Life as a Hip-Hop Feminist*. New York: Simon and Schuster, 1999.

Newton, Huey. *To Die for the People*. New York: Random House, 1972.

Oates, Stephen. *Let the Trumpet Sound: The Life of Martin Luther King, Jr.* New York: Harper and Row, 1982.

Parks, Sheri. "In My Mother's House: Black Feminist Aesthetics, Television, and *A Raisin in the Sun*." *Theater and Feminist Aesthetics*. Eds. Karen Laughlin and Catherine Schuler. Madison, N.J.: Farleigh Dickinson University Press, 1995, 331.

Piccone, Paul. "From Youth Culture to Political Praxis." *Radical America* 3, no. 6 (November 1969): 15-21.

Rich, Adrienne. "The Problem with Lorraine Hansberry." *Freedomways* 19 (1979): 247-55.

Roczak, Theodore. *The Making of a Counter Culture*. Garden City, N.Y.: Anchor, 1969.

Rose, Tricia. *Black Noise: Rap Music and Black Culture in Contemporary America*. Hanover, NH: Wesleyan University Press/University Press of New England, 1994.

Smith, David Lionel. "Black Arts Movement." *Encyclopedia of African American Culture and History*. Jack Salzman, et al., ed. New York: Macmillan Library Reference, 1996, 325-32.

Tate, Greg. *Flyboy in the Buttermilk*. New York: Simon and Schuster, 1997.

Unger, Irwin, and Debi Unger. *Turning Point: 1968*. New York: Scribner, 1998.

Walker, Alice. *In Search of Our Mothers' Gardens*. San Diego: Harcourt, Brace, and Jovanovich, 1983.

Washington, Mary Helen. "Black Women Image Makers." *Black World*, August 1974, 10-18.

Wilkerson, Margaret. "The Dark Vision of Lorraine Hansberry: Excerpts from a Literary Biography." *Massachusetts Review* 28, no. 4 (Winter 1987): 642-50.

———. "Lorraine Hansberry." *African-American Writers*. Eds. Valerie Smith, Lea Baechler, and A. Walton Litz. New York: Charles Scribner's Sons, 1991, 147-158.

Woodstock: Three Days of Peace and Music. Videorecording. Dir. Michael Wadleigh. Burbank, Calif.: Warner Home Video, 1994 (1969).

Yinger, J. Milton. *Countercultures: The Promise of a World Turned Upside Down*. New York: Free Press, 1982.

Index

About the Contributors

Jennifer Drake holds degrees from Brown University and the State University of New York at Binghamton. Currently, she is an assistant professor of English and women's studies at Indiana State University. She is co-editor of *Third Wave Agenda: Being Feminist, Doing Feminism*, and has written published or forthcoming essays on the work of Anna Deavere Smith, Guillermo Gómez-Peña, Coco Fusco, Bharati Mukherjee, Edwin Torres, Adrian Piper, and Lorna Simpson.

Henry A. Giroux is the Waterbury Chair Professor of Education and Cultural Studies at Penn State University. His latest book is *Breaking in to the Movies: Film and the Culture of Politics*.

Margaret Henderson teaches in the Bachelor of Contemporary Studies Program at the University of Queensland's Ipswich campus. She is currently writing a book on the remembrance of the Australian women's movement. Most importantly, she has surfed for ten years and only rides short boards.

Angela E. Hubler is an associate professor of women's studies at Kansas State University. Her research and publications focus on the literature and culture of female adolescence. You can email her at lela@ksu.edu.

David M. Jones is an assistant professor of English at the University of Wisconsin at Eau Claire. His scholarly interests include African American nonfiction and romance texts, themes of protest in American literature, and black feminist thought. He is also interested in critical theory on masculinity, whiteness, literature, and performance.

Elizabeth Kleinfeld teaches composition, literature, and humanities at Red Rocks Community College in a suburb of Denver. She is working on a Ph.D. in English studies at Illinois State University.

Andrew Kurtz teaches literature and popular culture at Bowling Green State University Firelands College. He is currently working on a critical analysis of addiction discourse as deployed by players of massively multiplayer role playing games.

Bill Osgerby is a senior lecturer in cultural studies at the University of North London. His publications include *Youth in Britain since 1945*, *Playboys in Paradise: Masculinity, Youth, and Leisure-Style in Modern America*, and a co-edited anthology, *Action TV: Tough-Guys, Smooth Operators, and Foxy Chicks*.

Jerry Phillips is an associate professor of English, Latin American and Caribbean studies at the University of Connecticut. He has published articles on Christopher Columbus, Herman Melville, Matthew Arnold, and Thorstein Veblen. He was the recipient of the Children's Literature Association Award for the Best Critical Essay of 1993.

Timothy Scheie has published numerous articles on French and American theater, and on the work of Roland Barthes. He teaches French, theater, and film at the University of Rochester's Eastman School of Music.

Gary L. Smith is a freelance journalist who lives in central Illinois and has written frequently about juvenile court cases. His article grew out of research for a book-in-progress on the twentieth-century management of marginalized children.

Ronald Strickland is a professor of English at Illinois State University. He co-edited *After Political Correctness: The Humanities and Society in the 1990s*, and he is currently working on a book about teaching the humanities in the corporate university.

Astra Taylor received her M.A. in liberal studies from the graduate faculty of the New School For Social Research and resides in Brooklyn, New York. Her writing has also appeared in *The Politics of Community*, edited by Michael Strysick. She is a part-time faculty member in sociology at the University of Georgia.